Colonialism and Race in Luso-Hispanic Literature

Colonialism and Race in Luso-Hispanic Literature

Jerome C. Branche

University of Missouri Press
Columbia and London

Library of Congress Cataloging-in-Publication Data

Branche, Jerome.
   Colonialism and race in Luso-Hispanic literature / Jerome C. Branche.
     p. cm.
   Summary: "Branche examines a wide variety of Latin American literature
and discourse to show the extent and range of racist sentiments throughout the
culture. He argues that racism in the modern period (1415–1948) was a tool
used to advance Spanish and Portuguese expansion, colonial enterprise, and the
international development of capitalism"—Provided by publisher.
   Includes bibliographical references and index.
   ISBN-13: 978-0-8262-1613-7 (hard cover : alk. paper)
   ISBN-10: 0-8262-1613-7 (hard cover : alk. paper)
   1. Latin American literature—History and criticism.   2. Racism in
literature.   3. Race in literature.   4. Slavery in literature.   5. Blacks
in literature.   I. Title.
   PQ7081.B68 2006b
   860.9'3552—dc22   2005036360

Designer: Douglas S. Freeman for Foley Design
Typesetter: Phoenix Type, Inc.
Printer and binder: Thomson-Shore, Inc.
Typefaces: Adobe Garamond and Berhnard

*The University of Missouri Press offers its grateful acknowledgment to the Richard D.
and Mary Jane Edwards Endowed Publication Fund of the University of Pittsburgh
for a generous contribution in support of the publication of this volume.*

for my grandmother
Constance
(in memoriam)

for my mother
Doreen

for my son
Djibril

Contents

Acknowledgments

In the process of writing these pages I came to realize how important it was to have the time to step away from teaching or family duties, and read, think, and write. My first debt of gratitude, therefore, is to the Center for Latin American Studies at the University of Pittsburgh, for buying me time in the spring of 2001 to do just that. Having that semester off also allowed me to do some work in the Spanish National Archives in Madrid. I would also like to thank the University Center for International Studies for offering the fellowship competition in the spring of 2004, which again allowed me another precious semester to bring this project closer to fruition.

As my friend and colleague Ronald Dathorne insists, this work is lonely work, especially if the things that are on your mind are not what people generally want to talk about. Maybe I should just get over it—the solitary nature of the work, that is. This being said, it would be remiss of me to not register my appreciation for the many friends and colleagues who provided encouragement, insights, and "hard copy" information on the realities of race in Latin America, and those who helped nudge my morale along in the latter months of the (rite of) passage to publication. Of the former group I acknowledge Ifeoma Nwankwo, for her patience in listening to me, as well as my Puerto Rican friends and colleagues Dolores Aponte, Kelvin Santiago-Valles, Gladys Jiménez, and Magali Roy-Fequiere; Gislene Santos of São Paulo, Brazil; and Miriam Gómez, of Buenos Aires, Argentina.

For their moral support and encouragement, I also thank John Beverley and Gerald Martin of the Department of Hispanic Languages and Literatures at the University of Pittsburgh, Edward Mullen and Marvin Lewis of the University of Missouri, Michael Handelsman of the University of Tennessee, and Marcus Rediker of the History Department here at Pitt. The following journals have granted me permission to reprint articles that have previously appeared in Chapters 1 and 3 respectively, and for this I thank them. They are *PALARA: Publication of the Afro-Latin/American Research Association,* for "Inscribing Contact: Zurara, the Africans, and the Discourse of Colonialism," 5 (2001): 6–19; *Afro-Hispanic Review,* for "Ennobling Savagery? Sentimentalism and the Subaltern in *Sab,*" 17, no. 2 (1998): 12–23; and the *Bulletin of Latin American Research,* for "'Mulato entre negros' (y blancos): Writing, Race, the Antislavery Question, and Juan Francisco Manzano's *Autobiografía,*" 20, no. 1 (2001): 63–87. Translations in the text, except where otherwise indicated, are my responsibility.

COLONIALISM
AND RACE IN
LUSO-HISPANIC
LITERATURE

Introduction

What's in a Name?

In one of the novels I discuss in this study, Alejo Carpentier's *Ecué-Yamba-O,* we meet a character referred to as "el negro Antonio" (black Antonio). The reader might, though he or she might just as well not, pause and take note of the curious syntactic coupling of *negro* with Antonio, in the identification of this individual, or the absence of the more customary binary of name and surname(s). Why would a racial label precede his "name," or be part of it, one might ask, if it is essentially our name that identifies us? Confronted by the knowledge that it is not customary in Hispanic culture for the inverse to occur, that is, to refer to someone as "el blanco Antonio" (white Antonio), except perhaps when *negro* (black) is deployed to distinguish the referent from another Antonio who happens to be *blanco* (white), we are forced to recognize that for "el negro Antonio," his "name" is not meant to identify him in the normal sense. Part of its underlying function, rather, is to point him out from among the anonymous mass of *negros,* even as it confirms whiteness and the binary names of the (white) patriarchal tradition as normative. Antonio's name and his casual, offhand naming in the novel, as indeed occurred in society, remit us to the time in Hispanic culture when the *what*ness of Africans and their American descendants was more important than their *who*ness. That the writer's intention might in all likelihood have meant the appellative more as a *nickname* makes little difference. "Among people of obscure origin," proffers Cuban Afrologist Fernando Ortiz, "nicknames were enough."[1] And here we would do well to take note of

---

1. Fernando Ortiz, *Hampa afro-cubana: Los negros esclavos; estudio sociológico y de derecho público,* 166. I return to the matter of slave naming in Chapter 2.

1

Ortiz's pun on "obscure." Slavery's power to objectify its captives conferred on the dominant culture the power to name, define, and categorize them. And just as the slave's laboring body was what mattered to the mercantilist mills of capital accumulation, his or her bodily exterior offered the slave traders the most evident content for the sign that would identify them as *negros* or *negras*. What the narrator has done, in introducing Antonio to us as "el negro Antonio," is to invite us to accept as normal the two contrasting and hierarchically opposed systems of social identifying.

This book is about the writing of the *negro*. It is about five hundred years of an expression of deep thought and feeling in Luso-Hispanic culture, which, under the aegis of coloniality, inscribed blackness as negative difference.[2] Harlem Renaissance poet Countee Cullen's painful record of a young white boy's socialization into racism as he hurls the "N word" at his equally young compatriot in the poem "Incident" might not be as recognizable as the mid-century reflections of Frantz Fanon. It does not, however, make the little event in Baltimore less significant than the ones that haunted the Martinican psychiatrist in Paris half a century later. Cullen's and Fanon's objection to racialized and racist identifying is equally evident in Puerto Rican critic Isabelo Zenón Cruz's complaint, in 1974, about Puerto Ricans of African descent being referred to as *negros puertorriqueños*. For him the term essentialized their blackness and minimized their nationality, an uncomfortable echo of their lived marginalization. They should, he felt, be more properly referred to as *puertorriqueños negros*.[3]

The burden of racialized naming, of *becoming* black, was expressed again, almost a hundred years after Cullen's unhappy experience, by Colombian intellectual Mara Viveros Vigoya as she confronted the memory of the reductive gaze of the Other, the experience of experiencing being through others, and the epithet that accompanied it. What the name *negra/negro* reflects, in a word, is a practice that obtains across the diaspora and wherever transracial contact has established race naming as a primary parameter for establishing difference. What it provokes is a response that might literally be applicable

2. Although in institutional academic practice "Hispanic studies" includes Portugal and Brazil, I am adding *Luso* to *Hispanic* for greater clarity, to indicate that my area of reference covers the Iberian Peninsula and Ibero-America. It does not include Portugal's former African colonies, nor does it include the rest of her former overseas empire. See Catherine Davies, *The Companion to Hispanic Studies,* 1–3, on the matter of defining Hispanic studies.

3. Although both terms would commonly translate as "black Puerto Ricans" in English, the nuance the writer has in mind has to do with the difference between "black Puerto Ricans," and "Puerto Ricans who are black." Isabelo Zenón Cruz, *Narciso descubre su trasero: El negro en la cultura puertorriqueña,* 1:22–23.

in millions of cases. Viveros Vigoya's anguished response to the racial appellative, like those of the individuals mentioned above, is a case of making the
personal political through the autobiographical documentation of the event.
She writes: "And like everyone who has had the experience of being labeled,
I had to struggle with this oppressive category, in many and various ways,
with diverse personal and intellectual resources, by rejecting it, wanting to
ignore it, trying to fill it up with a different content, widening its inner frontiers or 'deconstructing' it throughout the trajectory of my life."[4]

While the customary contrary argument might be raised, namely, that a
term like *moreno* ("dark" or "darkie") is often used in the Hispanic world to
indicate a desire to be polite, or that variants of *negro/negra* like *negrito/negrita*
express affection between speakers,[5] it is more important, I believe, in this
context, to recognize the potential for aggression inherent in racial naming.
After all, the decision as to where and when to employ the racialized name
is still fully within the power of the ones using it. Indeed, the persistence
over the centuries in the Latin American vernacular of expressions such as
"the black man is a brute" *(el negro es bruto),* "the black man is coal" *(el negro
es carbón),* or "the black man only thinks on Fridays" *(el negro solo piensa los
viernes),* speaks eloquently to the enduring nature of the racist structure of
thought, even as it renders unimportant the class origin of those who think
and speak in these terms. If we regard this dynamic in the Ibero-American
oral tradition, as social interpellation at the "micro" level, as Howard Winant
might call it, and consider its written counterpart as an expression of the
same phenomenon at the "macro" level, it would help situate both levels
of Luso-Hispanic discourse within the broader Occidental imaginary on
race. My feeling is that if we can delegitimize this dynamic at the individual, oral level, we can also delegitimize and decolonize the literature that
reifies and often celebrates it. Calling attention to the epistemic violence
that such writing has perpetrated and continues to perpetrate, given the
permanence of the written word, accounts for much of the motivation behind this book.

Indeed, despite the fact that the United States has often been cited as the
quintessential home of racism by apologists of racial discrimination in Latin
America, one of the remarkable fruits of black activism in this country, over
the past half a century, has been the forcing into existence of protocols of

---

4. Mara Viveros Vigoya, "Y así nació este libro," 8. For more on the "third-person consciousness" imposed by this kind of interracial contact, see Frantz Fanon, *Black Skin, White Masks,* 110.

5. The suffix -*ito* or -*ita* is a diminutive in Spanish.

racial identification, which, at least in public discourse, fall under the category of "political correctness." The clearest evidence of this goes back to the cap-italization of the *N* in *Negro,* and the more recent sequence of such terms as *Afro-American, black, Black,* or *African American* when referring to people of African descent. Analogous designations like *afrodescendientes* (people of African descent) in Latin America, or *afroecuatorianos/as* (Afro-Ecuadorans) or *afro-colombianos/as* (Afro-Colombians) reflect a similar aspiration to civility and interracial respect in Latin America. It would be erroneous to think, how-ever, that they have the same moral force as their cognates do in the United States. The fact that epithets and racialized name-calling in this country can have legal repercussions for the speaker is hardly a matter to be taken lightly, or one that can be overlooked. To the best of my knowledge, there is no leg-islation in Latin America that sees and sanctions racialized name-calling under the rubric of "hate-speech." Far from proposing a thoughtless appli-cation of U.S. standards of race relations on Latin American polities, what I am pointing to, rather, is the naturalization of a negatively charged racial nomenclature there.[6]

If the social designation of *negro* can be so loaded, what scale do we need to weigh a written tradition that over five hundred years reified it and its neg-ative connotations? *Colonialism and Race in Luso-Hispanic Literature* holds up for examination racially partisan works of the Luso-Hispanic canon in an attempt to document just how deep, widespread, and durable these struc-tures of feeling they expressed were held, and how important, in the final analysis, race as *narrative* has been and continues to be. Its premise is that modern race-making was consonant with the colonial enterprise and with the international development of capitalism. In this book I point out where race was also integral to national discourse both in the metropoles and in their colonial and ex-colonial areas of influence. The present volume will therefore pay attention to the racial inflections in Portuguese travel writing in the middle fourteen hundreds, in Spanish drama in the fifteen and sixteen hundreds, and in an array of texts from the Latin American colonial and postcolonial world, which exemplify these processes. It will look at biracial characters in nineteenth-century "abolitionist" writing, to try to capture their flight from the social identity of blackness, and will end up with the twentieth-century phenomenon called *negrismo,* whose implicit affiliation

---

6. The use of derogatory racial appellations among populations "of color," interesting a topic though it is, is outside the scope of the present discussion.

to black subjectivity often hid a distinct disaffinity with its Afro-Hispanic referents, and a correspondingly guarded posture regarding the pretensions of the latter to the full and equal rights of citizenship. In this regard the book is wary (and weary) of affirmations of racial democracy which hold to the premise that in Latin America slavery was "benign," and that postslavery race relations were subsequently cordial and harmonious. I feel that the familiarity of the quotidian suggested by such expressions as *el negro Antonio, mi negro,* ("black Antonio," "my black") and so on, ought never to desensitize us to cross racial customs of control and the power they wish to perpetuate. The colonial determinant, then, and its legacy of disempowerment, and the marginalization of blacks in the context of nation-making and the discourse of the nation will be my frame of reference throughout.

Race, Modernity, and Marginality

For the purposes of this study, it is important to underscore the significance of the concept of "racial democracy" in Latin America, not only for the role it has played in buttressing the hegemonic discourse of the nation at various times and in various places, but also to the degree that it has served similar interests in academia. Latin American exceptionalism (racial democracy) evolved from a defensive, proslavery discourse, which during colonial times engaged in an intermetropolitan comparison of colonial regimes, in which Iberian, French, British, and Dutch apologists for slavery sought to establish that *their* system was less inhumane to its captive laborers than that of the others. Through the promotion of *mestizaje,* or the idea of the continent as a homogenous racially amalgamated collectivity, liberal Latin American intellectuals early in the twentieth century distanced themselves from more overtly exclusionary elite identity politics of earlier generations, as I will point out. They continued to maintain, however, that the state of race relations in Latin America, deriving from the purportedly paternalistic and benign slave-owning tradition, was nonconflictual, at best, or mildly strained, at worst. Their point of comparison, by then, was the racial dictatorship institutionalized in the United States's Jim Crow South, or in the South African model of apartheid that followed later. Among the intellectuals who articulated versions of this position, and whose primary works I discuss briefly in this introduction as they relate to Afro-Latin citizenry, are Gilberto Freyre of Brazil, José Vasconcelos of Mexico, and Fernando Ortiz of Cuba.

For North American historians, racial democracy found one of its most important academic anchors in sociologist Frank Tannenbaum's 1946 study *Slave and Citizen: The Negro in the Americas*. Tannenbaum in effect drew on Freyre's early work and the dominant Latin American tradition, repeating the paternalistic argument. He suggested that relative to Anglophone America, Latin American slaves had found it easy to get manumission, that their culture and their humanity were respected, and that they were allowed to preserve their African traditions and to assimilate smoothly into the larger society when freed. Much of this was made possible as a result of a historically more receptive and humane Catholic culture, he stated, and a legal framework for slaves that dated back to the thirteenth-century Hispanic monarch known as Alfonso X the Wise. Most certainly because of its easy generalizations vis-à-vis Protestant Anglophone U.S. culture, chattel slavery, and subsequent race relations, Tannenbaum's book generated much criticism among comparative studies of the Americas and fell largely out of favor among North American historians, though of late it has attracted renewed interest.

Notwithstanding all that has been said in the decades-long polemic surrounding Tannenbaum, given the global transformations wrought by conquest and colonialism, and the way race came to be crucial in separating Europe from its subjected Others, it is pertinent to point out at least three areas of concern in the Tannenbaum premise, all of which have a bearing on the objectives of this study. The first has to do with the supposedly moral determinant in the Luso-Hispanic cultural outlook, based on the Christian idea of the "natural equality" of all humans and enshrined in tradition and law, from which its racial cordiality derived. The second is related to manumission, social mobility, and the idea that the "taint of slavery proved neither deep nor indelible" for free (or freed) *afrolatinos/as* during or after slavery. The third concerns the degree to which an argument for benign enslavement, beyond the evident contradiction housed in the term itself, presupposes acquiescence and submissiveness in the enslaved, along with the absence of agency that goes with it. Proposing an analogous relationship between a poorly ventilated thirteenth-century slave regimen in the Iberian Peninsula, to go back to the first observation, and the racial aspect of forced labor and capitalist production in the colonial world seems at best an error in historical analysis. This is especially so to the extent that the analogy overlooks the more immediate, and more pertinent, historical antecedent in Spain and Portugal, even if we were to suppose that the institution as practiced in Iberia survived the Atlantic crossing "intact." This mismatch between the modern and the premodern is replicated when we take into consideration the fact that it is in racialized modernity that whatever precept of sameness might have previously obtained in thirteenth-century Hispania, of "equality of men under the law of nature," was discarded in favor of discursive and epistemological strategies aimed at fixing biological difference in race as an ideological aid to exploitation. It is this articulation of negative difference, which began in the early modern period, and which has survived slavery and the colonial crucible with which I am concerned in this book. Robert Conrad's critique of the Freyre/Tannenbaum postulate attempted to defeat the rhetoric of partisan scholarship by reproducing a large variety of documents from the period, and letting the records speak for themselves, as it were, and thereby "reveal historical truth."[7] To the degree that I seek recourse in historical documents, for example in my discussion of Zurara's *Chronicle of the Discovery and Conquest of Guinea* (1453) in Chapter 1 or of colonial documents in Chapter 2, my objective is similar, even though I am quite aware that "documentary evidence" can be found to support widely contradictory opinions. I hope, however, in my analysis of said documents, to highlight a particular consistency in relation to the broader narrative of racialized power in Luso-Hispanic culture.

The polemics around Tannenbaum in terms of the writing of history have been detailed elsewhere and need not detain us much. One of my primary interests has to do with the extent to which the premise of cordiality in Latin American race relations is reflected directly and indirectly in generations of literature and studies of literature, and the way they minimize or sentimentalize the material and symbolic violence of slavery and its aftermath. As it relates to literary criticism, this is a discourse that spans generations of commentators on the black presence in Hispanic literature, from Emilio Ballagas and José Juan Arrom in the 1940s, to Mónica Mansour and Rosa E. Valdés Cruz in the 1970s, and to Roberto González-Echevarría in the 1990s, and it plays a complementary role to the power principle behind the historical writing of the *negro*. It does bear pointing out, however, to go back to the writing of history proper, that to characterize Latin America's diverse and

7. Frank Tannenbaum, *Slave and Citizen: The Negro in the Americas*, 56, 45. Alejandro de la Fuente discusses the polemic and notes the resurgence of interest in the Tannenbaum postulate. His own article takes a neo-Tannenbaum point of departure; see his "Slave Law and Claims-Making in Cuba: The Tannenbaum Debate Revisited"; and María Elena Díaz's rebuttal, "Beyond Tannenbaum." See also Robert Edgar Conrad, *Children of God's Fire: A Documentary History of Black Slavery in Brazil*, xxiii.

multiethnic social formations as racial democracies, has to be regarded somewhat as an expression of wishful thinking, especially considering the long periods of military dictatorship that have defined the region's political life.

Even the promise of the dissolution of class hierarchy that has been held out by the socialist revolution in Cuba can be shown to have foundered, and disturbingly so, on the racial question, in spite of the revolution's energetic efforts to equate the erasure of the class problem to an erasure of the race problem. It is effectively the postcommunist scenario, in the broader context of a postmodern multicultural politics in the United States, which also falls short of delivering power to its heterogenous "people," that has prompted at least one call for a retheorization both of the nation and its implied community. Taking as his point of departure the failure of communism as an alternative to capitalism, and capitalism's current and mostly formal concessions to difference and hybridity by way of the multicultural paradigm, John Beverley offers a suggestive restatement of the communist premise. This would dispense with the utopian principle of the many "becoming one" and replace it with the concept of the one "becoming many." In this case, however, "the people" would be an empowered ("heterotopian") heterogeneity.[8]

To be sure, a critical counternarrative, such as the one proposed herein, is by no means new. *Colonialism and Race in Luso-Hispanic Literature* comes in the wake of decades of work in Afro-Hispanic studies that has offered points of departure for rereading the Luso-Hispanic canon and rethinking the role of race therein. Richard Jackson's important study, for example, *The Black Image in Latin American Literature* (1976), and Miriam DeCosta's *Blacks in Hispanic Literature: Critical Essays* (1977) were part of a wider upsurge in the interest in black diasporic cultures that emerged with the civil rights movement. They were preceded by important critiques of the canonical perspective as seen in Wilfred Cartey's *Black Images* (1970) and Lemuel Johnson's *The Devil, the Gargoyle, and the Buffoon: The Negro as Metaphor in Western Literature* (1971). These studies drew theoretically from the binary of the white aesthetic/black aesthetic that was being advanced in African American literary criticism as a generation of black intellectuals sought to reclaim a racial space and perspective based on what Jackson at one point called the "true black experience." They also pointed the way to the writerly presence of blacks in Latin American countries. And although in a general sense the editors of college-level anthologies have been atrociously slow in including the latter, the mapping of Afro-Latino/a writers and their concerns that

8. John Beverley, "After Communism."

Jackson initiated in 1979 with his *Black Writers in Latin America* continues apace and has irreversibly altered the spectrum of Latin American literature.[9]

The present volume is also indebted to the more recent critical cluster around power, race, coloniality, and literary practice, from Angel Rama's *La ciudad letrada* to John Beverley's *Against Literature* and Charles Mills's *The Racial Contract*, to name but a few sources. It takes into consideration perspectives from subaltern studies and postcolonial studies, as well as psychoanalytic theory, and includes for analysis colonial newspapers, bodily inscriptions, travel writing, the law, and literary hermeneutic itself—cultural texts that have a bearing on what *el negro* has signified over time. The binary that interests me, then, has little to do with a purportedly black aesthetic vis-à-vis a white aesthetic. (This book is only marginally about black writers. Neither does it go back to representations of blackness at the beginning of Western civilization as Addison Gayle Jr. urged when he wrote his seminal essay, "Black Literature and the White Aesthetic.") My objective, though related, is the more limited one of looking at the binary created by white colonizing selfhood in the modern period, in representing its racialized nonwhite counterpart, and of an interpretive paradigm that sees the black Other as distortion and antithesis of this signifying self, created often by way of the stereotype and in the interest of distinction within a colonial or national episteme. It is about the objectives of this trajectory and its results.

The elements of a repressed selfhood, to the degree that they emerge in the process of this representation of the Other and complicate it by redounding back on the site of enunciation, following Sander Gilman, are also of interest to me. I shall be using, as well, the argument that the discursive re-presentation of antithetical models of the self was a necessary and fundamental ideological complement to the material depredation at the heart of coloniality and has persisted in the racialized division of power at the global and local (national) levels. The space between the "real" subject and his or her representation, as a function of the signifier's will to power, acquires here its epistemological importance, as Edward Said points out in his important study of Western colonial writing on the East, *Orientalism*.[10] Accordingly,

9. See Richard L. Jackson, *Black Writers in Latin America*, xi. See also Richard L. Jackson, *The Black Image in Latin American Literature*. The more notable examples of this development are seen, for example, in the work of Marvin Lewis, Laurence Prescott, Edward Mullen, Miriam DeCosta-Willis, Ian Smart, and William Luis, as well as recent studies by Michael Handelsman, Dorothy E. Mosby, and Dawn Stinchcomb.

10. See Sander Gilman, *Difference and Pathology: Stereotypes of Sexuality, Race, and Madness*, 23; and Edward Said, *Orientalism*.

negrismo, a top-down, colonially tinged twentieth-century discursive approach to blackness, which I discuss in Chapters 4 and 5, might translate as a *Negrist* "take" on the subject, with all its attendant anxieties, aggressions, and ambiguities.

If indeed I deem necessary the interjection that this book represents, it is in recognition of the need to continually refine the countercanonical critical perspective, to expand the index of the racially deleterious text(s), and to unsettle the suppositions of hegemony of a purportedly liberal academic tradition that, even if not color blind, is resistant to recognizing its own privilege or to acknowledging the forms of epistemic violence that it endorses. Academic institutions, it is no secret, play a supportive role in perpetuating the dominant ideology in all its multiple aspects, and racialized power is a major axis of social differentiation and privilege in Latin America. I hardly expect, however, that a position such as the one I have taken will go uncriticized, especially by those who subscribe to or benefit from this status quo. It merely confirms the presumptions of power, the permanence of coloniality, and the idea that the dominant ideology thrives upon the silence of those within its range of influence. That more dissonant voices have not been heard on matters relating to racism in Latin America is by no means an indication of their nonexistence. It is an existential reality that subalterns, racialized or not, struggle with, have struggled with, and *talk* about on a daily basis. Writing books about it, or continuing the challenge against what used to be a monopoly of Latin Americanist discourse on race in literature is a different matter. In this regard, let it be said, it is certainly relevant that in almost four hundred years of slavery in Latin America, there is only one extant slave autobiography that we know of. Juan Francisco Manzano's life history, an aspect of which I explore in Chapter 3, is a long tale of "sufferation." His being an autodidact makes him an important exemplar of the magnitude of the task of overcoming, and of the subaltern speaking. When we consider the limited charges he made against his masters and against the regimen, against the truths that he dared not utter, we can only imagine the content of the millions of untold stories from within captivity. The analogy with *afrodescendientes* today is not hard to imagine either, given the similarities that would obtain between slave society in colonial Latin America, and a contemporary hypothetical confrontation with political regimes known more for brutality and repression than for freedom of expression.[11]

---

11. Jerome Branche, "Sub-*poena:* Slavery, Subjection, and Sufferation in Juan Francisco Manzano." It is significant that the group of Afro-Brazilian writers and poets *Quilombhoje* (literally

The *negro* as object of study and discourse in the Hispanic literary and extraliterary tradition is a product of the broader experience of the new worlds created by the European voyages of exploration and expansion and the global demographic changes produced by the colonial process that followed. What has been referred to as the "absence of race as an organizing idea" in the Greco-Roman and Medieval periods was fundamentally replaced by its opposite from the fifteenth century onward—that is, the detailed and prolonged consideration of Europe's Others as subjects of difference. This multidimensional and multileveled discursive operation took place in the context of social, political, and economic domination, and it often served in effect to ground this domination ideologically. The construction of empires "upon which the sun never set," the massive commercial success of the mercantile system, the triangular trade, slavery, and the superexploitation of the colonies served as the backdrop—and often a catalyst—to modern race-thinking.[12]

Commenting on modernity as material and technological progress in the West, Andre Gunder Frank has observed, "it is impossible to calculate the size of the contribution of the colonial trade and the commercial revolution to the process of capital accumulation, industrial revolution, and economic development." The body count of African casualties of the slave trade has been recently recalculated from around 12 million to a conservative 36 million, and that of Native American victims of European conquest and settlement in the Americas as more than 90 percent of an estimated 75,000,000 to 100,000,000 in 1492, the year of Columbus's arrival. It is a stark index of the human cost that underlies modernity's narrative of progress. Inherent to this submerged text is the history of underdevelopment for vast sections of the planet, and of the wealth of nations today. The gross contradictions of core and periphery, resulting from what Immanuel Wallerstein calls "the axial division of labor in the world economy," has its roots in European colonial expansion and the racially hierarchical world order that it created. Corresponding racial wealth accompanying uneven development worldwide is also part and parcel of this binary.[13]

Quilombo, "today") emerged in Brazil in the latter 1980s, that is, at the end of the period of dictatorship, during which open discussion of racial matters had been not only taboo, but also illegal.

12. Ivan Hannaford, *Race: The History of an Idea in the West,* 8; Frank Snowden, *Before Color Prejudice: The Ancient View of Blacks.*

13. Andre Gunder Frank, *World Accumulation, 1492–1789,* 225; Eric Williams, *Capitalism and Slavery.* See also David E. Stannard, *American Holocaust: Columbus and the Conquest of the New World,* x, 11, 317; Walter Rodney, *How Europe Underdeveloped Africa;* and Eduardo Galeano, *Las venas abiertas de América Latina.*

For a study of black subject formation, it is imperative to appreciate the centrality of race-thinking and notions of white supremacy to the Western worldview, both in terms of the West as a supranational imagined community and in the context of its discourses of the nation. Racism, as Albert Memmi reminds us in his critique of colonialism, comes out of a relationship of power in which real or imagined differences are valorized in a generalized and permanent way, to the benefit of the dominant subject and to the detriment of its subordinated Others. Just as its objective is material and symbolic privilege, its mode of operation, whether through real or rhetorical means, is the denigration of its victims. For Mills, racism, coming out of European expansion and colonial domination, cohered into a political system of white rule and socioeconomic privilege, whether formal or informal, producing "norms for differential distribution of material wealth and opportunities, benefits and burdens, rights and duties," following a binary premise of whiteness and nonwhiteness. The racial contract emerging from it is transnational in scope and puts into action certain agreements that may be formal (juridical) or informal and unspoken, but whose objective is white privilege and its preservation. He stresses that all whites benefit from it, though not all are signatories to it. Further, according to Etienne Balibar and Immanuel Wallerstein, the theorization of racism is "indispensable" in the formation of the racist community, and it contributes in an important and incalculable way to produce "one of the most insistent forms of the historical memory of modern societies."[14]

A detailed account of the lengthy list of European "race theorists"—philosophers and scientists who for four hundred years contributed to the racist ideology—is beyond the scope of this discussion. Although they have received much attention in recent similar studies, it is nonetheless important to dedicate some attention to them because of their iconic and canonic importance to the Western intellectual tradition, as well as the practical application of their opinions into real politik, both in Europe and in its colonial zone of influence. The extent to which the racial hierarchy they theorized and advocated is directly or indirectly imported into the texts to be studied, and these texts' contribution to the broader regime of truth in Luso-Hispanic culture, is important to the final focus of this book.

The discursive construction of race in the modern period involves a basic duality. On the one hand, it entails the essentialization of an originally multi-

14. Maxim Silverman, "Mechanisms of Oppression: Interview with Albert Memmi," 29; Mills, *Racial Contract,* 3–11; Etienne Balibar and Immanuel Wallerstein, *Race, Nation, Class: Ambiguous Identities,* 18, 45.

ethnic Occidental identity into a singular and superior whiteness, and on the other, there is the corresponding negative projection of the Other through hyperbole. Homi Bhabha has written about the important role of stereotyping and of the excesses of this negative projection. He sees them as necessary to the "fixing" of the inferiority of nonwhites. The metaphorical operation of fixing is of the greatest importance to racial hierarchization, since it removes the need for the premises of racism to be empirically grounded. Print culture's ability to endlessly reproduce the same text provided a technological means of unsurpassable usefulness in the projection of this fixed, distorted image of the Other—that is, a re-presentation whose effect for its audience was to displace the object of which it spoke. In *Orientalism,* Edward Said reiterates this "delivered presence," its monological premise, and the various aspects of its institutionalized power.[15]

Paradoxically, it was the methodological change that accompanied the scientific revolution in the seventeenth century, with its promise and presumption of objectivity, that served as the securest anchor for racial hierarchy. The age of Copernicus, Descartes, and Galileo, and the Enlightenment revolt against ecclesiastical hegemony produced a paradigm shift in which the world could no longer be seen in simple terms of Christian and heathen, or via the Aristotelian binary of political man and barbarian. Scientific discourse, through the disciplines of natural history, anthropology, geography, phrenology, physiognomy, and later craniology and cephalometry, came to offer the necessary guarantees about race and racial difference. Stuart Hall has addressed this cultural function of science. "Since the Renaissance at least," he states, "and especially since the Enlightenment, it is the signifier Science that bears the indicator of the truth. . . . [W]hat people look for in science is not the truth about race, but the sanction of truth about race, i.e., that which will make what they cannot make true in any other way, come true as an effect. Science here is not consulted, but invoked." The invocation of a dubious science in any of its many disciplinary and discursive guises gave credence to the supremacist premise, ascribing permanence to supposed racial characteristics. At the turn of the twenty-first century, science as trope and epistemological point of reference still served this traditionalist ideological function in the face of DNA technology that renders biological bases of race-thinking archaic.[16]

15. Homi Bhabha, "The Other Question," 18; Said, *Orientalism,* 21.
16. Stuart Hall, *Race, the Floating Signifier.* Regarding the new racism in America, embodied in judicial and legislative processes, the media, and aggressive activism of right-wing intellectuals

What Kalpani Seshadri-Crooks has called the "conceit of whiteness," a formulation that implies equal measures of narcissism and deceit in discourse on race, began to take shape in the taxonomical listings of early natural history. The classification and tabulation of the animal kingdom by John Ray, François Bernier, Carl von Linné, Gerges Louis Leclerc de Buffon, and other scientists in the sixteen and seventeen hundreds took medieval hierarchical metaphysical suppositions of a Chain of Being that extended from God and the angels, through man, to the lower orders of animals, and reelaborated them around rational criteria. Enlightenment philosophers such as Johann Blumenbach, Immanuel Kant, David Hume, and Friedrich Hegel continued an important narrative of racial distinction even as they propounded Enlightenment principles of freedom and equality. On the matter of blacks, their impact might be summarized in the ninth edition of the *Encyclopaedia Brittanica's* (1884) statement under its entry for *Negro*. It had been nearly a hundred years earlier that Hume had written, in "Of National Characters," that "there never was a civilized nation of any other complexion than white, nor even of any individual eminent in action or speculation. No ingenious manufactures amongst them [the Negroes], no arts, no sciences." The *Encyclopaedia Brittanica* accepted this idea, gravely pronouncing that "No full-blood Negro has ever been distinguished as a man of science, a poet, or an artist, and the fundamental equality claimed for him by ignorant philanthropists is belied by the whole history of the race throughout the historic period." Other common "scientific" observations of the Enlightenment, such as pronounced black prognathism, cannibalism, decreased cranial capacity, an inherent malodorousness, and government by despotism and superstition, complete the picture offered by the encyclopedia. Black racial difference, and racial difference as a whole, according to the encyclopedia's point of view, is "fixed by heredity."[17] The authoritative role of encyclopedia in providing truth-value and permanence to its definitions is sufficiently resounding to preclude further comment.

---

and politicians, see, for example, Richard Herrnstein and Charles Murray, *The Bell Curve: Intelligence and Class Structure in American Life;* see also the critique by Henry Giroux and Susan Searles, "Race Talk and The Bell Curve Debate: The Crisis of Democratic Vision."

17. Kalpani Seshadri-Crooks, "The Comedy of Domination: Psychoanalysis and the Conceit of Whiteness"; Emmanuel Chukwudi Eze, ed., *Race and the Enlightenment;* Cornel West, *Prophesy Deliverance: An Afro-American Revolutionary Christianity;* Henry Louis Gates Jr., "Introduction: Writing 'Race' and the Difference it Makes"; Leon Poliakov, *Aryan Myth: A History of Racist and Nationalist Ideas in Europe;* Leon Poliakov, "Racism from the Enlightenment to the Age of Imperialism"; and *The Encyclopaedia Britannica: A Dictionary of Arts, Sciences, and General Information,* 318, 317.

Equally powerful were the implications of post-Darwinian theories of social hygiene propounded by British founder of eugenics, Sir Francis Galton, in the nineteen hundreds. For Galton, the "unfit" should not be allowed to reproduce, whereas the birthrate of the "fit" should be encouraged by all means possible. This idea corresponded to the spirit of the age as expressed in the self-explanatory title of Count Joseph Arthur de Gobineau's *Essai sur l'inegalité des races humaines* (1853–1855). By the late nineteenth century, Hegel's compatriot and Galton's contemporary, the zoologist Ernst Haeckel, who was convinced that Germans had evolved more than any other people from humanity's apelike beginnings, would also advocate the practice of eugenics "on behalf of the superior [German] race."[18]

It becomes clear upon examination that racial bias was a constant in the scientific and philosophical discourse of some of Europe's most illustrious thinkers in the modern period, and over time it cohered into a concrete ideology. Many scholars have taken note of the resistance that has greeted any challenges to their iconic stature in the academic field. The intellectual incest that an intertextual examination of their writings reveals, however, makes clear the extent to which their value-laden assessments share a common interest in material and symbolic racial aggrandizement and derogation. From the era of colonial expansion, through the industrial revolution, and after, their writings inscribe a postethnic, transnational community of European-originated whiteness that is defined in contradistinction to the natives of the colonial contact zone or to socio-racial subordinates within national borders. Indeed, a racialized right to conquest proved to be the discursive and ideological foundation upon which the exploitation and expropriation mentioned above would rest, and which would drive the burgeoning capitalist quest of industry and settlement. As Charles Mills observes, white superiority was not only a theoretical abstraction, it was inscribed from as early as the fifteenth century in the papal donations that sought to regulate colonial partition of the globe. It was also inscribed into the colonial slave codes that followed, into racially segregationist legislation, and most recently into apartheid, all of which institutionalized and supported de facto political and socioeconomic power.[19]

In this light, for example, British philosopher John Locke's seventeenth-century declaration that God gave the world "to the use of the Industrious and the Rational" accomplished two goals. On the one hand it legitimated

18. George Mosse, *Toward the Final Solution: A History of European Racism*, 87.
19. Mills, *Racial Contract.*

Anglo-American nullification of Native American sovereignty over ancestral lands, thereby advancing a primarily material objective. On the other hand, as discourse, it helped segregate the racial imagination of the future national community. In addition, Locke's statement is perfectly congruent with the fact that he had investments in the slave-trading Royal Africa Company, and with his participation in crafting Carolina's Lord Proprietors' "Fundamental Constitutions." The latter gave his peers, as colonial English freemen, "absolute power" over their black slaves.[20] The eighteenth-century planter-historians and intellectuals Edward Long, Bryan Edwards, and Thomas Jefferson, while energetically subscribing to the racialized trope of civilization and barbarism, also underscored the ideological function of discourse in terms of the power relations in society through their writings. Voltaire, a Negrophobe and anti-Semite, and one of the most influential of the eighteenth-century French philosophers, had investments in the trade while the others owned slaves themselves.

In the twentieth century, the supremacist delirium would come to a chilling climax as a generalized whiteness gave way to the Aryan concept as the active metaphor for racial superiority. Under the Nazis, science, instead of rationalizing racial oppression after the fact, as it often did during the colonial period, was invoked a priori to justify projected world domination. Alongside a highly sophisticated and methodical ultranationalist and anti-Semitic propaganda onslaught, it is important to note the Nazi invocation of anthropological principles that were two hundred years old in the state-sanctioned pursuit of the Aryan ideal. The SS ethnographer Bruno Berger, complaining that skull collections existed for every race except the Jews, not only measured the skulls of his subjects when they were alive, but also hastened to advance his scientific research by gassing them so that their skulls could be prepared for further study.

Hitler's first phase of national and racial purging, in which euthanasia was officially decreed, on September 1, 1939, to "free the Aryan race of any potential weakness," led over the next four years to forced labor camps for Jews and other undesirables. It also led to the gas chambers and the mass murder of close to six million Jews. Effectively, during the period 1934 to 1937, around 225,000 individuals suffering from blindness, epilepsy, feeble-mindedness, physical deformity, and alcohol or drug problems were sterilized

---

20. See John Locke, "Of Property," 291; and Robert A. Williams Jr., "Documents of Barbarism: The Contemporary Legacy of European Racism and Colonialism in the Narrative Traditions of Federal Indian Law," 104.

in Germany. This "public health" initiative was applauded by many in the United States and Britain. Between 1905 and 1972, some 70,000 American citizens were ruled eligible for sterilization on similar grounds. Hitler's enslavement of Poles during the occupation was a harbinger of a more generalized slavery under future Nazi domination. It is significant to note that Hitler's megalomaniac dedication to future Aryan hegemony rested on the theoretical foundation of races having "inborn, genetically transmitted" values. Political supremacy, as he told the Industry Club in Düsseldorf in 1932, alluding to colonialism as theory and praxis, was a "natural phenomenon" and "peculiar to the white race:"

> You can choose any single area, take for example India: England did not acquire India in a lawful and legitimate manner, but rather without regard to the natives' wishes, views or declarations of rights; and she maintained this rule, if necessary, with the most brutal ruthlessness. Just as Cortés or Pizarro demanded for themselves Central America and the northern states of South America not on the basis of any legal claim, but from the absolute, inborn feeling of superiority *(Herrengefühl)* of the white race. The settlement of the North American continent was similarly a consequence not of any higher claim in a democratic or international sense, but rather of a consciousness of what is right which had its sole roots in the conviction of the superiority and thus the right of the white race.[21]

To the extent that the discourse of racism in the modern era is susceptible to genealogical reconstruction, it reveals an unseemly underside to the gravity and grandeur of the Enlightenment and to the Occidental discursive tradition as a whole. To the degree that this tradition inscribed a dominant racialized selfhood (whiteness) identifiable with the values of civilization, especially as these values evoke colonization and its aftermath of two world wars, the 1940 comment of one of the casualties of the Nazi Holocaust was as timely as it was appropriate. To the German Jewish cultural critic Walter Benjamin we owe the terse, if poignant, observation that "there is no document of civilization that is not at the same time a document of barbarism."[22] The broad background of a supranational consensus around racial hierarchy facilitates the understanding of the phenomenon as it is manifested in the

21. Hannaford, *Race*, 362, 366; Hitler quoted in Max Domarus, ed., *Hitler: Speeches and Proclamations, 1932–1945*, 96; Mills, *Racial Contract*, 106.

22. Walter Benjamin, *Illuminations*, 258.

narrower, nationalist, framework. Accordingly, it serves the purposes of this introduction to further point out the nationalist marginalization of blacks as it is manifested in erstwhile colonial centers, "mother countries," as well as in the Latin American countries with which this study is primarily concerned.

In studying its evolution in the recent European context, Balibar and Wallerstein point to the discourse of the nation as another important site for the articulation of racism. Their suggestion is also applicable to nineteenth- and twentieth-century foundational discourses of the nation in Latin America, in which blackness and national identity are overwhelmingly regarded as conflictive categories. Like racism, they assert, nationalism involves itself obsessively in a quest for an essential, authentic core. It is a search that, as history has shown, ultimately proves elusive. Balibar and Wallerstein draw our attention to the way the exclusionary national project focuses on the morphology of otherness, language, religion, and race, and they observe that in spite of this exaggerated focus "the fact that the 'false' is too visible will never guarantee that the true is visible enough."[23] Although it is not necessary to analyze contemporary European literature to illustrate this point here, I shall briefly mention the nationalist marginalization of nonwhites in the present-day European context, as well as the writings of twentieth-century Latin American ideologues in the elaboration of a regional or national ideology of race.

Thousands of settlers from the Caribbean responded to the labor shortage in Britain that was occasioned by World War II. Their reception was less than accommodating, despite a black presence in Britain that goes back hundreds of years, and despite the implied universalism of colonial notions of commonwealth. Jamaican vernacular poet Louise Bennett aptly observed at the time, in her customary tongue-in-cheek manner, that the influx of West Indians in this process of "colonization in reverse" might prove a greater test to native British sensibilities than the apocalyptic threat of Hitlerian hegemony that had just recently been overcome. The sometimes veiled and often open invocation to "Keep Britain White" effectively began to be made as early as 1955. These appeals came from the highest political sources, as West Indians, East Indians, and Africans—all fellow colonials—were unwelcome aliens deemed to be "incompatible with authentic forms of Englishness."[24]

23. Balibar and Wallerstein, *Race, Nation, Class,* 9, 99.
24. Bennett's poem "Colonisation in Reverse" reads, "What a devilment a Englan! / Dem face war an brave de worse, / But I'm wonderin' how dem gwine stan' / Colonizin' in reverse" (Louise Bennett, *Jamaica Labrish,* 180); see also Paul Gilroy, *"There Ain't No Black in the Union Jack": The Cultural Politics of Race and Nation,* 46.

The contradiction that was felt to be inherent to the notion of British national identity and blackness, the anxieties arising from day-to-day racial coexistence and miscegenation, as well as a late-1950s recession in Britain, were all factors underlying white aggression in the first race riots, as at Notting Hill in 1958. The crisis subsequently provoked by unemployment, substandard housing, racialized police harassment, the Ku Klux Klan, the neofascist National Front, and systemic exclusion climaxed in the decade of the 1980s, with further riots at Notting Hill in 1981 and in 1985 in Tottenham, Brixton, and Handsworth. It all took place in a political climate in which spokespersons for Britishness referred to former colonial subjects and their British-born children as "the enemy within," and the appeal to white national homogeneity was frequently resorted to in the face of an increasingly multicultural landscape in Britain. Not surprisingly, as Gilroy comments, parties and other forms of leisure and recreation in the black communities were demonized and represented in mainstream media in terms of vice and hedonism. Even crimes committed by blacks were depicted in public discourse as an innate "expression of black culture."[25]

Not surprisingly also, the "crisis in national identity" in contemporary France, according to cultural critic Julia Kristeva, herself an immigrant, is also directly associated with the immigration flow from non-European sources that responded to the national labor shortage after 1945. The postwar influx into France from the Magreb, sub-Saharan Africa, and Asia soon overcame native levels of tolerance, notwithstanding the French universalist ethic and the "blood tax" previously paid by soldiers from the colonies through their participation in the two great wars. Overwork and underpay were characteristic of the experience of the immigrants, as well as their relegation to slum dwelling on the outskirts of major cities. This soon gave way to racist attacks and official calls for their repatriation, seen most notably in violence against Algerians in 1973 and a series of deportations of Malians in 1986. In the search for national (racial) homogeneity in France, not only has the far-right National Front taken a racist stance, but also administrations from both ends of the political spectrum have proven to be conservative when it comes to the foreign, specifically non-European presence.[26]

25. Gilroy, "*There Ain't No Black,*" 45, 109.

26. See Julia Kristeva, *Nations without Nationalism,* 5. Richard Burton uses the term "blood tax" in referring to the willingness of French West Indian enlistees in the 1914 and 1939 wars to prove their dedication to France, in Richard D. E. Burton and Fred Reno, eds., *French, and West Indian: Martinique, Guadeloupe, and French Guiana Today,* 3. As might be expected, assimilation, anti-immigration, and anti-Semitism are the pillars of the National Front's political platform.

The discomfiture caused by non-European settlers in the present post-colonial period is also a significant feature of life in contemporary Spain. Spain's quest for a racially homogenous (white) community in the phase of national consolidation, as reflected in literary discourse, dates back to the Renaissance, and it will be treated in a substantive manner in Chapter 1 of this study. But recent demonstrations of Spanish anti-Moorish xenophobia and racism are illustrative and are worth mentioning. Reports of "long-smouldering hatred" characterize descriptions of mob violence that erupted in the El Ejido community of Almeira as recently as February 2000, as the local population responded to allegations of the murder of a local woman by a Moroccan male. Vociferous calls for repatriation of the Maghrebi ("Moors out!") were made "as local people ran rampage through immigrant neigh-bourhoods, setting homes on fire, looting shops, wrecking the offices of organisations known to be sympathetic to the workers, and generally just tearing the place up, without any regard for whose property or health might suffer."[27]

Donato Ndongo, an immigrant writer and historian from Equatorial Guinea, has, like Kristeva in France, reflected on the meaning of race and nation in Spain today. Ndongo has commented on the myth of a nonracist Spain and on the low tolerance levels for nonwhite foreigners by native Spaniards, in spite of the importance of these immigrants to the economy. He refers to the fact that in 1999 there were over two million unemployed Spaniards when laborers from North and West Africa were sustaining the Spanish agro-industry. Ndongo's observation brings to mind similar situa-tions in the globalized dynamic of North-South migrant labor in which the native populations of the overdeveloped world refuse to take low-paying or low-prestige jobs. The value of the produce (eggplants, cucumbers, and toma-toes) of the Almeira region, set at $1.5 billion by Snowdon, and the wages of the laborers, who receive three hundred dollars a month and live "in hovels with neither running water nor electric lights," also reflects the wider condition of migrant laborers.[28]

In the twentieth century, the ideal of a racially homogeneous white national community in former colonial centers was disrupted by the (postcolonial)

Electoral successes in the spring of 2002 revealed increasing grassroots support, and a recurrence of demagogic discourses using "traditional" precepts regarding the racial difference mostly of the North African foreigners.

27. Peter Snowdon, "The Moor That Meets the Eye."
28. Ibid.

nonwhite presence. To the extent that the philosophical and scientific discourses outlined above had historically informed first the broader racial ideology and then the national identity of these European countries, the diachronic relationship of these discourses to the colonial ideologies of domination is also fundamental. Correspondingly, in nineteenth-century postindependence Latin America, discourses of national identity were marked by the colonial legacy of white supremacy, as well as by the influence of contemporary European racial theories deriving from Social Darwinism and Positivism.

As several studies indicate, the dominant ideology of whiteness in Latin America provoked a massive inferiority complex in elite intellectuals in the latter nineteenth century. Because of their nations' sometimes-high percentages of blacks, Amerindians, and racially mixed individuals (mestizos), intellectuals from Mexico to the Southern Cone were convinced that they were poorly equipped to face the challenges of development and modernization considering the economic and political setbacks brought about by the independence struggle. Immigration policies in Argentina, Brazil, and Cuba, for example, assumed that "whitening" the population was necessary for this development and that the current mestizo, black, and Amerindian masses were a hindrance to progress. These policies are reflected in the fact that between 1880 and 1930 Argentina mobilized the entrance of over three million European settlers while waging a genocidal campaign against the remaining Amerindian population. In an analogous situation, turn-of-the-century Cuba, despite fighting a prolonged war against Spain for independence in 1868–1898, turned to Spain itself to import white immigrants, while denying entrance to blacks from neighboring islands in spite of an acute labor shortage in the sugar industry. The Cuban immigration policy, aimed at correcting what was seen as a racial imbalance, yielded some 900,000 Spaniards and Canary Islanders between 1900 and 1929. It was only after more than a decade of government resistance, and the realization that without sugar the economy was in danger, that the desperate sugar lobby prevailed and recruitment of black workers from the Caribbean was fully legalized in 1917. This allowed for the importation of some 300,000 West Indians into Cuba by 1930.[29]

29. On the scientific racism behind nineteenth-century immigration policies in Latin America, see Thomas E. Skidmore, "Racial Ideas and Social Policy in Brazil, 1870–1940"; Aline Helg, "Race in Argentina and Cuba, 1880–1930: Theory, Policies, and Popular Reaction"; Alejandro de la Fuente, "Two Dangers, One Solution: Immigration, Race, and Labor in Cuba, 1900–1930," 34; and Martin Stabb, who quotes the following from Argentina's Jose Ingenieros's candid, if typical, rationale for the nation's racial problem. In 1908 he wrote: "Anything that might be done for the inferior races would be un-scientific; at best they should be protected so they

What is important about the race-thinking of Latin American intellectuals, as far as it pertains to the questions of national identity and black marginalization in the early twentieth century, is its shift in relation to the trends prevalent at the turn of the century. The unabashedly racist premises of ideologues like Argentina's José Ingenieros, Brazil's Joaquim Nabuco, Venezuela's César Zumeta, and Bolivia's Alcides Arguedas were replaced by raciological models that, instead of dismissing Afro-Latinos and Amerindians out of hand, sought to reevaluate their contribution to the nation from a purportedly antiracist standpoint. The three models with which this introduction concludes illustrate this change while showing the importance of the transatlantic colonial determinant and the permanence of the supremacist assumption. They concern the ideas about hemispheric and national racial identity articulated by Mexico's José Vasconcelos, by Gilberto Freyre's interpretation of Brazil as a "racial democracy," as well as by Fernando Ortiz's theories about racial diversity and transculturation in Cuba.

José Vasconcelos is mostly remembered for his ideas on the Mexican cultural and racial mix put forward in *La raza cósmica* (1926). During 1921–1924 he was Mexico's education minister and exercised a profound influence on cultural policy after the revolution of 1910–1920. Vasconcelos was also instrumental in the implementation of literacy programs aimed at bringing millions of indigenous Mexicans into the national mainstream by teaching them Spanish. *Indigenismo,* the term by which the revolution's vindication of Mexico's Indians is known, celebrated their cultural legacy in literature, cinema, and mural paintings. It also sought to liberate them from domination by rural priests and political bosses or *caciques.* Although it was an important historical development in itself, it has been suggested that the focus of the Mexican revolution on the symbolic value of Indianness helped further obscure an already demographically reduced Afro-Mexican population. This population was only "rediscovered" in the middle 1940s due to the ethnographic studies of Gonzalo Aguirre Beltrán.[30]

---

might disappear peaceably, facilitating the adaptation of the capable, exceptional ones. To be sure, democratic spirits are not flattered by the basic education that is given. Men of color should not be our equals, not politically nor legally; they are inept for exercising the civil capacity and should not be considered "persons" in the legal sense" (Stabb, *In Quest of Identity: Patterns in the Spanish American Essay of Ideas, 1890–1960,* 426).

30. See Gonzalo Aguirre Beltrán, *Cuijla: Esbozo etnográfico de un pueblo negro;* Marco Polo Hernández Cuevas, "The Afro-Mexican and the Revolution: Making Afro-Mexicans Invisible through the Ideology of Mestizaje in *La Raza Cósmica*"; and Marco Polo Hernández Cuevas, *African Mexicans and the Discourse on Modern Nation.*

Two of Vasconcelos's ideas in *La raza cósmica* stand out. They are largely responsible for the democratizing intent mistakenly imputed to his thinking. They have to do, first of all, with his antiracist defense of *mestizaje,* or racial intermixing, in the face of Herbert Spencer's nineteenth-century Social Darwinist theories that felt that miscegenation brought about racial degeneration. In doing this, Vasconcelos invoked the achievements of the mestizo cultures of Egypt, Golden Age Greece, and imperial Rome under Julius Caesar. His point was that Latin America, because of its high levels of racial amalgamation, could also produce a "higher" human type, capable of similar civilizational feats. Vasconcelos cautioned, however, that since the Spanish and Amerindians came from such radically different stocks, a longer period of synthesis would be required to achieve the required result. He also defended the tropics as a site for civilization. This theoretical location of civilization in the tropics is significant in that it went against prevalent notions of geographical determinism that had been propagated since Kant and Hegel. For the latter, climatological factors consistent with the Temperate Zone and its white peoples were key to these peoples' progress, and life in the tropics was inimical to such advancement. Vasconcelos pointed to the pyramids and to other cultural artifacts of America's ancient civilizations to support his argument.

However, Vasconcelos's attribution of the marvels of Aztec and Inca civilizations to the disappeared race of the mythical Atlantis introduces a problematic note in his thought. In describing the Aztecs and the Incas that the Spanish invaders met as "diminished," and "totally unworthy of the ancient and superior culture" (of the Atlanteans), Vasconcelos was effectively denying historical agency to the ancestors of his indigenous compatriots, and he revealed the race and class prejudice of his own *criollo* background. His discomfort with the apparently uninspiring postcolonial present led him to dismiss Darwinian selection, which he saw as limited to the "inferior species," and not humans endowed with free will. He therefore proposed a theory of aesthetic eugenics for Latin America, invoking the work of Austrian botanist Gregor Mendel (1822–1884) as well as the Greco-Roman classical standard. In this vision, the principles of beauty, emotion, and refined aesthetic taste would dominate in the production of a new "cosmic" race, and in the process the more advanced types of humans would absorb the more backward ones. Vasconcelos's program of aesthetic eugenics would make ignorance, misery, and ugliness disappear. Consequently, he thought, the (ugly and inferior) black race would disappear after a few decades of voluntary submission to the process, and the present-day Indians would be able to make the quantum leap and bridge the civilizational gap between the days of Atlantis and the present.[31]

Not surprisingly, the white Hispanic element in the mestizo mixture would be dominant in the new Latin American cosmic breed, especially since it was the historical bearer of the Greco-Roman aesthetic sense, the transcendental values of Christianity, and the valor and strength of the conquistadors. The Vasconcelos racial model, in summary, suppressed both Africa-derived people and their culture, and it suppressed the culture of the Amerindians, although in the broader public sphere, the latter were accorded folkloric value and an attempt was made to bring them closer to the political mainstream. Most importantly, and in keeping with older hegemonic forms, for Vasconcelos, it was Spanishness, or *hispanidad,* albeit diluted, that remained preeminent in an ostensible reversion of Eurocentric values, which, over time, shifted even further to the right of the political spectrum as he went on to support fascism under Franco in Spain.

Postcolonial ambivalence and an inability to rise above inherited schemes of racial hierarchy are also typical of Brazil's most important interpreter of the national cultural identity, Gilberto Freyre. Freyre's creative answer to absolutist racial differentiation also involved an apparently nondismissive role for Brazilians of African and Amerindian descent. His *Casa-grande e senzala: Formação da família brasileira sob o regime patriarcal* (1933) stands in significant contrast to the anxiety over the racial character of the nation that the country's leading intellectuals had expressed at the turn of the century and contrasts with their calls for whiteness and the progress with which this was associated.[32] These calls had determined current immigration policy and produced three million European settlers between the 1880 and 1920. It is noteworthy, therefore, that Freyre in 1933 not only accepted Brazil's multiracial mix, but also went out of his way to selectively assign affirmative value to the contributions of Amerindians and enslaved Africans in the formation of the national culture during the colonial period. His positive assessment of the agricultural, mining, and metallurgical skills of many of the enslaved African males, and of the value of the enslaved black women who served as surrogate mothers of the children of the colonials, is significant in this regard.

31. José Vasconcelos, *La raza cósmica,* 16, 43.

32. Page references in the following paragraphs refer to the 1956 English translation, Gilberto Freyre, *The Masters and the Slaves: A Study in the Development of Brazilian Civilization.*

Freyre's race-thinking is most beneficially analyzed in terms of the broader hemispheric and colonial scheme. In *The Masters and the Slaves,* a consistent underlying theme to his assertive acknowledgment of Brazilian racial hybridity is the proposition that the Portuguese colonialists who founded the nation were themselves cultural and racial hybrids who were accustomed to and accepting of racial and cultural difference. The Portuguese past, with its mixed Moorish, Mediterranean, and Nordic elements, serves as the basis for his assertion that "hybrid from the beginning, Brazilian society is, of all those in the Americas, the one most harmoniously constituted so far as racial relations are concerned" (81). Freyre's Brazil emerges in a morally more favorable light when compared to the separatist racial model of colonial and postcolonial United States, defined by hypodescent, or the "one drop" rule. Since the U.S. model of legalized segregation and its overt public pursuit of white racial purity was not operative in Brazil, his country was, by implication, nonracist.

But the argument for Portuguese "miscibility" on the basis of their cosmopolitanism and traditional absence of prejudice is immediately undermined by Freyre's reference to the process of military and politico-economic occupation of Brazil in terms of the archetypal "civilizing mission" (28). As the European colonial master narrative does, Freyre frames intercultural contact among Europeans, Amerindians, and Africans as an encounter between an advanced race and two backward ones. Indeed, the book's claims to harmonious socio-racial relations are placed in question even by its title, inherent to which are explicit and implicit signifiers of hierarchy along racial, class, and gender lines. First, to the extent that *The Masters and the Slaves* juxtaposes the respective dwelling places of the masters and the slaves as central locations of the typical colonial plantation, it is also projecting them as symbolic spaces where the emerging nation is housed. Inevitably this "national" community, symbolized by the *casa-grande,* or manor house, and the *senzala,* or slave quarters, is dominated by the plantation economy and its very particular relations of production, inherent to which, as the writer himself often notes, is the built-in potential for coercion and brutality on the part of slave masters and slave mistresses. In addition, the title's reference to the national community as a patriarchal family system by definition evokes an uneven balance of power between the paterfamilias and his wife, daughters, and sons, that is, despite the connotations of affection that the metaphor of family invokes. When one makes the colonial core family an "extended family" through the addition of Africans and Amerindians, the potential for phallocentrism and misogyny that is already there acquires new layers of influence and subalternity with the two groups of socio-racial subordinates.

It is important to emphasize that the key element in the family trope of *The Masters and the Slaves* is one of affect, and that this acts rhetorically to disguise the otherwise crude manifestations of power in the symbolic plantation-nation. In this regard it bears noting also that even the affirmative observations about the racial underclass are undercut by negative ones. Hence black wet nurses are portrayed as loving to the white children of the plantation owners that they take care of, although they are also seen as a bad influence in teaching them to be superstitious and to speak improper Portuguese. More importantly, despite Freyre's reference to them as having a "place of honor" in the manor house (324) (as will be further discussed in Chapter 2), the importance of black mammies to white settler families is premised upon them not having families of their own; a point that *The Masters and the Slaves* seems to overlook. Freyre's authorial ambivalence emerges again as he identifies slave children as indispensable playmates of the offspring of the slave-owning class, while they are also seen as a source of moral and physical corruption for them. Slave boys teach their young masters obscene language, and the slave girls introduce them to sex and often to syphilis.

The repeated image of interracial childhood interaction in *The Masters and the Slaves,* as putative metaphor for racial democracy among the young by way of the effect of affect, is by no means watertight. Its purported sincerity is exploded by the sadism that often characterizes the relationship between the young slave owner's son and his black slave companion and in his uninhibited sexual access to black and mulatto girls at the onset of puberty. In fact, the unevenness of such relationships is vividly depicted by Freyre's nonchalant reference to the belief among diseased young males of the slave-holding class that having sex with a twelve- or thirteen-year-old black virgin would cure their syphilis. Considering the vigilance exercised in preserving the virginity of white colonial fifteen-year-old females, and the importance given to their marriage, juxtaposing the destiny of black and white young women gives a graphic indication of racial disparity in Freyre's happy colonial family.

Freyre's misogynist and racist nonchalance is again evident on the question of the sexual basis of the *mestizo* national identity when he describes the initial contact between the Portuguese colonizers and the native women.

The encounter offers him the opportunity to extol the hypervirility of the Portuguese males, while the sexual availability of the Amerindian women is reportedly realized by means of "some trinket or other" (19). Indeed, Freyre's implicit endorsement of this sexual dimension of the colonial conquest is reinforced by the racial scale of sexual virility that he propounds. In contrast to the Portuguese, who are seen as "unbridled stallions," the male Amerindians and Africans are reported to be relatively weak sexually, since "it is indeed a known fact that among primitive peoples the sexual organs are generally less developed than among the civilized" (93).

Considering Freyre's uncritical acceptance of the material and symbolic violence that are part and parcel of the white-male-dominated colonial sexual economy that forms his book's central trope of a multiracial national family, it comes as no surprise that racist colonial myths find unedited inclusion in his analysis. These include the idea of the happy black slave and the notion that blacks are unaffected by the tropical heat and are thus perfectly suited by nature for slave labor. The proposal carries the trace of the proslavery argument that held that blacks were better off in civilized Brazil as slaves than they were as savages in heathen Africa, or that their condition was preferable to that of many in the European working class. Effectively, the most recent proponent of this position had been historian João Ribeiro, whose 1900 history of Brazil was adopted as an advanced textbook and which still served this function in 1966, in its nineteenth edition.[33] Writing in 1933, Freyre would clearly have been under its influence. The inability or reluctance to recognize pain and suffering in the subordinated racial Other is a cornerstone of the racist outlook, as Mills has observed; in *The Masters and the Slaves,* it is a discursive constant. While there is little, if any, overt discursive demonizing of racial subalterns in Freyre's text, it is clear that the latter are devalued and are feminized as a function of the rhetorical aggrandizement of the Portuguese element of the national mix. In *The Masters and the Slaves,* the classical racist negation of the Other is replaced by a rhetorical zigzag between assertion and negation in keeping with the objective of establishing an absence of racial animus. It is doubtful, however, whether the writer's claims for the paternalism and "mildness" of the regime would have been endorsed by the victims of the longest-lasting slave regimen in the Americas.

In summary, what Freyre achieved with the image of the *bom senhor,* or

33. Conrad makes this point in *Children of God's Fire,* xxii.

"good master," of the Brazilian slave past, and his happy plantation family, was to help legitimize a ruling-class consensus about race relations in colonial Brazil, whose parameters were presumed to apply to the present. Where Vasconcelos's new Americans of the cosmic race still harbored a dream of eugenic elimination and purification, Freyre's model appeared to embrace Brazil's miscegenated subjectivity, even upholding it up as a counter to U.S. segregation. By rhetorically removing the problem of racism, the Freyreian effect was that it was deemed to not exist. Future evocation of it would be discordant, producing a tradition of denial and minimization of the existence of racial discrimination and stratification in Brazil. Indices from every area of life in contemporary Brazil confirm its baleful existence, however, whether in white-black disparities in education, housing, employment, income distribution, imprisonment, and police violence, or in terms of numbers of elected political officials.[34]

The work of Cuba's Fernando Ortiz was singular in that it was multidisciplinary and spanned several decades, from the turn of the century to his death in 1969. Ortiz was a cultural anthropologist, jurist, historian, and public intellectual, and his thought reflects not only the international theoretical trends and changes in race-thinking over the period, but also the important impact race had on socio-political developments in Cuba, and on the definition of the national identity. His writings have been influential at both levels. One of Ortiz's most well-known theoretical contributions to the question of Cuba's cultural identity revolves around his active espousal, from the late 1920s onward, of the concept of a racially hybrid (Hispano-African) national culture. Coinciding with the flourishing of the *negrista* movement (which will be further discussed in Chapters 4 and 5), his public vindication of Africa-derived elements of Cuban culture during this period marked an important contrast with the cultural and political persecution and marginalization of Afro-Cubans that was the legacy of the colonial past. It formed an important point of departure for claims that seek to establish the democratic intent behind his writing.

In his 1940 essay "Los factores humanos de la cubanidad," Ortiz detailed the diverse ethnic origins of the national population—American, European, Asian, and African—and pointed out that this heterogeneity was essential to any definition of the national population. His analysis subverted the dominant, white-nonwhite colonial and neocolonial binary, and it amounted

34. Jan Fiola, "Race Relations in Brazil: A Reassessment of the 'Racial Democracy' Thesis."

to an important antiracist declaration, since it publicly challenged long-prevalent notions of racial separateness and hierarchy in Cuba. Ortiz's remarks were even more effective, coming as they did from an academic and highly regarded public intellectual. Critiquing the concept of racial purity itself, he likened Cuban cultural diversity to the national dish, *ajiaco.* His comparison sought to highlight, on the one hand, the "democratic" nature of the dish, since it is composed of a variety of raw materials and is consumed by everyone, and on the other, its dynamic nature, since constant additions make *ajiaco* a perennially unfinished and constantly renewed product. In another 1940 essay, he reinforced the egalitarian thrust of his analysis when he spoke of Cuban culture, not in the then-current hierarchic anthropological terminological framework of deculturation and acculturation, but more in terms of a give-and-take process of transculturation.[35] For Ortiz, Cuba's racial and cultural diversity should be appreciated and its potential for cohesiveness valued.

It is important to observe, although the details cannot be fully discussed here, that Ortician antiracism in the 1930s and 1940s was motivated by events both at home and abroad. The Fascist offensives of Mussolini and Hitler in the late 1930s, for example, had awakened latent anti-Semitism in Cuba, producing calls for the expulsion of Jews and state confiscation of their property. In 1939, Ortiz came out against this scandal; citing Cuba's patriot and martyr of the late nineteenth century, José Martí, he called for national racial unity. Martí was undoubtedly a source of nationalist and antiracist inspiration. The moral and intellectual integrity of Martí had been stimulated by his experiences in the armed struggle for Cuba's independence against Spain. It was a project in which the participation of black Cubans, the famous *mambises,* was overwhelming. Martí's response to the historical moment put the national interest above racial division, and his sense of social justice prompted repeated declarations against the Social Darwinism and the Positivism espoused by the Latin American intellectual elite mentioned above. In two articles in 1945 and 1955, "Martí y las razas de librería" and "La sinrazón de los racismos," Ortiz endorsed Martí's deconstruction of racist precepts by quoting him verbatim and by placing his thinking of several decades before in line with that of the most recent antiracist pronouncements of the international anthropological community:

35. See Fernando Ortiz, "El fenómeno social de la transculturación y su importancia en Cuba."

"Races have no innate hierarchy of intelligence, feeling, ethics, or personality. There are no 'predestined,' 'chosen,' nor 'cursed' races, in spite of the millennial racisms of theologies, of philosophies, of politics, of custom, of folklore, or of the premature conclusions of scientists."[36]

It is perhaps ironic that Ortiz, patriot and "social scientist," had already, by the time of his period of antiracist crusading, made indelible contributions to the scientific foundation of racial oppression in Cuba. As I point out in Chapter 5, his analysis of Afro-Cuban religion in his criminological study *Hampa afro-cubana* (1906) made a lasting contribution to vernacular and juridical stereotyping of blacks in Cuba. Early Ortician writings are also vital to the literary representation of blacks in twentieth-century Cuban literature. Despite the revolution's successes decades later in acknowledging the worth of Afro-Cuban cultural and religious practices, whether merely as folklore or for their inherent epistemological value, many such practices are today still placed under the rubric of "social pathologies," in keeping with official policies of the Ministry of Health. They are associated with such criminal activities as juvenile delinquency, drug abuse, child abuse, and truancy.[37] The criminalizing of certain aspects of African culture in colonial and postcolonial Latin America had been a governmental constant. Under the racist paradigm of turn-of-the-century Positivist criminology, energetically endorsed by an influential young Ortiz, it acquired the respectability of scientific sanction in newly independent Cuba.

A significant feature of the Cuban revolution of 1959 was the erosion of social disadvantage, especially in such areas as education, housing, and employment. Indeed, the revolution's orientation towards the removal of class privilege under socialism has over the years overridden concerns felt and sometimes expressed by Afro-Cubans concerning racial disadvantages they have experienced. But with the now-dominant notion of hybridity at the service of national homogeneity, and with the tabooing of serious intellectual discourse about race, public discourse in Cuba about the concerns of black racial specificity under socialism often proved to be risky. European-oriented cultural and aesthetic preferences still prevail. Further, the fall of communism brought a sharpening of the economic crisis in the island, and increased competition in a changed and "dollarized" economy also meant an often-racialized reformulation of alliances and networks in the struggle for

36. Fernando Ortiz, "La sinrazón de los racismos," 173 (emphasis in the original); see also Fernando Ortiz, "Defensa cubana contra el racismo antisemita."
37. Gayle McGarrity, "Race, Culture, and Social Change in Contemporary Cuba."

goods and services, in which broad masses of Afro-Cubans are still left behind. Like Ortiz's *ajiaco,* the racial question in Cuba, revolution notwithstanding, is still in an "unfinished state," one in which the historically inevitable flux and tension still obtain.

This introduction has pointed to the connection between racism as theory and practice in the modern period and as a coeval and integral feature of colonial expansion, the slave trade, and the development of capitalism. It has highlighted the corresponding importance of the ideology of racial whiteness to the national identity of metropolitan centers and to Latin American nations subordinated to the colonial determinant. This background is important for the fullest appreciation of the texts to be analyzed, since they speak to black and colonial subjectivity during the respective historical phases during which the *negro* was written, even as they alert us to the diversionary effect of the racial democracy postulates. The initial moment of colonial expansion in the fifteenth century, the colonial culture of slavery, and the changes that came with the politics and ideology of abolitionism in the nineteenth century are important stages in this historical process. This background also provides a context for the national discourse about race and diversity in Latin America as far as they impacted national identity at the end of the nineteenth century and at the beginning of the twentieth, when *negrismo* made its appearance.

1

Iberian Antecedents

Some touched my hands and limbs, and rubbed me with their spittle to discover whether my whiteness was dye or flesh. Finding that it was flesh they were astounded.

    Alvise Cadamosto, c. 1455

I saw in a city market place here, some 50 of these animals, piled up in a circle, their feet forming the circumference and their heads the center. Tied at the feet, they were dragging themselves and struggling to reach a large barrel with water. I stopped to see what they were doing. The entire effort of these unfortunates was aimed at licking the staves of the barrel, through which water seeped. Between them and a herd of pigs fighting over a mud hole, whether it was the way they did it, or because of their color, there was no difference whatsoever.

    Filippo Sasseti, *Lettere,* 1580

Gomes Eanes de Zurara's *Crónica dos feitos de Guiné* was completed in 1453 and has been described as the "first book written by a European on the lands south of Cape Bojador."[1] It provides the "most complete and authentic record of exploration down the West African Coast approximately up to

---

1. Page references in the following paragraphs will be to Charles Beazley and Edgar Prestage's translation of Gomes Eanes de Zurara, *The Chronicle of the Discovery and Conquest of Guinea.*

the year 1448," according to J. W. Blake, and has been of use mainly as a source for historical research. Blake and other historians have cited it to highlight the decades of Portuguese exploration that preceded Columbus's New World find, as well as the intense Portuguese and Castilian rivalry that produced the first colonial war between European powers and characterized this early scramble for Africa. The historic treaty of Alcaçovas, signed on September 4, 1479, brought Castilian and Portuguese competition momentarily to an end after four years of fighting. It limited Castile to the Canaries, while Portugal's claim to the other islands of the Atlantic archipelago and to the as yet "undiscovered" parts of Africa remained intact. Portugal's outthrust from 1415 to the turn of the century, and the eventual establishment of its vast seaborne empire, are important in the context of Ibero-American studies. The achievement of Portugal's captains Bartolomeu Diaz, Vasco da Gama, Pedro Alvarez Cabral, and Fernão de Magalhães contest the centrality of Columbus to the broader narrative of exploration and discovery, and to 1492 as the signpost of the modern period. In the same way, Portugal's production of sugar and its establishment of the slave plantation as an institutional complex in Madeira and the other Atlantic islands stand as important historical antecedents to conquest and colonization in the Americas.[2]

The relevance of this Ibero-African background to Ibero-American studies, or the value of Zurara's chronicle as a resource for historical research, is not difficult to establish. It may be observed, however, that when historians or cultural critics cite or comment on *Discovery and Conquest,* it is rare to find an engagement with Zurara's writerly intentions in the text, or with his rhetorical praxis in what is clearly a discourse of power. This seems to be the case irrespective of the degree to which his commentators endorse or critique the obvious ideological elements that undergird his narrative, or the triumphalist tenor of the macrotext that it supports.[3] The apparent gap in Zuraran

2. See John William Blake, trans. and ed., *Europeans in West Africa, 1450–1560,* 3–4. The first voyage of Alvise de Ca' da Mosto took place in 1455. Unlike Zurara, Cadamosto (as he is called in the English historiographic tradition) was both chronicler *and* adventurer. Although Cadamosto's firsthand testimony of Portuguese ventures was regarded as one of the primary authorities on West Africa, Zurara's chronicle is of greater importance to the present discussion on account of its ideological content and, obviously, because it covers an earlier period. On the early Portuguese and Castilian conflict, see P. E. Hair, "Columbus from Guinea to America." Bartolomeu Diaz rounded Africa's southernmost tip, the Cape of Good Hope, in 1488; da Gama reached Calicut in 1498; Cabral landed on the Brazilian coast in 1500; and Magalhães went around the globe between 1519 and 1521.

3. See, for example, A. C. de C. M. Saunders, *A Social History of Black Slaves and Freedmen in Portugal, 1441–1555;* Hugh Thomas, *The Story of the Atlantic Slave Trade: 1440–1870;* A. J. R. Russell-Wood, "Iberian Expansion and the Issue of Black Slavery: Changing Portuguese Attitudes,

scholarship is important, especially since his chronicle evidently occupies an important place in the broader European master narrative of discovery, colonization, and the creation of a worldwide racial order. In a more specific sense, the extent to which it also inscribes a paradigm of social and cultural hierarchy, of conquerors and conquered, as the captive Africans are forcibly inserted into fifteenth-century Portuguese society, is also important to my discussion.

The African presence in the Iberian Peninsula has, of course, been attested to since Roman times, but it is the modern history of this presence, and the relation between writing and subjectivity, that is of greater importance to the present discussion. Zurara's account of Portugal's venture in the Atlantic and down the West African coast is therefore significant as an early inscription of the modern encounter of European and non-European peoples and also for what this encounter reveals in terms of the dialectic of identity and difference. The fact that the "us and them" dichotomy that it expresses is articulated within a discourse of domination and conquest is what makes the document historically important as an act of signifying. Postcolonial critic Mary Louise Pratt has called attention to the way in which European travel and exploration writing produced the "rest of the world" for European readerships, encoding and thereby legitimating Europe's aspirations to "economic expansion and empire." In a similar vein, Homi Bhabha has pointed to colonialist stereotyping as a tactical and textual strategy designed to "construe the colonised as a population of degenerate types" and to (re)produce them in terms of an enduring racialized subalternity.[4]

The intervention of postcolonial critique as a deconstructive emancipatory response to what Said has referred to as the "knitted together" strength of varying colonizing enterprises is aptly summed up by Chris Tiffin and Alan Lawson in their introduction to *De-Scribing Empire: Postcolonialism and Textuality*. They remind us, "Imperial relations may have been established initially by guns, guile and disease, but they were maintained in their interpellative phase largely by textuality, both institutionally... and informally. Colonialism (like its counterpart, racism) ... is an operation of discourse, and as an operation of discourse it interpellates colonial subjects by

1440–1770"; Margarida Barradas de Carvalho, "L'idéologie religieuse dans la 'Crónica dos feitos de Guiné' de Gomes Eanes de Zurara"; Luis Felipe Barreto, "Gomes Eanes de Zurara e o problema da 'Crónica da Guiné"; and C. R. Boxer, *The Portuguese Seaborne Empire, 1415–1825.*

4. Mary Louise Pratt, *Imperial Eyes: Travel Writing and Transculturation*, 5; Bhabha, "Other Question," 41.

incorporating them in a system of representation."[5] This section of the chapter examines some of the ways in which Zurara's chronicle, in recording an early instance of exploration-associated plunder, trade, and capital accumulation, prior to colonization proper, labels blacks and other colonized people as inferior, under various rubrics, and articulates a justification for their subjection, thereby setting a discursive precedent for subsequent colonial writing. It stresses the degree to which the deployment of military adventurers, fortune seekers, and members of the nobility, by Portugal's Prince Henrique (Henry the Navigator), defines the venture in terms of a national protostatist alliance, as well as in terms of the incipient imperial project that this alliance made feasible. Three decades later, in 1492, the contents of Columbus's letter to the royal scribe Luis de Santangel, in which he details the human and natural resources of the first islands he stumbles upon, would speak to the same process.

The analysis of Zurara will be followed by a discussion of the insertion of blacks into Renaissance Spain, that is, at the moment of its formation as a nation-state. My reading of *Discovery and Conquest* sees the triumphalism of the text as essential to the ideological objectives of the chronicler in his role as panegyrist and national propagandist. Accordingly, the Prince, or Infante, Henrique, to whom it is dedicated, and the men who represent him abroad become the avatars of civilization and official defenders of the faith. The subjected Others are represented as barbarous, less than human, and somehow deserving of their subordination in the new imperial order. The section also explores the extent to which the contradictory motifs of the civilizing mission, the expansionist quest for profits, and the fundamentalism of the anti-Islamic crusade lay bare the ambivalence attendant to the textuality of colonialism.

Zurara was appointed royal chronicler in 1448 when he replaced his predecessor, Fernão Lopes. He was commissioned by King Affonso V with the writing of the chronicle to honor the king's uncle, the Infante (1395–1460) in order that his deeds, "so noteworthy among the many actions of Christian princes in this world," might be remembered forever (1.3). The zeal with which Zurara undertook the task of telling the story of the discovery and conquest of Guinea gets its fullest expression in his portrayal of the Infante. The fact that he was personally familiar with the prince and with the other aristocratic protagonists of the events he described added to his enthusiasm as a writer. Dom Henrique is a heroic extract from the

5. Said, *Orientalism,* 6; Chris Tiffin and Alan Lawson, "The Textuality of Empire," 3.

medieval novels of chivalry. His heroic status is built upon his exemplary service to God and king. In his eulogistic portraiture, Zurara does not distinguish between the terrestrial and celestial dimensions of the Infante's praiseworthiness; he is a visionary, a strategist, a statesman, and a military exemplar. Since many of his successes are achieved in the context of the confrontation with Islam, or may be so construed, his symbolic importance is also calculated in terms of the crusading ethic of eliminating the Infidel and spreading Christianity. The honor that the Infante accumulates in his life's work is therefore both earthly (national) and celestial.

The dual aspects of Henrique's persona are interwoven in the relation of two of his early triumphs: the prince's valiant performance in the conquest of Ceuta in 1415, in which the blows he delivered against the Infidels were "conspicuous beyond those of all other men," and his successful deployment of an armada he sent out against the Canaries some years later "to show the natives there the way of the holy faith" (1.16, 18). These events occupy the same narrative space as the relation of the churches he erected around Portugal.[6] Zurara recalls the hagiographic as he stresses the prince's wisdom and humility, his hardworking nature, his moral strength in abstaining from drink and sex, his generosity to guests and the members of his court, and his thirst for knowledge (1.12–13). In pinpointing the prince's more mundane objectives of finding new sources of trade, bringing new peoples into the Christian fold, and undermining Islamic geopolitical power, Zurara combines the two dimensions of the prince's actions into a single profile.

Zurara's celebration of Henrique's service to God and king—he refers to him at one point as "little less than divine"—calls attention to the very nature of the panegyric (1.6). A less-idealized version of the Infante's résumé, however, might draw attention to the degree to which the chronicler builds his song of praise around distinct features of selection and omission. Such an account might point out where the prince's motivations were more material than spiritual and also consider the facts of his deliberate, if patient, entrepreneurship and his political dexterity. These are shown by his persistence in sending out expeditions of exploration until they returned a profit, and in his subsequent acquisition of the monopoly over the licenses to trade in the newly discovered areas through his influence at court and at the papal curia. Despite his relative disadvantage in the royal hierarchy (he was King João's third son), Henrique also managed to appropriate the royal fifth, traditionally the king's purview, of the proceeds from the new ventures overseas.

6. Eanes de Zurara, *Discovery and Conquest,* chapter 5.

With his political titles (Duke of Viseu, Lord of Covilhão), and the revenues he derived from them, as well as his monopolies over tuna fishing in the Algarve and over soap production in the Realm, the Infante over time became "the third richest magnate in the kingdom," according to Ivana Elbl's estimates. When one considers, in addition, that a dispensation from consanguinity had been granted in relation to wedding plans in which the Infante had been involved, both his celibacy and his disinterest in material gain, underscored by Zurara (1.12–14), are placed in doubt.[7]

Zurara's rhetorical selectivity and elision are equally apparent in relation to the cognitive space accorded the Other in the narrative, whether these are the Idzâghen tribesmen of the Moroccan coast that the Portuguese encounter, the sub-Saharan Africans among them, or the Guanche natives of the Canaries. In his chapter summarizing the Infante's works, the chronicler is notably brief in describing how the Canary Islands were brought to "the way of the holy faith." His juxtaposition of the "great armada" employed in the task, however, and the claim for proselytism that follows it (showing them "the way of the holy faith"), is what betrays here the central paradox of his text as colonialist apologia (1.18). Although the settlement and the productivity of the previously uninhabited Madeiras are mentioned almost in the same breath, the triumphalist passage fails to mention the means by which the large supplies of "wheat, sugar, wax, honey and wood, and many other things," were produced. Henrique's expedition in 1425 against the Grand Canary continued a process that by 1450 had exported two-thirds of the native Canarians as slaves. The productivity and "great profit" of the Madeiras at Zurara's time of writing had been made possible primarily through Guanche slave labor (1.18).

To the degree that his syntax asserts the agency of the emerging metropolitan forces in the production of colonial wealth and denies the natives historical recognition as the producers of this wealth, Zurara's account can be seen as a sort of figurative erasure of the group. Their rhetorical suppression in the text parallels the real process of extinction of the native Canarians over the course of the fifteenth century. By implication also, the mention of the newly colonized lands primarily in terms of their productivity for the colonialist project signals their inclusion within the orbit of the incipient

7. Ivana Elbl, "A Man of His Time (and Peers): A New Look at Henry the Navigator," 78. Hayden White, in *The Content of the Form: Narrative Discourse and Historical Representation,* and "The Historical Text as Literary Artifact," alerts us to the writerly strategies of characterization, motific repetition, suppression and exaggeration of events, and so on, and the way they contribute to the creation of meaning in the historical text.

capitalist industrial order. By implication, their previous patterns of production might be disregarded as subsistence-level and prerational. Later, when he discusses the way of life of the Canarians in greater detail, Zurara invokes their barbarism and bestiality to justify their conquest and enslavement, as he again does in the case of the sub-Saharan Africans.[8] Considering the reference made earlier to Lockean invocation of industry and the rational in the heyday of continental expansion on the American continent, Zurara's early articulation of the colonial ideology of divinely approved expropriation of indigenous lands and labor is to be underscored.

A shifty rhetorical platform is the inevitable product of the irreconcilable ideological objectives of the expansionist text. The song of praise to the expansionist hero and the account of his triumphs impose a compromise with the empirical, as pointed out above. When Zurara identifies and represents the colonized, his discourse is similarly restricted by the requirements of triumphalism. While slave raiding *(razzias)* had been a Mediterranean tradition for centuries and has in all likelihood characterized intercultural conflict universally, in Zurara's postmedieval, expansionist text, the phenomenon of the manhunt is sandwiched between the discourse of evangelism and the clear and concrete desire for material gain. The conundrum that comes out of representing captives both as colonial booty and as souls for Christendom provokes elaborate ideological justifications, as well as semantic instability in identifying them.

In 1434, Henrique's squire Gil Eannes rounded the dreaded promontory at Cape Bojador, situated at twenty-six degrees north on the Saharan coast, after over a decade of patient and persistent effort and investment. It was the most important moment of the enterprise of exploration before the discovery of the gold trade at El Mina four decades later. The feat put to rest myths that had formerly haunted Venetian, Genoese, and Portuguese sailors, not only as to the impassability of the promontory, but as to what lay beyond it.[9]

8. A. J. R. Russell-Wood puts the number of Canary captives at fifty thousand ("Before Columbus: Portugal's African Prelude to the Middle Passage and Contribution to Discourse on Race and Slavery," 140). By midcentury, the consensus among Portuguese explorers, following Cadamosto, would be that the Senegal River separated "the Blacks from the brown people called the Azanaghi," (27). See C. R. Crone, ed. and trans., *"The Voyages of Cadamosto," and Other Documents on Western Africa in the Second Half of the Fifteenth Century,* 27.

9. In relating the event, Zurara claimed credit for Portugal's maritime leadership, suggesting that its seamen had gone "where none had gone before" (chapter 7), presaging thereby a motif that would be a constant in the national epic *Os lusíadas* (1572), by Luís de Camões, and, of course, reappear most recently in twentieth-century Western popular culture of space exploration (the television series *Star Trek*).

The maritime milestone apart, the event also marked a qualitative and quantitative change in the exploratory enterprise. Beyond lay the sub-Saharan populations and the captives for the future transatlantic trade.

What is remarkable about the narration of this stage of events is the growing speculation and excitement as the expectations of spoils are fulfilled. The voyages between 1434, when Cape Bojador was circumnavigated, and 1444, when the first major shipment of captives was brought to Lagos for sale, are marked by findings of increasing value. The findings range from mere herbs, plucked as evidence of landfall at the new site in 1434, to seals, and finally to humans (1.34). It is the narrator's collapsing of the different categories of items—vegetable, animal, and human—into the single class of "booty," however, that is noteworthy in the description of events. So, too, is the bloodlust of the adventurers. Zurara's relation of Gil Eannes's and Goncalvez Baldaya's return to Rio d'Ouro after they saw "footmarks of men and camels" (1.34) at Bojador carries the unmistakable mark of the predatory even though that particular hunt was eventually unsuccessful. His juxtaposition of the two kinds of "game" that they acquire two years later is equally revealing: "And because he saw...a great multitude of sea-wolves...he caused his men to kill as many as they could, and with their skins he loaded his ship—for either because they were so easy to kill, or because the bent of our men was towards such an action, they made among those wolves a very great slaughter. But with all this Affonso Gonçalvez was not satisfied, because he had not taken one of those Moors, so going on beyond this for a space of fifty leagues to see if he could make captive some man, woman, or child, by which to satisfy the will of his Lord" (1.37).

People and animals coalesce semantically again as Zurara reports on an expedition in 1443 that reached the island of Arguim. Discovering the island and seizing its natives, and discovering a neighboring one and capturing numerous royal herons, all form part of a seamless narrative in which islands, birds, and human captives are all registered as booty. The explorers' success in "making booty," as a primary topic, allows the narrator to foreground the actions and experiences of the Portuguese parties. Subsequently the remaining chapters of the narrative become an almost monotonous chronicle of the geography of conquest; that is to say of place names, the list of Portuguese adventurers involved, and a detailing of the number of Moors that they took. As "objects" in this narrative of mercantile speculation and predatory success, the humanity of the captives is again submerged.

While it is important to point out the suppression of the humanity of the natives in Zurara's protocolonialist account, it is also important to recognize that this depiction of them as less than human is only an attempt at objectification, one that is ideologically necessary to narrative triumphalism and that is rooted in the will to power. As Leonard Cassuto argues in the analogous case of the discourse of slavery and racism in the United States, "humans just can't see other people as nonpersons for long," suggesting, further, that such human objectification in fact "never fully succeeds." Cassuto locates the objectification principle in the "desire for superiority," since our anthropomorphic instincts predispose us to recognize our common humanity.[10] It turns out that the text's restoration of the humanity of the captives, in spite of the chronicler himself, perhaps, is never far away, as he narrates how the Moorish natives at the island of Naar flee in panic before the Portuguese onslaught: "Then you might see *mothers* forsaking their *children,* and *husbands* their *wives,* each striving to escape as best he could. Some drowned themselves in the water; others thought to escape by hiding under their huts; others stowed their children among the seaweed, where our men found them afterwards, hoping they would thus escape notice" (1.66; emphasis added).

The terms designating human family members in this passage betrays the recognition of the essential humanity of the Moors. A careful tally of the surviving ones is made immediately, however, and we are told that some are "stored" (as merchandise would be) in small boats to await the arrival of the larger caravels for eventual transport to Portugal. What the passage also highlights is the narrator's semantic instability in naming them one way and then another. In the denial and subsequent acknowledgment of their personhood, the Moors as captives are suspended somewhere between the animate and the inanimate.

It turns out that location in the narrative is a key factor in the ontological appreciation of the prisoners. If in describing them in the islands and on the African coast they are seen primarily as material spoils of conquest with eagerly anticipated market value, and thus objectified, on the mainland they are rehumanized. When the first group is put up for public auction at Lagos, the contradiction of a campaign to Christianize that is also a campaign to conquer and enslave is exposed. The chronicler's rhetorical premise of praising the prince who brought so many pagans into the way of salvation is thrown off-kilter by the ethical and moral problem that emerges. In spite of a tradition in commercial law that made slaves marketable as *cousas* (things),

---

10. Leonard Cassuto, *The Inhuman Race: The Racial Grotesque in American Literature and Culture,* 16–19.

and in spite of his prior placement of them in the class of plants and animals, as Zurara relates the episode of the auction, the human subjectivity of
the prisoners imposes itself. Their loud lamentations are too striking to be
ignored. So, too, is the graphic image of children struggling with their captors to resist separation from their parents, or that of mothers who cling to
their offspring for as long as possible, valiantly disregarding the blows they
receive from their captors. That this brutality violates a wider moral consensus, and that the townsfolk who had come to witness the novelty empathize
with the tragedy of the captives *as fellow humans* to the extent of disrupting
the proceedings, emphasizes the ultimate failure of the legal and narrative
attempts at objectification. In the end, the commoners have to be restrained
for the mass sale to be successfully completed. The chronicler, spokesperson
for the business interests of the aristocracy, finds it an opportune moment
to commiserate with the captives as he also claims that he wept "in pity for
their sufferings" (1.81).

This, however, is one of the few moments that the narrative recognizes
their victimization. Although some historians highlight the chronicler's
response to their plight, it is pertinent to note that Zurara's sympathy is short-
lived.[11] His role as apologist reasserts itself as he extracts the Infante from
any moral responsibility and advances justification after the fact for the capture and enslavement of the foreigners. He clarifies for posterity that the
pleasure the Infante expresses at the success of his captains is based purely
on the "salvation of those souls that before were lost" (1.83). The human
agency of mercantile speculation is therefore replaced in the narrative by the
workings of fate, and the goddess Fortune is assigned a role in the present
predicament of the prisoners and in their future deliverance.

Faced by the morally unbecoming image of the prince astride his powerful steed, claiming his "royal fifth" of the wailing men, women, and children,
and his redistributing them in lordly fashion among his followers, Zurara
resorts to stressing the compensatory value of Euro-Christian culture for the
captives. It is a device that is often used, in obvious dismissal of the prisoners'
own heritage and cultural specificity, and it anticipates proslavery justifications
that appear in later centuries. Zurara emphasizes the spiritual as well as the
material superiority of Christendom and inscribes, at the same time, the
notion of the European space being the civilized one, with the corollary that,

---

11. See, for example, Saunders, *Social History,* 35. Thomas uses Zurara's rhetorical question
"What heart could be so hard (as not to be pierced by piteous feeling to see that company)?" as
title and epigraph to his first chapter (*Story of the Atlantic,* 22).

notwithstanding the means employed, their habitation of European space is needed for the savages' sake. The chronicler's claims regarding the compensatory value of Christian culture for these foreigners range from assertions of their benign treatment as slaves and their happy integration into Portuguese society to their joyful acceptance of Christian sacraments and their dismissal of the false prophet Muhammad. On one occasion, in a remarkable display of cognitive dissonance, Zurara laments that some Moors choose to flee upon witnessing the decimation of their companions, rather than surrender to the Christian slave hunters and thereby guarantee eternal salvation for their souls: "And finally of all the people there were taken, fifty-seven; some others were killed and again some others escaped. Oh, if only among those who fled there had been some little understanding of higher things. Of a surety I believe, that the same haste which they showed in flying, they would then have made in coming to where they might have saved their souls and restored their things in this life" (2.201).

Zurara's compensatory arguments are premised on Aristotelian notions of the natural inferiority of some people, that is, their natural enslavability, and on the thinking of medieval theologians that further justified the subjection of nonbelievers. According to thirteenth-century thinker Egidio Colonna, unacceptable norms of dress, housing, and diet, as well as the lack of laws and a stable government, placed some peoples closer to the beasts than to civilized humanity. Bestiality meant enslavability. Zurara's colonialist justification is both derivative and prescriptive, as he details not only the foreigners' paganness, but also their apparent lack of reason and industry, their nakedness, lack of houses, and the fact that they seemed only to know how to live "in a bestial sloth" (1.85). The gross cultural chauvinism apparent in assuming that the surviving captives would be better off living among Europeans "under an alien rule," or that, on account of their ignorance of Christianity and their bestiality, their own culture represented "much greater captivity" (1.10, 2.201), would later become ideological cornerstones of colonialism and the Atlantic slave trade.[12] According to Thomas Aquinas, the thirteenth-century Aristotelian scholar to whom Zurara often alludes, to the extent that unbelievers might, however indirectly, stand in the way of the diffusion of

12. Political and cultural superiority is also taken for granted in the Spanish *Requirimiento,* an imperialist document that called for political and cultural surrender from natives in America. The accompanying demonization of Aztec gods by sixteenth-century Spanish priest Bernardino de Sahagún offers a striking example of this; see *Historia general de las cosas de Nueva España.* Anthony Pagden and Jan Nederveen Pieterse study the supremacist premise in French and British colonial and travel writing.

Catholicism, war might justly be waged against them. Additionally, deterring the possible proliferation of any non-Christian doctrine, or reducing the lands or goods of the adherents to alien religions, was seen as justification for Christian offensives.

Zurara's ideological framework also incorporated the Augustinian doctrine that enslavability is premised on divine punishment for sin. The Idzâgen tribesmen of the Moroccan littoral were the approved enemy because they were Muslim and the offshore islanders might be preyed upon because they were seen as primitives. Justification of the enslavement of the black Africans in this process, however, is sought in the original sin of Noah's son Ham for staring upon his father's nakedness. A millennium before Christ, the ancient Hebrews had used Noah's mythical curse upon the descendants of Ham's son Canaan to celebrate their military conquest in the Land of Canaan and to justify the enslavement of its inhabitants. This power myth originated in a racially homogenous context but would come, over time, to apply to Syrian, Slav, and black African captives. It would also be assumed by Islamic slave ideology. If, in fixing itself upon black Africans in the context of modern Atlantic slavery, this anti-Hamitism might be referred to as a deformation, its essentially mobile and mythical nature is confirmed in its application to Native Americans in the nineteenth century. Their exploitation was also justified in terms of Ham's cursedness.[13]

The anti-Hamitic myth makes its appearance earlier in the text to explain the presence of some enslaved blacks among Moorish prisoners. The reason, Zurara asserts, is "the curse which, after the Deluge, Noah laid upon his son Cain [sic] ... that his race should be subject to all the other races of the world" (1.54). It buttresses an also prevalent racial prejudice that he expresses at Lagos, that associated whiteness with beauty and the divine, and blackness with the polar opposites of ugliness and deviltry: "And these, placed all together in that field, were a marvelous sight; for amongst them were some white enough, fair to look upon, and well proportioned; others were less white like mulattoes; others again were as black as Ethiops, and so ugly, both in features and in body, as almost to appear [to those who saw them] the images of a lower hemisphere" (1.81). The racial diversity of the group he described would most likely have been the result of the presence of white European Christians, victims of similar raids during the period of Islamic

13. See William McKee Evans, "From the Land of Canaan to the Land of Guinea: The Strange Odyssey of the 'Sons of Ham'"; for references to sub-Saharan Africans as sons of Ham in Muslim cosmology, see James H. Sweet, "The Iberian Roots of American Racist Thought," 149. See also Cassuto, *Inhuman Race*, 37.

hegemony, and thereby absorbed into the Muslim empire of North and sub-Saharan Africa. The Manichean projection by which blacks are assigned a negative aesthetic value and associated with evil or a "lower hemisphere" had been articulated by theologians like Origen and Jerome as far back as the fourth century.[14] It persisted in the popular imagination in contemporary Spanish and Portuguese lyric poetry. In its coherent articulation of past and present ideologies of racial and cultural superiority, Zurara's chronicle of discovery and conquest, written at the beginning of the expansionist age, becomes an important foundational document for colonialism and trans-atlantic slavery.

In his panegyric to the Infante, Zurara stresses the geopolitical value of the 1415 conquest of Ceuta and the strategic importance of finding an Atlantic sea route to an undefined point in southern "Guinée" that would allow the Portuguese to attack the Infidels from the rear. Ceuta was not only the launching point for Henrique's fame as the "Navigator," but was also pivotal to his prestige in terms of statesmanship. Located at the northern-most tip of a centuries-old trans-Saharan trade route, it was an important commercial entrepôt. The prisoners from the Ceuta campaign confirmed the old supposition that the source of the gold trade controlled by the Mus-lims lay south of the Sahara, as had been represented in the 1375 Catalan Atlas, which showed the emperor of Mali with a golden orb in his hand. The ensuing gold trade that Henrique's voyages made possible allowed the mint in Lisbon to strike gold coinage in 1457; this was an important event, since Portugal had not had its own gold currency since 1383, and it was thus a fundamental step toward state consolidation. Significantly, the coin was called the *cruzado*—the crusader.

Zurara's chronicle brings together the interrelated topics of Portuguese maritime protocapitalist expansion, the Crusade, and the civilizing mission, along with the religious and secular alliances around which the national state was coalescing. It also provides us with an early example of writing the *negro* and descriptions of other casualties of maritime outthrust and colo-nialism. Zurara quotes at length the bull by which Pope Eugenius IV in 1442 granted the Infante the monopoly over exploration and trade in the as-yet-unmapped areas from which Antão Gonzalves and Nuno Tristão had brought the first captives the year before. The papal citation highlights the ideological oneness and the close structural relationship between the curia and the Por-

14. See St. Clair Drake, *Black Folk Here and There: An Essay in History and Anthropology,* 2: 58–59.

tuguese royal house. In the case of the Ceuta campaign of 1415, a similar letter from the pope had authorized the venture in terms of a crusade and provided plenary indulgences to the soldiers involved. Such bulls would become the legitimizing instruments for future colonial (dis)possession, most notably at the end of the century, when the transatlantic voyages of Columbus initiated the period of Spanish imperial ascendancy.[15]

The papal bulls were premised on the evangelical principle of the world as a potential "City of God," with the pope, as God's earthly representative, empowered to apportion material and spiritual prerogatives to designated Champions of the Faith. At the time, the Christian world order, as Anthony Pagden observes, knew no natural frontiers. "Propagating . . . Christian religion to such people as yet live in darkness and miserable ignorance of the true knowledge and worship of God," or, more candidly, "plant[ing] Christian religion, to traffic, to conquer," became almost a formula by the end of the sixteenth century. Here Pagden's quotation from the writings of Richard Hakluyt, British colonialist geographer, confirms a unanimity of intent and content in colonial discourse, both within and without the papal orbit, that had been expressed by Spain and France, the other major colonial powers, in the intervening century and a half. In the fifteenth century, God handpicked the Infante for this mission. Portugal was charged with the responsibility "of transforming the world into an immense City of God."[16]

A. J. R. Russell-Wood shares this idea of Christ becoming a nationalized deity, or "warrior god" for postmedieval Portugal, one who would provide strength and protection to the nation in exchange for a commitment to defend and extend Christendom.[17] The bull "Romanus Pontifex," issued by Pope Nicholas V on January 8, 1455, came after the challenge by Castilian interlopers in 1452–1453 for access to the Atlantic trade. It confirmed the pope's previous letter, "Dum Diversas" of 1452, congratulating Henrique

15. Eanes de Zurara, *Discovery and Conquest,* chapter 15; Valentin Mudimbe, *"Romanus Pontifex (1454)* and the Expansion of Europe."

16. Anthony Pagden, *Lords of All the World: Ideologies of Empire in Spain, Britain, and France, c. 1500–c. 1800,* 36. In 1554, the chronicler of John Lok's voyage to Guinea reported, for example, repeating the formulaic narrative dismissal of black African natives: "It is to be understood, that the people which now inhabite the regions of the coast of Guinea, and the middle parts of Africa, as Lybia the inner, and Nubia, with divers and other great & large regions about the same, were in old time called Aethiopes and Nigritae, which we now call Moores, Moorens, or Negroes, a people of beastly living, without a God, lawe, religion, or common wealth, and so scorched and vexed with the heat of the sunne, that in many places they curse it when it riseth" (quoted in Anthony Barthelemy, *Black Face, Maligned Race: The Representation of Blacks in English Drama from Shakespeare to Southerne,* 4–5). See also Barreto, "Gomes Eanes de Zurara," 335.

17. Russell-Wood, "Iberian Expansion," 27.

for his "most pious and noble work" and endorsed his monopoly of discovery and trade. Because of its specificity, it has been termed "the charter of Portuguese imperialism."[18] As it turns out, the bull offers a remarkable intertextual and ideological counterpoint to Zurara's narrative. The stylized fictionalization of *Discovery and Conquest* projects the Infante as an epic hero. He is also a privileged and faithful instrument of God in the eternal cause of good against evil. But in the bull, the Infante is not the hierarchical superior that he is for the chronicler, he is the highly approved "son" of Nicholas V, the ecclesiastical "father."

Pierre Bourdieu's notion of legal discourse as a creative speech that "brings into existence that which it utters," and that consequently supports "the dream of absolute power" seems an apposite frame of reference for the sledge-hammer legality of this document.[19] Based on the notion of papal infallibility, and of the pope's apostolic authority as God's representative and spokesperson on earth, the "Romanus Pontifex" admits no question as to the righteousness of its premise or the status or identity of the Other. The Saracens (Muslims), Guineamen (blacks), "enemies of the faith," gentiles, or pagans that it refers to all share the common denominator of being subject to Christian domination and conversion; apparently by the most direct and effective means available—violence. Neither the harm to their physical selves, nor the destruction of their material belongings, implies a moral or ethical deterrent to the belligerence of this document. Henrique's and Alfonso's mandate is unambiguous. Its unambiguity is indicated in the semantics of repetition and emphasis and severely undermines the purported universalism of the faith. The Infante is authorized to "invade, search out, capture, vanquish, and subdue all Saracens and pagans whatsoever, and other enemies of Christ wheresoever placed, and the kingdoms, dukedoms, principalities, dominions, possessions, and all movable goods whatsoever held and possessed by them and to reduce their persons to perpetual slavery, and to apply and appropriate to himself and his successors the kingdoms, dukedoms, counties, principalities, dominions, possessions, and good, and to convert them to his and their use and profit."[20]

Considering that, in Zurara's account, surviving Moorish captives were regarded by Portugal's agents as divine "reward" for the "toil they had under-

18. Pope Nicholas V, "The Bull Romanus Pontifex," 23; Boxer, *Portuguese Seaborne Empire*, 21.
19. Pierre Bourdieu, *Language and Symbolic Power*, 42.
20. Pope Nicholas V, "The Bull Romanus Pontifex," 23.

gone in [God's] service" (1.66), and that their military attacks were accompanied by loud invocations of "Santiago" and "São Jorge" (Portugal's patron saint), the idea of Portugal's conversion of Christ into a warrior god hardly seems to be an exaggeration. The interpretation of Christian cosmology by the sixteenth-century African convert King Afonso I of the Kongo appears to confirm the idea of this particular value of the Christ-figure to post-medieval Christians. The Kongolese king's military victory over his half-brother, a non-Christian, and his consequent accession to the throne, were entirely attributed to the divine intervention of the new God, by way of the miraculous appearance of Santiago (St. James Major) leading an army of armed horsemen. Upon seeing this vision, the forces of Mpanzu a Kitumu, the half-brother and putative usurper, fled.[21]

To the extent that Zurara's *Discovery and Conquest* confirms the papal premise of the non-Christian world being a *terra nullius,* or unclaimed land, available for conversion and domination, it assumes a foundational role in a broader discourse of power yet to be expressed through other such travel accounts from other sources in the emergent expansionist European community.[22] This documentation would include the discourse of colonial administration, of cartography, and of popular fiction, and it would be expressed at various levels of the vernacular. In its aggrandizement of the protagonists of colonialism, and its reduction of the Other to the status of tabula rasa, the chronicle bridges the gap between force and apologia in the colonial enterprise. Equally important are the omissions, accretions, and ambiguities that characterize its triumphalist rhetoric, especially to the extent that these promote (European) racial supremacy or misrepresent colonialism in terms of benefaction and the civilizing mission. The sometimes-unsubtle sophistry that produced such myths as that of happy slaves, their benign exploitation, and their equally happy integration into colonial society produced a discourse based on the silence of the subordinated. Even in attempting to conceal the relations of domination they describe, however, these myths highlight them.

The question of integration and immigration is key to the issue of the diaspora of Africans. If, as indicated earlier, globalization in the new millennium continues to give evidence of their status as personae non grata in Western nationalities, this unwelcomeness also draws attention to the collapse

21. See John Thornton, "Perspectives on African Christianity," 173.
22. See Mudimbe, "*Romanus Pontifex.*"

of Euro-Christian universalist projections defended in Zurara's apologia five and a half centuries ago. In Portugal, the earliest diasporic site associated with the European trade in Africans, immigrant gender imbalances, low marriage and reproduction rates, a high infant mortality, and a generally unfavorable sexual economy had an important negative impact on the populations of African descent. The "disappearance" of the descendants of tens of thousands of Africans forcibly removed to Portugal from the fifteenth to the eighteenth centuries is indicated by the fact that there are few, if any, somatic indicators that would point to black African ancestry in today's Portuguese population.[23] This assessment, of course, does not refer to the new waves of immigrants from Portugal's former African colonies.

Recent research into African-ancestored Portuguese has resorted to gene technology in its pursuit of an African presence for which only the nation's toponymy bears witness in an evident manner.[24] The existence of African-inspired place names in Portugal, from Negrais and Póvoa da Preta in Aveiro, to Pretarouca in Viseu, represents the inscription of an absence that goes to the heart of the dynamic of diaspora; that is, the resulting liminality of the enslaved migrants in their new environment. The fact of their exclusion is most starkly revealed in the fifteenth-century practice of tossing the cadavers of the deceased into the Tagus, burying them on the beach at Santos, or disposing of them in such locations *outside of* the host community. This de facto declaration of their outsiderness speaks as eloquently as the toponym of the Rua e Travessa do Poço dos Negros in Lisbon, which recalls the decision by Dom Manuel I to put an end to such arbitrary and hazardous practices and established mass burial sites for them, hence the Poço dos Negros, or "pit" for blacks. "We are informed," said the king, "that the slaves that die in this city, brought from Guinea, like others, are not buried as well as they should be in the places where they are thrown, and they are thrown on the ground in such manner that they are discovered . . . and eaten by dogs; and a large number of these slaves are thrown in the dung heap . . . and still others in the fields of farms."[25] Just as informative is his (belated) royal edict in 1514 that slaves of African origin be baptized.

---

23. In 1550, the number of enslaved blacks in Lisbon was estimated at ten thousand, or 10 percent of the city's population. By 1700, this had risen to thirty thousand. Lisbon was the premier European center for sale and transshipment of African captives at the time. See Maria Christina Neto Didier Lahon, "Os escravos negros em Portugal," 72.

24. See António Amorim, "Escravos africanos em Portugal: Que descendentes (lhes) deixaram (ter)?"

25. Quoted in Sweet, "Iberian Roots," 159.

Imperial Spain: The Other Within

In Zurara's text, the difference of blackness and of other Others is inscribed against the background of a Euro-Christian identity (that of Christendom) that highlights the royal figure of Dom Henrique as a combined political and religious icon. Santiago, the patron saint of Portugal, plays a similar role. Zurara's and other expansionist texts from Europe, like the philosophical and scientific discourses that came later, constitute, each in its own way, a continuing call to consciousness of a racialized selfhood and collectivity, vis-à-vis non-European Others. In turn, Spanish literature of the sixteenth and seventeenth century, in this early phase of the supranational construction of power/race relations under the colonial determinant, offers a more specific statement of racialized identification, whose orientation is nationalist.

Spain's Renaissance and Baroque literature participates in, and may be seen against, a broad historical spectrum of social and racial othering. As discourse, it added to the emerging repertoire of signs that would eventually produce a transgenre, as well as transnational, syntax, or code, for writing blackness. The earliest victims of expansionist slave-raiding were a racially diverse group, as seen at Lagos, for example. They were composed of Guanches, Moors, and blacks. The eventual focus on sub-Saharans, as the process of exploration and slave trading down the coast of West Africa continued, and an increasingly racialized Spanish nationalism would link two ontological operations evident both in literature and society.[26] They are that the ethnic and "tribal" diversity of the captive sub-Saharans (Mandingo, Wolof, Dahomey, and so on) would be collapsed under the single generic label of *negros,* just as the Iberian vernacular imaginary would essentialize this collective, making their historical condition as slaves into a "natural" one, following the Aristotelian premise that some people(s) are by nature slaves. Literature as product of and creator of social consciousness, operating as an early modern version of "mass media," would be the vehicle that broadcast the relationship of blackness to whiteness as well as what the *negro* was.

In Spain, the process of consolidation of the nation-state began with the union of the kingdoms of Castile and Aragon in 1469. It continued with the elimination of Jews and Muslims and the imposition of a white male Christian hegemonic order, which sought to identify itself as the quintessence of

---

26. With the Alcaçovas treaty of 1479, mentioned above, Spain ceded the right of exploration and exploitation to Portugal. For several decades after, the latter would exercise, "officially," a monopoly of slave acquisition in Africa.

the nation. The purification of the social body that national homogeneity required was effected around such categories as religion, language, and culture, with skin color and gender also playing a role.[27] As the paramountcy of old Christian lineage was established, the Inquisition and the separatist, biological notion of race through blood purity *(limpieza de sangre)* emerged as its primary instruments. The ideological role played by literary practice would complement the absolutist program of allegiance to God and king and would help establish the symbolic boundaries of the national community.

While the fall of the last Moorish stronghold at Granada in 1492 is generally held to be the final material and symbolic event of the *reconquista,* it is important to note that the first targets in the absolutist quest for religious orthodoxy at the moment of state formation were the Jews and Jewish converts, the *conversos.* The problem of the *moriscos,* a potentially dangerous conquered minority who stayed after the *reconquista* and whose conviction to Catholicism was always suspect, would be finally resolved in the expulsions of 1609–1614. To the extent that the eviction of these minorities signified a renunciation of plurality in Spain, the fate of blacks as newcomers in an acutely heterophobic environment actively engaged in identifying and sanctioning otherness is a question that looms large. This section will therefore look at Renaissance and Baroque literary discourse of blackness with a view to answering two basic questions: What forms did absolutist orthodoxy (through the Inquisition and the *limpieza* principle) take vis-à-vis blacks as outsiders? And what does the literary *negro* reveal about the experience of blacks and their reception in Spain, if indeed they left no significant cultural traces as a social group (as Antonio Domínguez Ortiz states) or were the beneficiaries of an ethos of cultural flexibility (as other scholars suggest). Bearing in mind how unlikely it would have been for them to write about their experiences, their confrontation with the Inquisition, an institution so central to life in Spain, becomes an important site for the ensuing intercultural interlocution.[28] The charges they faced and their tes-

27. As a minority, the gypsies, who entered Spain in the latter 1440s, refused to sign on to the social contract and have remained marginal to mainstream society ever since; see Antonio Domínguez Ortiz, *The Golden Age of Spain, 1516–1659,* 162–67. For a discussion of misogyny and gender control in the construction of the early Spanish nation, see Yvonne Yarbro-Bejarano, *Feminism and the Honor Plays of Lope de Vega.*

28. Antonio Domínguez Ortiz, "La esclavitud en Castilla durante la edad moderna," 392. Juan Latino, the best known of the few black writers in the period under study, was African born and a former slave in the family of the third Duke of Sessa. He is remembered primarily for his *Austriadis Carmen,* a poem written in Renaissance Latin hexameters. His decision to write in the

timonies at the same time reconfirm their marginality and provide an albeit limited opportunity to hear their voices, even if these come to us as reported speech. The section begins with a look at the question of the Jewish and Moorish minorities in the broader context of the racialization of the nation. What follows is the effect on blacks of this process in society, and their representation through literature.

The Jewish presence in what became Spain dates back to the destruction of Jerusalem in the year 70 of the Common Era. In the interim to the Moorish occupation of 711, this presence was marked by periods of persecution, segregation, and forced conversion by the Christian majority, more notably in the fifth and seventh centuries. Hundreds of years later, the generalized trauma experienced in Europe as a result of the plague found a convenient scapegoat in Judaism as its adherents were rumored to be the source of the Black Death, and mass burnings with thousands of victims ensued in several European cities in the fourteenth century.[29] In Seville in 1391, ferocious anti-Jewish preaching helped trigger mob violence that claimed the lives of over four thousand Jews, synagogues were ransacked or converted into Christian churches, and the rich Jewish quarter was appropriated and settled by Christians. The pogroms across Spain provoked the birth of the *converso* community as two hundred thousand Jews embraced the Catholic faith.

By around 1400, policies of structured segregation were (re)enacted, with badges being required for Jews and Moors so that they might be identified in public, and restrictions on the latter against their moving out of their *aljamas*. Holding of titles or office was forbidden to Jews, as was ritual bathing, their participation in various trades, and talking, eating, or drinking with Christians. Behind the outbursts in 1449, 1467, and 1473—the burning, pillaging, and massacres of Jews—was fervent sermonizing around the topic of the passion of Christ, and a vicious process of anti-Semitic myth-making and criminalizing. Alonso de Espina's *Fortalitium fidei contra judaeos,* for example, written in 1454, detailed such crimes as blasphemy, usury, child-murder, homosexuality, poisoning (while practicing medicine), and treason as specifically Jewish evils.[30]

---

old imperial language may be seen as an effort to place himself above the pressures of racial diminishment. His life story was dramatized by playwright Diego Ximénez de Enciso.

29. Hannaford, *Race,* 118–19.

30. See Lee Ann Durham Seminario, *The History of the Blacks, the Jews, and the Moors in Spain.*

Eventually it would be anxieties surrounding the supposed penetration and "contamination" of the higher reaches of the Church and the Spanish nobility by *conversos* that would prompt the establishment of the Inquisition in Spain in 1478. Queen Isabella, under pressure from her former confessor, Tomás de Torquemada, and the higher Sevillan clergy, solicited and received a bull from Pope Sixtus IV to authorize the *Santo Oficio* in Spain. It is significant that in the negotiations between Castile and Rome, final authority regarding administration of the institution remained the purview of the state. Accordingly, revenue deriving from confiscation of goods of heretics, a customary penalty since heresy was regarded as treason, went to the royal treasury and not to Rome.[31] In effect, the Inquisition became a powerful source of income for the crown not only during the reign of the Catholic Kings, but throughout the sixteenth and seventeenth centuries. The Jews had long been objects of hate and envy due to their financial success in commerce, revenue collection, money lending, and perceived public ostentation. Clergy-induced hysteria regarding an apocalyptic takeover of Christianity by relapsed *conversos* or active Judaizers, and stories of a conjuration to this end involving the heart of a murdered Christian child and a consecrated Host, played a significant part in the final Edict of Expulsion in March 1492. According to Isidore Loeb, some 50,000 individuals accepted forced conversion and 165,000 emigrated, with 20,000 dying on the forced trek out of Spain.[32]

Spanish "purity of blood" as the badge of supremacy for the dominant group, the Old Christians, and the pernicious notion that "one drop" of alien blood signaled infection and inferiority, is a foundational concept in the modern politics of race and racism. As an instrument of exclusion, *limpieza* was evident early in the 1400s, when the university college of San Bartolomé of Salamanca, established by papal bulls in 1414 and 1418, forbade admission to those whose Old Christian lineage was in any way suspect. Over the course of the century, different towns promulgated statutes preventing *conversos* and *moriscos* from access to various privileges until, with the Inquisition, public office, holy office, military orders, attendance at most

31. Tomás de Torquemada was the first Inquisitor General, and two thousand burnings were attributed to his tenure. Of this reign of terror within the *civitas dei,* Manuel Chaves y Rey writes: "The activities of the tribunal of the Faith, in Seville in the sixteenth century, are beyond description. Imprisonment, torture, and the autos in which innumerable victims were brought out daily, accused of Lutheran heresy, of being Molinists, Judaizers, iluminati, etc., were an ongoing phenomenon" (*Cosas nuevas y viejas [apuntes sevillanos],* 107).

32. Quoted in Durham Seminario, *History,* 62.

universities, and a range of other positions required certificates of *limpieza*.[33] With the blood purity standard came a sense of paranoia among the wider population, as anyone who was a candidate for religious and public office had to provide the Holy Office with detailed genealogical records, while at the community level, arbitrary accusations of heresy and religious dissidence could prove calamitous for ordinary individuals. Under the inquisitorial regime, a de facto spy system developed in which depositions from friend or foe, themselves subject to torture for further evidence if necessary, could send the accused to the *quemadero,* the ostentatious centerpiece of the auto-da-fé, where the guilty, so condemned, were burned alive. With the advent of the Reformation, the categories of religious dissenters and potential suspects naturally grew, as did the sense of individual insecurity among the populace.

The Inquisition's scrutiny of candidates for office included detailed interviews of the neighbors and acquaintances of the person concerned. This bore the risk for the candidate that any bit of damning evidence that might be revealed, whether true or false, could result in ruin for him and his family. The process resulted in the downfall of many highly placed Christians, since the mere accusation that one or various of their foreparents had been Jewish created doubts as to their own continued faithfulness to Catholicism. The tenacity of the Holy Office in this regard is dramatically illustrated by the fact that if a candidate's lineage was found to be suspect, it could result in the bones of the purported Jewish ancestor being disinterred and burned, and in his estate being confiscated. Antonio Domínguez Ortiz reminds us of the thinking behind this policy: "[J]ust as nobility was inherited, so the tendency to relapse into Judaism was hereditary. . . . The general opinion was that one drop of Jewish blood carried a perpetual contagion."[34]

The hypothesis that blood purity was the equivalent of racial or religious purity raises at least two important questions: First, that racial purity exists and can indeed be empirically established and certified as attempted by the Inquisition, and second, that blood is a racially separating biological agent that corresponds to bodily somatics and to behavior. The absurdity that

---

33. Jan Read, in *The Moors in Spain and Portugal,* asserts that blood purity was a Jewish "implant," since "Official Jewry . . . had always adhered rigorously to its scriptures in preserving the purity of blood" (204). The Royal Pragmatic of 1501 extended the *limpieza* requirement to every civil post. Included were royal councilors, judges in *audiencias* and chancelleries, *alcaldes, alguaciles, mayordomos,* and lesser local officers such as *corregidores* and *regidores;* see Ann Twinam, *Public Lives, Private Secrets: Gender, Honor, Sexuality, and Illegitimacy in Colonial Spanish America,* 46.

34. Domínguez Ortiz, *Golden Age,* 219.

the ideas of "Jewish blood," "White blood," "Black blood," "Asian blood," "Indian blood," and so on are still part of the twenty-first-century vernacular signals the triumph of the ideological in modern racial and racist categorization. And this, in spite of it being common knowledge that differences in blood types, which have no respect for epidermic considerations, are a more scientific basis for categorization among humans. "Impure" blood, that is to say, blood that is corrupt or degraded, whether inside the body or out, and whether or not it signals the presence or absence of disease, is a determination that more properly belongs to the realm of the biological or the biomedical. The use of the notion of impure blood in the service of a purportedly empirical enterprise such as religious or cultural identification, is therefore an exercise in impossibility. Since it seems clear, however, that in fifteenth- and sixteenth-century Spain the empirical aspect of the premise of blood purity was of less importance than its metaphorical value, we are left with the ideological function of the metaphor and the displacement of the empirical by the ideological. In effect, it is from the ideological drive to naturalize and fix (negative) difference, as indicated earlier, that racist practice emanates. In addition, to the degree that nationalist consolidation made the identification of true Christians and Spaniards a function of heredity, nationalism buried the universalist premise of the religion. What is important, however, is to appreciate *limpieza*'s instrumentality in creating distinction and difference in the name of the nation, in a manner analogous to and derivative of feudalism's prior reification of class and pedigree using the fantasy of "blue" blood or of superior bloodlines.

As a political tool, the focus of blood purity was on Jews, Muslims, or cultural hybrids in Renaissance and Baroque Spain. It forced them underground, erected barriers to their social advancement, subjected them to forced conversion, or sought their elimination through exile or execution. Language for the *moriscos* or *mudéjares* was a primary marker of difference and would play an important role in the prolonged process of their expulsion. Under the terms of the capitulation at Granada in 1492, the bulk of the Moors who did not choose exile were guaranteed continued government under their own laws, freedom to practice their religion, and protection of life and property. These concessions, however, were soon revoked as Queen Isabella's representative, Cardinal Ximénez de Cisneros, in antiheretical zeal, assembled and publicly burned huge quantities of Arabic theological and scientific treatises and artistically rendered copies of the Koran in Granada's town squares, proceeding thereafter to implement a unilateral policy of forced conversion and mass baptism. The ensuing Moorish discontent erupted in the 1499 Alpujarras rebellion, which was summarily quashed, producing a 1502 decree governing Castile and Leon that required Muslims to either leave or convert, or face death or confiscation. In 1525, Valencian Moorish leaders approached Charles V and managed to secure an agreement, on payment of fifty thousand ducats, that *moriscos* would have a forty-year moratorium from Inquisitorial persecution. This agreement, which would have provided a breathing space for baptized Moors, was also violated, as the period from 1532 to 1540 saw *moriscos* involved in 441 trials out of which 50 were burnt at the stake.[35]

Durham Seminario points to the financial problems of the crown in the 1550s and relates it to the stepping up of Inquisition property confiscation from Moorish *reconciliados,* that is to say, *moriscos* who were "reconciled" to the Church after their Inquisition trials. The relentless pressure for cultural uniformity, however, was further expressed under Philip II in 1567 by an edict that demanded that *moriscos* learn Spanish within three years and abandon Moorish names and any ceremonies that might be associated with Islam. This included a ban on public baths found in all Moorish towns. *Moriscos* were also required to wear Spanish-type clothing and refrain from speaking, reading, or writing Arabic. In fact, during the great Alpujarras uprising of 1568–1570 that these new pressures provoked, persecution and identification of *moriscos* of Granada included a test in Spanish pronunciation in which the individual was made to say *cebolla* (onion). The Arabic-accented *xebolla* usually gave the convert away.[36] The uprisings of 1499 and 1568, apart from the dislocation of large sections of the Moorish population, also yielded thousands of prisoners of war who were subsequently divided up among the triumphant forces and reduced to slavery.

Another *concordia* (agreement) in 1571 sought to pacify the Inquisition by means of a twenty-five-hundred-ducat payment per annum, but the hoped-for ease in Moorish persecution for heresy or relapsing had disappointing results. The expulsion resolution was finally put into effect under Philip III in Valencia, Castile, Extremadura, and La Mancha, in 1609. Granada, Andalusia, and Aragon followed in 1610, with Catalonia one year after and Murcia in 1614. Popular support for the expulsions, as in the case of the

---

35. Durham Seminario, *History,* 96.

36. Ibid.; Luis Antonio Santos Domínguez, "La minoría morisca: Apuntes de sociolingüística histórica," 286. In 1937, during a similarly murderous moment of Hispanist nationalist identification and expulsion, Dominican dicatator Rafael Leónidas Trujillo's generals would make Haitian immigrants say *perejil* (parsley) to betray their alien origin. See Susy Castor, *Migración y relaciones internacionales (el caso haitiano-dominicano),* 20.

Jews, was fueled by rumors of another child martyr, the Santa Niña Catalina de Oliva, allegedly sacrificed by the Moors in November 1600. Nine hundred years of coexistence had been insufficient to overcome cultural and religious difference, as *moriscos* in excess of a quarter of a million—many of whom, ironically, were descendants of Christians converted to Islam in previous centuries—became victims of what today we call ethnic cleansing.

While the homogenizing thrust of Spanish nationalism wanted to get rid of adherents to Judaism or Islam, the same cannot be said in relation to the Africans. Being a source of slave labor, they were actively imported. As a whole, Africans displayed neither the intention nor the potential to undermine the political or ideological hegemony of Catholicism that was associated with the Judaizers or *conversos*. Besides, their general acceptance of Christianity, save for the black Muslims, gained them a reputation for assimilability. The very reason for their presence, however, precluded a welcome. As a social group, they never grew in numbers nor apparently did they develop the kind of cohesiveness, except for the occasional *cofradía,* that might be cause for alarm among the dominant group.[37]

Although Antonio Domínguez Ortiz feels that the native population generally felt that "their behavior was seen as that of overgrown children," this is not to be taken to mean that blacks were benignly treated.[38] Religious and racist absolutism showed itself to be as intractable with the black Africans or with the black Spanish as with any other minority. Since a great proportion of them were located in the domestic sphere, there was no question of mandating their segregation into physically separate communities, as had been the case historically with the other minorities. There would, nonetheless, be concrete as well as symbolic barriers to their integration. Their being in Spain "to stay" brought into evidence the assimilationist imperatives of colonization; that is to say, conformity with the norms of dominant white culture and abjuration of their own.

The slave population in Spain has been calculated as being in the vicinity of 100,000 in the year 1565. The archbishopric of Seville showed at that time a mixed, mainly *morisco*/black slave population of 14,670, which was proportionally 1 in 30 of a wider population of 429,362, with the city of

---

37. A *cofradía* was a mutual aid group of Christianized blacks sanctioned and monitored by the authorities. A series of royal *cédulas* during the course of the sixteenth century sought to prevent the entry of (black African) Muslims into the New World, on account of their general rebelliousness and resistance to Christianization. See Leslie B. Rout Jr., *The African Experience in Spanish America: 1502 to the Present Day,* 24.

38. Domínguez Ortiz, "La esclavitud en Castilla," 391.

Seville, itself a primary slave market, hosting 6,327, or a ratio of 1 to 14. Smaller concentrations were to be found in other southern cities such as Málaga, Granada, or Cartagena, or in the provinces of Valencia and Catalonia. Unlike the situation in the Americas, slave employment in Spain was seldom agricultural but mainly urban, and it never came to be pivotal to the economy. Apart from the king's slaves, they were distributed among the rich and the artisan classes. While some slave owners restricted their charges to the domestic arena, others rented out their labor. Several categories of tradesmen used them in this way or in their own service. The array of trades in which slaves performed included work as stevedores, shoemakers, carpenters, masons, tailors, rope makers, soap makers, blacksmiths, and silk weavers. The king's slaves were employed mainly in the construction of forts, in the mines, and in the galleys. The institution peaked in the sixteenth century and in the first half of the seventeenth, falling into decay by the beginning of the eighteenth century.

José Luis Cortés López states that the virtues deemed to be of greatest importance by Spanish slave owners were faithfulness and gratitude. His assessment of slavery and race relations in the 1600s is based on archival documents as well as literary works from the period. Citing the absence of a current codified system of laws applicable to specific slave misdemeanors, he suggests that custom dictated punishment, with the whip being the most frequent instrument, and the *pringado,* or application of melted pork fat to open wounds, often accompanying the whip. Escape attempts were punished by the loss of an ear, and branding, in addition to identifying the enslaved as property, also served as a means of punishing runaways. Although not all slaves were branded, it was customary for an *S* and a line representing a nail (*es/clavo* = Spanish for slave) to be applied to one cheek, while the owner's mark or initial graced the other. Ruth Pike, for example, cites a 1539 record which spoke of an individual whose face bore the entire name of his owner as well as the date, "Francisco de Aranda en Sevilla 29 de mayo de 1539" (Francisco de Aranda, Seville, May 29, 1539). Slaves found guilty of banditry were hung and quartered, their remains left in the public roadway. Slave movement and association were also zealously monitored. This is revealed by local ordinances that placed them under curfew, prevented citizens from harboring them overnight, restrained tavern keepers from serving them wine, and regulated various aspects of their life outside of work, including assembly in houses and in public places in groups of more than ten. Upward social mobility for freedmen was almost an impossibility as various guilds excluded them on grounds of their previous slave status or on grounds of "blood purity."[39] It is significant that Cortés López's assessment seems unencumbered by the need to sugarcoat the institution by importing assumptions and conditions of Hispanic slave society four centuries prior.

There seems to be little to distinguish the Inquisition's authoritarian treatment of blacks from that meted out to other groups.[40] While there was no reason to single them out as political or financial targets, as was the case with the minorities discussed above, the moral and doctrinal dictates of the Holy Office nonetheless bore upon them heavily. This was so despite the scant religious education that their condition allowed, or in spite of their limited juridical status. Antonio Domínguez Ortiz's affirmation that "widespread religious ignorance" prevailed in the countryside among native Spaniards makes the infractions of the faith committed by lower-class Spaniards seem comparable to those committed by the enslaved blacks, who had themselves received little or no instruction in the fundamentals of Christianity.[41] Their very foreignness to Euro-Christian culture, however, suggests that their conscious rejection of religious domination, or of values alien to their own cultural legacy, should be recognized as such. Like anyone else, individual enslaved blacks were brought up on charges of sacrilege, blasphemy, and heresy, evidently because as outsiders they failed to appreciate the mysteries of Christianity, or often because they were merely echoing sentiments and turns of language already current in the vernacular. Some were punished with apostasy for having "turned away from" the perfunctorily imposed Catholicism, while others received penance for declaring that sex outside of holy matrimony was not a sin, or for questioning the existence of hell or the supposed virtues of the saints and the Holy Family.

In a 1612 *relación,* for example, eighteen-year-old Domingo, a native of Guinea, was penanced for having twice renounced God "and the blessed Apostles Saint Peter and Saint Paul," while being castigated by his master. His punishment was a further fifty lashes. In a similar case, an enslaved mulatto,

39. José Luis Cortés López, *La esclavitud negra en la España península del siglo XVI;* Ruth Pike, "Sevillian Society in the Sixteenth Century: Slaves and Freedmen," 348; Fernando Ortiz, *Los negros curros,* 158.

40. I am basing this conclusion on my study of Inquisition records for Seville for the years 1559–1577 and 1602–1603 at the Archivo Histórico Nacional (AHN), Madrid.

41. Slave baptism was reported by ships' captains who were involved in the slave trade; they describe such baptisms as being perfunctory and literally meaningless to Africans, who knew no Spanish and who shared the ceremony with hundreds of other captives aboard ship or in a holding factory. Regarding the state of religious instruction in the Spanish countryside, see Domínguez Ortiz, "La esclavitud en Castilla," 392, 206.

Francisco Rodriguez, was penanced in November 1604 for renouncing "God and his saints" while being held prisoner for attempted escape from his master. The master had come to retrieve him at the prison and was threatening further physical violence when Francisco allegedly uttered the blasphemous words. The punishment by the Inquisition was that he appear in the auto-da-fé gagged, that he abjure Judaism, and that he receive a hundred strokes of the whip. In the same auto-da-fé, Tome Lovato, a mulatto from Lisbon, also received a hundred strokes for renouncing God and the saints.[42]

Since the Inquisition also had jurisdiction over what today would be considered civil matters, among its victims were included persons accused of disorderly conduct, that is, of being a *perturbador,* as occurred with Jorge, an enslaved black man in Seville, in the auto-da-fé of July 28, 1562. In the following year, María Rodriguez, a mulatto woman, was sentenced to appear, gagged, candle in hand, and with the ignominious halter around her neck. She was also required to abjure Judaism, was sent into exile for five years, and received two hundred lashes. Being an integral part of the public ceremony, application of corporal punishment to the individual so sentenced was done with him or her mounted on an ass, and naked to the waist. They were then led through the streets preceded by the town crier as the executioner applied the whip. María's crime had been that of bigamy and of saying that living with a sexual partner was not a sin. Bigamy was also the charge against the mulatto woman Beatriz Gomes in 1602, although her punishment was not spelled out in the *relación.* In similar fashion, Juan Domínguez, a free mulatto from Seville, received the gag, two hundred lashes, and two years of unpaid labor in the galleys in 1563, for fornication and for saying that the act was not a mortal sin. Magdalena de la Cruz, a free black woman from Lisbon, was also punished for declaring that fornication was not a sin. In addition to the candle, gag, and halter, she received a hundred lashes.[43]

Trauma and the bewilderment of captivity, exile, and forced labor all define the condition of the victims of Atlantic slavery, even as freedom and the desire for freedom have been their responses to it. The degree to which the slave owner made personal faithfulness and gratitude on the part of his slave the cornerstone of their relationship, as José Luis Cortés López suggests

42. Inquisición, Sevilla, Relación de causas de fé, a 1612, legajo 2075, no. 22, folio 1; Inquisición, Sevilla, Relación de causas de fé, Nov. 30, 1604, legajo 2095, no. 15, folio 20; both AHN.

43. Inquisición, Sevilla, Relación de personas que salieron anos 1560–1562, folio 6; Inquisición, Sevilla, Autos de fe relacion de personas anos 1574–1577, Noviembre 1574, legajo 2075, no. 5; both AHN.

above, and applied corresponding rigor at the latter's attempts at escape, inevitably contours the power relationship between captor and captive, regardless of other aspects of the relationship. While maroonage became an established practice in the diasporic experience of the enslavement of Africans in the Americas, and is a well-researched topic, the history of the efforts of captive Africans to regain freedom while at sea is not so well known. From the sequestered individuals who threw themselves overboard in a desperate attempt at freedom through suicide, to those other victims whose bodies, dead or alive, were hurled into the sea by ships' captains, the story of the sea as final resting place, or as liquid frontier and endless horizon, marks a definite yet elusive frame of reference for African diaspora studies. The case of the *Amistad,* recently rendered in film, dramatically illustrates the 1839 plight of Sengbe Pieh of the upper Mende country and his fellow captives. After a successful revolt on board, the Africans were left at the mercy of two of their erstwhile captors, who unlike them, knew some navigation, and attempted to steer their ship back to Cuba. Gale-force winds finally blew the vessel northwards to the U.S coastline. Inquisitorial records for the periods indicate, through the third-person relations of its scribes, the experience and voices of putative escapees who braved the (unknown) seas in a desperate attempt to return "home," just as they bring us fragments of the lives of those others who broke the moral codes.

The example that appears in the *auto de fé* of 1603 is of Manuel Veira, who, with four companions, took over a ship by force with the intention of going to Barbary. According to the *relación,*

> He and other Moorish and Christian slaves had agreed to go to Barbary and that to that effect they had taken a boat from a boatman by force, with which they had sailed two days and two nights as a result of contrary winds they had arrived at one of the coasts of Spain where they had been taken prisoner by His Majesty's justice in the hearing he confessed having taken flight as accused intending to go to Barbary to live in the (illeg.) of Mohamed. . . . Upon conclusion of his case . . . it was decided that he be admitted as reconciled with a painted cloak . . . and be given a hundred lashes and he was . . . to his aforementioned mistress to be instructed in matters of the Catholic faith.

A similar case is recorded in the same *relación* of 1603 concerning Francisco, a black man from Alcalá, who was arrested and detained by a Spanish marine official on the coast, and who, it was discovered, had been waiting for a Moorish ship to take him to Barbary. From that point he thought he could "flee homeward."[44]

"Performing" Blackness: Civilization, Barbarism, Nationalism, and Racial Ventriloquism

The study of Spanish literature in the sixteenth and seventeenth centuries, in its nationalist function, highlights a racialized vernacular self, signifying against the foreign Other. Where this Other is the free or enslaved African or Afro-Spanish, the power differential deriving from the social class of the writer becomes evident, as does the desire to reify the superiority and inferiority attached respectively to the social identities of whiteness and blackness. Through literature, white aggrandizement, and the corresponding, dialectical diminishment of blackness found expression through every imaginable rhetorical reference, with a stereotypically comical role assigned to black subjects, especially in the drama. In this way, the symbolic order of the nation, while materially ridding itself of its Jewish and Islamic elements, came to erect instead a wall of laughter against the African presence, as the racist drive enacted its fantasy of superiority.

Stereotypes that associate blacks with dance and song, caricatural representations of their incorrect Spanish, and general black comicality are the cornerstones of the literature under study. To the degree that these stereotypes underscored their otherness and devalue and marginalize them, they also defined the transcendence and centrality of the signifying subject. As postcolonial and critical race theorists have pointed out, the racist stereotype in action reduces its object to a few easily identifiable characteristics, which it repeatedly projects in order to achieve a fixed, permanent, and ahistorical image of the Other. Often reflecting the repressions of the signifying subject, the racist stereotype, as indicated above, is premised on the silence of its object, and this displacement of the real by the rhetorical leaves him or her with a denied or distorted subjectivity. Accordingly, it is perhaps a tribute to the success of the stereotype of blacks in Spain on both the diachronic and the synchronic planes that otherwise highly informative studies have uncritically replicated sixteenth-century evaluations of the

44. Inquisición, Relación de causas de fe a 1603, Noviembre 30, 1603, legajo 2075, folio 15, AHN.

black slave population. According to Domínguez Ortiz, for example: "Literature popularized *the most salient characteristics of black psychology*... their halfway language was an easy target for satire; their superstitious fear of darkness and ghosts also provided laughter on stage; but *the most outstanding feature of the black soul,* the one which even today constitutes its originality, is their sense of rhythm, their musical instinct." Fernando Ortiz's assessment concurs with that of Juan R. Castellano, when he states that their primary attributes were "happiness, loquacity and the dance." For Castellano, the most striking impression one got from the black of the *entremés* subgenre was that "he was a jovial and happy fellow."[45]

The symbolic violence inherent to distortive representations as a whole acquires a particular objectivity when the distortion is expressed by way of the burlesque in Spanish Renaissance and Baroque literature. The "bozalic" interjections, the contrived situations, and the conventional comicality of black characters in the drama and in other genres point to the core of postmedieval Spain's response to what Lemuel Johnson has termed "blackness in human form." "Laughter," as Michael Neve observes, taking his cue from Freud, "is the opposite of itself, or can be." Psychoanalytical theory posits that when we laugh at other people, we are also making them targets of our repressed aggression. Reducing them to absurdity affords us a "pleasurable sense of the superiority which we feel in relation to them." The distortive imitations of black speech, the primary marker of black comicality in Spanish drama, were meant to attest to the superiority and centrality of the surrounding indigenous community. These derogatory imitations, as a means of demeaning real-life Afro-Spanish individuals, affirmed the linguistic normativity of Castilian. Highlighting the bozalic made black speech serve as a cultural borderline. It reprised the binary of the mythical barbarians and the civilized, while the ever-present "correct" linguistic model implicitly showed them the road to assimilation.[46]

45. Domínguez Ortiz, "La esclavitud en Castilla," 392 (my emphasis); Ortiz, *Los negros curros,* 159; Juan R. Castellano, "El negro esclavo en el entremés del Siglo de Oro," 63.

46. *Bozal* refers to those Africans who had not yet learned to express themselves in Spanish or Portuguese. Sebastián de Covarrubias, *Tesoro de la lengua castellana o española* (1611), gives as its meaning "a black man who knows no language but his own." See also Lemuel Johnson, *The Devil, the Gargoyle, and the Buffoon: The Negro as Metaphor in Western Literature,* 28; Michael Neve, "Freud's Theory of Humor, Wit, and Jokes," 36; and Sigmund Freud, "Jokes and the Comic," 168. The myth-making nature of the bozalic convention and the factor of audience expectations are both evinced in the fact that, by the fifteenth and sixteenth centuries in Spain, the majority of the country's black residents would have been speaking Spanish "with no distinctive accent." See John Lipski, "The Golden Age 'Black Spanish': Existence and Coexistence," 10.

But cross-racial ventriloquism and song and dance mimicry, as a manifestation of the hegemonizing pretensions of the dominant culture, is hardly to be regarded as a clear-cut, unidirectional phenomenon. Colonial derision, as Homi Bhabha asserts, reveals the traces of desire. Also, hidden beneath the repressed unconscious of racist representation, may be the troubling temptation to see blacks as "really supermen, better endowed than whites." In other words, within the binary logic of stereotypical representation, co-exist both the notion of the black as puerile simpleton and the corollary idea of blacks as somehow overendowed and larger than life. Susan Gubar's recent study of racial impersonation in the primitivist dimension of twentieth-century American modernism reveals an "ontological fullness" imputed to blacks. Her book is an attempt to illuminate "the powerful attraction of black people and their culture within the white imagination."[47]

Gubar highlights the tension between the racist legacy of blackface minstrelsy, and the approximation and identification with blackness and black culture attempted by many contemporary white writers in the period that African American poet Langston Hughes has referred to as "when the Negro was in vogue."[48] As is well known, modernism's enthusiastic and unprecedented adscription of cultural capital to blackness reflects both postwar pessimism and a temporary turning away from the master discourse of Western cultural transcendence. Regarding the black-white cultural divide, there is no reason to not see elements of a foreshadowing of this cross-cultural phenomenon at the very beginnings of the modern period, when a similar "ontological fullness" in black culture began to be appreciated in the Iberian Peninsula. Paradoxical though it might seem, the cross-racial impulse here, albeit a tentative one, would signal the fissures in the hegemonic project, and the eventual instability of a master text aimed at domination through derision and demonization.

Venetian travel writer Cadamosto noted his admiration for the dance of the natives of the "Kingdom of Senega" in the mid-1450s. Even at the beginning of that decade, in 1451, black Africans in Lisbon were among the Canarian and Sanadja (Moorish) captives who performed tribal dances and songs at the public festivities celebrating the wedding of Afonso V's sister, Leonor, to Emperor Frederick III. Effectively, the earliest extant Hispanic poem on the black theme in the modern period was written to accompany

---

47. Bhabha, "Other Question," 18; Stuart Hall, "The Spectacle of the 'Other,'" 263; Susan Gubar, *Racechanges: White Skin, Black Face in American Culture,* xviii.
48. Langston Hughes, *The Big Sea,* 223–32.

similar performances at a subsequent royal marriage in 1455. By the early 1500s, and taking into consideration the sizeable black populations of Lisbon and Seville and their appearance in popular festivities as well as in royal entertainments, it is hardly surprising that there had developed what P. E. Russell calls "a taste for the music, singing and dancing of Black Africa" in Spain. In his study of Sevillian theater between 1564 and 1659, in fact, Sentaurens records close to two dozen dance performances whose titles allude to blacks and Spain's encounter with Africa.[49]

With this in mind, Domínguez Ortiz's assessment, previously alluded to, of the imported blacks having made no significant impact on Spanish culture, might well bear revision. Effectively, even beyond native Iberian writers' ignorance of African languages, or these writers' caricatural intent, the more easily appreciated structural element of the call-and-response in African oral culture was often attempted in their works. The most significant example of this that one might find, perhaps, would be the closing lines of Simón de Aguado's *Entremés de los negros* (1602), in which the happy ending sought by two enslaved lovers is celebrated. The male protagonist, Antón, mirrors the rhythm and repetition of call-and-response with an onomatopoeic interjection.

> Todos: A la boda de Gasipar
>   y Dominga de Tumbucuto,
>   Turo habeme de bailar:
>   Toca, negro.
>
> Antón: Toca tú;
>   Tu, pu tu tu, pu tu tu, pu tu tu,
>   tu, pu tu tu, pu tu tu...
>
> (Solo) Dominga más beya...
>   tu, pu tu tu...
>   que una crara estreya...
>   tu
>   casamo en eya,
>   tu,
>   y como es donceya
>   tu,

---

49. Alvise Cadamosto, in Crone, "*Voyages of Cadamosto*," 50. P. E. Russell, "Toward an Interpretation of Rodrigo de Reinosa's 'poesía negra,'" 226. Included among the dances are the *guineo*, the *chacona*, the *zarambeque*, the *ye-ye*, and the *zambapalo*. Such dances were prohibited and often criminalized. Jean Sentaurens, *Seville et le théâtre: De la fin du moyen age à la fin de XVIIe siecle*, 1179–222; Baltasar Fra Molinero, *La imagen de los negros en el teatro del Siglo de Oro*, 50.

hijo haremo en ella,
    tu,
que Seviya venga
    tu[!] . . .

[All: To the wedding of Gaspar
      And Dominga of Timbuktu
      We will all dance.
          Play, black man!

Anton: Play, tu!
      Tu, pu, tu, tu, pu, tu, tu, pu, tu, tu!
      Tu, pu, tu, tu, pu, tu, tu!

(Solo) Dominga, more beautiful!
      Tu, pu, tu, tu!
      Than a bright star,
          Tu!
      In matrimony we'll unite,
          Tu!
      And since she is a virgin,
          Tu!
      A child we'll make in her,
          Tu!
      Let her come to Seville,
          Tu!][50]

Similarly, Góngora's final lines in his *letrilla* "En la fiesta del Santísimo Sacramento" (1609) prefigures the rhythmic intentions as well as the African-sounding innovations of the *negrista* movement of the 1930s (which I will discuss in Chapters 4 and 5):

    Zambambú, morenica del Congo
    Zambambú.
    Zambambú, que galana me pongo
    Zambambú.

    [Zambambu, little black woman from the Congo
    Zambambu,
    Zambambu, how pretty I make myself,
    Zambambu.][51]

---

50. In Emilio Cotarelo y Mori, ed., *Colección de entremeses, loas, bailes, jácaras y mojigangas desde fines del siglo XVI a mediados del XVIII,* 1:235. Translation taken from Edward Mullen, *Afro-Cuban Literature: Critical Junctures,* 203–4.

51. Quoted in Mónica Mansour, *La poesía negrista,* 45.

Transracial voicing in the drama and a generalized cross-cultural impulse in popular culture were evidently features of the historical presence of Africans in Spanish society. In the unwilling attraction, perhaps, lies much of the rejection expressed in the literature. In the course of the sixteenth century, as the national theater developed and the structure of dramatic performances became established, blacks, or mostly their white surrogates, became structurally "integrated" into the shows. In addition to an albeit peripheral role in plays proper, black faces might appear in the *tono,* the musical introduction to these plays, and in the *entremés,* a humorous skit presented in the interlude before act two. They might also appear in the *baile,* or dance that came after the second act, and finally the *fiesta,* or *mojiganga,* which concluded the performance. The presence of the song and dance motif in the literature might well be seen, therefore, as evidence of a measure of "acceptance" of Africans and their culture, on account of their exotic allure and their appeal to repressed native Christian sensibilities.[52] The use of the voice in the drama, however, represents the opposite side of the coin.

Black talk became an object of desire for the white, twentieth-century, modernist writers desirous of flaunting their nonconformity with high culture and with bourgeois linguistic norms. In the Hispanic Caribbean, as I discuss in subsequent chapters, the primitivist vogue also included the wish to "talk real black talk" *(hablar en negro de verdad),* to quote a line from Cuban poet Nicolás Guillén in his 1929 poem "Pequeña oda a un boxeador cubano." In Renaissance Spain, however, during the process of nationalist consolidation, the establishment of linguistic and racial hegemony militated against such concessions to subalternity. Several studies point to the development of a comedic repertoire in relation to black characters that revolved around their skin color, their general ignorance of Hispanic and Christian culture, their incompetence in the Portuguese and Spanish languages, as well as any situational combination that highlighted their incongruity as outsiders. Social and racial debasement would be expressed through dialogues in which they were referred to as "dog," "hound," "greyhound," "whippet," "mastiff," or other semantic allusions to the canine.[53] Direct racial name-

---

52. Ortiz, *Los negros curros,* 167. For Cotarelo y Mori, *Colección,* they became the "gravy and main adornment of these funny pieces," clxxx.

53. In Diego Ximénez de Enciso's play on the life of Juan Latino, the protagonist's personal liberation and his rise to social recognition as a lettered individual provided the occasion for particularly egregious verbal assaults. His persistent animalization by his interlocutors—"brazen dog" *(perro atrevido),* "ill-born black" *(negro mal nacido),* "big dog" *(perrazo),* and "animal" *(El*

calling to invoke lower animal forms would be complemented by color-based references to dirt or darkness (soot, coal, ink, shadow, nighttime, and so on), to tropologically pun on their blackness. Baroque conceits, as Fra Molinero points out, with their concern for mental ingenuity and contrast, took the unadorned racial insults to sophisticated levels of artistry. It is seen in the work of such authors as Lope de Vega, Andrés de Claramonte, and Francisco Gómez de Quevedo.

Whereas the staged black body itself served as a metasign of incongruity and negative difference, in the drama the black voice was its primary complement. Known to writers, their audiences, and to the critical tradition as "Guinean" *(guineo),* "black talk" *(habla de negro),* or "half talk" *(media lengua),* it replicated the comic effect of the *Sayagués* spoken by the *pastores* in the liturgical poetry of the late 1400s. Its speakers joined such marginal figures as the *bobo,* the *gallego,* the *villano,* and the *gracioso* as the drama developed and became increasingly secularized and popularized in the sixteenth century. Many writers, starting with Diego Sánchez de Badajoz, Gil Vicente, and Lope de Rueda, who regularized this "Africanized Spanish" in their works, and continuing with other Golden Age stalwarts like Lope de Vega, Simon de Aguado, and Quiñones Benavente, used it primarily in their one-act *pasos, farsas,* or *entremeses,* otherwise known as the *género chico* in the Spanish theatrical tradition. *Género chico,* which served to poke fun at the provincial ignorance or the cultural inadequacy of lower-class characters, stood in counterpoint to the more prestigious *comedias de teatro.* In these, the elevated concepts of honor, dignity, heroism, emotional love, and correct speech defined the patrimony of the political and religious elite. "Guinean" has been well studied from the standpoint of its phonological and morphosyntactic elements.[54] Its valency as an ideological device, however, is just as important, and its reductive and formulaic nature is evident in such plays as Lope de Rueda's *Eufemia* and *De los engañados* and Luis Quiñones de Benavente's *Entremés famoso: El negrito hablador, y sin color anda la niña.*

Encubierto y Juan Latino: Comedias de Don Ximénez de Enciso, 268–69)—is only surpassed in vitriolic content by their reaction to his accession to the language of power and the prestige of the poetic. Don Martín, a rival, registers the paradox of the impermissible combination of blackness and brains as he asks on one occasion, "The dog speaks Latin?" *(¿Latín sabe hablar el mastín?),* 182.

54. See Castellano, "El negro esclavo"; Edmundo de Chasca, "The Phonology of the Speech of the Negroes in Early Spanish Drama"; Luis Monguió, "El negro en algunos poetas españoles y americanos anteriores a 1800"; Germán de Granada, "Sobre el origen del 'habla de negro' en la literatura peninsular del siglo de oro"; Frida Weber de Kurlat, "El tipo cómico del negro en el teatro prelopesco, fonética"; and Frida Weber de Kurlat, "El tipo de negro en el teatro de Lope de Vega: Tradición y creación."

In reminding us that the majority of black residents in Spain in the sixteenth and seventeenth centuries would hardly have sounded any different from the people around them, John Lipski hints at an important psychological motive underlying much of Spain's ridiculing of "Africanized" Spanish in a convention that lasted more than two hundred years: It was to bury the nation's African (Moorish) roots. To the extent that Lipski's point recalls Christian ascendancy, it also invokes Pierre Bourdieu's observation that "the official language is bound up with the state, both in its genesis and in its social uses."[55]

Renaissance nationalism made language an important focus in Spain, both in its vernacular as well as in its classical aspect. National linguistic unity and the elevation of Castilian to the prestige of the imperial languages of old was an important counterpart to the cultivation of "good Latinity" (la buena latinidad) under the Catholic Monarchs.[56] Although Cardinal Ximénez founded the University of Alcalá de Henares in 1508 to encourage the study of Latin, Greek, and Hebrew, the production of three grammars— Nebrija's in 1492, Villalón's in 1558, and Correas's in 1625—would signal the demise of Latin as the language of power and prestige. Correas attested to the eventual de facto and de jure triumph of the vernacular, as official correspondence and philosophical and scientific treatises began to be published in Castilian. The corresponding repression by ridicule of the speech models of the lower classes and of racial minorities, Jews, Moors, guineos, gypsies, sayagos, lacayos, pastores, and so on in favor of Castilian dominance can only underscore the role of literature as a ruling-class tool for cultural and linguistic assimilation and conformity.

Language apart, the nationalist tenor of Baroque literature in Spain— that is, its thematic and often propagandistic emphasis on God, king, and country—is observable in the historiography and, of course, in the texts themselves. In this regard, the work of dramatist Lope de Vega is exemplary on account of that writer's prolificacy, his studied engagement with the audience as the drama became a professional endeavor and catered to an eager public, and his consistent defense of the status quo. Lope de Vega's innovations included condensing the slow-moving dramatic models of antiquity into three-act plays in which the plot was not resolved until the last act, and employing a polymetric technique that varied in accordance with the mood

55. Lipski, "Golden Age," 10; Bourdieu, Language and Symbolic Power, 45.
56. It was, of course, the desire that Castilian replace Latin in this role that underlay Nebrija's famous retort to Queen Isabella in 1492 that language is the "companion" of empire. See his nationalistic intentions in Antonio de Nebrija, Gramática de la lengua castellana, 81–82.

of the work. In *El negro del mejor amo,* one of his three saint-plays involving black protagonists, history and the hagiographic tradition converge in the playwright's most nationalistic statement.[57] Although the play was set in Africa and on the island of Sardinia, its historical trajectory and central issue, that of the triumph of Christianity over Islam, make clear its nationalistic conception, taking into consideration Spain's self-projection as international champion of the faith.

Mejor amo is the story of Antiobo, a Moorish prince who deserts his culture and fights for Christianity. Antiobo is the son of a black African princess, Sofonisba, and Dulimán, a Muslim prince in exile. His story is designed, in part, as Molinero points out, to highlight the moral corruption of the Islamic world in which custom demands that, for "reasons of state," the king's first-born, the successor to the throne, eliminate his brother, as the latter is a potential competitor for the crown. Dulimán's flight to Libya reflects this plight. As the twists of the plot make clear, he is also fleeing from a world in which lust, intrigue, greed, and betrayals are the norm. These elements portray an image of Islamic culture that diametrically opposes the moral rectitude and high ethical obligations of Christian and Hispanic nobility. The most important aspect of the protagonist's transformation, therefore, would consist of his recognition of Christianity's higher moral order and the superiority of the Christian God. Also, as a social newcomer, he would reaffirm the transcendence of Christianity for his fellow blacks and for the general populace, while his blackness serves as its own apologia for his enslavement. The catalysts of Antiobo's conversion are an enslaved captive Christian woman, who breast-fed him as an infant and secretly baptized him, and a rosary that he coincidentally recovers from her years later. The event that marks his definitive move across politico-cultural borders is his defense of the Sardinians as the ships of the Turkish sultan approach to attack. His subsequent hermitage and miraculous posthumous protection of the island confirms his saintly status.

But if Antiobo's defection confirms the magnetism of the Christian moral order over that of Islam, it bears mentioning that from the standpoint of the erstwhile prince's culture of origin, freeing Christian galley slaves and arming them to kill the soldiers he commanded also confirms him as traitor. In the ebb and flow of power over the centuries of Muslim occupation in the Peninsula, self-interest and unstable intercultural politico-military alliances

---

57. Félix Lope de Vega y Carpio, *El negro del mejor amo.* The other plays with black protagonists are *El prodigio de Etiopia* and *El santo negro Rosambuco.*

were no novelty. While Antiobo may well have been modeled on the historical figure of Moroccan prince Don Felipe of Africa, a similar deserter, the very nationalist thrust of Lope's argument in *Mejor amo* imposes a recollection of two foundational moments in Hispanic history with which the playwright would easily have been familiar, especially since he himself was a priest, former soldier, and assiduous investigator into the national past. These episodes concern the collaboration of the legendary Count Julian of Ceuta with the advancing Muslim forces, against Roderick, the Visigoth king of Christian Hispania, at the time of the eighth-century Muslim conquest. They also concern the inability of the national icon King Alfonso X to muster support among his own rebellious nobles in the face of the Moorish offensive in the Sevillian borderlands centuries later, in 1273.[58]

Lope uses a rhetorical commonplace from the centuries-old trauma of Muslim incursion and Christian defeat as he describes the Islamic host advancing "como hacen en redil hambrientos lobos" (as do hungry wolves around a sheepfold). The reference appears most notably in the thirteenth-century lamentations of Alfonso X, as his translation of the chronicles of the Archbishop of Toledo, Rodrigo Ximénez de Rada, *Historia de rebus Hispaniae*, employed the same image of the conquering Arab as "the wolf among a flock of sheep." Olga Impey has pointed out the extent to which contemporary events influenced the pain and anxiety that pervaded Alfonso X's thirteenth-century jeremiad. Those events include successful Muslim offensives at Jaén and Sevilla, and the Alfonsine lamentations are also suffused with the continuing anguish over the (black) Almoravid invasions of 1108. They also reflect the inability of Alfonso X to rally his nobles to the defense of Christianity and the "nation" almost two hundred years after. In fact, the Christian nobles, Alfonso's brother Don Felipe included, gave their support to the invader Aben-Yúzaf. While such events point to a vulnerable past and confirm how imprecise alliances could be as geopolitical power flowed back and forth across the peninsula as a zone of conflict, they relativize Antiobo's desertion and underscore the propagandistic orientation of Lope's play.[59]

---

58. Condemning the "false crescents" (*falsas medias lunas*) of Islam, Antiobo at one point declares: "Know children, that it is my intention: / that you cast my Moors all, disarmed, into the sea" (Sabed hijos, que es mi intento: / que a mis moros, desarmados, / al mar arrojéis todos) ("El negro del mejor amo," 484). See also Fra Molinero, *La imagen*, 104, on the matter of unstable alliances. Domínguez Ortiz reminds us that Lope "ransacked ancient and contemporary chronicles and national and foreign histories in his search for plots" (*Golden Age*, 260).

59. Lope de Vega, *El negro del mejor amo*, 473; Olga Tudorica Impey, "Del duello de los godos de Espanna: La retórica del llanto y su motivación."

There is an important merging of specifically antiblack references with the general anti-Islamic images attendant to the Moorish menace as seen in King Alfonso's narrative, to which Lopean nationalism appears also to respond. The wolfish rapacity of the Muslim horsemen serves to highlight Christian victimhood in the account, and their agility and overwhelming physical presence is described through yet another fearsome animal image, that of the leopard. It is the emphasis on their blackness, however, in expressing the feeling of dread that the invaders inspire in the native populace that is most important in terms of Lope's historical subtext. Alfonso's narrative focuses on the blackness of their faces: "[L]as sus caras dellos negros como la pez" (Their faces [were] as black as a fish), one passage declares. Another states, "el mas fremoso dellos era negro como la olla" (the most handsome of them was as black as a pot). The description is a simultaneous reference to blackness as the supreme antiaesthetic value (ugliness) and, following the millennial association of darkness and the diabolical in the Christian tradition, of blacks as the incarnation of evil. As far as the specific historical presence of black Muslims is concerned, this is probably most clearly marked in the Medieval accounts of the twelfth-century Almoravid invasions recorded in Christian and Muslim chronicles, as well as in statues, paintings, church murals, and manuscript illustrations studied by Miriam DeCosta. The medieval *cantigas,* didactic religious poems, also reprise the image of Almoravid invaders as "chus negros que Satanas" (as black as Satan), paralleling Alfonso's rendering of them in his discursive flashback to the eighth and twelfth centuries.[60]

The historical antecedent, then, explains the metaphorical merging of a primary narrative that projects Islamic political and cultural hegemony in the Alfonsine account and portrays (Islamic) blacks as complementary negative icons of evil. That is to say that to the degree that Antiobo, a biracial Muslim from a family of black(a)moors on his mother's side, combines the elements of now-vanquished traditional enemies, he is the perfect "antagonist" in a nationalistic discourse that has self-consciously moved from lamen-

---

60. The objective of Impey's study was to emphasize Alfonso's use of rhetorical techniques aimed at dramatizing the tragic effects of the Moorish invasion in his translation of the Toledan's chronicle. She points out that Ximénez records the Arab soldier as being faster than a leopard, while Alfonso transfers these qualities to the invaders' horses (ibid., 298). The *OED* reminds us of the close semantic relationship between ugliness and evil, with one definition of *ugly* being "morally offensive and repulsive." This definition of ugliness is useful in this regard; it is also a cause of "horror, dread, loathing." Reference from the *cantigas* quoted in Miriam DeCosta, "The Portrayal of Blacks in a Spanish Medieval Manuscript," 195.

tation in Alfonso X to triumphalism in Lope de Vega. The key to the reversal of symbols inherent to Antiobo's crossover lies in the agency of the Holy Virgin Mary. Her miraculous intervention had often ensured survival and victory for Christian Hispania during the period of occupation and Islamic hegemony. She would also be the one to claim Antiobo's devotion upon his defection.

Antiobo's declaration of dedication to the Virgin Mary is an unambiguous racialization of the medieval literary trope of slavelike devotion to God as it appears in the hagiographic tradition. That the term *negro* is now the semantic equivalent of *slave* is emphasized by its capitalization in Lope's text: "Virgen María, / en vuestras manos me pongo. / Vuestro negro quiero ser" (Virgin Mary / into your hands I place myself. / I want to be your Negro). Lope's application of Aristotle's natural slave thesis to black Africans is reiterated by the protagonist's further declaration of abjection. Although there may be a surfeit of (white) slaves already serving Mary in heaven, he declares, as proof of his even more fervent devotion, that he would occupy a still lower rung in the upside down "hierarchy" within servitude. While they serve *at* her feet, he wishes to serve *under* her feet. He would be the carpet she walks upon.

> . . . a servir por vos me pongo.
> Hartos blancos hay allá
> que a esos pies sirvan de trono
> poned a un negro que sirva
> de alfombra a esos pies hermosos.
>
> [. . . I place myself at your service.
> There are more than sufficient whites there
> who serve as a throne to those feet.
> Put a Negro to serve
> as a carpet for those beautiful feet.][61]

Upon his successful rebuff of the Muslim invasion, the Sardinians offer to crown Antiobo king. Acceptance on his part, however, would run counter to the ideological thrust of the work. Following the projected essentialist credo for blackness—"I serve therefore I am"—Lope's black saint articulates the message that gives title to the play, declaring that he is "el negro del Mejor amo" (the slave of the better Master), serving the Christian God.[62]

---

61. Lope de Vega, *El negro del mejor amo*, 473.
62. Ibid., 486.

The rejection of Allah had already been expressed through his reference to the false crescents displayed from his ship. He then humbly withdraws to his seaside hermitage to miraculously rise again after death as the protection of the island requires.

If, in Zurara's foundational text, the civilizing mission of colonialism brought the savages to the light of Christianity, so much so that the writer could boast of the fact, as pointed out above, then in Lope the final logic of evangelization is fulfilled as the community of savages has produced a saint. It is to be noted, however, that the religious determinism of Antiobo's role as hermit constrains him to isolation and celibacy. In other words, there is no question of granting phallic power to this putative man of arms, as is made clear in his "rejection" of the advances of two native white women.[63] His symbolic castration apart, it is his blackness that continues to be the major determining factor of his identity in his new community. As the antithesis of all that is pure and white and good, the playwright constantly reiterates his character as an oddity and a lesser being among the indigenous community of white Christians. Predictably, the customary test of faith that all saints must face is articulated around the association of blackness and moral impurity. Antiobo's response to Lidonio, the devil's agent, as the latter questions the anomaly of a black with supernatural moral power, is confident and straightforward as the future saint gives his credentials: "Tiznado no, mas lavado / de su sangre, de quien fuí, / aunque negro, rescatado" (Blackened no, but cleansed / by his blood, by whom I was / though black, rescued). As Molinero has observed, however, even with the "original sin" of blackness removed so that acceptance by the white community might be obtained, his destiny is still essentially one of service.[64]

While Antiobo is a perfect symbol for post-Reconquista triumphalism as it might pertain to blacks, Moors, and Afro-Arabs, the direct rejection of black Africans in Spanish Golden Age literature is most acutely expressed in the poem "Boda de negros," by Francisco de Quevedo y Villegas. The principle of blackness incarnate as an unwelcome and unsightly blot or stain on the body politic is the metaphorical axis upon which Quevedo's famous poem turns. Cosmetic lactification, or the spiritual whitening or whitening of the soul, remains the cultural imperative, a literary equivalent of the

63. Daniel Boyarin discusses the symbolic power of the phallus versus the merely biological penis in "What Does a Jew Want; or, The Political Meaning of the Phallus."
64. Lope de Vega, *El negro del mejor amo*, 499; Fra Molinero, *La images*, 124.

Fanonian insight that the colonized must "turn white, or disappear." Accordingly, there is little room, if any, for the inclusion into Spanishness of the present objects of his attention, given the well-known phobia that Quevedo felt for all foreigners.[65] Much of the poem's forcefulness is derived from the testimonial pose adopted by the poet. What the speaking "I" saw personalizes and thus lends credibility and emotional intensity to the narrative.

> Ví, debe de haber tres días,
> en las gradas de San Pedro
> una tenebrosa boda,
> porque era toda de negros.
>
> [I saw, it must have been three days ago,
> on the steps to Saint Peter's cathedral
> A fearful wedding,
> because it was of all blacks.][66]

There is an unavoidable sense of dread in which the reader is invited to participate through this evocation of the forces of darkness (the wedding is *tenebrosa,* "fearful"), poised, as it were, almost in the doorway of the cathedral, the house of light. The threat of invasion by the blacks can only be viewed with revulsion, that is, as a sacrilegious violation of the sanctity of a place of worship, especially bearing in mind their association with the demonic in the popular imaginary. Ever since the fourth century, as indicated, with the speculations of Jerome, Origen, and other church fathers, the Ethiopian (black) had been regarded as "no other than the devil." Medieval painting and poetry repeated this association, as expressed in a poem by Pedro Cartagena in a fifteenth-century *cancionero.* Cartagena's lines were unambiguous: "Vade retro, Satanás / no tientes a mi señora" (Get back, Satan, tempt not my mistress).[67] The black as bogeyman, or *coco,* was also a constant in the literature of the period. The double use of the metaphor in the introduction to Quevedo's "Boda" thus unified both the demonic

---

65. Gerald Brenan speaks of Quevedo's sympathy for the cause of the Amerindians even as he notes his ardent support for the Inquisition and his "irrational hatred" for all foreigners; see *The Literature of the Spanish People: From Roman Times to the Present,* 270–72. See also Fanon, *Black Skin,* 100. Blacks "with a white soul" *(de alma blanca),* is a cliché that accompanies the black presence in Hispanic literature from Medieval times to the present; see, for example, Alberto Insúa, *El negro que tenía el alma blanca.*

66. Francisco de Quevedo y Villegas, *Obras completas: Verso,* 2:242–43. Quotations in the following paragraphs are from this edition.

67. See Drake, *Black Folk,* 58–59; and DeCosta, "Portrayal of Blacks"; Cartagena quoted in Mansour, *La poesía negrista,* 32.

extreme (the devil, with the religious anxiety it carried) and the more attenuated fear of imaginary monsters. The presence of the unholy and the antithetical in this black wedding party sets the tone for the rest of the poem.
Its objective hardly goes beyond describing the rest of the event and saying
what an obnoxious anomaly all of this was. What follows is a brilliant display of baroque binaries that oppose humor with fear, black with white, the
holy with the unholy, purity with impurity, civilization with savagery, and
the sublime with the ridiculous.

Quevedo's exposition in "Boda de negros" exploits two traditional topoi
present in both folklore and high culture. They have to do with the theme
of the upside-down world, and that of the grotesque body. In the former,
the divinely ordered hierarchy in the universe, God's Chain of Being, from
the heavenly host through man, the animals, plants, and stones, is upset
and disrupted. The literature in which the absurd and the incongruous
dominate expresses this world out of order; chairs sit on men, servants rule
their masters, children berate their parents, and the nonsensical displaces
reason, all to produce a comical effect. When the discord and unreason are
associated with deviltry and witchcraft, this inversion of values assumes its
most serious form.[68] In Quevedo's vision of Spain here presented, the world
has to be upside down if savages are taking marriage vows and if these subjects, more properly speaking (synecdochial) representatives of the underworld, are celebrating a holy sacrament on the church steps. The second
verse reiterates, "Parecía matrimonio / concertado en el infierno" (It seemed
to be a wedding / contracted in hell).

Philip Thomson has characterized the grotesque as simultaneously con-
veying the notion of the laughable and the horrifying, expressed by way of
hyperbole. "Boda de negros" qualifies for such a characterization, especially
since, considering the relatively harmless nature of the party in question,
the scene is intended to be more funny than fearful, and it is the element of
(word)play that, in the final analysis, matters most. Rather than to express
fright, its authorial intention turns out to be more akin to that of the ten-
dentious joke, whose hostile impulse, according to Freud, operates on the
basis of an a priori "us and them" dichotomy that appeals to sameness and
separates difference. Accordingly, discursive differentiation resorts here to
the tradition of the comic genre in European folk discourse, where mockery
and abuse focus on the grotesque body. In Bakhtinian theory, this revolves
around "the genital organs, the anus and the buttocks, the belly, mouth,

---

68. See Helen F. Grant, "The World Upside-Down," 110.

and nose."[69] Since the context is not that of a fairly monochrome indigenous Europe, however, the epidermic specificity of the subjects is a primary element in their depiction.

Blackness as a chromatic effect has an almost totalizing and apocalyptic result in "Boda de negros." It radiates from the body surface of the couple itself, affects the patio where the reception will take place, and inhabits the plates, tablecloth, wine, and food of the guests. Quevedo's eschatological buildup leads us to a climax in which the party wash their hands after their meal and the opportunity is provided for the penultimate racial insult: "y quedó el agua / para ensuciar todo un reino" (and the water that remained [was filthy enough] to soil an entire kingdom). Following the grotesque premise, a similar exaggerative procedure is applied to associate the subjects with lower life forms and with the lower bodily functions. A particularly striking metaphor relates how, as the group passes by, the street is drowned in sneezes as a reaction to their intolerable body odor. This would reflect the "customary sidewalk jeer" *(estornudo)* with which "whites showed contempt for Negroes." The striking sensory combination of drowning and smell (they are also compared to the notoriously malodorous bird, the *grajo,* or rook)[70] is complemented by the graphic visual image likening them to black crows:

> Hundíase de estornudos
> la calle por do volvieron
> que una boda semejante
> hace dar más de un pimiento:
>
> Iban los dos de las manos,
> como pudieran dos cuervoz;
> otros dicen como grajos,
> porque a grajos van oliendo.
>
> [The street whence they came
> was drowned in sneezes
> for a wedding like this
> brings out more than one pepper.

69. Philip Thomson, *The Grotesque,* 3; Leonard Feinberg, *The Secret of Humor,* 9; Sigmund Freud, *Jokes and Their Relation to the Unconscious,* 90, 102–3; Simon Dentith, *Bakhtinian Thought: An Introductory Reader,* 228.

70. Ortiz observes that the comparison survived the Atlantic crossing, in spite of the fact that the birds referred to do not exist in Cuba (*Los negros curros,* 159). Regarding the sidewalk jeer, see Pike, "Sevillian Society," 357.

They went by hand in hand
as two crows might;
like rooks others say,
because they smell like rooks.]

The following depiction of them as flea-bitten dogs—"los abrasaban pul-
gas, / por perrengues o por perros" (fleas embraced them / for being niggers
or dogs)—is only surpassed by Quevedo's final animalistic reference, which
puts them on the same level with swine. Even then, however, the simple
simile seems insufficient to express the poet's disdain. The allusion to pigs is
arrived at in a roundabout way. The black pudding *(morcilla)* was served,
states the text, but some of them were afraid to eat it, thinking that they
might be eating other cooked blacks: "y hubo algunos que, de miedo, / no
las comieron, pensando / se comían a sí mesmos" (and there were some,
who out of fear, / did not eat it, thinking / that they were eating each other).
Following the allusion to cannibalism, the bacon is then brought in, which
is also related with a similar quip.

> . . . cuando llegó el tocino
> hubo grandes sentimientos,
> y pringados con pringadas
> un rato se enternecieron.
>
> [. . . when the bacon arrived
> there was much lamentation,
> and *pringados* and *pringadas*
> for a moment were sad.]

Here the poetic conceit goes beyond the mere merging of the abstract qualities of squalor, and moral or physical defilement that would be conveyed in
Quevedo's metaphorical association of blacks with swine. Their animalization, and the ultimate success of the Baroque trope, is effected through the
more accessible mental picture of melting pig fat being dropped on the
open wounds of the enslaved as a form of punishment. They, the *pringados*
and *pringadas,* whose bodies had already been, as it were, dipped in the fire,
are saddened to see the remnants of their fellow swine, now made into bacon
by deliberate exposure to heat. While an alternate reading of this passage
might personify the bacon instead and make them all *(tocino, pringados,*
and *pringadas)* respond sentimentally upon seeing each other, what is remarkable about the image is the deliberate and prolonged contemplation of the

black body with imaginary open wounds made by the lash, and with burning oil being applied thereto. The image takes the narration beyond the
cynicism and contempt that the speaker obviously feels for his subjects and
introduces the element of sadism and scopophilia into his narrative.[71]

In this context the suggestion that there is a libidinal element being pursued by Quevedo in his depiction of the black wedding is by no means far-
fetched. The naked bodies of the bride and groom together in bed had
already been invoked in an earlier stanza. While much of the general focus
is to establish the overwhelming physical and metaphysical blackness of the
entire ensemble, a later stanza identifies them by name, albeit the stereotypical ones given to literary blacks of the period. He is Tomé and she is Francisca. It is the wordplay on *es/clavo,* however, and the new groom's ostensible
purpose in marrying, that is worthy of note. In introducing them—"El se
llama Tomé, / y ella Francisca del Puerto; / ella esclava, y él es clavo" (His
name is Tomé, / and hers is Francisca del Puerto; / she is a slave, and he is a
nail)—the poet takes advantage of the visual image of the mark of the *S*
and the nail, *clavo,* that was customarily branded onto the faces of slaves.
His syllabic separation of "slave," or *esclavo (es clavo),* not only restates their
social status and maintains the interior parallelism of the line, it also provides an easy phallic image for the context of newlyweds: Francisco "es
clavo / que quiere hincársele en medio" (is a nail / who wants to impale her
in the middle).

Heinrich Schneegans has commented on the tendency in the grotesque
artist to become "intoxicated with his own creation," and to lose sight of
the satirical object while language and the concept of art for art's sake take
over.[72] The degree to which "Boda de negros" might be merely an accumulation of clever conceits and linguistic overkill, or alternatively, a deliberate
study in unbridled contempt and xenophobia, hardly mitigates its effec-
tiveness either way. As a one-sided demonstration of social power between
the implied interlocutors, however, it is Francisco's metallic erection that
shows the fissure in the powerhouse of language being unloaded upon
Quevedo's subjects in the "Boda." Underlying the sick sadism (redundance
notwithstanding) of a phallus that wounds and ultimately kills, are two
things: the age-old male fantasy of superhuman sexual prowess, and the

---

71. For a discussion of scopophilia as libidinous looking, see Otto Fenichel, *The Collected
Papers of Otto Fenichel,* 1:373–79; Freud, *Jokes,* 98.
72. Quoted in Thomson, *Grotesque,* 42.

unrestrained animal sexuality that Quevedo is here projecting on his *negros*. Penis envy, as Susan Gubar and Stuart Hall have pointed out, is an aspect of the ontological fullness imputed to the black Other and confirms the ambivalent nature of the racist colonial stereotype.

If the text of domination can be said to flounder here on the sexual question, the projection of uncleanness onto the Other also redounds back to the speaker. The banning of daily ablutions among the Jewish and Islamic communities under Cardinal Ximénez and the Catholic monarchs, and the abolition of public baths in Muslim towns after the 1568 Alpujarras rebellion, hardly speak to an ethic of high hygiene among the constituency for which Quevedo spoke. In fact, among the Franciscans, the Cardinal Ximénez's own brotherhood, "physical dirt" was considered "a test of moral purity and true faith," and the height of their ambition was achieved by "dining and sleeping from year's end to year's end in the same unchanged woollen frock." Cadamosto, on the contrary, had found the Wolof men and women "clean in their persons, since they wash themselves four or five times a day."[73]

While the latter observation can only be of relative pertinence in the objective context of exile, captivity, and enslavement of Africans, it is the ideological intention of the text of the "Boda" and its thematics of debasement that matter most for this discussion. The projection of black people as generically unwashed, unwashable, and malodorous reveals the ignorance and visceral irrationality of prejudice, the conceit of epidermic whiteness, as well as the role of the literary in producing knowledge. As an exercise in symbolic violence, however, its significance is probably overridden by the gross materiality of social and political relations in sixteenth- and seventeenth-century Spain. Practices such as the roasting alive of religious nonconformists at the public *quemaderos* and the disinterring of the bones of the deceased so that they, too, might be subjected to public purification by fire certainly relativize the importance of literary imaginings. José Luis Cortés López also recalls the casual, unpunished murder of a black slave in Seville in 1520, when he and his companion defended themselves verbally against the customary sidewalk slurs, and the pursuit and subsequent slaughter, in a church, of the Good Samaritan who came to their defense.[74] Events of the Spanish Golden Age, in conclusion, in both their material and their literary

73. Cadamosto, in Crone, "*Voyages of Cadamosto*," 27. The observation on the Franciscans was quoted in Read, *Moors;* Read adds that inhabitants of the land of Castile soap "may have foregone the practice of regular washing well into the nineteenth century" (234).

74. Cortés López, *La esclavitud negra*, 95.

expressions, confirm a still-extant nationalist hysteria of the injunction "Moors get out!" *(fuera moros).* The literature's ceaseless linking of African-ness to subordination has also been an enduring contribution to modern race-making, whether by taking black skin as the Aristotelian sign of the natural slave, by way of the anti-Hamitic pretext, or just through the un-adorned will to power.

2

Slavery and the
Syntax of Subpersonhood

I wanted to be a man, nothing but a man.

    Frantz Fanon

They were all doomed to remain on the spot, like sheep in a pen, till they were sold; they have no apartment to retire to, no bed to repose on, no covering to protect them; they sit naked all day, lie naked all night, on the bare boards, or benches, where we saw them exhibited.

    Robert Walsh, *Notices from Brazil in 1828 and 1829*

  Literary stereotypes of blacks can be shown to have had a conspicuous role in race-making and racial domination in the Peninsular Hispanic tradition (as in other modern European national traditions). It is important to point out, however, that literature's fictionality, its made-up nature, its determinants of form or genre, and its embedded pleasure principle, are all capable of attenuating the more or less implicit political message it carries. That creators of literary stereotypes reduce their object to its barest essentials and from that point reproduce them tirelessly for maximum results is arguably a conscious or unconscious strategic response aimed at (re)infusing political dynamism into the literary text. Notwithstanding the presence of blacks in colonial Latin American literature, therefore, I shall pay attention in this chapter to other, nonliterary aspects of discourse pertinent to Africans and their descendants and to other nonwhites in race-making in the Latin American colonial context. I propose that these aspects of discourse are arguably of much greater potency than merely "literary" ones, since they go to the heart of subject formation especially for the forced migrants as they inhabit their new material and social environments as slaves and ex-slaves and are designated identities in the dynamic of social stratification and its taxonomies. My objective is to highlight a certain experiential dimension to subjectivity that is often forsaken when under the academic "historiographic" focus, in which process the individual frequently recedes into the background as an object of study.

The aspects of discourse that interest me here include the legal language of empire and the racial presumptions projected by royal edicts, the colonial racial nomenclature, as well as the commercial language of slavery itself. I suggest that all the varying registers of this broad colonial discourse bear a coherent syntactic relationship to each other, to the degree that they produce a code and a consensus as to racial identity within the Latin American polity and to black racial identity in particular, and undercut the premise of a generalized cordiality in Latin American race relations. In a social formation in which racial identity had such an important bearing on status and eventual quality of life, how benign, indeed, could the mechanisms of separation be? Identity, we recall, concerns not only how one sees oneself, but also how others see one. It is in the racialized West and its colonial zone that the black-as-body, for instance, as Frantz Fanon reminds us, becomes the naturalized (visual) symbol of negative social and moral value and of servility.[1] Correspondingly, in Latin America, we find the colonial power of naming and its panoptical gaze producing a vocabulary of difference as a strategy of domination. This physiognomic rationale would operate on the premise that the body is legible and subject to diagnosis, constituting a textuality that attests to the binary of superiority and inferiority according to various rubrics of social, moral, and ethical worth.

Charles Mills, in his critique of the Enlightenment revolt against the social theory and practice of the Occidental ancien régime, points out the limitations of the movement's rights-based individualism, especially with regard to the moral egalitarianism of philosopher Emmanuel Kant, its premier theo-

---

1. Fanon discusses the reductivism of the "corporeal schema" in his chapter "Fact of Blackness" in *Black Skin*, 109–40; see also Charles Johnson, "A Phenomenology of the Black Body."

rist on race. He asserts that the Enlightenment's rejection of feudalism's veneration of lineage and wealth, its entitlement of the individual to respect, and to an inherent moral worth and social personhood, although purportedly "universal," was meant, in reality, to refer only to white males. The remaining social subjects were the *Untermensch,* or subpersons. While within the European ambit, women and children continued to be relegated to this secondary status, it is the colonial encounter with racial difference, and more specifically slavery, which exemplifies, in most dramatic form, the marginality and disempowerment of subpersonhood. If colonial production was subpersonhood's primary raison d'être, in other words, then racial ideology was one of its main political strategies, and discourse its primary location. The following discussion will therefore highlight the extent to which the language of a normative racial and cultural whiteness—written, read, and "seen" in the first instance as moral and biological *limpieza*—legitimized Hispanic imperial rule.[2] The whole was effected by projecting and reifying racial alterity as inferiority in various textual registers in Latin American colonial life.

During the Renaissance, in the process of formation, the Spanish nation was identified as white and Christian, as Jews and Moors were expelled. Feudalism's strong legacy still prevailed, however, internally stratifying nobility, clergy, and commoners, as well as guilds and corporations, in this society of estates, in which honor *(honra)* was the single most important concept that set individuals apart. *Honra,* a shifting, multivalent signifier, bore connotations as to the legitimacy of one's birth, one's nobility or lack thereof, as well as one's whiteness. To be born of unwed parents, for example, constituted a grave social blemish, and since the days of Alfonso X's Siete Partidas, illegitimates were labeled *infamados* and therefore were unqualified for prestigious public or ecclesiastic positions and could never acquire *honra.* The same stigma and corresponding sanctions applied to those whose religious orthodoxy was questionable, as pointed out in the previous chapter. The king's intercession could provide rank for the *infamados* and relieve them of the burden of genealogical dishonor. It could also provide the requisite purification for individuals who lacked *limpieza de sangre* (blood purity). Contemporary observers have taken note of the oppressive nature of the legal statutes

2. My reference to the racialized colonial gaze here subsumes into the question of corporeal surveillance as an instance of differentiation, the genre of paintings known as *cuadros de castas* (caste paintings) in eighteenth-century Mexico. See Ilona Katzew, et al., eds., *New World Orders: Casta Painting and Colonial Latin America;* and Magalí Carrera, *Imagining Identity in New Spain: Race, Lineage, and the Colonial Body in Portraiture and Casta Paintings.*

supporting the regimen in Europe and have attested to the socioeconomic and political paralysis suffered by those lacking *honra*.[3] In the multiracial milieu of the New World, whiteness, as an element of identity, would assume unprecedented importance, and institutionalized royal intervention would also participate in the dynamic of the negotiation and establishment of the social worth or honor of individuals.

The Premise of Whiteness

In Latin American historiography, it is axiomatic that the politico-military domination of the conquest provided the opportunity for the colonists, in their majority of peasant and artisan origin, to get rich and even buy titles of nobility, along with the package of privileges these titles provided. Inevitably, specifically racial domination also played a role in the general erection of the colonial power structure. The top-down control of the labor force and of the distribution of labor, and the racialized appropriation of lands, mines, and other natural resources, are only the more notorious aspects of the colonial contract and of its legacy of social and racial inequality. Other aspects include the racially exclusive access to higher education that provided entry to the professions, as well as the role of race in accessing the political favor required for the higher reaches of the bureaucracy. In 1542, fifty years after the arrival of Columbus, the human status of the American natives was still an issue of serious intellectual debate in Spain, and the generalized racial intermixing that came with the Spanish invasion produced a colonial population that was deemed doubly defective; first, because they were the issue of unwed parents, and second, on account of the nonwhite origin of either mother or father. In the libidinal economy of conquest, defined more often than not by brute force, it was not unusual for encomienda holders or conquistadors themselves to have dozens of children by native women, or even for friars and priests to hold concubines. As late as 1806, on the eve of Latin American independence, monarchic absolutism, ancien régime stratification and racial discrimination, as well as the discursive and legal superstructure that upheld these principles, were reasserted. According to the Council of the Indies:

> If it is impossible to deny that the different hierarchies and strata are of the greatest value because their gradual and connected links of subor-

3. See Twinam, *Public Lives,* 45.

dination and dependence support and substantiate the obedience and respect of the lowest vassal towards the King, this system is required for many reasons in America. This is so not only because of the greater distance from the throne but because of the great number of people who by their vicious origin and nature cannot be compared with the simple people in Spain and do constitute a very inferior species. It would be utterly reprehensible if those known to be the sons and descendants of slaves sat down with those who derive from the first conquistadors or families that are noble, legitimate, white, and free from any ugly stain.[4]

Indeed, individuals of non-noble birth, nonwhites, and those with the "ugly stain" (a simultaneous reference to miscegenation and questionable cultural and religious orthodoxy of individuals) had been institutionally disenfranchised quite early in the setting up of the colonies. While most of the major administrative offices for the running of the colonies were already created by 1535, by 1570 they were fully developed, to suffer little structural modification until the Bourbon reforms of the middle eighteenth century. The racial regimen, however, remained basically unruffled throughout the colonial period. Although local circumstance, the great distance that spanned the empire, and the crown's chronically impecunious state continually compromised the royal will to absolutism, the law remained a formidable instrument of racialized privilege and a powerful contributor to group identity, as it erected a boundary between the whites and the so-called *castas*. The "inferior species" referred to in the above statement of policy, for example, had been spelled out since 1549 in a royal decree, which stipulated that "No mulattos, mestizos, nor illegitimates may have either Indians, or royal or civic appointments, unless they have our special permission."[5] It reinforced the diminished status of the native population as a collectivity subject to payment of tribute and to exploitation as a result of conquest, while restating the moral and racial restrictions regarding employment opportunities for other nonwhites.

The presumed immorality and incompetence of the nonwhites was again expressed some decades later (1584), as loyalty, trustworthiness, and intelligence were the prerequisites declared for the position of collector of judicial fees or *receptor de penas*. Here, the crown warned the Audiencia of Santa Fe to try "as much as it could" to exclude mulattoes and mestizos. Similarly, the governor of the province of Venezuela was exhorted in 1576 in the

---

4. Magnus Morner, *Race Mixture in the History of Latin America*, 28, 48.

5. In Richard Konetzke, ed., *Colección de documentos para la historia de la formación social de hispanoamérica*, 1:256.

name of "good governance" to decommission all mestizo notaries and to desist from making similar appointments in the future. Such posts were to be made only to persons "who possess the qualities of loyalty, legitimacy and such others as required by the laws of these kingdoms."[6]

The racial inflection to colonial legislation assumed, perhaps, its clearest form when treating the question of public safety. The 1566 decree or *cédula* to the Audiencia of Perú, in revoking any licenses that might previously have been issued to Indians, mestizos, and mulattoes to bear arms, made explicit the white normativity to which it catered. It also sought to reiterate the principle of keeping the racial boundary between the colonizing class and their social subordinates militarized. Racialized political and civic power, and power in arms, were further reinforced at the level of the various guilds of tradesmen and in the everyday dress codes that mandated that individuals dress in accordance with their position in the social hierarchy. In 1570 and 1584, the reiterated ban on blacks and mulattoes in Mexico from learning the art of silk weaving, to cite but one example, had its corollary in legal stipulations that forbade the wives of the latter from sporting ostentatious adornments, such as pearls and gold jewelry, or from wearing silk garments. Effectively the element of white male dominance in this particular rubric was evident in the fact that if the black women were wives of Spaniards, they were exempted from this rule according to a 1571 ordinance.[7]

As with the bureaucracy, the prominent role of the Church in the colonial enterprise was reflected in its selectivity in relation to the personnel deployed to undertake its mission. If, as might be expected, the moral character of its agents was a priority in recruitment, the New World context compounded such traditional criteria as orthodoxy and legitimacy of potential churchmen with a heightened sensitivity to their racial identity. The royal *cédula* rebuking the archbishop of Granada (Colombia) in 1576 for ordaining individuals who did not meet the appropriate criteria spoke to more than their lack of virtue and moral temperance. To these general demerits, which might afflict all applicants, white ones included, it added the specific category of *mestizo* as a nonqualifying characteristic: "We have been told that you have given holy orders to many persons who do not sufficiently qualify for such, and to mestizos and persons of that ilk." The characteristics of "temperance," "virtue," and "sufficiency" appear in almost formulaic fashion in edicts such as the ones directed to Quito and to Chile in 1578

6. Ibid., 1:555, 498.
7. See Manuel Alvar, *Léxico del mestizaje en hispanoamérica*, 29.

and 1588, respectively, which were explicitly intended to keep mestizos out of the priesthood.[8]

What is perhaps most noteworthy about these and similar royal pronouncements is the racial binary upon which they were premised. The detailed naming of the other racial groups—*mestizos, indios, mulatos*—establishes the normativity of whiteness, even as these groups stand, in the texts, in counterposition to the unnamed, but very present, dominant white minority. Though unstated, the white subtextual presence is again distinctly inferable in the moral qualifications attached to bureaucratic positions, the priesthood, guilds of craftsmen, and so on, for which euphemistic terms such as "sufficiency," "necessary qualities," and "the common good," are semantic stand-ins for whiteness. As statements that invoke a white/nonwhite binary, but which are addressed primarily to white official and extra-official agents in charge of their implementation, it is also significant that the other extreme element of the binary, the blacks, are rarely mentioned in these documents. Black unmentionableness is no doubt due to the fact that, especially earlier in the colonial period, the greater percentage of this group would have been in bondage, hence it was needless to mention them in regard to paid occupations that were often socially elevated. Their textual invisibility, however, bearing in mind the increasing numbers of free individuals of color as time went by, attests to a practice of social and racial domination that made it literally unthinkable, for example, that *negros* might be linked ontologically with the concept of the priesthood.[9]

Whiteness as the metaphor for the absence of contamination in colonial Latin American legal discourse regarding personnel for church and state needs to be seen in terms of its idealism in at least two respects. First, as a metatextual reference to the point of enunciation, it remits to the projection, or pursuit, of an imperial Hispanic white essentialist core. Threadbare conquistadors in the New World, Stuart Schwartz reminds us, would sometimes reach backwards beyond an Afro-Islamic presence of over seven hundred years to claim racial anchor in the Visigoths to establish their pedigree.[10] Second, in terms of its practical application, the principle of white racial purity highlighted an absolutism that was, though desired, rendered impossible by the material conditions of the colonial enterprise.

The defeat of absolutism is seen in the repetition—time and again, and

---

8. In Konetzke, *Colección*, 1:491, 514, 588.

9. Frederick Bowser, "Colonial Spanish America," 36, points out the extent to which the population of freedmen exceeded that of the enslaved by the second half of the eighteenth century.

10. Stuart Schwartz, "Colonial Identities and the Sociedad de Castas," 189.

in different places—of the same ordinances, a fact that indicates their non-compliance. These ordinances were notoriously inconsistent as to the sanctions they sought to apply, further indicating a weakness at the top. While the scarcity of white colonizers opened access to lower-level occupations for racial subalterns in a way that white numerical preponderance in the colonial United States, for example, did not allow, the paucity of female Hispanic immigrants imposed limitations on the potential for white separatist endogamy in the Latin American colonial scenario. At the beginning of the colonial period, the crown had encouraged the conquistadors to marry the daughters of the indigenous nobles, but even as independence approached, some 250 years later, royal pragmatics of the 1770s continued to rail against racially unequal marriages, since these were presumed to be prejudicial to the state and to the family.[11]

Regarding the absolutist premise, it is perhaps important to bear in mind that the draconian model of what became Jim Crow segregation in the United States drew much of its strength from white numerical dominance in all socioeconomic levels in colonial American society, a fact that effectively impeded the integration and upward mobility of free blacks. Of related importance is the fact of the availability of white wives for the colonists, to the degree that it tempered interracial intercourse and miscegenation there. It becomes clear, consequently, that the supremacist impulse in colonial Latin America was hindered from its initial stages by these two important factors—the absence of the white immigrant family, and a relatively low white demographic presence. When whiteness became an object of purchase with the introduction of the *cédulas de gracias al sacar* in eighteenth-century colonial Spanish America, it blurred even further the lines of racial difference already made vague after the first century of miscegenation.

Related to the low percentage of women among the early migrants to Hispanic America as a factor of the region's intensive race mixing are the high levels of concubinage that came with this interracial contact. They are, in and of themselves, a significant reflection of peninsular racial disdain, taking into consideration the association between matrimony and female *honra* in peninsular Hispanic culture and the elevated percentage of white intermarriage when white women were available in the colonies. The mentioned shortage of white males to fill the multiplicity of middle- and lower-range positions, especially in the military and trades, also explains the gradual

11. See Jaime Jaramillo Uribe, "Mestizaje y diferenciación social en el nuevo reino de Granada en la segunda mitad del Siglo XVIII," 38; and Twinam, *Public Lives.*

access that was gained by those individuals deemed otherwise racially unfit by the royal *cédulas*.[12] The *peninsulares'* aversion to manual labor, however, and their vigorous attempts to exclude *casta* competition from any lucrative endeavor, were equally important elements in the structuring of socioracial power.

An interesting illustration of the tensions besetting racial hegemony lies in the *cédulas de gracias al sacar,* which were often used as certificates of whiteness that gave their holders access to privileges otherwise denied them by their racial condition. The crown's desperate need for revenue in the sixteenth and seventeenth centuries led to the sale of a wide range of offices that, by 1700, had even ascended to the level of the viceroyalty. With the crown facing bankruptcy in 1557, for example, Philip II ordered a thousand *hidalguías* sold, regardless of the class origin or the supposed defects of the buyers, setting thereby a precedent for subsequent sovereigns. By 1795, Bourbon financial reforms brought a fixed tariff for some 71 categories of these certificates into being. The acquisition and use of certificates of whiteness by an albeit small minority of colonials to pass, in combination, of course, with such other qualities as having a good reputation, or having a record of loyal service to the crown, illuminates the principle of settled expectations in whiteness. It made the epidermic condition more than just a passive aspect of identity and converted it into an asset, or "property."[13]

Official and popular resistance to these invasions of privilege, however, shows the tenacity with which the creole and peninsular elite sought to hold

12. Carrera speaks to the issue of Spanish endogamy in the Sagraria parish in Mexico City. In 1665–1670, Spanish-Spanish marriages accounted for 96 percent of unions involving Spaniards, in 1752–1754, 75 percent, and in 1781–1783, 72.7 percent (*Imagining Identity,* 39). See also Twinam, *Public Lives;* Morner, *Race Mixture;* and Jaramillo Uribe, "Mestizaje." Rout, in *African Experience,* stresses not only the role of slaves and ex-slaves as cannon fodder in local and international struggles in Latin America, but also the fact that, although they labored in the trades as journeymen, they could not get certification as master craftsmen.

13. See Clarence Haring, *The Spanish Empire in America,* 213; Bowser, "Colonial Spanish America," 46; Mark Burkholder and Lyman Johnson, *Colonial Latin America,* 86; and Twinam, *Public Lives,* 19. Cheryl Harris proposes that the "right to exclude" is a premise shared by whiteness as property. Its expectations of power and control are enshrined in law. Her reference to the famous case of *Plessy v. Ferguson* in the United States, in which the former claimed that "the mixture of blood (was) not discernible in him," hence his entitlement to "every recognition, right, privilege, and immunity," speaks to an issue not fundamentally different from the dozens of cases to which Jaramillo Uribe refers in eighteenth-century Colombia, in which colonials appealed to the crown to have their (pure) white lineage recognized ("Mestizaje"). Among the rewards anticipated were certain immunities like the right to not be imprisoned on account of debts owed, the guarantee of the right to inheritance, the right to use a coat of arms, or simply to be socially recognized as an *español* and not a *mestizo* or *mulato* (Harris, "Whiteness as Property," 1714).

back *castas* from contaminating their exclusive racial sphere. Several studies refer to the case in which a *mulata,* dressed above her station, ignored the injunctions of the *señoras* in the town of Córdoba to "dress down." One of the latter tricked her into visiting her house and made her servants undress her, whip her, burn her fineries, and finally dress her appropriately. In similar fashion, the Lima city council prohibited, in 1614, the use of coffins among the African population as a "serious affront to the superior status of the Spanish," and a church synod ruled that nonwhites were not to be buried in the cathedral. It is also significant that often the certificates only bought symbolic gains, such as the ability of the ladies of one mulatto family to wear mantillas in church.[14]

The Gramscian proposal that hegemony is based on coercion as well as persuasion remits us to the technologies of the symbolic as a function of the apparatus of power. Undeniably, in Latin America, the colonial racial taxonomy, as a verbal and symbolic representation of social stratification and power, is the most complete and representative cultural text in this regard. It endorsed legal proscriptions, and over time it also served to naturalize negative racial difference. These racial epithets reflect and complement the *casta* genre of paintings ordered by the Spanish botanist José Celestino Mutis in the middle 1700s. Mutis, the personal physician to the Viceroy of New Granada, was a disciple of the natural scientist Carl von Linné, who, as previously discussed, was a firm believer in racial hierarchy and a primary exponent of polygenesis, even in the face of interracial "crossbreeding." Among the objectives of the paintings, powerful visual signifiers that they were, was the ordering of the increasingly miscegenated colonial populace, a fact which, given the economic expansion of the eighteenth century, was blurring traditional lines of racially acknowledged hierarchy.[15] While the series of paintings, varying from sixteen to twenty, represent but a limited mimetic expression of the imaginary, the verbal signifiers of the racial taxonomy encompass a wider gamut of racial difference. They constitute an even more graphic illustration of the binary of personhood and subpersonhood. It can be argued that the completeness of the verbal taxonomy points to the success with which the (imposed) idea of the transcendence of whiteness was accepted and reproduced by the colonial population at large.

14. Alvar, *Léxico,* 29; Bowser, "Colonial Spanish America," 41, 46.

15. It is to be observed that *españoles,* a category that included both Spaniards and white creoles, were always placed at the beginning of the *casta* series, as Katzew observes, to indicate their dominance over the other groups. Family units of *castas* of lower social status, and presumably of lower racial status, followed, along with flora and fauna of the region (*New World Orders,* 13).

Effectively, it was the bodily absence of melanin, or an individual's white-ness, as an adjunct to the racialized facial morphology, that signaled their worth in the absence of material manifestations of honor (such as wealth, office, slaves, lands, and so on). The rising colonial expectations of erst-while Iberian commoners were pointed out by Alexander von Humboldt, a nineteenth-century observer, when he remarked on the coincidence between the obsession with rank on the Peninsula, and the racial arrogance Peninsulars displayed in the New World situation. "In America," he noted, "the skin, more or less white, is what dictates the class that an individual occupies in society. A white man, even if he rides barefoot on horseback, considers him-self a member of the nobility of the country."[16] Peninsular *donomanía,* in the presence of a population deemed a priori to be *infamados,* was taken to new heights as Spanish sailors, cabin boys, shoemakers, tailors, and potters, once in the New World, claimed to be aristocrats, infecting in turn the creole and *casta* population with the preoccupation over status.

The socioracial dynamic described above resulted in an atmosphere of heightened anxiety in which people fought to have their whiteness recog-nized and their African or Indian origin somehow overlooked or excused. This, in turn, produced collective and codified operations of reading the body that sought to identify and inscribe the minutest shade of racial dif-ference. Erring on the side of darkness in referring to someone could be the cause of grave personal offense and effectively resulted in numerous and prolonged lawsuits as individuals felt their material and symbolic worth jeopardized. In the process of these lawsuits, the outcomes would often hinge on hearsay and the (slippery) enunciations of the vox populi as town elders and neighbors were called upon to testify as to the lineage of either defender or accused. The possibility of unequal marriage was also a concern that often produced such court hearings, as the communicative dynamic of gos-sip assumed its role in the preservation of group ethic and the status quo. For those concerned, it was more than a question of personal honor—the defense of the social order was at stake. That the honorific title *don* might be withheld from someone who held or claimed nobility or *hidalguía* could also furnish the content for a typical case, and it could even lead to blood-shed, as people tenaciously defended their racial and social pedigree.[17]

16. Quoted in Morner, *Race Mixture,* 56.

17. On the question of gossip and group ethic, see Jorg Bergmann, *Discreet Indiscretions: The Social Organization of Gossip;* see also Jaramillo Uribe, "Mestizaje," 34. *Hidalgo* (or *fidalgo,* in the Portuguese) refers to an individual of the lesser nobility in the Iberian Peninsula. The term, which contracts *hijo de algo,* literally means "son of something." See also Carrera, *Imagining Identity,*

The process of cognition and race naming that ensued often strained the denotative capacity of language. This is reflected in such racial categories as "I don't understand you" *(no te entiendo),* or "suspended in the air" *(tente en el aire),* as mathematical calculations of the most minute racial percentages mirrored the burgeoning empiricism of the natural sciences. While the famous paintings of the *casta* genre are kept in colonial and metropolitan museums, it is in such storehouses of language as the *Real diccionario de la lengua española* and the *Diccionario histórico de la lengua española* that one must look for the multiple labels that racially identified the colonial population, although their sheer numbers reflect the fact that their real home was in the vernacular. As Manuel Alvar, the primary source for the following discussion, observes, the recorded and available dictionary entries that reproduce them do so only inadequately. Besides, it was in the vernacular that the true denotative and connotative charge of these racial signifiers was most vividly manifest, although, as another compiler of racial and ethnic terminology observes, they were also spread out among epistolaries, parochial files, colonial censuses, and the chronicles of the explorers and the scribes.[18]

In spite of the fact that the classificatory labels often had no more than a local application or conveyed slightly different meanings in different parts of the empire, race-naming in colonial Latin America as a general rule was a clear index of the racial ideology of white superiority. Racial labels could be "congratulatory," as in the case of the term *castizo,* which in Mexico and Puerto Rico identified the product of the union of a Spaniard and a *mestiza,* and was a way of complimenting the individual on his white peninsular paternity, or they could be mocking. A *saltatrás* or *tornatrás,* in Mexico, Venezuela, and Colombia, for example, was a descendant of *mestizos* who had the genetic misfortune to have features that identified him primarily with his black or Amerindian ancestors—in the dominant ethic of whitening, he was going in the wrong direction.[19] As seen in these two examples, racial labels often expressed the scorn and disdain of a hypothetical white subjectivity vis-à-vis nonwhites or the "people of color" *(gente de color)* as

which begins with the case of Cristóbal Ramón Bivián, a Spaniard and resident of Mexico City, who in 1789 sought to repair the honor of his wife, whose name at baptism had been recorded "in the book of castas . . . not the book of Spaniards as it should have been." Bivián considered this a "most egregious falsehood" (1).

18. See Iris M. Zavala, "Representing the Colonial Subject"; and Thomas Stephens, *Dictionary of Latin American Racial and Ethnic Terminology,* 1.

19. Alvar, *Léxico,* 108–10, 190–94; Stephens, *Dictionary,* 55, 224–25.

they measured distance of the latter from the white ideal. If we consider three sets of racial categories—those that bordered on whiteness, those that express *casta* identity by way of the zoological paradigm, and those that ridicule particular racial mixtures—we can appreciate the extent to which they all reflected the peculiar hysteria of being that defined the regimen. They also expose its polygenist premise as it separated white personhood from nonwhite subpersonhood.

The very idea of referring to the racially mixed as *castas,* bearing in mind the term's etymological origin in the breeding of livestock, refers us to the binary that sets apart the quintessentially pure from the degraded products that result from matings with inferior strains. The terminology describing those who were white, "but not quite," to borrow a phrase from Homi Bhabha, both in its number and content, confirm the existence of a color line and the punctiliousness of dominant white normativity lest this line be breached. In this scheme of things, language itself became precarious and unreliable, since an individual designated a "white" *(blanco)* in Mexico, Cuba, and Peru did not really refer to a "pure white," which is to say a *blanco de pura cepa,* "from the Spanish kingdoms" *(de los reinos de España).* The term referred, instead, to a relational whiteness that had a broad colonial collective in mind that was less white. For individuals in this category, as indeed it turned out to be for many others, the acquisition of the title of *don* would be the crowning seal of arrival. Likewise, the label *gente blanca,* referring to an almost white person, stood in opposition to *gente de color,* though it also assumed a positive value in the term *gente,* since there were masses lower down on the social and racial scale who are not even regarded as *gente.* For this particular mixture, the offspring of a Spaniard and a *requinterona de mulato,* Alvar places the racial composition at 96.87 percent white and 3.13 percent black. Similar terms like *limpio* (clean) and *cuasi limpio de su origen* (almost cleansed of their origin), both of which refer to the offspring of whites and *gente blanca* in Peru and upper South America, reiterate the principle of purity in whiteness and the drive to underscore the smallest identifiable measure of racial otherness.[20] In the United States, a similar

---

20. The qualifiers around whiteness were to remove all doubt as to the subject's racial purity; see David Cahill, "Colour by Numbers: Racial and Ethnic Categories in the Viceroyalty of Peru, 1532–1824," 342. In 1818, Lima titles of *don* were available for fourteen hundred *reales,* according to Jaramillo Uribe, "Mestizaje," 47*n;* the title signified that the holder was not only white *(blanco)* but also clean *(limpio)* (46–47). See also Alvar, *Léxico,* 138, 153; and Stephens, *Dictionary,* 140.

"one drop" precept was enough to keep the racial rift; in Spanish America, however, the racial ideology of whitening allowed racial "improvement" to be a realizable goal.

Although the American continent was the theater of the hysteria of racial signifying and, indeed, of many of the actual labels, it is to be borne in mind that the Iberian Peninsula was its linguistic and ideological source, and archaic terms gained new life as they were deployed to designate new realities. Much of the traditional language of animal husbandry and cross-breeding comes into evidence as the racializing gaze sought to ontologically organize the myriad skin tones of miscegenation. Signifier and signified then combined to entrap the colonial subject in a prison of meaning under-lain by zoology, mockery, and the tropology of the anomalous. If signifiers of Moorish racial otherness in the suffix -isco, as in morisco and berberisco (Moorish, Berberlike), take us back to earlier moments of racial differentia-tion in Spain, the Mozarabic cultural presence is again invoked in the racial category cambujo, derived etymologically from the Mozarabic capuz. Since the term refers to a mask or a veil that covers the face, it metaphorically marks the dark-skinned person so identified (62.5 percent Amerindian and 37.5 percent black) as a human abnormality.[21] His face is not his own, it sug-gests; the color must be a dark veil that covers the faces of "real" humans—whose faces are white.

Peering through the skin of miscegenation and naming its diversity pro-duced such labels as cuatralbo, a term used in Mexico, which refers to a dark horse with four white feet. Presumably, according to the grim humor of colonial race-naming, this individual had been dipped in whiteness, though not fully so. The albarazado, another racial category, repeated this indulgence in humor and linked the imperfect whiteness of this triracial subject with leprosy, again duplicating a zoological designation applied to dark animals with white spots on their skin. The lunarejo, a reference to horses or cows with white spots or birthmarks, employs a similar metaphorical process. Many of the other varieties and combinations of reds and browns and yel-lows are also identified by names from the animal realm. The presumed multilayered nature of persons whose genealogical antecedents were 12.5 percent white, 70.3 percent Amerindian, and 17.2 percent black, for example, was called barcino, since they apparently called to mind the striped exterior of tigers, or some dogs, cats, or snakes. The labels of coyote, lobo (wolf), and cabro (goat), in turn, sought to match the colors of these animals, along

---

21. Alvar, Léxico, 104–7; Stephens, Dictionary, 46–47.

with their characteristics, to the groups that they named. That the multiplicity of the race labels could only be arbitrary, in spite, paradoxically, of their search for exactitude, is borne out, finally, in a term such as *ahí te estás* (there you are). The elusive nature of the term at once refers to the confusion (and despair) of the speaker at the fact that the subject, after some ten or twelve generations of mixture, has apparently condemned himself to *mestizaje* with no apparent possibility of racial improvement in sight. The racial composition of the *ahí te estás,* according to Alvar, is 15.62 percent white, 59.38 percent Amerindian, and 25 percent black. The varying racial proportions offered by Stephens only points to the essentially arbitrary nature of the race-naming project.[22]

If *castas* are the first field of reference in the duality that juxtaposes whiteness to otherness in the Hispanic colonial scheme, it is important to reiterate that the *indio* and the *negro,* as racial "absolutes," are what really constitute the opposing pole in the white-nonwhite binary. While the *castas* ontologically are constructed as less than human, the subpersonhood of blacks is intrinsically associated with their status as saleable beings, objectified by the act of commerce. The negative metaphysical attributes that their radical somatic difference called to mind were naturally compounded by their abject social status. Their condition has been described by Orlando Patterson as being literally and metaphorically one of "social death," as he emphasized the totalitarian premise that governed the relationship between slave and master, as well as the slaves' alienation from ascending or descending genealogical ties and their reduction in law to the status of a thing. Patterson's reference to the archetypal context of enslavement as being a substitute for death in war, or as punishment for a capital offense, is underscored by Robert Conrad's candid corroboration of other levels of the appropriateness of the "social death" comparison in his affirmation that most slaves who lived in Brazil "died in slavery."[23] The point signals not only the physical death of the subject, but also his or her death in terms of the (im)possibility of recuperating a social being outside of the framework of bondage. As the optical opposite of whiteness, the slaves symbolized the limit point of degradation and, in social terms, the opposite of honor. The dominant ethic of whitening

22. For *cuatralbo,* see Alvar, *Léxico,* 121; and Stephens, *Dictionary,* 91. For *albarazado,* see Alvar, *Léxico,* 91; and Stephens, *Dictionary,* 19. For *barcino,* see Alvar, *Léxico,* 97; and Stephens, *Dictionary,* 30. For *ahí te estás,* see Alvar, *Léxico,* 89; and Stephens, *Dictionary,* 17. Stephens offers different percentages (*Dictionary,* 17).

23. Orlando Patterson, *Slavery and Social Death: A Comparative Study;* Conrad, *Children of God's Fire,* 319.

ensured that blackness was what everyone else was running away from. The commercial language of slavery, both in the terms of the transatlantic trade and as articulated in colonial newspaper advertisements concerning sales, runaways, and the like, are privileged sites for the analysis of this phenomenon.

The Embodiment of Subpersonhood

The colonial racial taxonomy illustrates the degree to which pigmentation and skin color, as indicators of caste and class, were attached to honor and social value. As important as the body's surface was to the colonial episteme in this sense, the body's greatest significance lay, obviously, in its being the source of the labor that drove the economy. Slavery, whose features combined captivity and the multiple forms of violence necessary to enforce productive activity, thereby becomes a totally embodied phenomenon, premised on the splitting of the self and the separation of the body from the will of the agent it houses. This separation is the objective of the process known as "breaking in," in which "being for self" is transformed into "being for the dominant Other," the representative of the captor culture, and the body is transformed into a unit of colonial production. What Hortense Spillers has called the "theft" of the body in slavery therefore has both a literal and metaphorical aspect. Alienation of the self from the body, that is, the split between interiority and exteriority, is poignantly articulated in the state of suspended animation experienced by individuals in the process of purchasing their freedom while still in bondage. An example from Marília Pessoa Monteiro speaks of Innôcencia, an enslaved woman in Altinho, Brazil, who in 1833 "bought" 200,000 *milreis* worth "of her body," and continued to be a slave while waiting to save the rest to complete the purchase of "herself." She was valued at 300,000 *milreis.* The example might be multiplied, of course, a thousand-fold. Colonial labor in many of its technical aspects relied on the judgment, skills, and intellective capacity of the enslaved workforce. Undeniably, however, the degree to which its grosser aspects required mindless obedience in the performance of repetitive and burdensome tasks highlights the fact of its centering in the corporeal and the zombification it eventually produced.[24] As we see below, the *asiento,* or license to traffic in slaves, stands out as a primary instrument in the process of objectification.

---

24. See Hortense J. Spillers, "Mama's Baby, Papa's Maybe: An American Grammar Book"; Marília Pessoa Monteiro, "A mulher negra escrava no imaginário das elites do século XIX," 99. In

Zurara's discursive figuring of African captives as beasts of the chase in early Portuguese explorations came to acquire a more sinister dimension with the subsequent formalization and institutionalization of the slaving enterprise. A coalition of Western Europe's mercantile oligarchy, with the direct or indirect participation of royalty or its representatives, and the tacit or active involvement of the church, produced the forced migration of untold millions of Africans during the four hundred years that followed his chronicle. Henry's authorization by the pope and King Alfonso to explore and trade south of Bojador had redounded in the licensing of Lançarote de Freitas's Lagos Company in 1444 and the procurement of the 235 captives distributed by the Infante at Lagos. In 1468, the first *assento* (trade monopoly) over slaves, spices, and other such items, was sold by the Portuguese crown to Fernão Gomes. Shortly thereafter, in 1486, the Casa dos Escravos was set up in Lisbon to centralize and regulate the business. More than half a century before the oft-quoted 1517 suggestion by Bartolomé de Las Casas to the Spanish crown that black slaves be used to replace the rapidly dying Amerindians at Hispaniola, the African continent was already earmarked for its role as a source of forced labor for the massive colonial enterprise. Between 1518 and 1808, as Rout observes, thousands of licenses and the infamous *asiento* would be the instruments through which slaves were "legally" supplied to the Spanish colonies.[25] After an extended period of Portuguese dominance of the trade, which lasted until 1640, fierce competition among the Dutch, French, and English would regard the Spanish *asiento* as a major potential item of booty, just as they would the colonies themselves.

True to the imagery of the Zurara text, the royal reward to Fernão Gomes in 1471, upon his successful conquest of the territory of Sierra Leone, reflected the essentially predatory nature of the undertaking. Gomes was granted a

---

Cuba, this practice was also known as "coartación." It has been subsumed into a wider argument around manumission as a morally superior differential in comparing the Latin American and U.S. slave systems; see De la Fuente, "Slave Law." René Depestre offers a suggestive analogy between the psychological and physiological effects of intense and repetitive physical labor on the individual, and the myth of zombification in Haiti; see "Problemas de la identidad del hombre negro en las literaturas antillanas," 20.

25. Rout, *African Experience,* 61. By the middle of the fifteenth century, with the opening of the African trade, the Iberian Peninsula had corrected its handicap vis-à-vis the more northern kingdoms and their access to the traditional sources of European slaves from the Black Sea and the region of the Caucasus. The Caucasian flow of forced labor was practically halted with the fall of Christian Constantinople to the Turks in 1453. With the rise of Ivan the Great, a decade later, came further protection for potential captives for Western slave markets. See Sweet, "Iberian Roots."

title and a coat of arms that showed the "heads of three negroes wearing collars and pendants of gold." The British privateer John Hawkins, almost a hundred years later, replicated the predacious iconography as he himself acquired a title on the basis of successful raids against Iberian slavers. His coat of arms, granted under Elizabeth I, also dramatically featured the heads of three Africans with ropes around their necks, topped off with a crest that displayed the head and torso of a bound and captive African. Both insignia, as hunting icons as well as symbols of colonial triumphalism, represent the legitimation of a practice that after a century and a half was approaching genocidal proportions, even as the profits it generated suffocated any sense of moral dissonance. In this regard, one might observe that the most noteworthy cry of protest against the slave trade from Hispanic churchmen was that of Bartolomé Frías de Albornoz in his *Arte de contratos* (1573). Frías critiqued the crown's premise of certain peoples being "natural slaves" and its rationalization that the slaves were taken in "just war." His book was promptly placed on the Inquisition's Index Librorum Prohibitorum.[26]

The figurative decapitation in the representations of African captives on the coats of arms of slavers like Gomes and Hawkins simultaneously underscores their dehumanization ("heads" of cattle come to mind) as well as their reduction, in the colonial mercantile economy, to the status of objects of exchange. This status is most clearly brought out in ship invoices and in the records of slave trading companies such as the Portuguese Guinea Company, the Dutch West India Company, the French Royal Guinea Company, and the British South Sea Company. Africans acquired through the Spanish *asiento* were categorized as *piezas de Indias* if adults (eighteen to thirty-five years old), *mulecones* if between fourteen and eighteen, or *muleques* if between six and fourteen. They formed part of a colonial inventory that included ports, harbors, mines, plantations, islands, territories, and a wide array of tropical agricultural products subject to either purchase, exchange, or plunder as the case warranted. As the *asiento* stipulated, they could be traded for cash or kind, had duties levied on them at ports of entry, and, owing to the high rate of deaths during the middle passage, even had a precalculated "mortality allowance" on any given number of them that might be stipulated

26. Kim Hall discusses Gomes's coat of arms in *Things of Darkness: Economies of Race and Gender in Early Modern England,* 19. See Margaret M. Olsen's discussion of Jesuit missionary Alonso de Sandoval as he tried to reconcile his observations of suffering Africans upon their arrival at Colombia with the discursive legacy of savagery (Olsen, *Slavery and Salvation in Colonial Cartagena de Indias,* 122–52). Other dissenters were Tomás de Mercado and Luis de Molina (Rout, *African Experience,* 33).

by respective contracts.[27] The objectification that synecdoche had achieved through displaying the heads of blacks on the coats of arms of slavers would be replicated through the numbing repetitiousness of the discourse of book-keeping in ships' records and in slaving contracts.

Documents such as the published letter by a British West-Indian merchant in 1712 to a compatriot at Tunbridge lay bare the textual equivalence between black humanity and inanimate materiality in mercantile discourse. Also highlighted are the key issue of European agency in the intercontinental transaction and the real motivations that underlay the political economy of colonialism. The *Letter from a West-India Merchant to a Gentleman at Tunbridg, concerning that Part of the French Proposals, which Relates to North-America, and Particularly Newfoundland* was written a year after the formation of the South Sea Company in 1711 and a year before the Treaty of Utrecht brought the War of Spanish Succession to an end. This letter chiefly concerned the New World and not the European theater, where the War of Spanish Succession was being fought, and its focus on the carnivorous inter-imperial rivalry in the New World makes it important. The letter draws attention to the French turn-of-the-century push for hegemony and also highlights the beginnings of British imperial ascendancy as the eighteenth century advanced. In it, the high value of the *asiento,* one of the British gains of the treaty, stands out, as does the influence of the colonial merchant lobby for which the writer spoke.

In the letter, the seize-and-settle praxis of colonialism becomes clear, as does colonialism's antiethic of plunder and spoilage, as the writer recalled King William's declaration of war against France in 1689. William had charged Louis XIV with

> invading our Charibbee Islands, and possessing himself of our Territories of New York, and of Hudson's-Bay, in a hostile manner; seizing our Forts, burning our Subjects Houses, and enriching his People with the Spoil of their Goods and Merchandizes; detaining some of our Subjects under the Hardship of Imprisonment, causing others to be inhumanly kille'd, and driving the rest to Sea in a small vessel, without Food and Necessaries to support them; actions not becoming ev'n an Enemy.[28]

---

27. The losses expected in this way, for example, in Gómez Reynal's *asiento* in 1595, were placed at 17.6 percent. This does not take into account the death-inducing conditions during storage on shore on either side of the Atlantic (Rout, *African Experience,* 33).

28. *Letter from a West-India Merchant to a Gentleman at Tunbridg, concerning that Part of the French Proposals, which Relates to North-America, and particularly Newfoundland,* 2.

The writer dismissed any conciliatory generosity of the French that might be based on their proposal to restore several neighboring colonial territories to Britain and—invoking as colonialism's first principle, the "Law of Arms"—he underscores Britain's right to the part of the island of St. Christopher recently won from France.[29] Recalling recurrent French hostilities in 1697 and 1705, he cautioned against any policy that might turn out to be inimical to British trade and industry in the area. He then went on to stress the importance of reversing the advantage held by the French in the harvesting and curing of Newfoundland fish, and the great damage this caused to British shipping, commerce, and colonization. The letter insisted, finally, on the complete ouster of the French. As it turned out, with the Utrecht treaty, France gave up its territorial claims to Newfoundland and to mainland Nova Scotia.

A consideration of the *asiento* alongside the other British concessions won at Utrecht reveals more than just the political and economic importance of the British coup; it also sheds light on just how disengaged was the colonial mind-set, and the colonial discourse itself, from the essential humanity of its African referents. In the *Letter,* slaves and cod assume the same syntactic and semantic status in a textuality whose ontological center is wealth and the creation thereof. At no point are the former referred to outside of the register of the inanimate. As with the *asiento* contract, African subjectivity is not even recuperated through mention of the black interlocutors in the trade, as the discourse makes visible only the end product, that is, the captive bodies at one stage or another in the international process of exchange.[30]

The strenuous efforts of the Spanish to regain control over the monopoly during the next four decades would highlight the commercial and strategic value of the *asiento,* promptly sold by the British government to the South

29. Ibid., 1.

30. It is a historical irony, perhaps, that great quantities of Newfoundland salted cod, especially useful in commerce for its long shelf life, did indeed provide fuel as a staple for the enslaved bodies that were in turn consumed by the colonial capitalist mill in the British West Indies. The United Nations' 2001 *Report of the World Conference against Racism, Racial Discrimination, Xenophobia, and Related Intolerance,* in referring to slavery as a crime against humanity, emphasizes the institution's "negation of the essence of the victims." Its article 13 reads: "We acknowledge that slavery and the slave trade, including the transatlantic slave trade, were appalling tragedies in the history of humanity not only because of their abhorrent barbarism but also in terms of their magnitude, organized nature and especially their negation of the essence of the victims, and further acknowledge that slavery and the slave trade are a crime against humanity and should always have been so, especially the transatlantic slave trade and are among the major sources and manifestations of racism, racial discrimination, xenophobia and related intolerance, and that Africans and people of African descent, Asians and people of Asian descent and indigenous peoples were victims of these acts and continue to be victims of their consequences" (10).

Sea Company for 7.5 million pounds in 1712, and so would Britain's equally forceful efforts to retain it. Corporate interests apart, however, what attracts our attention is the curious individual claim on the lives and destinies of the persons that the contract stipulates for delivery. The callousness of the claim in the contract is accentuated, perhaps, when we consider the role of royalty in the enterprise. Philip V of Spain owned 28 percent of South Sea stock. Queen Anne of Britain owned 22.5 percent. The first article of the slaving monopoly, previously held by the French Royal Company, had gravely "permitted . . . the Kings of France and Spain, for the mutual Advantage of them and their Subjects, to import annually from the 1st of May 1702, to the 1st of May 1712, 4,800 Negroes of both Sexes and of all Ages."[31] The current agreement, concerning the delivery of 144,000 "Negroes" over a period of thirty years, merely needed to substitute the British sovereign and her subjects, in the place of Louis XIV, king of France. In the various versions of the *asiento,* the market forces that determined the destinations of the slaves, whether to the port of Barlovento, Cumaná, Maracaibo, Buenos Aires, Cartagena, Havana, Santiago, Caracas, Vera Cruz, or any such location in Spanish America, while reifying the object status of the captives, dramatically trace the cartography of diaspora also. If the role of the *asiento* as an actualization of the commercial intercourse between corporate elites, in converting slavery's captives into *negros,* is not as self-evident as it could be, then the role of the slave traders, the agents of these elites, helps make it so. Luso-Hispanic slave traders, *negreiros/negreros,* are locked into a morbid act of midwifery with their charges through the morphological constitution of their title.

In the same register as the *negrero,* the commercial reference to the African captives as *piezas* holds a singular place in the syntax of subpersonhood to the degree that, like other aspects of the colonial grammar under discussion, it effected the crudest incursion on their subjectivity. Intended originally to designate one adult male subject seven *palmos* tall and in good health, the *pieza* over time would fluctuate in significatory value, depending on such factors as the real size, age, gender, or body weight of the persons concerned. The 16,791 individuals, for example, delivered by the French Royal Guinea Company during its tenure of the monopoly, turned out to be considered only worth 12,798 *piezas* by Spanish fiscal authorities; a value, that is, of 1.31 persons per *pieza.* When the South Sea Company held the *asiento,* its numerical value again varied between 1.74 persons to as much as 11 persons.[32] Measurement

31. *Letter from a West-India Merchant,* 19.
32. Rout, *African Experience,* 62.

by body weight was inconsistent. The Spanish *tonelada,* for purposes of cartage, sought to achieve an appropriate ratio relative to available space on board a slave ship. A ton of slaves, however, could turn out, in practical terms, to be represented by any number between three and seven individuals.

The difficulties attendant to the commercial calculation and measurement of human cargo, by using a mathematical paradigm more appropriate for (dead) meat or for inanimate objects, go to the heart of slavery, race-making, and subpersonhood. They emphasize the degree to which the semiotics of the slave trade—expressed in texts like slave traders' coats of arms, the *asiento* contract itself, or the invoices of slave ships—inscribe and consolidate the association between Africans and the less-than-human. Terms like *pieza, muleque,* and *mulecón,* with their Brazilian equivalents, *peça, moleque,* and *molecão/molequinho,* evidently contribute to this effect. Such signifiers, created and shared by the international community of slave traders and slaveholders alike, and passed on from them to the wider vernacular, are of obvious importance to this discussion for their ideological and symbolic value. Their resulting practical effect at the level of slave-market transactions is evidenced in the handling of the captives by prospective purchasers "exactly," remarks British travel writer Robert Walsh, "as I have seen butchers feeling a calf."[33] His description of a slave ship is also effective in portraying the harsh reality of mercantile objectification and the profit motive in the transatlantic trade. The by now familiar images of slave ships transporting human beings packed like sardines present a disturbing visual image of the implacable logistics of slave cartage. Walsh's verbal account of the *Veloz,* bound for Bahia, is no less vivid. Nor is it a less troubling reflection of the torturous connection between mercantilism and modernity:

> She had taken in, on the coast of Africa, 336 males, and 226 females, making in all 562, and had been out seventeen days, during which she had thrown overboard fiftyfive. The slaves were all enclosed under grated hatchways, between decks. The space was so low, that they sat between each other's legs, and stowed so close together that there was no possibility of their lying down or at all changing their position, by night or day. As they belonged to, and were shipped on account of different individuals, they were all branded, like sheep, with the owners' marks of different forms.... These were impressed under their breasts, or on their

33. Robert Walsh, *Notices of Brazil in 1828 and 1829,* 2:179. In a footnote, Mary C. Karasch cites the term *cria,* a reference to young domesticated animals, colts, or fillies, as having also been used in Brazil to refer to young slaves (*Slave Life in Rio de Janeiro, 1808–1850,* 31).

arms. . . . But the circumstance which struck us most forcefully, was, how it was possible for such a number of human beings to exist, packed up and wedged together as tight as they could cram, in low cells, three feet high, the greatest part of which, except that immediately under the grated hatchways, was shut out from light or air, and this when the thermometer, exposed to the open sky, was standing in the shade on our deck at 89°. The space between the decks was divided into two compartments, 3 feet 3 inches high; the size of one was 16 feet by 18, and the other 40 by 21; into the first were crammed the women and girls; into the second, the men and boys: 226 fellow-creatures were thus thrust into one space 288 feet square; and 336 into another space 800 feet square, giving to the whole an average of 23 inches and to each of the women not more than 13 inches though many of them were pregnant. . . . The heat of these horrid spaces was so great, and the odor so offensive, that is was quite impossible to enter them, even had there been room.[34]

Walsh's commentary offers a valuable descriptive and affective response to the facts of human commodification in the mercantile system. By the later 1700s, with the groundswell of abolitionism, British abolitionist Thomas Clarkson publicized the cross-section of the slaving vessel *Brookes* as part of the antislavery campaign. To maximize the available space aboard the vessel, the plan of the *Brookes* allowed 6′ × 1′4″ for a male individual, 5′10″ × 1′4″ for a female, 5′ × 1′2″ for a boy, and 4′6″ × 1′ for a girl. The implications for cramping and claustrophobia and for deformity and disease in conditions that were coffinlike in their constrictiveness need no emphasis. If the slaves' cramped conditions have been likened to that of sardines in a can, then this metaphor is also relevant in that, like the tin can, the slave ship contained a cargo of human bodies that were for sale as well. The analogy ends, of course, as we take cognizance of the fact that sardines are dead fish. The *Brookes*'s plan allowed for stowage of 450 persons. On one of its voyages, it carried 609.[35]

If being denominated a *pieza* and being treated accordingly were initial events in the process of depersonalization of captive individuals, further branding upon arrival and the loss of one's name were no less significant in this regard. Both the physical mark, left by the heated iron, as well as the symbolic mark of the name may thus be seen as additional signs in the textuality

---

34. Walsh, *Notices,* 2:262–63; see also Gilberto Freyre, *O escravo nos anúncios de jornais brasileiros do século XIX,* 22.

35. Elizabeth Donnan, *Documents Illustrative of the History of the Slave Trade to America,* 2: 592n.

of their inferiority. Like the genealogical isolation that their new condition implied, branding and name loss for the enslaved were intended to wrest them from kith and kin, from cultural anchor and former identity, and to facilitate, from the standpoint of the slave owners, their transition to the culture of nonbeing and obedience. The new, singular, Christian name would therefore identify incoming Africans in the Hispanic colonies and would appear in plantation records, in the press, or in notary or police records whenever the need arose. These names would sometimes be accompanied by a reference to the "nation" or tribal origin of the individual, as in José Gangá, Macario Carabalí, or Rosa Lucumí, as Ortiz points out in relation to Cuba.

While the single Christian name indicated African birth in the individual, the absence of a Hispanic surname among locally born blacks marked them also as slaves. Those whose mothers had been known in the community in which they lived might additionally be identified as simply the daughter or son of Juana, Encarnación, or Francisca, as the case might be. In either event, their names signaled their not belonging to the normative, legitimate, white, patriarchal order. The absence of the family name, Orlando Patterson reminds us, was "the surest sign of slavery" in such diverse slave societies as Rome, Russia, China, the Near East, and pharaonic Egypt. Freed individuals, in their move toward civic personhood, adopted the former master's surname, but even here, the absence of the second surname, important to Peninsular custom, continued to stigmatize individuals in the postemancipation context. The tag "without other surname" *(sin otro apellido)* in notary and other public records, for example, effectively labeled black Cubans as second-class citizens well into the twentieth century, because of its association with illegitimacy and bondage. The thrust for inclusion into the symbolic order of the dominant culture is perhaps most evident in the political drive by black activists in 1890s Cuba to legitimize their access to the honorific title *don.* On the other hand, the recuperation of African names in twentieth-century American societies would also become an important counterdiscursive and countercultural gesture of affirmation of cultural selfhood, as seen especially in the United States, the Anglophone Caribbean, and Brazil. Early in his career, a Hispanocentric line of criticism would soundly chastise mulatto poet Nicolás Guillén for his lyrical experimentation with the idea of the lost African last name.[36]

36. Patterson, *Slavery,* 58. See also Michael Zeuske, "Hidden Markers, Open Secrets: On Naming, Race-Marking, and Race-Making in Cuba." On Nicolás Guillén, see Jerome Branche, "Soul for Sale? Contrapunteo cubano en Madrid."

The question of name semiotics and social pedigree apart, perhaps the most important public site for colonial textuality concerning blacks was the newspapers. Whether by way of advertisements of slaves for sale or rent, or to publicize their escape, colonial newspapers helped establish black liminality vis-à-vis normative white society. In the case of runaways, the necessarily reiterative and detailed descriptive focus on the black body for purposes of identification highlighted, among other things, the scars inflicted by the conditions of their captivity, whether these scars were the result of disease, punishment, or overwork. One might even propose that the scars themselves make the enslaved body a metatext of its bondage. Apart from being physical attestations to the necessary violence of the regimen of forced labor, these signs written on the body (as if it were a page) also articulate a message, direct or implied, of black imperviousness to pain, a notion already present in their animalization and the natural-slave theory. Between the rigors of an often-sadistic regimen of production and punishment, of racially discriminatory laws and imprisonment for blacks in postslavery societies, lies an important aspect of the historical development of racism.

In newspaper advertisements, bodily disfigurement that was the result of illness also helped confirm the association of blacks with disease for the white colonial public, that is, beyond the objective determinants of the conditions that produced their many maladies. In this way, the written enunciation, because of its potential for permanence as a signifier, helped reify, in turn, stereotypical connotations of blackness and the pathological. Thousands of announcements made in Brazilian newspapers in the nineteenth century confirm this role of the press. The entries, by pointing out only individuals who were fit enough to flee, however, provide only a partial picture of the general state of health of the broader slave population. The high incidence of deformity and disease that they confirm, notwithstanding, serves as a powerful indicator of the murderously insalubrious environment that the referents were exposed to, as, along with the often-disfigured somatic characteristics of the individuals identified, come a lengthy list of contagious and viral illnesses.

The notices for runaways were often accompanied by the dramatic little icon depicting the fugitive with his bundle of personal effects hanging from a stick over his shoulder. The descriptions themselves, forerunners of the camera and the mug shot of today, offered as graphic a depiction as possible of the escapee, producing a "black morphology," as it were, in its close attention to skin color, hair, height, build, breasts and buttocks (in women), facial features, tribal markings, and oddities of limb. As Gilberto Freyre observes, the entries also tell a compact, if sometimes sensational, story about the lives of the individuals, as well as about slavery in general in nineteenth-century Brazil.[37] A primary consideration in this regard is that these entries are statements from the slave owners themselves asserting dominion over their property. They address an implied white public and thereby invite consensus as to the premise of ownership and chatteldom that defines slave society. As they empower "any member" of this public to turn the fugitive in, they tend to naturalize the relationship of subjection between white and black. Arrayed against the freedom seeker would be the entire normative colonial apparatus consisting of the militia, the urban slave patrols, the specialized bush-captains or *capitães do mato* (*rancheadores* in Cuba), as well as individual opportunists or bounty hunters. In opposing potential slave catchers against fugitive slaves, the announcements therefore draw the line between the free and the enslaved, the white and the nonwhite, speakers and those spoken about, on-lookers and the objects of the gaze—in essence, between colonialism and its Others. It is important to observe, however, that as statements of power and objectification, announcements about runaways are partially nullified by the very act of agency displayed by the individuals themselves in fleeing. Their discursive residue, however, remains powerful. In the absence of the slaves' voices, speaking in the first person (a question to which we shall return in the following chapter), the candid voices of their masters offer an invaluable perspective on the institution.

As indicated, the announcements provide a stark biographical statement about the fugitives. The scars themselves are quiet but eloquent sites attesting to the terror of torn tissue and the violation of the integrity of the flesh in the service of the ideology of subjugation. Gilberto Freyre's study of advertisements for runaways stresses the importance of this "bodily hiero-glyphics" to the process of identification and apprehension of the fugi-tives.[38] The wounds on the back, the buttocks, the breasts, and across the entire body that he mentions, however, whether they were fully healed or in any of the stages of healing, go beyond the use of physical marks for pur-poses of identification. A consideration of injury and scarification as the material trace of the ideology of force takes us inevitably back through the vicious circle from scar, to wound, to weapon, and finally back to the inten-tionality behind the event of injuring.

Elaine Scarry's influential study *The Body in Pain: The Making and Un-*

37. Freyre, *O escravo.*
38. Spillers, "Mama's Baby."

making of the World highlights the terrible agency of torture in the language of repressive regimes. A cornerstone in the fiction of power, it takes on a life of its own for political prisoners and captives in analogous circumstances throughout the ages. Its instruments, which the victims of torture, as an intimidatory strategy, are often forced to look at before they are applied, come into action, as it were, even before they are effectively put into action. The psychological instrumentality of punitive injuring in slavery is therefore tellingly present in the mere cataloging of implements used in the institution. Freyre's list of tools for torturing of slaves in nineteenth-century Brazil, and the frightful refinements invented by the sadistic imaginations of slave owners, belie, if nothing else, the facile generalizations about the benign nature of the institution in that country, or in Latin America as a whole.[39]

While the felt experience of pain is unshareable from one individual consciousness to another, as Scarry points out, it is at the same time eminently knowable, since, as members of the same species, our neurological wiring is the same. If the pain of injury defeats language, reducing us to open-mouthed screams and moans, the scars that form over bodily rents and fissures, as highlighted in these announcements, effectively speak to the all-consuming agony previously inflicted by the lash, the stocks, thumbscrews, mutilation, dousing in boiling water, or the application of melting pork. Terminal punishments such as the breaking of bones on the rack, being thrown into a hot oven, or being eaten alive by insects attracted to a honey-coated body surface would leave no scars that might signify in the public landscape. But even when bodily annihilation has been the objective, as in the hanging of insurgents, the decapitated heads on the pickets at the entrance to towns, or at prominent sites on the roadway, unerringly convey the message, to the rest of the black population, about the vulnerability of the black body and the will to power of the dominant class. While the wounds on the bodies of the runaways cannot speak, we can doubtless work back through them to the initial moments of injuring and the sensory content of the pain that accompanied them. The repeated reference in the advertisements to "sad" looks as a facial feature of the escapees, alerts us unmistakably to the distress, past and present, of the subjects and to trauma that is as much physiological as it is psychological.

The case of João, advertised in the *Diario de Pernambuco* on March 23, 1834, is typical, in that it provided merely the Christian name of the referent, accompanied by his "national" origin, Angola. Just as typical is the

39. Freyre, *O escravo*, 86–87.

advertisement's lack of precision regarding his age, stated simply as "twenty-something years old," a fact that reminds us once more not only of the depersonalized character of captivity for the Atlantic slave market, but also of the existential uprooting and the radically altered life expectancy that the Brazilian reality connoted. João is further described as being blind in one eye and having several scars on one foot and on the forehead. The advertisement continues, noting that, judging from the way the left side of his face bulges out, it seems swollen; Joao may also have suffered from a pulmonary disorder, since "he pushes hard from the chest when speaking." The description concludes by saying that he was wearing a light-colored shirt of cotton waste, a torn dark serge vest, and a straw hat when he took his leave.[40]

Rosa, also a *bozal,* was roughly fifty years old when she was declared missing in the *Diario de Pernambuco* on January 30, 1850. She was described as short, full-bodied, with a high rump, a round, shiny face, apelike features, small feet, and a limp. The limp was associated with "an *estupada* on her right foot, a wound on her little toe on the left foot, and having the big toes on both feet eaten away by *bicho.*" *Bicho-de-pé* is an insect that can penetrate the foot and lay eggs, leading to infection and ulcers. Mary Karasch has referred to this malady as the most common cause of lameness among barefoot slaves in Rio, and Freyre confirms its frequency in the nineteenth-century newspaper announcements about runaways. The limp affecting another slave, Francisco, which was indirectly referred to when his escape was announced in the *Diario de Pernambuco* on May 12, 1843, was not acquired through parasitism or contagion, however. His disability was the direct result of the occupational risks of colonial agriculture—a box of sugar had fallen on his feet, causing him to lose two toes. Joaquim, reported missing in the *Diario* on March 31, two years later, apparently had no toes at all. According to the announcement, they had been eaten away by the lime in the mortar that he had been made to use his feet to mix. Going barefoot, as these slaves did, also exposed them to tetanus, a deadly disease, as did forms of punishment that broke the skin's surface.[41]

Being a slave porter bore its own hazards, since it made them "prone to

40. Ibid., 27.
41. I assume that the *estupada* on Rosa's foot refers to a bandage made up of cotton waste or rags, or *estopa,* from which one would get *estopada. Estupada* might therefore be a typical, nineteenth-century Brazilian rendering of the term, or a misspelling. Karasch refers to *bicho-de-pé* (*Slave Life,* 170); and Freyre mentions them regarding runaways in *O escravo,* 39 (Francisco and Joaquim are mentioned on pp. 66 and 67, respectively).

hernias and crippling of the lower limbs." It is what seemed to have afflicted sixteen-year-old Benedito, who took flight in 1835 and was described in the announcement on July 20 in the *Diario de Pernambuco* as having scrota that had swollen to an unnatural size. So, too, was the case with Pedro João, reported in the *Diario de Pernambuco* on November 14 the same year, and Inácio Catolé, whose case Freyre records as having been published on March 26, 1857. The debilitating effects of hoisting heavy objects, as seen in the lower body in the numerous cases of hernia and hydrocele reported, could also leave their mark on the head of the individual, as seen in the case of another Joaquim, reported in the *Diario* on November 10, 1843. This Joaquim suffered both from enlarged scrota and a "crown" or callus for fetching weights on his head. Twelve-year old Caetano, reported in the *Diario* on January 23, 1830, was bald in the middle of his head for the same reason, as was Pedro from the Congo, reported in the *Diario* on August 14, 1838.[42] A catalog of deformity and infirmity including (but not limited to) missing and decayed teeth; knock-knees, bowed legs, or misshaped heads produced by rickets or the cramped conditions of the middle passage; plus scurvy, scabies, smallpox, yaws, and the effects of other contagious diseases such as ophthalmia, is evinced in the descriptions of the runaways. Were they fictional, one might describe their combined effect as carnivalesque, but since they were not, they constitute a bizarre corporeal code for otherness, subjection, and inferiority that was based on reality.

Of particular poignancy, perhaps, is the case of Cândida, who was reported in the *Diario* on April 30, 1830, and whose main identifying mark was a padlocked mask over the head and face. The purpose of such masks was to stop the wearers from eating dirt, a frequently chosen mode of suicide. Cândida's aborted(?) suicide, frightful in its premeditation and deliberateness, might be compared to the practice of asphyxiation by swallowing the tongue that was also engaged in by many slaves across the Americas. Both cases highlight the emotional and psychological catastrophe of captivity and the cruel conditions of bondage. In this regard, Walsh's 1831 account mentions the fact that the harbor at Rio was "constantly covered with the bodies of blacks" who had chosen drowning to end their lives. The mask forcibly imposed on Cândida might be compared to the metal collars that adorned the necks of frustrated fugitives as a mark of their attempted maroonage. From these collars projected a long bar on both sides of the head, which ended with either a cross or a curve, the intricacy of the terminal

---

42. Freyre, *O escravo,* 58, 53, 66, 30, 61. Regarding hernias, see Karasch, *Slave Life,* 177.

ironwork making future flight through the bushes impossible. The bars on some of the collars, additionally, ended with five metal fingers, intended to signal that this particular individual was a thief, since he had provisioned himself with his master's food and other belongings in his attempted flight.[43] If newspapers and their announcements are site and instance in the syntax of subpersonhood, with a primary role in facilitating the iron restraint of slave society, the physical irons that restrained the slaves, that is, their face-masks, collars, shackles, chains, and so on, could also signify, as in the case of the message sent by the five fingers on the metal collar. In the context of this two-tiered textuality of oppression, imprisoning the bodies of the enslaved did not always require the physical enclosure of the jail. Slaves could carry their prisons with them, even as they continued to labor and create wealth for their owners.

Slave women were inevitably inscribed into the sexual economy of the colonies in their multiple roles as breeders, mammies, and sexual partners of the ruling class. Predictably, the otherwise direct and denotative discourse of the advertisement about escaped women is tinged with erotic overtones, as the female body is often written with a focus on the shape of their breasts as primary identifiers. Breasts of women that are described as either upstanding or fallen, large, elongated, round, or regular, or which bear evidence of the whip, speak to the sort of environment from which Brígida, for example, fled, in 1834, with her seven-month-old "little mulatto boy" as her announcement in the *Diario* of January 8 reports.[44] In all likelihood, the paternity of the infant was a major aspect of her decision to flee.

Advertisements for mammies are another aspect of gendered othering and objectification in which colonial newspapers participated. The following are typical for Rio de Janeiro in the middle nineteenth century: "Good wet nurse for rent. Gave birth *three weeks ago*. Very loving with children." "Black wet nurse for rent. *Gave birth one week ago*—with good and abundant milk." "Good wet nurse for sale. *Gave birth* to her first child *three weeks ago*." "Very good wet nurse for rent. Delivered *three weeks ago and has milk*. Very loving, sews to perfection, and treats infants with great care and all-night attention." "Black girl for sale, *with or without her two-month-old baby*."[45]

43. On slave suicides, see Walsh, *Notices,* 2:190. Regarding the metal collar, as might be imagined, it would be all but impossible to sleep with such a fixture attached to the body.

44. Freyre, *O escravo,* 36.

45. Quoted in Sonia Maria Giacomini, "Ser escrava no Brasil," 147 (emphases in the original). Citations taken from the *Jornal do commercio* in 1850, on August 1, 15, 7, and 8, respectively,

The commercial paradigm, described above in relation to other aspects of the slave regime, is perhaps what is most immediately evident in these advertisements for wet nurses. In this case, the impersonality and anonymity of both vendor and product stand out. While the black woman *(preta)* remains unnamed, as is appropriate to the generic register for goods and services, the passive syntax of "for rent" *(aluga-se)* operates at the same impersonal register, even as it hides the very active intention of her owner to sell or rent. The quality of the product, affirmed in all cases by stressing how good the subject is, how abundant her milk is, and by highlighting how recently she herself gave birth, is also an essential aspect of the commercial paradigm. The wet nurse as surrogate mother, however, in a linguistic sense, has necessarily corrupted the signifier *motherhood* to the degree that it erases the offspring of the slave mother from the field of the signified in favor of possibly several infants of the white slave-owning class. Additionally, not only is her maternity displaced, but the paternity of her male coparent is also rendered invisible and irrelevant by the text. A further assault on language is to be found in the advertisements' guarantee of affection *(carinho)* by the surrogate mother. While lactation may be a biological function of new motherhood, and in some cases babies were even hired to prolong the lactation period of "professional" wet nurses, affection is born of an entirely different impulse.[46] It cannot be guaranteed a priori.

It is significant that the eventual destination of many of the wet nurses' own children, as yet unfit for the labor force, many of whom were the progeny of the slave masters themselves, was the orphanage known as the Roda dos Expostos in Rio. These orphans, on the one hand, illustrate the crushing difficulties attendant to the formation of black family units under a regime defined fundamentally by relations of property. On the other hand, the fact that the mortality rate at these institutions was as high as 50 percent adds significance to the comparison that Patterson makes between slavery and parasitism.[47] In the case of institutionalized wet nursing, the African and Afro-Creole host body has not only provided labor, but also has supplied its very biological essence, mother's milk, to the sons and daughters of the master class.

---

except for the penultimate announcement, which appeared in the *O gratis: Publicador de annuncios,* May 16, 1850.

46. Giacomini, "Ser escrava," 149.

47. Ibid., 150; Patterson, *Slavery,* 335.

Black bodies in colonial Latin America, read in the context of racial stratification and *mestizaje,* written upon with the marks of slavery, or inscribed into the various registers of law and the colonial economy, operate as a sign in the colonial episteme that continually affirms their status as less than human. Hispanic colonial writing of the *negro* contributes in the creation of a multidimensional social and historical construct in which little independent agency is recognizable for the subject outside of its narrow parameters. Undoubtedly there are cases, extremely rare, in which these subjects managed to beat the odds and have a juridical personality recognized in appealing to the law and thereby acquiring freedom.[48] These, however, should be weighed against the lives of the untold millions who perished at any of the many stages between initial captivity and their eventual demise. As mentioned above, the great majority of slaves entering Brazil, the largest American slave market, were destined to die as slaves. Here it is pertinent to recall that homeless or wandering "unclaimed" blacks were included under Brazilian legal statutes governing stray cattle and beasts of burden and were considered "property of the wind" *(bens do vento).* They were therefore susceptible to seizure by the authorities followed by detention, forced labor, and eventual (re)enslavement, with the proceeds of their sale remitting to the state.

The maroon initiative, located beyond the geopolitical control of colonial authorities, offered a unique opportunity for a political and existential alternative for these new Americans. The methodical ruthlessness with which many maroon communities were eventually destroyed attests to the colonial constant regarding the role of blacks in Europe's New World. Many who survived the transition to the national state evince, in their marginality, a peculiar mix of tradition and modernity, whether in Jamaica, in Brazil, in Suriname, in Mexico, or in Colombia.[49] Saint Domingue, the marooning, counterhegemonic instance that did advance to statehood as the "first black republic in the world," continues to pay for the effrontery of defying the racial and political order of modernity. Its firstness has now been effectively nullified by contemporary mass media's references to Haiti, two hundred years after independence, as a "failed state." With abolition, independence, and the transition from slave to citizen came an epistemological opportunity

48. See Julio Ramos, *Paradojas de la letra;* and De la Fuente, "Slave Law."
49. See, for example, Richard Price, *Maroon Societies: Rebel Slave Communities in the Americas;* Aquiles Escalante, *El palenque de San Basilio: Una comunidad de descendientes de negros cimarrones;* and Gonzalo Aguirre Beltrán, *La población negra de México.*

for a "denegrifying" of *negros*. The overriding racial ideology would allow for little change, however, in what the term connotes.

There is an assumption, additionally, endorsed in many studies, that with independence and the Enlightenment-inspired constitutions of the new Latin American states, the racial taxonomy discussed above ceased to have functionality. The case is overstated. Writing in the middle of the twentieth century, Afro-Peruvian poet Nicomedes Santa Cruz, in several of his *décimas,* employed biting satire to comment on color prejudice in Peru. Isar Godreau, writing at the turn of the twenty-first century, highlights the euphemism and ambiguity that characterize the use of racial labels in Puerto Rico. While stressing context and interlocutor as important determinants in the inter-personal use and application of such terms as *trigueño* (wheat colored), *indio* (Indian), *negro* (black), and *blanquito* (white, whitish), she makes it clear that (notwithstanding the shiftiness of racial signifiers) racism in employ-ment, education, and various areas of public intercourse in Puerto Rico, is "real and concrete." The value judgment implied in the above terminology becomes explicit as the vernacular dispenses with euphemism when it wishes to indicate the unmitigated morphology of a particular black subject. These "ethnic extremities," presumably so black that their color is "violet," are referred to as belonging to *la séptima raza* (the seventh race), or the "ulti-mate" (expression) of "the race."[50]

50. Isar Godreau, "La semántica fugitiva: 'Raza,' color y vida cotidiana en Puerto Rico"; Isar Godreau, "Peinando diferencias, bregas de pertenencia: El alisado y el llamado 'pelo malo.'" See also Nicomedes Santa Cruz, *Décimas y poemas: Antologia.*

3

Tez de mulato

RACE, WRITING, AND THE ANTISLAVERY PREMISE

For "quo ad" morals, nothing can be worse,
But "quo ad" sugar, 'tis the sole resourse.
    Richard Madden

Rockstone a' river bottom no know sun hot.
    Jamaican saying

Given the overvaluation of whiteness and the accompanying melanopho-
bia of colonial Latin American society, it is not surprising to find in the
nineteenth century a perhaps paradoxical valorization of mulattoness even
in the creative writing that purported to promote the abolition of slavery.
Indeed, considering the way mulatto skin color, or *mula-tez,* is ideologically
manipulated in the works discussed below, one might well speak in terms of
a literary actuation or inscription of what sociologist Carl Degler once described for Brazil as the mulatto "escape hatch." The quest for or assertion
of skin privilege, whether in the autobiographical mode, as with Juan Francisco Manzano (1839), or as part of a top-down racialist gesture of the
omniscient narrator in Gertrudis Gómez de Avellaneda's *Sab* (1841), or in
Bernardo Guimaraes's *A escrava Isaura* (1865), is the thematic constant with
which this chapter is concerned. It pervades all three texts, the first two

Cuban, the third Brazilian, in spite of the differing circumstances of their production and the differences in form and content that characterize them. That all the protagonists are domestic slaves whose acquired cultural attributes—literacy and artistic sensibility and talent—turn out to be important complements to their somatic condition also constitutes a highly suggestive paradigm of racialized power, the flight from blackness, and the architecture of *blanqueamiento,* or whitening.

Alongside their reinscription of racial pedigree, per the taxonomy described in the previous chapter, nineteenth-century slave narratives in a general sense also allow us to see the *criollo* imagination at work, as its schemes for reform and its protonationalist projections attempt to give voice to the laboring slave bodies. While this gesture inheres a possibility of black agency in accordance with the nineteenth-century ethos of emancipation, independence, and a postslavery polity, I would argue that the *criollo* embrace of *mula-tez* hides a more serious problem: the suppression of the (darker) slave masses who might emerge as the protagonists of any real project for social change. As it did for the so-called antislavery writers, the often-muted but ever-present specter of the Haitian revolution, or a generalized *peligro negro* (black menace), would continue to haunt Creole projections of nation and independence into the twentieth century (as we will see in subsequent chapters). It is therefore important to appreciate the ambivalence attending this liberal *prise de conscience,* and the literary mulatto racial buffer zone that is created, as the *criollos* consider their own emancipation from the clutches of coloniality.

The biracial Manzano occupies a curious position at the intersection of the two projects of emancipation. As a *person,* he would advance his own agenda by tapping into the dynamism of social race, even as he puts into action the liberationist imperative that came with the reality of oppression for the wider collective. As a *persona,* however, his racialized life story would provide a model for literary creation. There is, then, more than a figurative sense to the elite Creole "giving of voice" to Manzano. And while the degree to which he identifies with either of the prevailing projects of emancipation (that of the slaves, or that of the liberal Creole masters) may never be known, it is less difficult to see that, for him, the accession to writing is also the occasion for racial identification per the taxonomy above. In this sense, both the slave (soon to be ex-slave) and the members of the slave-owning class participate in the same broad paradigm for writing the *negro* in their nineteenth-century national contexts. Other partisan interests aside, it is beyond doubt that the plan for nation founders on the question of race. The gross contradictions of *criollo* life, overdetermined by the imperatives of colonial production, and the specter of revolution from below end up scattering Manzano's bene-factors and the lettered elite, thereby postponing the arrival of national be-coming and deferring the dream of racial rapprochement.

Manzano: A "Mulatto among Blacks" (and Whites)

Situated as it is between the powerful and the powerless, between literacy and illiteracy, slavers and the enslaved, the life story of Juan Francisco Man-zano occupies a unique place in Cuban and Latin American literary history. The fact that it is the only extant autobiography of a person of African descent written during the period of Latin American slavery enhances the particularity of the document. The *Autobiografía* is also noteworthy because it is the historical point of departure for what has been canonized as early Cuban "antislavery" writing. It has also been regarded as having provided a narrative model for this genre. Cuban man of letters Domingo del Monte and the corps of literati (the *círculo delmontino*) who were instrumental in the production of these early texts have been remembered accordingly as exemplars of New World enlightenment and humanitarianism. Paradoxi-cally, Manzano, the only member of the circle who could describe slavery from a personal perspective, and who was central to the mostly derivative and fictional slave narrative, has had a somewhat limiting critical harvest in comparison with the historical protagonism accorded the other writers of the group. With few exceptions, the critical gaze, due almost certainly to his condition as a slave, has tended to see him through the prism of pathos and less in terms of his intellectuality or as a literary originator.[1] The intellectual lionization has generally been reserved for the white writers of the group.

In this section of the chapter, I propose a look at Latin American colonial cartography as a backdrop to the prestige of this group of Cuban writers and their writings, highlighting the power and prestige inherent to the insti-tution of literature and pointing to the eventual connections with race. My discussion will first take into account the occlusion of the unlettered under-class that is part and parcel of the canonizing process, and the implications for the latter as historical agents. The enhanced critical legacy of the Del

---

1. For Manzano's autobiography as literary model, see Salvador Bueno, "La lucha contra la esclavitud y su expresión literaria"; William Luis, *Literary Bondage: Slavery in Cuban Narrative,* 39; and César Leante, "Dos obras antiesclavistas cubanas," 175. As literary originator, see Luis, *Literary Bondage;* and Sonia Labrador-Rodríguez, "La intelectualidad negra en Cuba en el siglo XIX: El caso de Manzano."

Monte group and their prominence in the Cuban discourse of national literary foundation is also an important consideration here. So, too, is the extent to which the antislavery premise within this discourse has sought purchase and legitimacy in the larger moral and philosophical issues of the day: emancipation and the Rights of Man. Manzano's autobiographical construction of self in a textual and extratextual universe overdetermined by race and the subjugation of enslavement is also relevant to the broader context of this foundational moment in Cuban writing, and it will finally be seen in this regard.

In his 1944 study *Capitalism and Slavery,* Eric Williams referred to the historical inevitability of the ending of the latter institution, whether as a result of metropolitan lobbying "from above" or of slave insurgency "from below." Williams's observation not only points to the essentially heterogeneous nature of transatlantic abolitionism, but also highlights what later historians have seen as a major problem in Western antislavery studies, that is, the "projection of a hierarchical order" in the discussion of the antislavery question. According to the colonialist history of emancipation, it was enlightened European humanitarians and intellectuals who brought freedom to the blacks. When this discourse recognizes a protagonistic role for the enslaved, their action is regarded as marginal to the broad sweep of history, as mostly instinctive, material outbursts against oppression, in effect, "a lower species of political behavior, lacking in ideological cohesion, intellectual qualities, and a philosophical direction," as Hilary Beckles described it. Even within metropolitan abolitionism, the energetic contributions of Olaudah Equiano, an ex-slave and tireless antislavery agitator and militant, have been greatly overlooked by historians.[2]

It is interesting to find a not entirely dissimilar tendency to polarize and racially hierarchize the antislavery question in the approach of many scholars of Cuban literature. César Leante, for example, in "Dos obras antiesclavistas cubanas," extols the high moral and philanthropic impulse behind Anselmo Suárez y Romero's novel *Francisco.* He stresses the point that it was to the planter class that the white writer turned in his concern for social justice, and not to the class of the enslaved. Asserting that "it is difficult for it to

2. Williams, *Capitalism and Slavery,* 208; Hilary Beckles, "Caribbean Anti-Slavery: The Self-Liberation Ethos of Enslaved Blacks," 8, 3. Beckles illustrates the point by citing Robin Blackburn's *The Overthrow of Colonial Slavery,* which evokes Thomas Clarkson's seminal antitrade essay of 1808 and asserts that "it has been common to identify the origins of anti-slavery within the works of the learned men who first published critiques of slavery or of the slave trade" (8). See also Peter Linebaugh, "All the Atlantic Mountains Shook," 117.

have been any other way," Leante adds rhetorically: "What effect could a book possibly have in a totally illiterate conglomerate?" Leante's statement would of course be quite logical if indeed all enslaved blacks were illiterate or incapable of literary or intellectual expression. The same might be said if it were only the enslaved who took up arms for freedom, but the historical record indicates otherwise. Another critic, William Luis, while lauding the Del Monte literary project aimed ostensibly at changing slave society, seems to proceed in a similarly essentialist vein when he states, "it stands to reason that antislavery, as a concept or as a literary, political, or economic movement in Cuba, could only exist as a white movement."[3] Whereas both writers do recognize a role for unfree blacks in casting off the chains of bondage, one wonders if, in their analyses of the antislavery question, they are not privileging writing, writers, and the Cartesian premise along restrictive racial lines.

Contrary to the notion that antislavery protest operated along a racialized axis determined by literacy or literariness, empirical evidence suggests a much more complex and nuanced relationship between the enslaved and the dominant culture of writing not only in Cuba, but across the black Atlantic. Far from the exclusivism of the Eurocentric premise, or the plantocracy's blanket prohibitions to literacy for its slaves, writing as an intellectual tool was an effective and intrinsic element of the Afro-Creole project of liberation. Afro-Creole agency through writing is evident if one considers, for example, its role in the Bahia rebellion of 1835, led by literate Muslim slaves. The role of writing is also clear when one considers the different ways in which some Afro-Creoles appropriated colonial languages to communicate their sociopolitical concerns to the crown and to the slaveocracy, or simply by way of their accession to and use of writing in terms of standard literary practice.

The celebration of the Del Monte circle in the discourse of early nineteenth-century Cuban literary beginnings is better understood if we see its members as legatees of what Angel Rama referred to as the *ciudad letrada,* and in terms of the diglossia that characterized the social relations of production in colonial Latin America. Rama reminds us that in the urban/rural dichotomy of the colonial economy, it was in this "Lettered City" where political and administrative power was centered. In an overwhelmingly unlettered population, literacy and erudition among lawyers, royal functionaries, professors, priests, and creative writers played a crucial role in constituting a hegemonic apparatus located in the urban space. It was an apparatus

---

3. Leante, "Dos obras antiesclavistas cubanas," 181; Luis, *Literary Bondage,* 65; William Luis, "La novela antiesclavista: Texto, contexto y escritura," 114.

that kept colonial subalterns—slaves, blacks, Amerindians, mestizos—at an appropriate distance from the exercise of sociopolitical and economic influence. In the context of an economy based on forced labor, however, with a documented antislavery praxis of individual and collective acts of rebellion, it is impossible to deny the agents of this rebellion a corresponding antislavery consciousness, or discursivity.[4]

A full account of antislavery voicing from the fringes of the dominant scribal tradition is beyond the scope of this discussion. The challenges to the power of the crown and the colonial oligarchy that include the use of the written medium, however, were a constant in several areas of colonial Latin America. Perhaps the most significant threat to the status quo in Cuba, within living memory of the Del Monte group, was the Aponte conspiracy of 1812, which planned an uprising against the plantocracy and Cuba's colonial status. José Antonio Aponte was an *Oni-Shangó,* that is, a leader in the Nigeria-originated *lucumí* religious order. His coconspirators included other coreligionists, free Afro-Cubans, slaves, and poor whites. Aponte's inspiration lay both in the successes of the recently concluded Haitian revolution and in the progressive initiatives taken by Spanish American deputies to the liberal Spanish Cortes at Cádiz, Spain, to end the slave trade and slavery.

Historian José Luciano Franco's account of Aponte's arrest, trial, and execution provides additional information pertinent to this discussion. It refers to the presence of secret *abakuá* drawings among the conspirators as well as a proclamation in Spanish that the insurgents had posted up on the wall of the principal government building, the Government Palace, in Havana. The latter called upon the public at large to be "on the alert to overthrow tyranny." Another, more extended document was directed to the white business sector, inviting them to join with the rebels in the liberatory enterprise.[5] Aponte, a talented woodcarver and painter and the owner of a small library, had produced a large book of highly suggestive paintings containing Afro-diasporic motifs, images of Egypt and Haiti, and other illustrations that were used against him at his trial. Among the paintings considered seditious was one that depicted black and white soldiers in battle, in which the black general emerges triumphant. Another painting detailed the city of Havana, with its forts, castles, walls, storehouses, military installations, sugar mills, and so

---

4. See Angel Rama, *La ciudad letrada,* 22–67. See also Gordon Lewis's remarks on antislavery ideology in this regard (*Main Currents in Caribbean Thought,* 172–73).

5. See José Luciano Franco, "La conspiración de Aponte," 175. One recipient of this document, a businessman by the name of Pablo Serra, promptly turned it over to the captain general of the island, the Marquis of Someruelos.

on. Other paintings—portraits of Haitian revolutionary leaders Toussaint-Louverture and Henri Christophe—enhanced the incendiary symbolism of these illustrations.

Regarding Aponte as an antislavery protagonist, it is important that the materials seized by the authorities point to the variety of texts he used to communicate with his different groups of interlocutors: whereas the *abakuá* illustrations would have been decipherable only by religious initiates, the proclamations in Spanish would have communicated to his literate followers and to the public at large as well. Of course, it is easy to see how the graphic nature and content of the paintings could have been aimed primarily at those of his comrades who could not read. Meanwhile, the detailed interrogation to which Aponte and his followers were subjected by the colonial authorities indicates the seriousness with which these texts were regarded. For the authorities, they all constituted subversive acts of signifying.

Equally subversive of the slavocratic and colonial status quo was the role of Arabic in the 1835 *Malê* rebellion in Bahia, Brazil, described by João José Reis as "the most effective urban slave rebellion ever to occur on the American continent." It was an event imbued with a sense of Islamic millennialism in which many of the bodies of the insurgents were later found with amulets containing prayers and Koranic passages that spoke of hope amidst oppression. The rebels had entered the war with these amulets as mystical guarantees of invulnerability. The persistence of a West African Islamic intellectual tradition in these enslaved Muslims is manifest in the documentation that the authorities found that revealed their plans for the execution of the rebellion and in the Koranic schools they attempted to continue in Brazil. Researchers have also stressed the significance of *Malê* literacy in a context in which a large percentage of the Portuguese and white Creole community could neither read nor write.[6] It is significant that two of the seven leaders, Manoel Calafate and Elesbão do Carmo, were freedmen.

Much earlier, in Colombia, in the 1680s, maroon leader Domingo Criollo, with the help of Spanish clerics, had for a decade negotiated in writing with the local governor and the Council of the Indies before his village was finally destroyed in 1693. Also in the Guyanese county of Berbice, then a Dutch colony, rebel leader Kofi engaged in a protracted correspondence with Governor van Hoogenheim in 1763. Kofi's extended letter writing, according to

---

6. José João Reis, *Slave Rebellion in Brazil: The Muslim Uprising of 1835 in Bahia*, xiii, 106. *Malê* is a generic term referring to enslaved Muslims in Brazil. They were primarily of Nagô ethnic origin but included Jejes, Hausas, Tapas, and Bornus. See also Jack Goody, "Writing, Religion, and Revolt in Bahia," 324.

one commentator, was a delaying ploy by which it was hoped that an eventual peace treaty might ensue. Similarly, in Barbados, Bussa's rebellion of 1816 recalls that of Aponte, in the sense that its leadership was aware of the wider antislavery struggle. In this case, the uprising reflected the slaves' understanding of the effect of abolitionist agitation in England and the crisis facing the planter class, in many instances by way of information acquired from local and British newspapers.[7] The awareness of political developments in the local or metropolitan government circles, in the free and enslaved black communities, through print media, often influenced the nature and timing of their rebellions.

Complementing the texts that were directly related to armed insurgency were other kinds of Afro-Creole antislavery protests that used writing. These challenges to oppression may have been direct or mediated and may have taken the form of letters, complaints, or even lawsuits. They might have been aimed at obtaining autonomy for maroon sites, as indicated, at securing liberty for already freed individuals under threat of reenslavement, or at acquiring any number of the perceived rights denied by racially exclusionary colonial laws. Together they constituted a discourse aimed at nullifying the status of object to which Africans and Afro-Creoles had been reduced.[8]

The appropriation of written discourse demonstrates the awareness among free and enslaved Africans and Afro-Creoles of the relationship between writing and the politico-legal superstructure, as well as their determination to use whatever means were available to achieve their liberation. While learning to read and write may have been illegal in all of the Americas, there can be no question that there is a black antislavery archive in writing that is available for recovery, whether this consisted of letters, treaties, testimony at trials, or other papers. It is in the transcripts of the interrogations relating to the trial of Aponte, and its revelation of the degree to which he drew on a revolutionary counterdiscursivity circulating among Caribbean harbor cities and beyond, that allows us to posit the valency of an actively shared black Atlantic liberationist consciousness, even if its precise means and mechanism

7. Regarding Domingo Criollo, see Margaret M. Olsen, "*Negros horros* and *cimarrones* on the Legal Frontiers of the Caribbean: Accessing the African Voice in Colonial Spanish American Texts," 57. Alvin Thompson names an African ex-slave, Prins, and various whites and captives of mixed ancestry as the writers of Kofi's letters ("The Berbice Revolt, 1763–64"). See also Hilary Beckles, "Emancipation by War or Law? Wilberforce and the 1816 Barbados Slave Rebellion," 94.

8. Digna Castañeda documents the appeals of black women in nineteenth-century Cuba against sexual predation by their masters, or their refusal to honor the agreed price for the women's freedom; see "The Female Slave in Cuba during the First Half of the Nineteenth Century."

are not fully available at the moment.[9] The contents of this broader archive, therefore, would dramatically enhance our understanding of the nature of the relationship between the dominant and the subordinate groups in colonial Latin America. They would also allow for a more balanced view of who did what in antislavery history, while dispelling notions of unqualified illiteracy and unsophistication among the enslaved. The fact that these texts were part of a crucial existential necessity for those engaged in their writing underscores their importance as a discourse against slavery. Antislavery writing as an abstract fictional endeavor is an entirely different matter.

In the final analysis, action spoke louder than words as far as the antislavery question was concerned. In the foundational moment of Cuban literature in the 1830s, to the extent that fear of antislavery upheaval stalked the minds of the plantocracy and the colonial bureaucrats, it is to be recognized that it was the slaves themselves who were the agents of this unease and not the literati. Their potential for turning Cuban colonial society upside down is recorded in their increased rebelliousness over the preceding four decades. Indeed, it was the real or imagined threat that they represented that often hindered otherwise progressive thinking among the Cuban intelligentsia of the period. Although it is undeniable that this intelligentsia expressed antislavery ideas as they established a national discourse, it is crucial to specify the motivations underlying their antislavery proclamations and the implications of their ideas for the future nation. Meanwhile, conferring epistemological paramountcy on them as the founding fathers of Cuba's national literature on the basis of their presumed liberationist discourse seems to respond to an overvaluation of the role of literature and literati. It suggests the development of a hierarchy within the antislavery concept that correspondingly devalues the voices, consciousness, and the agency of the slaves who protagonized their own liberation. As indicated, liberation was achieved by means of an essentially heterogeneous praxis that, when necessary, combined the pen with the sword.[10]

The figure of Domingo del Monte (1804–1853) is pivotal to any discussion of Cuban literary beginnings. A litterateur par excellence, Del Monte

---

9. See Sibylle Fischer, *Modernity Disavowed: Haiti and the Cultures of Slavery in the Age of Revolution,* 51.

10. Cuba entered its "plantation mode" in 1792, when colonial statesman Francisco de Arango y Parreño issued a call for the sugar industry to be developed so that Cuba might take the place of Saint Domingue in the world market. It was an initiative that brought an unprecedented number of African captives to the Caribbean colony. Franco details the link between the 1792 initiative and the spate of rebellions in the later part of the decade ("La conspiración," 133–34).

was widely traveled, knew Latin and five modern languages, and is regarded as having been the most important bibliographer in the Caribbean in the nineteenth century. His passion for literature is seen in his reputation as a voracious reader and through his active promotion and discussion of literary works and theories among his friends. Recognized by scholars as Cuba's first professional literary critic, Del Monte used his discussion groups, or *tertulias,* and the journals with which he was associated to introduce Neoclassicism, Romanticism, and Realism to Cuba and to promote an aesthetic in which New World and Cuban motifs would be central. Antonio Benítez-Rojo suggests that it was from his literary circle that a definably Cuban body of works emerged in the latter 1830s.[11] Among the writers with whom he worked and whom he mentored were Ramón de Palma, José Zacarías González del Valle, José Antonio Saco, José Jacinto Milanés, Anselmo Suárez y Romero, and Félix Tanco y Bosmeniel. Occasional participants in his group were mulatto poet Plácido de la Concepción Valdés and Juan Francisco Manzano. The writing coming out of his athenaeum included articles on customs, drama, travel writing, poetry, novels, literary criticism, and, of course, Manzano's slave autobiography.

Del Monte's contribution to Cuban literary beginnings is also seen in his cofounding and coediting of such periodicals as *La moda ó recreo semanal del bello sexo* (1829–1831), *El puntero literario* (January–May 1830), and *Revista bimestre cubana* (1831–1834). These vehicles not only provided an outlet for local writing, but also entertained and educated an ever-widening readership as to the latest scientific and literary trends in Europe and the United States. Through them, authors and poets such as Scott, Byron, Zorilla, Hugo, and Balzac were introduced to the Cuban public, just as their merits were assessed among the new generation of would-be writers. Literary historians regard Del Monte as having achieved a major coup in winning the approval of the Regent Maria Christina for the establishment of a Cuban Academy of Literature in 1834. The proposed academy had grown out of his work since 1830 as president of the Commission on Literature of the influential and prestigious Sociedad económica de amigos del país. Due, however,

---

See also Luis, *Literary Bondage,* 2; and Antonio Benítez-Rojo, "Power/Sugar/Literature: Toward a Reinterpretation of Cubanness," 10. John Beverly, in *Against Literature,* argues for deemphasizing the perceived value of the literary text as an artifact of high culture. His premises would permit us to appreciate the historical specificity of subaltern modes of resistance.

11. On Del Monte as bibliophile, see Enildo García, "Romanticismo antillano: Domingo del Monte y 'The Harvard Connection.'" See also Antonio Benítez-Rojo, "¿Cómo narrar la nación? El círculo de Domingo Delmonte y el surgimiento de la novela cubana."

to a climate of severe repression of freedom of expression, and the high-handed action of powerful enemies of the proposed academy, the project never came into being.[12]

The subsequent defense, by Del Monte and his colleague José Antonio Saco, of the right of the Academy of Literature to exist constitutes an event of the highest significance. In the atmosphere of colonial suppression, it signaled liberal Euro-Creole determination to have independent opinions about art, politics, and a wide range of subjects, and to express these opinions. Saco pointed out in an erudite and forceful article that the arguments against official ratification of the academy in Cuba were specious, and that official ire had been inspired because the literati had shaken off "the domination that they [the Patriotic Society] wanted to exercise over them."[13] Saco's bold and public statement came only two years after he had used the *Revista bimestre cubana* to call for abolition of the slave trade because it was bringing too many potentially hostile blacks into the country. Impugning the pretended patriotism of the powerful slave traders, he called them instead *patricidas* (patricides), lambasting their lust for profits in an illegal trade, and attacking, in passing, the colonial officials who collaborated with them in the traffic. Spain had signed an agreement in 1817 with Britain to bring an end to its trade in Africans in 1820, and it was established custom that captains general accepted handsome bribes to look the other way. With slave imports about to peak in 1835, the fact that Captain General Miguel Tacón subsequently sent Saco into exile was not surprising.[14]

Del Monte added to this alienation of the powerful alliance of wealthy landowners, slave traders, and upper-echelon administrators with his own angry vindication of the proposed academy in the *Aurora de matanzas* newspaper on April 2, 1834. Five years later, he followed up with a call for freedom of the press and for equal provincial representation and constitutional rights for Cuba in Spain. Equally damning—from the standpoint of the sugar interests—was that he was known to have associated with British abolitionist Richard Madden, resident magistrate on the mixed commission

12. Larry R. Jensen discusses the severity of press censorship in nineteenth-century Cuba, especially in the 1820s, in *Children of Colonial Despotism: Press, Politics, and Culture in Cuba, 1790–1840.*

13. José Antonio Saco, "Justa defensa de la academia cubana de literatura . . . ," 25, 52.

14. José Antonio Saco, "Análisis por don José Antonio Saco de una obra sobre el Brasil," 202. Hugh Thomas reports that "63 slavers [left Havana] in 1828, 45 in 1829, and 80 in 1835" (*Cuba; or, The Pursuit of Freedom,* 200). The decade of the 1830s recorded the highest imports in the history of Cuban slavery. See also Christopher Schmidt-Nowara, *Empire and Antislavery: Spain, Cuba, and Puerto Rico, 1833–1874,* 4.

that had been established for liberating Africans rescued from captured slave ships. At Madden's request, Del Monte had some of his group members prepare works on the topic of slavery in Cuba, and in 1839 these were handed to him for publication in England. According to José Zacarías González del Valle, *tertulia* member, these works were to allow Madden to form "an exact idea of the opinion of the thinking youth of the country as to the treatment of slaves."[15]

It is the profile of Del Monte as defiant, autonomist, and at the same time cosmopolitan man of letters, that has made him an object of pride for many literary historiographers. Along with Saco, he has been seen as central to a "discourse of resistance" against the powerful sugar interests and as a promoter of a "literary anti-slavery campaign." It is an assessment premised primarily on economist Francisco de Arango y Parreño's 1792 proslavery initiative to the crown, the *Discurso sobre la agricultura de la Habana y medios de fomentarla,* which had advocated making Cuba a sugar-producing replacement for then-insurgent Saint Domingue. William Luis's *Literary Bondage: Slavery in Cuban Narrative* also vindicates Del Monte's project from the standpoint of its supposed counterdiscursivity.[16]

The Del Monte group has even been promoted in terms of the revolutionary paradigm of the Enlightenment, and its discourse of emancipation. In the opinion of José Zacarías González del Valle, he and his companions were young men "imbued with the principles of liberty, equality, and fraternity," who exchanged books and ideas in a clandestine manner, and who dedicated their "noble and generous hearts" to ending the slave trade and slavery. As local versions of the great European humanitarians and encyclopedists, according to González del Valle, they paved the way for the epic moment in 1868 when Cuban national hero Manuel de Céspedes launched the war for independence and declared his slaves free. For these reasons, he

15. Del Monte's later article was "Estado de la población blanca y de color de la isla de Cuba en 1839"; see pages 158–59. Del Monte's list for Madden included Manzano's autobiography and some of his poems and Anselmo Suárez y Romero, *Francisco: El ingenio, o las delicias del campo,* which was finally published in 1880, among other items. Félix Tanco y Bosmeniel's story "Petrona y Rosalía" (1839) was also a product of the group. Antonio Zambrana's *El negro Francisco* (1875) was inspired by Suárez y Romero's novel. See Adriana Lewis Galanes, "El album de Domingo del Monte (Cuba, 1838/39)." The letter from José Zacarías González del Valle to Anselmo Suárez y Romero, September 5, 1838, expresses the group's position (González del Valle, *La vida literaria en Cuba [1836–1840],* 57).

16. See Benítez-Rojo, "Power/Sugar," 22; and Luis, *Literary Bondage,* 3–81. The Saint Domingue rebellion started in 1791. At the time, it was France's richest colony and the leading producer of cane sugar in the world. Independence was declared in 1804, and the country's name was changed to Haiti.

suggests, "they deserve to be known by present generations, because they speak to us of a splendid era in our literary history that reveals the generous sentiments and advanced ideas of those young writers."[17]

The oppositional stance of the Cuban literati of the 1830s vis-à-vis the sugar barons and the colonial bureaucracy is undeniable. The abolitionist question is also a key point of difference between them. But here it is important to note that there is a difference between the idea of abolition as an end to the slave trade, and the idea of abolition as an end to slavery, and that neither of the two necessarily implies altruism. In the celebration of Del Monte's humanitarianism and his supposed antislavery dissidence, these distinctions have too often been glossed over. Further, in the particular context of Cuba at the time, the blurring of the difference—that is, describing him in unqualified fashion as "abolitionist"—can obscure the important implications of the two kinds of abolition for intellectuals like Del Monte. As it turns out, the Del Monte group's opposition to slavery as an altruistic vindication of the rights of the enslaved, an idea advanced in the studies previously cited, is a highly questionable proposition. So, too, is the suggestion that he and his literary group in toto espoused the vision of a democratic inclusion of black ex-slaves in a future Cuban polity.[18] On the contrary, the writings of both Saco and Del Monte repeatedly reveal a sense of paranoia over racial coexistence at the time, as well as the supremacist desire for a white and hence "civilized" future Cuba.

In the early nineteenth century, Cuban nationalist discourse was intimately tied to the question of political independence from Spain. Independence, in turn, was tied to the island's racial composition and to the possibility of union with the United States. It all resulted in an ideological bottleneck that would not be resolved for decades. Proslavery advocate Francisco de Arango y Parreño may have expressed confidence in Spain's ability to control Cuba's growing slave population due to increased imports at the turn of the century. But by the 1830s, Saco was expressing panic at the rising number of blacks and slaves in Cuba and at their demographic preponderance in neighboring countries. Considering it his duty as writer, intellectual, and patriot to warn his fellow countrymen of impending racial conflagration and financial ruin should the importation of Africans continue, he proposed several reforms aimed at modernizing Cuba's sugar industry in a subsequent essay. The key

17. González del Valle, *La vida literaria,* 6, 7, 5.
18. See, for example, Luis, *Literary Bondage,* 28–30.

element in these reforms lay in the importation of white labor and the elimi-nation of the blacks.[19]

Free white workers, he maintained, were more intelligent, dedicated, and motivated; the black slaves were lazy and prone to sabotage and rebellion. Arguing that beet sugar was being produced quite successfully by free labor in the East Indies, Saco exhorted his compatriots to save the Cuban father-land, describing its current population as "gravely ill" as a result of the black presence. The solution, he asserted in *La Supresión,* lay in closing "forever, the doors to all blacks," while opening them "freely to all whites."[20]

The self-interest and monetary gain of the entrenched power groups, however, militated strongly against Saco's admonitions. It was a situation in which a successful slaving expedition could net a profit of $100,000 in 1835, Captain General Miguel Tacón had amassed $450,000 in bribes during his four-year tenure, and sugar was showing unprecedented profitability for the saccharocracy. While Saco can certainly be described as having an antislavery ideology, he can hardly be described as a Negrophile. His essay "Contra la anexión," in fact, actually made a call for the "extinction, if this were possible, of the black race."[21]

Antonio Saco's monochrome nationalism was endorsed in all its impor-tant points by Domingo del Monte, in spite of the general endorsement by the *tertulia* of a racially inclusive Cuban literary landscape. Of the group, Félix Tanco y Bosmeniel seemed to be the most radical in this regard. He argued for a realist approach to writing (à la Balzac) by the *tertulia* and for stories that would include black characters. Even so, in his exposure of the cynicism and the cruelty of the master class in the successive father-and-son violation of a slave mother and daughter, his implied protest in the short story "Petrona y Rosalía" does not allow for more than a defeatist portrayal of the main black characters. Del Monte was as alarmed as Tanco was on the matter of Cuba's racial imbalance, and he supported the idea of import-

19. Franco details the frequency of uprisings in the 1790s and their bloody suffocation ("La conspiración," 133–34). The essay in question is José Antonio Saco, "La supresión del tráfico de esclavos africanos en la isla de Cuba, examinada con relación a su agricultura y a su seguridad, por don José Antonio Saco."

20. Saco, "Análisis," 196; Saco, "La supresión," 226.

21. On the profitability of slave trading in 1830s Cuba, see Thomas, *Cuba,* 96. The amount attached to Governor Tacón's venality was revealed in an interview Madden held with Del Monte, cited in Edward Mullen, ed., *The Life and Poems of a Cuban Slave: Juan Francisco Man-zano, 1797–1854,* 135. Saco, in "Contra la anexión," cited in Raúl Cepero Bonilla, *Azúcar y abolición,* 53.

ing European laborers to redress the issue. For this reason also, he felt that British-style abolition would be ruinous since it would make free people of the enslaved. As a plantation owner, Del Monte had more of a stake in the preservation of his personal property. In the early decades of the nineteenth century, Cuban sugar barons as a group deployed their political muscle, as generators of revenue for a debilitated Spain, to delay de facto prohibition of the slave trade, notwithstanding the wave of liberalism in Europe or the 1817 treaty. With the Saint Domingue antecedent in mind, however, they were acutely aware that their prosperity was precarious, and they saw the powerful United States, a slaveholding nation, as a potential source of security. Significant overtures in this regard took place in 1810, in 1822, and as late as 1868, when the rebel leader Carlos Manuel de Céspedes, on behalf of the sugar interests, wrote Secretary of State W. H. Seward to this effect.[22]

Del Monte's correspondence with the diplomat Alexander Everett, one of his American colleagues, shows how much he identified with the thinking that defined his class. Everett had been the U.S. minister to Spain in 1825 and had supported those members of the U.S. political elite desirous of annexing Cuba. When Del Monte visited the United States in 1829, Alexander Everett, along with his brother Edward, the president of Harvard University, was among a group of North American scholars and writers with whom Del Monte established a friendship.[23] A close correspondence covering personal, political, and cultural matters ensued thereafter between the two. In Cuba, writing for a public audience at the time might raise the question of censorship or self-censorship. In Del Monte's private correspondence to Everett, there is no reason to believe that such considerations obtained.

In a series of letters to the powerful diplomat covering a wide range of topics, Del Monte showed remarkable candor as he courted U.S. annexation of Cuba, all the while expressing a position on race in Cuba that was unambiguous. The slave owners, he asserted in August 1843, are united in their intention to seek "help and protection and support" from the great

22. Manuel de Céspedes said, "There will be no doubt, after constituting ourselves as an independent nation, that we, sooner or later, will form a part of such powerful States" (quoted in Cepero Bonilla, *Azúcar,* 193). See also David R. Murray, "The Slave Trade, Slavery, and Cuban Independence," 111, 117; and Thomas, *Cuba,* 100.

23. Everett asserted in a letter to President Adams that it was "the policy and duty of the United States to endeavor to obtain possession of Cuba" (Murray, "Slave Trade," 118). Henry Longfellow, George Ticknor, William Prescott, and Washington Irving were among Del Monte's North American friends. García refers to them as Del Monte's "Harvard Connection" ("Romanticismo antillano," 69).

northern confederation, should Madrid declare slavery abolished. Earlier, in November 1842, in an unsubtle appeal to the assumed racism of Everett, he described Cuba as "the youngest sister in the Great Western Confederation of Caucasian peoples of America." In this letter, Del Monte tried to persuade Everett that Cuba was a political pawn of the British, who were bent on freeing the slaves and setting up a black military republic in Cuba. With this in mind, he asked rhetorically: "Will the American people watch impassively, as one who contemplates the development of a play in the theater, while the astute Albion curiously and ably elaborates the loss of the largest of the Antilles . . . ? I think not." In the same letter he asserted Cuba's destiny as "the most brilliant star in the American flag," clarifying on a later occasion that his conversations about emancipation with British abolitionist agent David Turnbull, and with other liberals, were purely theoretical speculations. Supporting freedom for black slaves, he reiterated in June 1844, would be madness, since it would "sacrifice the tranquility of my country and the existence of my race." Del Monte, after all, had married into a family of "hardworking and honorable capitalists," and wished ardently to be cleared of all suspicions of being a "conspirator . . . abolitionist or revolutionary."[24]

Apologists for Del Monte's humanitarianism allude invariably to his role in rescuing Manzano from slavery and to his support of Manzano's literary endeavors as concrete proof of his abolitionist commitment and benevolence. Salvador Bueno, for example, in several articles supportive of the notion of Del Monte's altruism and enlightenment, quotes Cuban national hero José Martí on one occasion in describing him as "the most real and useful Cuban of his time." It is certainly to his credit that we have Manzano's invaluable writings. It bears pointing out, though, that in the context of the wider Atlantic, elite white sponsorship of enslaved blacks with literary ambitions was no novelty—nor was vindication of their intellect. It had been the case several decades before of Ignatius Sancho, Ottobah Cuguano, and Gustavus Vassa in England, Francis Williams of Jamaica, and Phyllis Wheatley of Boston, Massachusetts, among others. Besides, as owner of a hundred slaves and a nine-hundred-acre estate, and as a member of the

---

24. Del Monte, quoted in Enelda García, "Cartas de Domingo del Monte a Alexander H. Everett," 117, 113, 134, 133. Del Monte had been under suspicion of involvement in the Escalera conspiracy of 1844, a never-proven event used by Captain General O'Donnell as an opportunity to purge Cuba of foreign abolitionist agitators like David Turnbull and others whom he considered potential troublemakers in Cuba. The poet Plácido was tried and executed, Manzano was imprisoned, and hundreds of others died under torture or were exiled. See David R. Murray, *Odious Commerce: Britain, Spain, and the Abolition of the Cuban Slave Trade*, 159–80.

slave-trading, slave-owning Alfonso-Aldama-Madam clan, one of the most opulent family groups in Cuba, Del Monte's description of his family's creation of wealth as "honest capitalism" does little to enhance his humanitarian image.[25]

The spirit of emancipation that characterized the Enlightenment and is exemplified in the American (1776) and French Revolutions (1789) also saw the emergence of abolitionist societies in England, France, and the United States. The ideological radicalism of men like England's Thomas Paine and France's Henri Grégoire are examples of the democratic spirit of the age and of its abolitionism. Paine, noted for his political activism in both the American and French revolutions, also authored the anticlerical and antiaristocratic *The Rights of Man* (1791) and *The Age of Reason* (1794). As clerk of the Pennsylvania Assembly, he drafted legislation providing for the gradual emancipation of the state's slaves, and, nearly a hundred years before Lincoln, attempted to write a clause against slavery into the American constitution. Grégoire, a Jacobin and member of the French Societé des amis des Noirs, also wrote *De la littérature des nègres* (1808), a vindication of the intellectual achievements of Africans of the diaspora. Grégoire's essay was aimed at combating the burgeoning supremacist discourse that would culminate with Positivism and the pseudoscientific racism of the nineteenth century.[26]

Eric Williams has called metropolitan abolitionism "one of the greatest propaganda movements of all time." The famous seal of the Anti-Slavery Society, for example, depicting an African with one knee on the ground and in a pose of supplication, was reproduced by Josiah Wedgewood by the thousands. It bore the society's motto, "Am I not a man and a brother?" Supporters of the cause wore it to show their solidarity. Antislavery tracts, tallied by researcher James Walvin at 2,802,773 in the period between 1823

25. See Salvador Bueno, *Domingo del Monte, ¿Quién fue?* Bueno, "La lucha contra la esclavitud," and Salvador Bueno, *Las ideas literarias de Domingo Delmonte.* The first article contains the reference to José Martí (9). See also Luis, *Literary Bondage,* 36. Henri Grégoire, *On the Cultural Achievements of Negroes,* is a good example of current literature vindicating black achievement. By the decade of the 1860s, Del Monte's family clan owned 40 sugar mills, 15,000 slaves, railways, houses of credit, banks, and shipping lines, as well as 10 titles of nobility. Del Monte's estate, Ceres, was located at Cárdenas. Lisandro Otero, "Del Monte y la cultura de la sacarocracia," 724; Thomas, *Cuba,* 207.

26. See Michael Foot and Isaac Kramnic, eds., *The Thomas Paine Reader,* 12, 24. Among the Negrophobe writings Grégoire refutes in *Cultural Achievements* are Jamaican planter-historian Edward Long's *A History of Jamaica,* David Hume's "Of National Characters," and Thomas Jefferson's *Notes on the State of Virginia.*

and 1831, were complemented in formal literature by a plethora of poems, plays, and fiction. Seymour Drescher notes also the influence of the British masses, as their generalized mobilization through lecture and petition campaigns made candidates in British parliamentary elections of 1832 take careful note of the power of the antislavery constituency.[27]

As French philosophers of the later eighteenth century pondered the oppression of colonial slavery, they asked the rhetorical question, "Where is the new Spartacus?" The reluctant revolutionary in Victor Hugo's novel *Bug-Jargal,* however, and the defeatist and suicidal protagonists of Anselmo Suárez y Romero's *Francisco* and José Tanco y Bosmeniel's "Petrona y Rosalía" (all "antislavery" works), bear little resemblance to the reality of the Saint Domingue rebels described by C. L. R. James as "The Black Jacobins." As suggested previously, the image of a Toussaint-Louverture and like insurgents did not appeal to the literary imagination of the Del Monte circle. Wedgewood-like supplication, rather, was what characterized the persona of Juan Francisco Manzano as he fashioned the personal and racial self most likely to promote sympathy from his colleagues and thus eventual liberation.

In 1840, Manzano's first editor, Richard Madden, expressed the opinion that the autobiography conveyed "the most perfect picture of Cuban slavery," because it was "so full and faithful in its details."[28] Madden's observation alludes to the verisimilitude of the document as it relates to Manzano's lived experiences, but it also alerts us to the metatextual management by the writer of his persona as he develops it. Much critical discussion of the autobiography, in its appreciation of Manzano as a representative or generic black/slave, has bypassed an engagement with the subtleties attendant to the racial self with which he presents us. I propose that colonial determinants surrounding caste, class, and writing, complicate a final appreciation of Manzano's text, and that the subject's representation of himself as a "mulatto among blacks" (and among whites, I might add) are important to the fullest understanding of the autobiography.

When Manzano the poet confronts the occasion of the public and indelible inscription of the self that is implied by Del Monte's request for the autobiography, an inevitable tension arises. This tension derives from the

27. Williams, *Capitalism and Slavery,* 178; James Walvin, "The Propaganda of Antislavery," 60; Seymour Drescher, "Public Opinion and the Destruction of British Colonial Slavery," 31.

28. Mullen, *Life and Poems,* 79. Manzano's document has had many editions and corresponding modifications; for a fuller discussion of these, see Luis, *Literary Bondage,* 83–100. In the following discussion, I shall be quoting from Ivan Schulman's 1996 bilingual edition, Juan Francisco Manzano, *Autobiography of a Slave/Autobiografía de un esclavo.*

fact that the relative autonomy and distancing afforded by the lyric voice in his previously published work would be lost due to the heightened self-referentiality of the autobiographic mode. More importantly, as an enslaved person, the multiple dimensions of Manzano's victimization would necessarily claim precedence in an autobiographical relation. As a writer "testifying" to the grave injustices and brutality of the colonial regimen of slavery (and hoping to be rescued from its clutches), extreme care would therefore be required in the fashioning of his story. On the one hand, the manner of its telling should not alienate his benefactor and literary ally, the white patrician Del Monte.[29] On the other hand, its "accusatory" contents could arouse the anger of real and potential enemies in the planter class and among the colonial authorities.

The question of literary censorship in Cuba, particularly Manzano's self-censorship as it pertains to the autobiography, has been addressed in many studies. That Manzano's primary victimizer, Marchioness of Prado Ameno, was still alive and influential, that the repressive policy of the colonial authorities was still in place, and that Manzano remained a slave, dependent upon his benefactor for his freedom, are facts that have already been pointed out. What has not received comparable attention, perhaps, is the way in which these factors, in combination, influence the narrative strategy of Manzano as autobiographical writer in a very specific socio-racial dynamic of power.

In addressing Del Monte, as well as an implied audience consisting of the other white, upper-class members of Del Monte's literary circle, and a potential European readership, Manzano takes discursive recourse in a simple binary procedure.[30] His life story is divided into a happy period of childhood innocence, with good and caring masters, and a dramatically sad period that begins with his loss of innocence and delivery into the hands of

29. His previous work was contained in *Cantos a Lesbia* (1821) and *Flores pasageras* (1830). Manzano's freedom was purchased with a collection raised by the Del Monte group between 1835 and July 1836. His correspondence with Del Monte of June 25 and September 29, 1835, suggests that the first part of the autobiography was completed in the course of the year preceding his freedom. A letter dated October 16, 1834, reveals Manzano's frustration and despair over his deferred liberation and the lack of control over his intellectual property. In the letter, reproduced by Franco, he confides to Del Monte: "If one day God willing I had a chance to speak with you: in private, your Grace would see: that I have not lost my mind perhaps because my time has not come yet, I have suffered greatly within" (Juan Francisco Manzano, *Obras: Juan Francisco Manzano*, 78).

30. Manzano already knew that Del Monte was sending his poetry to Europe; this is apparent in his letter dated December 11, 1834. He had no reason to believe that his autobiography would be any different, as happened eventually.

an obsessive and tyrannical mistress. Underlying the narrative of the unhappy enslaved speaker is the premise that there are "good" slaves—that among slaves, there are model individuals who, like himself, deserve a better lot in life (freedom). By implication, there is another category of slaves who do not.

In placing himself in the first category, Manzano stresses those virtues and values that are important to his presumed readership. We thus learn of the natural literary talents of his persona and his love of and devotion to letters. He exemplifies this by stressing that at the age of ten, he could already recite Fray Luis de Granada's sermons by heart, imitate passages from French operas for his mistress's guests, and knew "many lengthy passages, short plays and interludes, dramatic theory, and stage sets." When, under the Marchioness Del Prado's ownership, his creative impulse leads him to produce his own *décimas* poetry, and he gives rein to his penchant for performance in front of the other servants and the children of the house, we are told that he is forced to withstand punishment—blows, isolation, a gagging (49, 57). Beyond this early composition and memorization of his own poems, devotion to the literary vocation is further underscored by the fact that he eventually painstakingly teaches himself to write, persevering in this endeavor in the face of his master's injunctions to the contrary.

His talents are not limited to the literary, as is pointed out repeatedly. Just as the rich and powerful applaud his childish flair for the theatrical and his orality while he lived at the Marchioness of Santa Ana's home, they also encourage his potential as a portrait painter. As he grows older, he is congratulated and rewarded for his subsequent accomplishments as manservant, sick nurse, fishing companion, confectioner, and seamster of tunics, chemises, draperies, mattresses, trimmings, and so on. It turns out to be entirely consistent with the self-centering and self-promotional rhetoric of the autobiography that he should declare that he was a model slave at nineteen. At that time, he says, he was responsible and "took a certain pride in knowing how to fulfill my duties. I did not like to be told twice to do something or to be shamed for trivialities" (111). This assiduousness, he stresses, is what allowed him to ascend in the slave hierarchy. It also gained him the envy of other house slaves, even of those much older than he was.

To the extent that Manzano's narration foregrounds a deserving and multitalented self, the other black slaves, with the exception of his family, are anonymous. They are a part of the background; a plurality to which he refers with the generic marker of *negrada*. These slaves are generally identified only in association with a significant event, such as the accident in which Andrés, a black Creole, or *negro criollo*, dies (99), or when a stone thrown by a *moreno* accidentally wounds the protagonist (67). Their anonymity is hardly a rhetorical coincidence, however, since it is what allows his intelligence and his talent to stand out. Neither is it a coincidence that the speaker adheres closely to the colonial nomenclature of caste in describing them. He refers to himself as a *mulato* or a *chinito* or a *mulatico* (115), terms that all carry the association of "pedigree" and its implications for upward socio-racial mobility. His use of these terms is quite conscious. It allows us to appreciate a distinction between the speaker and the aforementioned subjects, especially the category referred to as *negros*—the ones occupying the lowest rung of the socio-racial ladder. Manzano's projection of a self that is *different* from the rest of the slave body comes into sharpest focus, perhaps, in these references.

As putative member of a group of writers whose racial ideology associated intellectuality or *razón* (reason) with whiteness, his own interests could be served in pointing to the distance between himself and the purported baseness of the *negros*. To the degree that his autobiography is a rhetorical construction designed to highlight his suffering to an imaginary white readership and garner sympathy from them, it could be confrontational and counterproductive to associate that readership with the source of the cruelties that he details. Primary agency in his degradation (and that of his delicate, "poetic" persona) is therefore often associated with the brutality of the black males incorporated in the system of oppression. Hence he reminds us of the regularity with which they were the ones who administered the beatings: "More than a few times I have suffered vigorous floggings at the hands of a black man" (59).

Later, on the occasion of another of his unjust punishments, his mother comes to his defense; when she is herself rebuffed and punished, attention is drawn to the four *negros* who manhandle her and hurl her to the ground prior to her whipping (73). After the capon incident, during which he was made, unjustly, to suffer a *novenario,* or nine-day whipping, for a chicken that had gone missing, his innocence and constantly evoked frailness make a sharp contrast with the cruelty of his punishment and his punishers. On that occasion, it is the overseer, his assistant, and "five black men" (97) who deliver the heartless thrashing. The role of the black men as victimizers is invoked in his relation of yet another incident of excessive punishment, when he remarks, "a black man was already waiting for me, I was handed over to him" (81). To the extent that the black men, together with the overseers and the Marchioness, are specified as the source of his misery, slavery as an institution recedes as the basic reason for his unhappy condition. Slavery's subjugation of a collective, of which the speaker is a part, is also attenuated in the process of the relation. Indeed, one might even speak of a rhetorical tactic of scapegoating of the whip-wielding *negros,* as the victim seeks a place to locate blame, while highlighting the wretchedness of his own condition.[31]

Following the binary structure of his story, the early years of his childhood, in which he was the object of affection and the center of attention in the home of an apparently doting Marchioness of Santa Ana, are evoked in glowing terms. He refers to them poetically as a "garden of very beautiful flowers, *a series of joys*" (51). However, his eventual transferal to the power of the tyrannical Marchioness of Del Prado, and to the rural plantation of El Molino, where he says "the true story of my life" began (57), does more than signal a radical change in fortune. Manzano's reference to the rupture that begins with Santa Ana's death as the period in which his "true story" begins also serves the metatextual function of enhancing the degree to which his destiny has changed. It functions as a rhetorical platform upon which to stress the regularity with which he is now beaten and imprisoned in the dark and forbidding coal shed (two to three times a week) (57), and the tears and nosebleeds that have become his daily lot (85).

The more scandalous of his cruel and unjust punishments include the infamous *peseta* incident, for which he is condemned to a nine-day period of fifty lashes daily (they are eventually not delivered) (73). They also include the incident of the crushed geranium, for which he is placed in the stocks and eventually sodomized,[32] and the incident of the misplaced capon, for which he is almost eaten alive by dogs and does receive the *novenario.* All contribute to the image of powerlessness and abjection in the speaker. If we can regard this autobiographical enunciation of the pathetic subject as a kind of "open letter" to a more or less unknown public, it is only in his private letters to his benefactor Del Monte that we find a comparable quality of pathos.

In this regard, Sylvia Molloy has characterized as "excessive" Manzano's expressions of gratitude to Del Monte as literary mentor. She highlights, as

31. In similar fashion, not wanting to name his real victimizers, he often places blame on himself and sees his punishment as a result of his lack of religious devotion (87).

32. Robert Ellis makes an entirely plausible argument regarding the rape that Manzano may have suffered at the hands of the sadistic don Saturnino and the veil he draws over such events in his relation. Ellis's reading of Manzano's uninhibited affection for his younger brother Florencio (in the poem "Un sueño") as an expression of "reciprocal homoeroticism" and "racial solidarity" (433), however, is not quite as persuasive. An expression of love and empathy for parents and siblings, as in Manzano's case, is hardly to be confused with an intention to vindicate all of the enslaved. See Robert Ellis, "Reading through the Veil of Juan Francisco Manzano: From Homoerotic Violence to the Dream of a Homoracial Bond."

do Roberto Friol and Edward Mullen, the personal and socio-racial chasm between them expressed in Manzano's likening of himself to a leaf exposed to the inclemency of nature that finally finds asylum under the "robust trunk" that is represented by Del Monte. Friol even speaks of Manzano's infantilization as he prostrates himself in his letters to Del Monte, as if the latter, a younger man, had become a surrogate father.[33]

Undoubtedly there is a mix of the "strategic" and the "temperamental" in Manzano's posture. But it is important to point out that Manzano's abjection is not total, and that the system may not have beaten the rebelliousness out of him, as Sylvia Molloy's rebuttal of Richard Jackson's argument suggests. There is more than enough evidence of a continuing rebellious strain beneath Manzano's meek exterior in his two escape attempts. It is also visible when he confronts the terrible Marchioness with his demand for a letter of *coartación,* and in the times when he drops the mask of submissiveness and pounces like a lion in defense of his mother's honor (73). Like the very act of learning to write, in defiance of orders to the contrary, his management of his persona in his autobiography offers evidence of a dogged sense of resistance. In this regard, it is significant that he consistently rationalizes or justifies his misdemeanors to his readers. If we juxtapose his hesitation and apprehension at the thought of writing his autobiography with his decision to write a fictional account that would tell all, once he achieved his freedom and felt safe enough to do so, the meekness of the persona in the autobiography becomes clearer. So does the writer's manipulation of his reader(s) through this persona. As Sonia Labrador-Rodríguez observes, the writing in Manzano's autobiography is neither spontaneous nor naive.[34]

If my analysis of Manzano's assumption and portrayal of a racial selfhood that sees the *negro* as Other is correct, it follows that he is not as ambivalent about his racial identity as some critics have been wont to assume. His avoidance of blackness in relating his story and his espousal of the cultural markers of whiteness point to a conscious constitution of self as a racial subject, one that is in strict accordance with the dictates of the dominant ideology of whitening. It is important to remember that the blood-purity ethic that evolved in tandem with national consolidation in Renaissance Spain produced a Manichean taxonomy of race that grew ever more complex in the

---

33. Sylvia Molloy, *At Face Value: Autobiographical Writing in Spanish America,* 39. See also Manzano's poem "A D. Domingo Del Monte," reproduced in Roberto Friol, *Suite para Juan Francisco Manzano,* 96–97, and his remarks regarding Del Monte, 57.

34. Molloy, *Face Value,* 40; Jackson, *Black Writers,* 29; Lorna Valerie Williams, *The Representation of Slavery in Cuban Fiction,* 27; Labrador-Rodríguez, "La intelectualidad negra," 15.

colonies in associating racial pedigree with social, political, and economic privilege.[35]

Regarding the ideological aspect of the race question, Louis Althusser's proposal that people work unconsciously or "by themselves," in the way they assume subjectivity in a given social order, may explain Manzano's sense of difference in relation to an unlettered collective of *negros*. The writer's insistence on his own specificity as *mulato* in the autobiography is quite conscious. Manzano, in other words, is clear about what he is not, racially speaking. His access to and use of the medium of writing, therefore, can hardly be seen as an abandonment of his "own," that is, "African" frame of reference, as William Luis suggests.[36] He could not abandon an ethnic identity that he had never assumed. His emphasis on his in-betweenness—what he "is" within the racial order—is what is important. This recognition may also be taken as an awareness of the relative fluidity of colonial racial barriers and as an indication of his intention to negotiate racial identity and racialized privilege vis-à-vis an overarching white subjectivity.

Key to his self-definition would be his emphasis on the elevated status of his parents as household slaves. His mother is a *criada de razón,* and his father is the *primer criado* of the house—she was endowed with "reason," and he was the "head servant." Ivan Schulman also indicates in a footnote that Manzano had underlined the reference to *razón* in his manuscript, in his reference to his mother, while Roberto Friol intimates that Manzano had clarified for Madden that his maternal grandparents were "mulatto" and "black." Manzano's concern for registering socio-racial value or distinction is further evident in the way he speaks of his second wife to Del Monte in his letter dated December 11, 1834. Delia is a "free brown, daughter of a white man, and pretty as a grain of gold from her feet to her head."[37] Also noteworthy in this regard is the fact that the Marchioness of Justiz Santa Ana claimed him as the "child of her old age" (47), often displacing his biological parents as a source of both parental affection and authority. He, in turn, recognized her in these terms calling her "my mama" (49), thereby closing the Althusserian circle of mutual intersubjectual recognition. As surrogate

35. See Molloy, *Face Value,* 45.

36. See Louis Althusser, "Ideology and Ideological State Apparatuses," 248. Postrevolutionary Cuban critic Roberto Friol takes care to remind us that Manzano was not a "pure black," stressing that he was recorded as a "pardo" (brown) in his publications, on his marriage licence, and in the official documents of the Escalera trial in which he became involved (*Suite,* 153). See also Luis, *Literary Bondage,* 65.

37. Schulman, in Manzano, *Autobiography,* 44; Friol, *Suite,* 49; Manzano, *Obras,* 82.

"son" of the Marchioness, he reminds us, he spent more time in her arms than in those of his own mother, and he would often throw a tantrum if he was brought back home from school too late for his daily visits with her. His father's attempts at disciplining such unruly behavior met with Santa Ana's disfavor, and it was the older man who required an intermediary to return to the Marchioness's favor.

The uncommon process of socialization and the formation of a socio-racial consciousness in Manzano the slave are further detailed in the facts that his godparents are white aristocrats and that he attends school and plays with the Marchioness's grandchildren. He also notes that he is forbidden to play with little black children by both his father and doña Joaquina, a member of the extended white family to which Manzano belonged. His juxtaposition of Joaquina's personal attention to his hair and dress, and her vigilance that he avoid contact with other *negritos* (little blacks), while she herself treated him "like a *niño*" (child) (55), further confirms a de facto treatment beyond his socio-racial condition as he describes it. One might recall here that *niño*, in plantation terminology, also referred specifically to white children of the planter class.

Although we cannot be sure if, by using the term *niño*, Manzano really meant to insinuate that he was treated as a "white" child by Joaquina, his sense of the availability of white privilege, and his insertion of self into that world of power, is clearly evident. His recurrent use of the metaphor of the family—that he "belongs to" or is "part of" a white family—is therefore revealing both in the sense of this strategic subjective identification with whiteness and as a skillful manipulation of the system of *padrinazgo,* or patronage, that characterized the patrician universe of the colonial plantation. As the text indicates, his appeals to influential intermediaries or *padrinos* (godfathers) are many, given the frequency with which he gets into trouble. Such occasions all too often derive from the contradictions inherent to his being a slave who is aware that social and racial privilege is negotiable and that the ideological imperatives concomitant to his identity as slave are subject to rupture.[38]

Bearing in mind Manzano's insight into the relation between power and racial definition, and his own assumed subject position in this regard, it comes as little surprise in the end that it is the renewed threat of being reduced to

38. Manzano's insight here might be related to Althusser's observation that "all ideology represents in its necessarily imaginary distortion not of the existing relations of production (and of the other relations that derive from them), but above all the (imaginary) relationship of individuals to the relations of production and the relations that derive from them." Althusser, "Ideology," 242.

the lowest common denominator of enslavement that fuels his resolve to escape. The final pages, which describe his punishment for taking an unauthorized bath, his accidental breakage of the water barrel, and his impending banishment to the El Molino plantation, illustrate this question. Having already been shorn and stripped of the outer vestiges of his privilege—shoes, clothing—it is the observation by a free servant that he was being treated worse than any *negro bozal* that deals the final blow to his dignity. Here it is pertinent to note not only the distinction that his putative benefactor is establishing between the generic black slave, or *negro,* and the *bozal,* the recently arrived captive who did not speak Spanish, Portuguese, or French and knew nothing about the dominant culture, but also the stigma that the latter designation bore among the slave community. The prospect of returning alone and unsupported among the field slaves, of being a mulatto among *negros* (131), along with the dangers posed by the sadistic overseer Don Saturnino, wreaked havoc on his vivid imagination.

If Manzano's negotiation of race serves to reveal the lack of fixity to the concept, then paradoxically it is his success in securing freedom that confirms racism's rigidity in structuring social power in the Latin American colonial context. As a theoretically free person or *liberto,* his vulnerability as a black male outside of the protection and patronage of the plantation "family" structure becomes tragically evident when he is accused of being involved in the alleged Escalera conspiracy of 1844. The months of imprisonment, torture, and interrogation between 1844 and 1845 must have impressed upon him that literary passing was not enough to place him beyond the clutches of a racialized system of oppression that saw every black person as a possible conspirator in the supposed uprising. I propose that this is a major factor in his silence after Escalera. Manzano may have read the code on race and written according to its dictates, but as Ivan Schulman, his most recent editor, observes, he failed to "grasp the limitations colonial society placed on members of his class and race." To the extent that his intellectual, ambitious, artistic, and culturally "assimilated" autobiographical persona represented a vehicle for ideological crossover, its success was therefore limited. His benefactor Domingo del Monte, writing from Paris, expressed dominant racial ideology most succinctly in 1845, when he dismissed both Manzano and Plácido, another *mestizo* poet, as *dos poetas negros* (two black poets).[39]

39. Schulman, in Manzano, *Autobiography,* 12. Ideology involves not only the "subjection to the Subject [by the subject]," but also the "mutual recognition of subjects and Subject," according to Althusser, "Ideology," 248. See also Del Monte, quoted in Friol, *Suite,* 226.

The analysis of Juan Francisco Manzano's autobiography affords us a unique example of the politics of race in a Latin American colonial setting. The place of the document in the Latin American scribal tradition is undoubtedly important. While writing may have been one of his tools for assimilation and upward socio-racial mobility, it is clear that, for Manzano, citizenship in the republic of letters required more than being a gifted creative writer or having friends in high places. It is perhaps ironic that more than two decades after he responded to the suggestion that he was a *mulatico fino* (cultured little mulatto) who had no place among *negros bozales,* this is precisely what his destiny was. The unified and unmitigated reaction of the colonial authorities to the supposed Escalera threat reduced him first to the status of *bozal* (in the sense of "he who does not signify"), and second to the status of *negro* (in the sense of "he who has no political significance"). Unlike thousands of slaves and black Cubans who lost their lives as a result of the Escalera persecution, Manzano did have a white lawyer (another *padrino*) to defend him.[40] His subsequent invisibility and silence as a writer after Escalera suggest, however, that what he now occupied was a zone of existential liminality in which he was neither slave nor free.

Sab: Sentimentalism and the Subaltern

If Del Monte and his circle of literati, through the circumstances surrounding the production and publication of Manzano's autobiography, are an important illustration of the anxieties associated with the question of the postslavery presence of blacks in the foundational discourse of the Cuban nation, Gertrudis Gómez de Avellaneda's *Sab* (1841) is no less significant. Unlike Manzano, who never had the opportunity to write the national novel that he dreamed of, or the freedom to do so, plagued as he was by the multiple insecurities attendant to his socio-racial condition, the two upper-class intellectuals Del Monte and Avellaneda were able to take advantage

---

40. One of the Peninsular Spanish meanings for *bozal* is "muzzle." The lawyer appointed to him was Julián María Infanzón. Manzano's letter dated October 5, 1844, written to Del Monte's mother-in-law, Doña Rosa Alfonso, from the prison at Belén, shows the harsh treatment he received as a political prisoner. Besides the hunger and material deprivation arising out of months of imprisonment, Manzano registers his anguish at his inability to find a godfather *(compadre)* for his baby daughter. His complaint raises the interesting question of whether his erstwhile associates of the Del Monte circle would have accepted this role had the immediate political situation been less volatile, especially since it would have meant recognizing him as a part of the paternal order, and free (Manzano, *Obras,* 91–96).

of a broader sense of extranational belonging. They migrated to Europe (France and Spain, respectively), while Manzano's (and other blacks') claim of a national home in Cuba would remain repressed and denied for the next several decades, as we shall see in Chapters 4 and 5. In contrast to the nonfictional realization of the power dynamic in the relationship between Del Monte and his protégé Manzano, however, Avellaneda's novel *Sab,* though fictional, is equally evocative of the binary of liberation and bondage. Written into its main story about Sab, a sensitive, literate, and noble individual, is also a subtext about the privileging of mulattoness and skin color, through the racialization of the moral, the intellectual, and the ethical. In other words, Sab's enslaved counterparts, to the extent that they are *negros,* are proportionally less endowed with these qualities on account of their racial identity. Avellaneda, one of the more important Cuban, and indeed Hispanic, nineteenth-century writers, thereby adds a noteworthy paragraph in the broader writing of the *negro* through her portrayals or misportrayals of black and biracial identity. Just as significant, historiographically speaking, is the novel's articulation of the gender/race complex in the Cuban colonial context of the nineteenth century.

In spite of what seemed obvious to a contemporary reading of Gertrudis Gómez de Avellaneda's first novel, there is a preponderance of critical evaluations today that, with greater or lesser adamancy, proclaim it to be a discourse of liberation. *Sab* as liberation discourse is thereby read as a pioneering abolitionist novel, an early demonstration of modern feminism in literature, and an exemplary articulation of Enlightenment vindication of human liberty and equality. The trend in liberationist critical readings of *Sab* may well be seen in terms of what Stuart Hall refers to as the process of the "fixing of the meaning" of visual images through the way in which the media represents events past and present. We may see Hall's highlighting of the determinative role of ideology and power in his discussion of the media as a signifying practice, as analogous to that of the interpretive function of literary criticism vis-à-vis its own texts or "raw material," and note, on this basis, its relevance to the process of canonization in literature.[41] The implications for

---

41. Stuart Hall, *Representation and the Media.* According to Nicomedes Pastor Díaz, writing in 1842, *Sab* "might have been more interesting if it had more verisimilitude" (quoted in Helena Parcas Ponseti, "Sobre la Avellaneda y su novela *Sab,*" 349). Spanish poet Alberto Lista, to whom Avellaneda dedicated the novel, in a letter to the author in 1842, saw the story's "chief merit" in the drama of unrequited love (quoted in Williams, *Representation of Slavery,* 89). For Stacy Schlau, the novel is "clearly and irrevocably abolitionist" ("Stranger in a Strange Land: The Discourse of Alienation in Avellaneda's *Sab,*" 495); and for Mary Cruz, it is a "flaming denunciation"

power in knowledge production, as we consider such matters as abolition or racial identity, are no less relevant, whether looked at from the standpoint of creative writing and representation or through the assumptions of literary critics. In this section, I reexamine the abolitionist-feminist premise that is imputed to Avellaneda's novel and that underlies current tendencies toward its extolment. I draw attention to the power and gender relations in the text, positing that, as a function of the racialized social relations of a Caribbean slave colony—Cuba—these relations have not been sufficiently accounted for in previous readings and are critical to a reconsideration of the novel.

As suggested in the discussion on Cuba and Juan Francisco Manzano, the abolition of slavery in former New World colonies is undoubtedly an important, if contested, topic, in not only national but also hemispheric historiographies. Notwithstanding the marginalization of black historical agency in dominant antislavery discourse, and the fact that there were important economic and political considerations motivating governments to end the slave trade and slavery itself, there is little gainsaying the moral and political capital accruing to protagonists of abolition like Granville Sharp, Thomas Clarkson, or William Wilberforce. The same may be said of the dozens of Quaker antislavery societies in England and the United States, and of the French Societé des amis des Noirs. Clarkson's courageous exposé of the appalling conditions within slave ships at Bristol and Liverpool and Wilberforce's leadership in the British parliament at the turn of the century were instrumental in ending the British slave trade in 1807. For their part, the role of the Ladies Anti-Slavery Society, whose members were "the leading figures in the social protests against the slave trade between 1788 and 1792," has also been documented; the political work of the organization included boycotting slave-grown produce and promoting a reduction of materialistic consumption. By 1838, there were forty-one such auxiliary societies in Massachusetts alone.[42]

Women's antislavery work in the United States included energetic fundraising through the sale of handicrafts that were didactic in design and in-

---

of slavery ("*Sab,* su texto y su contexto," 119). Regarding abolitionism and feminism, see Edith L. Kelly, "La Avellaneda's *Sab* and the Political Situation in Cuba"; Nara Araujo, "Raza y género en *Sab*"; Susan Kirkpatrick, "Gómez de Avallaneda's *Sab:* Gendering the Liberal Romantic Subject"; Elio Alba Bufill's "La Avellaneda y la literatura antiesclavista"; and Beth Miller, "Avellaneda, Nineteenth Century Feminist."

42. Anne K. Mellor, "'Am I Not a Woman and a Sister?' Slavery, Romanticism, and Gender," 315. See also Karen Sánchez-Eppler, "Bodily Bonds: The Intersecting Rhetorics of Feminism and Abolition," 34.

tent, propaganda campaigns that produced "hundreds of images dramatizing the violence related to the institution of slavery," as well as public lectures and conferences. There is, as well, an important connection between Quaker-inspired women's abolitionist work, described above, and the nineteenth-century beginnings of feminism.[43] Although the antislavery contributions of the more notable proponents of abolition have over time been subsumed under the broader (national) discourses of Enlightenment celebration of liberty, it should be noted that Quaker abolitionist philanthropy, and its insistence that slavery violated the inalienable rights of humankind, emerges by itself as an important transracial stance against the dominant order. It was a telling indictment of the betrayal of Christian morality that the planter classes and the slaveholding nations purported to espouse.

Regarding Latin American literature, it is hardly surprising in this light to find, to the extent that a Cuban literary abolitionist canon might be constructed, for example, that it would be construed around concepts of moral and political correctness. It is the idea of "moral progress," for example, that frames William Luis's discussion of the Cuban antislavery novel, as he proposes a "genealogy" of Cuban antislavery writing that extends through the nineteenth century to include the twentieth century as well. The members of the Del Monte group, as we have seen, were often portrayed as enlightened individuals and as beacons of change in an oppressive and racist society. Avellaneda is frequently included in this abolitionist grouping, even if only by association, since she was not a member of the Del Monte's *tertulia*. Her abolitionist credentials, in the wider hemispheric context, are taken for granted, however, in the repeated reference to *Sab* as having preceded Harriet Beecher Stowe's *Uncle Tom's Cabin* (1851–1852) by ten years.[44] In the local

43. Jean Fagan Yellin, "Women and Sisters: The Antislavery Feminists in American Culture," 5. Sánchez-Eppler points out that according to legend "the idea of a women's rights convention—not realized until 1848—was first discussed in the London hotel rooms" of the women excluded at the World's Anti-Slavery Convention in 1840 ("Bodily Bonds," 52).

44. In an epigraph, Luis quotes "antislavery" writer Antonio Zambrana: "art has the privilege of warming souls, of taking them out of their apathetic coldness, because only it, and not cold reason, can usually provoke noble anger, fervent enthusiasm, effective compassion, inflexible and intransigent antipathy, necessary levers for the work of moral progress" (Luis, "La novela anti-esclavista," 103). See also William Luis, "The Antislavery Novel and the Concept of Modernity." Avellaneda, along with her family, left Cuba for Spain in 1836, where she completed *Sab*. It is likely that she was in contact with Del Monte or with members of his group, since she is recorded as having sought and gotten endorsement for the artistic merit of the book from a Cuban gentleman familiar with the genre. Kelly, in "La Avellaneda's *Sab*," speculated that this gentleman might be José Antonio Saco, Del Monte himself, or Salustiano de Olózaga (306). See also Cruz, "*Sab*, su texto," 43, regarding the comparison with *Uncle Tom's Cabin*.

context, it is her feminist convictions that serve to locate her in the vanguard of the mostly male Cuban writing on slavery.

To the extent that the latter portrayals constitute further attempts, on behalf of Cuba's "abolitionist" writers, to procure for them the prestige of the "counterdiscursive" in relation to a dominant ethic of race and class oppression (slavery), it is important to reiterate that neither as citizens nor as writers were they free of contradictions. As pointed out, notwithstanding his liberal leanings, for Del Monte, the unfortunate Africans who happened to be enslaved had no place in a future Cuban republic. Their immediate release from slavery (abolition), as abominable as the institution might be in moral terms, would have meant economic ruin for his family and the members of the planter class, as he asserted in 1845. Not unlike the French revolutionary assemblies that had declared the Rights of Man but then rejected, in 1789, the petitions from their West Indian delegates "of color" for full citizenship, abolitionism in practice differed greatly from the idealism of humanistic theory. Again, like Napoleon's decision to reinstate slavery in 1802 in order to restore the productivity of rich Caribbean colonies, for those who benefited from the institution, it was the economic factor that mattered most in the final analysis.[45]

David Haberly observed that the major abolitionist works in Brazilian literature could easily fit on a "single bookshelf" compared with the "thousands of novels and poems assailing the slave trade and slavery itself" that were produced by intellectuals in Europe and the United States. His assertion opens an important window on Cuban literary abolitionism, whose sparseness in production is just as noteworthy. Notwithstanding the fact that the publishing industry in Latin America in the nineteenth century was less developed than that of the United States or Europe, the observation is significant both in terms of the push for prestige for its abolitionist writers (referred to above), and in terms of the broader issue of the mythification of race relations in the Americas. The paradox that Haberly notices in Brazil-

45. In 1845, in a letter to Captain General O'Donnell, Del Monte defended himself vigorously against charges that he had been involved in the Escalera plot to free slaves in Cuba and had been a coconspirator with mulatto poet Plácido de la Concepción Valdés: "I hold slavery to be an evil in my country... but I have never even remotely entertained ideas of violent upheavals which would put an end to my fortune and to that of my family; neither have I had dealings or intimate communications with lower-class people, not with him, nor with other subversive subjects" (quoted in Ileana Rodríguez, "Romanticismo literario y liberalismo reformista: El grupo de Domingo Delmonte," 52). See also Salvador Bueno, prologue to *Acerca de Plácido,* 9; and Murray, *Odious Commerce.*

ian abolitionist literature, of its being simultaneously "anti-slavery and anti-slave," may well apply to the Cuban case. Richard Jackson likewise detects an "actual aversion to the black man" in the latter body of antislavery works.[46] It is such contradictions in the writing (and reading) of Avellaneda's *Sab* that are most striking in relation to the intersection of race, gender, and power in the Caribbean colonial context.

In many critical discussions of the novel, despite an apparent anxiety to vindicate *Sab* as either abolitionist or feminist, abolition as "putting an end to slavery" is almost never defined. Neither is it explained how Sab, the protagonist, an individual sworn to slavery, becomes a universal symbol of freedom. Similarly, feminist readings of the novel demonstrate a remarkable blind spot for the black women lurking in the shadows of the narrative. It is also interesting to find that many of the anomalies of plot and narration in the story find easy explanation by way of the excessive sentimentalism of the Romantic paradigm.

Celebration of *Sab* as an abolitionist-feminist text has centered around its ideological position, which critiques the dominant patriarchal order from the standpoint of the rigidity of its property laws and the permanence of the bond(age) of marriage. The limitations placed therein on the freedom and personhood of the wife are equated to a similar loss of integrity suffered by the slave. This is the story that is told of Carlota Otway, the white wife who is sadly deceived by an opportunistic husband (Enrique), and of Sab, her black slave. That it is also the story of the impossible love that the male slave holds for his mistress has prompted the observation that the novel is a feminist reversal of the Romantic paradigm. Here, in addition to the fact that it is the male who dies brokenhearted, the females are depicted as the subjects rather than the objects of desire. In similar fashion, Avellaneda's characterization of the white husband/rival, by self-interest and opportunism, and her imbuing the black slave with noble traits, has prompted the claim that she has ruptured traditional canons of racial coding, thereby becoming a traitor to her race and class.[47] Additionally, the noble slave's outbursts

---

46. David Haberly, "Abolitionism in Brazil: Anti-Slavery and Anti-Slave"; Jackson, *Black Image,* 22.

47. See, for example, Pedro Barreda Tomás, "Abolicionismo y feminismo en la Avellaneda: Lo negro como artificio narrativo en *Sab.*" For the wife/slave analogy, see Schlau, "Stranger in a Strange Land," 495. Regarding Romantic inversions, see Kirkpatrick, "Gómez de Avellaneda's *Sab,*" 120; Sharon Romeo Fivel-Démoret, "The Production and Consumption of Propaganda Literature: The Cuban Anti-Slavery Novel," 8; and Doris Sommer, "Sab c'est moi," 116.

against oppression, taken as the primary reason for its banning by Cuban authorities in 1844, are seen as final proof of the book's subversive abolitionist nature.

Notwithstanding *Sab*'s claim to fame based on its early publication as a woman's abolitionist novel, and Avellaneda's protest against injustice by way of the wife-slave parallel, it bears pointing out, as with the celebrated liberation of Manzano by the Del Monte circle, that *Sab* was neither unique nor unprecedented in either regard. On the one hand, a similar claim for "abolitionism" may be made for the first novel by a woman, Aphra Behn's *Oroonoko* (1695), while many have considered Lydia Maria Child's short story "The St. Domingo Orphan" (1830) the initiator of the genre in the United States. On the other hand, it is a fact that the slave-wife analogy had been an integral part of women's abolitionist discourse since the early 1800s. It was British writer Mary Wollstonecraft, who, in 1792, in her *Vindication of the Rights of Woman,* first described wifely dependence as "slavish." Women abolitionists' metaphorically equating (European) wifely subordination with that of slaves allowed their public to more readily empathize with the plight of the unfree.[48] It became a rhetorical point of reference for the abolitionist cause both in Britain and the United States. In the women's movement, the image of laboring black women slaves helped undermine patriarchal discourse that would exclude the female sex on the traditional grounds of their supposedly "delicate" constitution.

For the purposes of this discussion, what is most important in this discourse is that although it was not without its contradictions, the metropolitan women's abolitionist movement saw and foregrounded black slave women. Their stories "condemned slavery because it violated the domestic affections, separating mothers from their children, husbands from their wives, subjecting black women to sexual abuse from their white masters."[49]

48. Regarding *Oroonoko,* see Firdous Azim, *The Colonial Rise of the Novel;* on Lydia Maria Child, see Sánchez-Eppler, "Bodily Bonds," 54. Sánchez-Eppler points to some of the exaggerations that were produced by the easy equivalence between chattel slaves and bourgeois wives, when even the length of fashionable skirts for the latter became an "antislavery" rallying point (ibid., 31). The hierarchy between these two subaltern groups is most clearly borne out in the women's version of the Wedgewood abolitionist medallion. Its caption, "Am I not a Woman and a Sister?" was accompanied by a figure of a black woman and a white woman. It is the agency of the latter that is stressed, however, for she is the one who stands and speaks the liberating words; the black woman kneels before her. See Mellor, "Am I Not a Woman?" 319.

49. Harriet Beecher Stowe exemplifies one such contradiction in her 1863 article "Sojourner Truth: The Libyan Sybil," in which her nativization of Truth is as condescending as it is obvious. Nell Irvin Painter raises the point of race and class rivalry by indicating that Stowe's article incorrectly stated that Truth was dead (she died in 1883) and described her as "African" (Libya was

In light of this visibility, the suppression of the Sabbian mother is remarkable. In Avellaneda's story, no text of sisterhood or sympathy emerges to vindicate the enslaved black women in their hapless condition. In a purportedly feminist-abolitionist story, this absence, in relation to the group that best qualifies for attention on account of their double exploitation, cannot be without significance.

Avellaneda's avoidance of the Sabbian mother may well lie in the class and race differential that explodes the (uneven) slave-wife analogy. That the laboring black women around her may be invisible to her elitist eyes is suggested in her own abhorrence of domestic chores. Her often-quoted autobiographical comment in Spain, which is used to highlight her love of letters and to garner sympathy in the face of relatives who scoffed at her inability to cook and clean, also clearly exposes the fact that, for herself, as for any young lady of her class, such housework was considered degrading.[50] Evidently it was fit only for the poor and the black women slaves.

Class, as well as racial distinction, may again explain the lack of sisterly solidarity for a subject whose interaction with the dominant white males within the colonial sexual economy was more likely to be the result of rape than romance. It is significant that in the description of Sab's origins, it is his black mother's "deep and powerful passion" that is foregrounded and not that of his father, who is represented as "good and pious."[51] Notwithstanding the presumed purity of this romanticized encounter between the parents, we are told that the mother maintains a chilling silence to her son as to the identity of his father.

It has been argued that it is the symbolic potential of black women, and not the perceived threat of black males, that presents the greater menace to the dominant white patriarchal order in its need for "perfect self-replication."

---

synonymous with Africa) when she was in fact born in New York State. See Painter, "Representing Truth: Sojourner Truth's Knowing and Becoming Known," 477. See also Mellor, "Am I Not a Woman?" 315; and Sánchez-Eppler, "Bodily Bonds," 54.

50. According to Avellaneda: "The upbringing that young ladies are given in Cuba is so different from what they are given in Galicia that a woman, *even one from the middle class, would think that she had degraded herself* in my country by doing things that the most aristocratic women in Galicia regard as an obligation of their sex. My stepfather's female relatives said, therefore, that I was good for nothing, because I could not iron, nor cook, nor knit; because I did not wash glasses, nor made beds, nor swept my room. According to them, I needed twenty servants and I put on the airs of a princess. They ridiculed my liking to study and they called me the bluestocking." Quoted in Williams, *Representation of Slavery,* 87 (emphasis mine).

51. Gertrudis Gómez de Avellaneda, *Sab and Autobiography,* 31. Unless otherwise noted, I shall be citing from this edition, translated by Nina M. Scott.

Addressing racism and miscegenation in the English literary tradition, Lynda Boose observes, "in the untold story about the son produced by a 'faire Englishman' and an 'Ethiopian woman as blacke as cole' lurks the impetus for a patriarchal culture's profound anxieties about gender to spill over into a virulent system of racial anathema. While such anathema would eventually apply to everyone thus stigmatized, the locus of the transfer would not be the black male but the black female, whose signifying capacity as a mother threatens nothing less than the wholesale negation of white patriarchal authority."[52] Sab's mother as an "unrepresentable" black woman would seem to respond to this capacity for subversion. Further, her suppression in the text may also be due to Romanticism's requirement to extol beauty in women, especially women of royal blood. When Sab is made to comment on the appearance of his mother, an African princess, his assertion of her beauty is undermined by the accompanying qualifier referring to her color: "In spite of her color, my mother was beautiful" (31). Avellaneda's failed attempt at paradox, which one might paraphrase by saying: "Although black, she was beautiful," betrays her complicity with an ethnocentric value system that could not see beauty in blackness.

If, in her depiction of the hero's black mother, Avellaneda was reluctant to break with tradition, her allegiance to the dominant order is made more evident in the way she represents race in depicting Sab himself. With both his mother and his father conveniently removed from the narrative at a very early stage, Sab is (re)made in the idealized cultural image of the latter, described early in the text as an "excellent young man" (31). Sab is well-spoken, artistic, loves reading, and is given to lofty philosophizing on liberty and equality. Culturally, he is as faithful to the paternal model as is possible. The way Avellaneda writes his body is just as revealing.[53] In his first meeting with Sab, Enrique Otway, a total stranger, "reads" Sab's body—his phenotype, his manner of speech, his dress—in strict accordance with the way it is coded by its creator. As a slave, Sab is atypical. His body is not written in scars and stripes. As we have seen, there is more than a figurative sense to the idea of a "written" slave body, since physical markings or abbreviations of words served to identify them both in Europe and the New World. Born a mulatto, the unmarked and well-clothed Sab is dressed in the fashion typ-

52. Lynda Boose, "'The Getting of a Lawful Race': Racial Discourse in Early Modern England and the Unrepresentable Black Woman," 46.

53. Here I am using Hall's idea of the racialized body as text, and the idea that we are "readers of race" (*Race, the Floating Signifier*).

ical of the white peasants. Indeed, Enrique's first impression is that he might be either peasant or proprietor.

The reluctance of the narrative to fully incorporate the Africanness of the protagonist is evident in the tentative language and the negative markers that accompany his introduction to the reader and to Otway. He is described as not being white *or* black *or* Amerindian, but as a unique mixture, without being a "perfect mulatto" (28). Here Avellaneda's ambivalence in relation to a somatic norm with which she was familiar is seen in her hesitancy about labeling him. Any product of the parents described here would be a "perfect mulatto," but by marking him as racially "unique," while insisting on his "yellowish-white" complexion, his "shiny hair," and "aquiline nose," the text suggests that his creator is invoking artistic license in his reproduction. That Sab, an individual accustomed to a life in the outdoors in the tropics, can still be (mis)taken for a white landowner (30), speaks to the cosmetic process to which he has been subjected.

In denying Sab a body, which as a Caribbean woman she knows would correspond to what she calls a perfect mulatto (in the tropics), Avellaneda has again repressed the generative and symbolic power of the black woman. The genetic anomaly that the text presents seems plausible only after generations of miscegenation, and not as a result of the union of an indigenous black African mother and a white European father. The hero's raven-like hair is the clearest evidence of his creator's foray into the unempirical.[54] The repeated attempts in the text to set him apart from the "degradation and coarseness which is the norm in people of his sort" (44), and his references in the third person to the other slaves as *negros*,[55] are symptomatic of his and the text's desire to underscore his racial difference. The extent to which this difference is associated with the character's "nobility" reveals the subtext of racial hierarchy to which the narrative subscribes.

Nicomedes Pastor Díaz's observation, cited at the beginning of this section, in which he also describes *Sab* as "an American novel, like its author," is

54. Orlando Patterson downplays the importance of color differences in multiracial New World societies. However, he underscores the "symbolic potency" of differences in hair (*Slavery*, 61). *Sab* has often been seen as a palimpsest of Aphra Behn's *Oroonoko* (1695), by way of Victor Hugo's *Bug-Jargal* (1826). Oroonoko, an indigenous Black African, is also presented "cosmetically," with shoulder-length hair. Similarly made-up are his nose and mouth, which are unlike "the rest of the Negroes," 12.

55. Gertrudis Gómez de Avellaneda, *Sab* (1976 edition), 128. The nuance between *negro* as "slave" and *negro* as "black" is lost in translation. In other words, Sab, like Manzano, is a slave, but he is not a *negro*.

correct. Her depiction of race in her characters conforms unerringly to colonial hypersensitivity to color and to contemporary racialist schema. Accordingly, Enrique's "northern" origin automatically accounts for his blond, blue-eyed beauty and his classic Greek profile (27, 60). Like Sab, racial belonging for the Amerindian woman Martina is also denied: "[Her] skin color, moreover, was all that supported her pretensions of being Indian, for none of her facial features appeared to match her alleged origin" (78). Caught in the limbo between the racially superior colonizer and the racially inferior colonized, Avellaneda's Creole speaker, a "local white" *(blanco de la tierra),* becomes prey, like Carlota and the writer herself, to the angst that eventually breeds exile.[56]

As indicated above, the banning of *Sab* in 1844 has also been read as after-the-fact evidence of Avellaneda's subversiveness. The first of seven letters composing the censor's file on *Sab* and *Dos mujeres* delineates the following reasons for the banning of the two novels: "[B]ecause the first one contains doctrines Subversive to the System of slavery on this Island, and contrary to morality and good custom; and the Second one is plagued by immoral doctrines."[57] Many abolitionist readings of *Sab* have stressed the importance of the censor's reference to slavery at the expense of his equally concrete reference to "immoral doctrines" in these books. But here it is important to emphasize that the immorality imputed to *Sab* is also imputed to *Dos mujeres.* In the case of the latter, Hilario de Cisneros Saco, the censor, is more explicit in accusing the novel of attacking the permanence of matrimony and of promoting adultery.[58] Both cases, however, represent an act of repression, on the part of the patriarchal order, of the female writer's freedom of expression regarding sexuality.

In the New World colonial situation, what is even more important in terms of power and gender politics is the fact that it is the black male slave who is the object of speculation and desire by the two white women of the

56. Actually, a *blanco de la tierra,* according to Hispano-Caribbean colonial classification, is a (sardonic) reference to someone whose black African ancestry is barely perceptible. I am using the term here in its literal sense. It is pertinent to observe, however, that Fanon, in *Black Skin,* while discussing race and the colonized mentality, focuses mainly on the black colonized, the white colonized are also evidently not free from colonialism's effects. The impulse to move away from the colonized space often coexists with a longing for the metropolitan "mecca."

57. Quoted in Edith L. Kelly, "The Banning of *Sab* in Cuba: Documents from the Archivo Nacional de Cuba," 350.

58. The August letter reads: "[T]he Second one, because it is infested by doctrines that are prejudicial to Our Holy Religion and attacked conjugal Society and canonized adultery." Quoted in ibid., 350.

planter class. If this by itself is a slap in the face of the sexual hegemony of the white male slave owners, the fact that the women in question, Carlota and Teresa, have more or less clear blood ties to the hero, only deepens the potentially reprehensible nature of this desire. This invocation of the incest motif, added to the book's endorsement of the forbidden model of interracial desire, could only provoke the worst reaction from the colonial authorities. Embedded in *Sab* is a story that must have reminded them of one of slavery's shameful secrets, that of the rape of black slave women, and of the dismissal of the ensuing offspring by their white slave-owning fathers. The fact that the subtext of *Sab* seemed to take such a situation to its horrifying logical conclusion—intercourse between the denied illegitimate son and a (legitimate) female member of the family—could only seem apocalyptic.

Since Sab, by his own admission, was not going to lead a slave rebellion, and Avellaneda's white female readership in Cuba would be an unlikely constituency for armed insurgency, antislavery elements in the story pale in comparison to its hints at a transracial sexual transgression that could indeed shake the patriarchal order to its foundations. Regardless of the often-invoked fear among the planter class of a Haitian-style revolt among the slaves, slave unrest or the threat of revolt were constants that were dealt with swiftly and decisively. Official reaction to the alleged Escalera conspiracy in 1844 is ample evidence of this. The image of a (black) slave, however, as an object of desire for white women who read for entertainment what Avellaneda herself wrote as a pastime, was an enemy of a different nature. Banning the book could achieve an objective that material violence could not. Similar sanctions applied to U.S. writer Lydia Maria Child in her challenge to white male sexual hegemony bear this point out in no uncertain terms.[59]

The misapprehension, evident in some critical readings of the novel, of the importance of transracial sexual politics in *Sab* may be traced, in part, to

---

59. Cuban historian José Luciano Franco makes the Escalera plot the brainchild of the recently arrived Captain General O'Donnell and the slave-trafficking oligarchy. The ensuing purge was aimed at the white liberal anticolonial faction and the free, incipient middle class of color. It was also designed to send an unequivocal message to the slave population after a spate of uprisings in 1842 and 1843, and to stifle British abolitionist interests in and out of Cuba. The result was seven thousand whipped to death, seventy-eight executions, and deportation and exile for hundreds of black and white Cubans.

Avellaneda stated in the introduction to *Sab* that the work was written as a distraction from moments of "leisure and melancholy," 26. Child's abolitionist tract *An Appeal in Favor of that Class of Americans Called Africans* (1836), in which she critiqued the "freedom [of the white male] to choose his sexual partners," resulted in her expulsion from Boston's literary society and the cancellation by "horrified parents" of subscriptions to her abolitionist series, the *Juvenile Miscellany*. See Sánchez-Eppler, "Bodily Bonds," 43.

the sentimentalist paradigm in which the book was written. It is the sentimentalist motif that is at work in the telling of a story in which the hero,
son of a fallen princess and a fine young colonial gentleman, is orphaned at
a tender age and is taken in and cared for and educated by a good and
benevolent family. That the hero is a disenfranchised slave who cannot as-
pire to the hand of the woman he loves because of prevailing race and class
prejudices, and is further driven to martyrdom as a result of his plight, is
also appropriate to the sentimentalist paradigm. What is occluded by the
Romantic framework in which the story is told, however, is the fact that
Sab, the poor slave, is also a slave driver *(mayoral),* that is, an integral part of
the structure of oppression, who consciously disassociates himself from the
racial group whose suffering he would appropriate to give voice to his own
misfortune. Also covered over by the sentimentalist rug is his deification of
the slave mistress, under the guise of the motif of impossible love.

Avellaneda's use of the trope of mysticism to illustrate Sab's adoration of
Carlota is revealing. In Sab's relating to Teresa of the events of the night on
which he witnesses Carlota raise her head to heaven in prayer, his and the
narrative's customary reference to her as an "angel" are taken beyond the level
of Romantic metaphor. In a suggestive juxtaposition of their bodies, hers on
the inside of the house, and his on the outside at ground level, both individuals offer their souls to heaven in sequence. The replication of earthly and
heavenly hierarchies is inescapable as the text describes her union with God in
the style of the Spanish mystics, and then his union with God. In the midst
of his mystical ecstasy, however, the figures of God and Carlota become
confused in the slave's mind: "A confused feeling of vague, indefinite, celestial
happiness filled my soul, lifting it to a sublime ecstasy of divine and human
love, to an indescribable ecstasy in which God and Carlota fused in my
soul" (102).

To the extent that sexual contact between the white female and the black
male in the social context of *Sab* is taboo—Sab's tryst with Teresa has to be
celebrated under cover of darkness, and her suggestion that they elope is only
conceivable in "remote climes" (108)—Carlota's sublimated union with the
protagonist would seem to be an instance of the female version of white sexual hegemony in New World slave culture. While the "predatory sexuality of
white men" made the bodies of black female slaves available to them, prevailing sexual mores militated against a similar expression of sexual power by their
female counterparts. In this case, it is expressed by way of the imaginary.[60]

---

60. Barbara Bush, *Slave Women in Caribbean Society, 1650–1838,* 107.

Sab's subjection to what Lorna Williams has called the "gentle tyranny" of his mistress, however, is undeniable. Disregarding declarations of his freedom by his owners, he swears to remain Carlota's slave forever. In voluntarily giving up the lottery that he wins in order to secure her a dowry, while he himself dies a virgin, he confirms the lack of free will that defines the model slave. His self-abnegation also confirms the slaveholder's dream of absolute power. Further, his perversion of the reality of the other slaves, in affirming that they have greater access to liberty than the married white women of the planter class (144), only serves to demonstrate the extent of his (idealized) subjection.[61] Avellaneda's Romantic tale about life in her native Cuba portrays slavery as a place where an African princess can meet and fall in love with the archetypal prince, in this case, a white aristocrat of the planter class. That the representatives of this class are depicted as humane, benevolent, and enlightened individuals, while the slaves themselves are represented as docile and even happy in their condition, raises the question of whether *Sab* was not in effect ennobling a particularly savage system of human exploitation.

The narrative's portrayal of the black slaves as subhuman and somehow incapable of sociopolitical consciousness is more a reflection of the racist ideology underlying the system than of the historical record. In their conversation, Sab earnestly assures Teresa, "you are not threatened by any danger. The slaves patiently drag their chains: in order to break them they might need to hear one voice which cries out to them 'You are men,' but I assure you that voice will not be mine" (97). On the one hand, his declaration is as much a denial of the reality of slave rebelliousness as it is of their capacity for such. On the other, the text's glorification, through him, of an affective component to a master-slave relationship defined essentially by force, can only respond to what Pierre Bourdieu and Jean-Claude Passeron

61. Williams, *Representation of Slavery*, 95. When Enrique suffers an accident while riding through a storm, Sab is tempted to dispose of his rival under cover of darkness, but he is arrested by the memory of his obligation to Carlota. Here the cold power of master-slave subjection takes on an interestingly "magical" form as Carlota's will is expressed by the narrative through a "mysterious spell" and an "invisible spirit" (51). Some of the elements pertinent to the asymmetrical slave-wife analogy have to do with, first, the objectivation of the slave as an article of sale; second, the brutality of a system that could reduce the life expectancy of a healthy enslaved person to five to seven years after purchase; third, the fact that the legal possibility of manumission was by no means available to all slaves in Cuba (or in Latin America for that matter); and fourth, Sab, the supposed spokesperson for slaves, had never personally experienced the degradation and brutality of forced labor. When Carlota complains about the constraints of matrimony, it is as a result of her discovery that Otway is ignoble and materialistic, and that he is manipulating her inheritance (which is the product of slave labor).

call the symbolic violence that occurs when a text "generates the illusion that it is not violence."[62]

It is pertinent to stress that, notwithstanding the "liberationist" emphasis that has united some liberal, feminist, and socialist readings of *Sab,* the only freedom that the protagonist is allowed is in death. A parallel may be drawn between Carlota's sentimental proclamation that when she gets married to Otway she will free her slaves, and the equally good intentions of the slave-owning members of the Del Monte group, none of whom freed the slaves on their plantations. Sab's martyrdom falls into a pattern for Cuban anti-slavery novels like *Francisco* and *El negro Francisco.* While the death of these protagonists in love may be explained by Romantic determinism, it may also respond to the ideological need, on the part of their creators, to project docile (and expendable) black male and female slaves, as Jackson suggests. Sab's immolation may appear to mimic the observed behavior of enslaved Africans on New World plantations, but there is a difference in objective that is crucial.[63]

Slave suicide was a response to the trauma of deracination, exile, degradation, and overwork. The concept of transmigration of the soul—that in death the subjects' souls would be projected back to Africa—held a profound individual and collective spiritual and psychological value that was endorsed by many. Fredrika Bremer's 1853 travelogue documented the group suicide of eleven enslaved Lucumí in Cuba and the endorsement of their comrades: "Many female slaves, therefore, will lay upon the corpse of the self-murdered the kerchief, or the head-gear, which she most admires, in the belief that it will thus be conveyed to those who are dear to her in the mother-country, and will bear to them a salutation from her. The corpse of a suicide-slave has been seen covered with *hundreds* of such tokens."[64]

Sab, the product of the slave-owning imagination, whose most significant bond of affection was to his mistress, died very much alone. His aloneness highlights two points. The first is that, in this purportedly liberationist discourse, it is not the plight of the slave collective that is emphasized, but that of a romanticized and privileged individual whose story, sad though it may be, overshadows that of the mass of slaves in a way that parallels the sense of superior selfhood that the protagonist projects in relation to the ordinary

---

62. Pierre Bourdieu and Jean-Claude Passeron, *Reproduction: In Education, Society, and Culture,* 17.

63. Jackson, *Black Writers,* 25–35. See also Luis, "La novela antiesclavista," 111.

64. Frederika Bremer, "The Homes of the New World: Impressions of America," 116–17 (emphasis mine).

negros of the plantation. The result is that the necessarily oppositional posi-
tioning of the abolitionist narrative, vis-à-vis the locations of power in the
slave colony, are severely compromised in *Sab.* This silencing of the subaltern group (of which I have chosen to highlight the mother) is to be
underscored, since the protagonist (Sab) is too often seen by critics to be
representative of the wider slave body; a misreading, one might add, trig-
gered by the very attenuation of antagonism in the narrative.

The second point that his aloneness highlights is that the life and death
of the slave who was not a *slave,* bears inevitably on his biracial genesis and
the way this functions in terms of the Latin American colonial dynamic of
race and class. It is the colonial imperative of racial and cultural assimila-
tionism or whitening that produces his despairing cry at the end that "there
is no love or wife for me either" (107). That Sab never considers black or
mulatto women as possible mates, and that he acknowledges his inability to
break the taboo governing sexual union with white women (he tells Teresa
"I am unworthy of you" (108), combine to make extinction seem the only
option for this racially hybrid male. Hybridity then, under the assimilationist impulse, seems to create the double bind of alienation from a wider
black collective, even as it precludes progeniture.

Sab's dismissal from the symbolic order as a father and as a biracial ethnic
subject creates a cruel counterpoint to the too-often real banishment suffered by *mulato* subjects in the social order. Although the smothering of the
African mother enhances the transcendence of the white patriarchal order
through the slave son in this fiction, in the real world that the slaveholders
made, in interracial unions it was all too often the white slaveholding fathers
who dismissed their paternity in order to keep their offspring subject to the
social identity of slave. The dismissal of Sab as a possible progenitor in the
symbolic order mirrors the liminality of the mulatto son in the social order,
as it reflects his banishment from a possible black ethnic identity.

Perfect Brazilian, Perfect Slave: Isaura

Inspired by the idealism and reputation of European Romantics George
Byron and Victor Hugo, and more particularly by the slave protagonist
Bug-Jargal of the latter, Félix Tanco y Bosmeniel in 1836 declared to the
other members of the Del Monte group that the slaves on the island of
Cuba should be their muse. "[N]ot only the blacks," he suggested, "but the
blacks and the whites, all mixed together, to form thereby pictures and

scenes that would necessarily be diabolical and hellish, but evident and true. Let our Victor Hugo be born, and let us know once and for all who we are, painted with the truth of poetry." The rebellious spirit that Tanco y Bosmeniel displayed, and of which he provided further evidence in his exposé of sexual predation in "Petrona y Rosalía," deserves mention on two accounts, notwithstanding the rather dubious abolitionism of Victor Hugo that motivated him. The first concerns the willingness, by a writer of the elite, to confront the "diabolical and hellish" nature of the colonial contract as it was manifested in the world of the plantation, and the second concerns the affirmative imagining of an inclusive nationalist collective that he hints at in his reference to the literary mixture of the blacks *with* the whites. Even with all its reformist limitations, the determination in Cuban foundational writing to see the slaves and promote a black literary subjectivity is to be noted. In Brazil, in contrast, not only was the forced labor collective left invisible throughout the colonial period, with the foundational discourse focusing instead on the romanticized Amerindian as noble savage, but also black literary invisibility before 1850 would be followed by a curious combination of denial and dismissal for the next eighty years.[65]

If the enslaved were regarded more as livestock than people and thus were unimaginable as literary subjects, the British-imposed cessation of the trade in 1850 and the slow growth of an abolitionist ambience among the intellectual elite in the ensuing decades did not do much to help humanize their eventual portrayal. Nor was this elite disposed toward confronting the contradictions produced by an institution that was over three hundred years old. The curious slant on abolition taken by the writers would include the poems of Antonio Castro Alves, remembered, interestingly enough, by Brazilian literary historiography as "Poet of the Slaves." Alves's "abolitionist" work "Vozes de Africa" (Voices of Africa), however, includes oddly dissonant references to distant North African sands and to biblical antiquity. And the tragic scenes of his "Navio negreiro" (The Slave Ship), albeit of greater historical relevance, take place in mid-Atlantic, rather than in the more concrete locations of production on the shores and in the heartland of Brazil's midcentury empire. Even so, in "Navio negreiro," it is the fact that the slave ship flies the Brazilian flag that seems to constitute the major cause for concern in the poetic speaker. The poem, written in 1868, would remain

---

65. Tanco y Bosmeniel quoted in Cruz, "*Sab,* su texto," 46. José de Alencar's Indianist novels *Iracema* (1857) and *O guarani* (1865) are paradigmatic expressions of the Indianist interest. See Zilá Bernd, *Literatura e identidade nacional.*

unpublished until 1880. Just as revealing is the motivation behind the call to end slavery made by Joaquim Manuel de Macedo in his introduction to *As vítimas-algozes* (1869) (The Executioner-Victims). Macedo believed that abolition was necessary not to bring freedom to slavery's overexploited victims, but more as a means of forestalling the moral decay of white Brazilian families that was supposedly brought on by the proximity of blacks. "Forget Bug-Jargal, Toussaint-Louverture, and Pai-Simão," he warned in his prologue to the three cautionary tales in *As vítimas-algozes,* "the slave that we are going to reveal to your eyes is the slave in our homes and on our plantations, a man who was born human, but whom slavery turned into a beast and a pestilence. . . . If you ponder these stories well, then you must banish slavery so that they might not be repeated."[66]

At a juncture in which the end of the supply of slave labor and the increasing acceptance of the economic unfeasibility of the institution combined with growing national self-consciousness about being one of the last slave-holding nations, the movement toward republican status finally made the continuation of slavery an untenable proposition. The scientific racism of the latter half of the nineteenth century, however, with its assertions of the innate inferiority of blacks, forecast a discomfiting future for a nation that had experienced centuries of miscegenation. Massive European subsidies therefore not only promised to solve the problem of cheap labor, but also allowed republican discourse to entertain the fantasy of progressive whitening to the degree that the spectral memory of slavery and its personae could be conveniently distanced from the national consciousness. "We cannot believe that such a noble country [as ours] / in olden times had slaves" sang Medeiros e Albuquerque's "Hymn to the Republic" in 1890, two scant years after abolition was finally declared.[67] The 1890 and 1891 burnings of slavery documents in Rio's customhouse by the statesman and former abolitionist Rui Barbosa is as eloquent a gesture as any to betray the desire to forget the institution and its moral burden.

As members of the lawyer elite, Castro Alves, Barbosa, and Joaquim Nabuco may have acquired abolitionist reputations. But it was the tireless campaigning of biracial autodidact Luis Gama—both in terms of his courtroom advocacy, which rescued over five hundred individuals from slavery, and in his satirical journalism and poems—that remains the most persuasive example of abolitionist activism in Brazil. Gama, sold at ten into slavery by

---

66. Joaquim Manuel de Macedo, *As vítimas-algozes: Quadros de escravidão,* 5.
67. Quoted in Roberto Reis, *A permanência do círculo: Hierarquia no romance brasileiro,* 19.

his own father, provides an interesting combination of the rebellious impulse from below and of the deployment of writing and the legal instrumentation of the dominant culture in the service of freedom.[68] If we were to set aside Gama's *carapinha* (nappy-headed) aesthetic and his celebration of the African muse, there would be no affirmative recognition of a black cultural presence in academic and public discourse to speak of in Brazil until Gilberto Freyre's interventions of the 1930s. But even Freyre, as we have seen, is notably partisan in his interpretation of the Brazilian cultural mélange.

Written in 1875, Guimaraes's *A escrava Isaura (Isaura the Slave)* is an intriguing reflection on race, slavery, and the national condition. It is a melodramatic, Cinderella-type account of good over evil as the tragically vulnerable heroine is rescued by a modern-day knight from the clutches of a menacing and unyielding antagonist. It is perhaps emblematic of the broader literary dismissal of the ordinary bondsmen and -women in Brazilian literature of the period, and of the institution itself, that the story, set in the 1820s, focuses on the (mis)fortunes of another mixed-race house slave who is not really a *slave*. Guimaraes's title, *Isaura the Slave,* establishes a provocative, if subtle, counterpoint to the way his narrator refers to the protagonist throughout the novel. Her condition is consistently resemanticized in terms of captivity. She is a *cativa* (captive), which implies that her dilemma, while distressing, is subject to resolution, whereas that of her "peers" is not. If her release is somewhere on the horizon, on account of her many racialized attributes, the bondage of the others is permanent, because for blacks, slavery is a natural state. There can be no overemphasizing the degree to which Isaura's beauty, her refinement, her skin color, her modesty, and her innate nobility are represented as antithetical to slavery and to blackness. This premise is endorsed not only by all the males and females of the slaveholding class, but also by the slaves themselves. Leôncio, her owner and putative lover, is unequivocal in his evocation of a divinely decreed natural order when he asserts on one occasion: "You're free, because God could not create such a perfect being to then toss her into slavery."[69] His rival, Alvaro, takes the argument a step further by arguing that it would be sacrilegious for man and for society to demean such a magnificent example of God's handiwork—Isaura—through enslavement (132).

---

68. See James Kennedy, "Luiz Gama: Pioneer of Abolition in Brazil." Gama's mother was Luisa Mahin, a leader in the 1835 Malê rebellion.

69. Bernardo Guimaraes, *A escrava Isaura,* 48. Subsequent page citations refer to this edition.

But "real" slavery in *A escrava Isaura* is not as far off as some critics have opined, nor is Guimaraes's narrative as disengaged from the institution as his disregard for its enthralled black subjects might suggest. It may well be that the essential contradictions of the institution, and the uncompromising nature of slavery's property relations, still get past the story's Romantic rhetoricizing and its plot twists, despite the writer's lack of attention to the slave ensemble. Leôncio's relentless and frustrated sexual pursuit of the heroine leads, for example, to a moment of unguarded candor, in which he exclaims: "[Y]ou belong to me, body and soul," revealing once more the slave owner's dream of absolute power (49). His subsequent imprisonment and torture of the unwilling Isaura remits us to the suffering of her mother, Juliana, a generation earlier, as she was similarly accosted by the father of Leôncio, and to the realities of colonial rape, which explode the sugar-coated interpretations of scholars of Brazilian miscegenation like Gilberto Freyre. That Leôncio and his brother-in-law almost come to the point of challenging each other to a duel over the house slave illustrates the depth of the libidinal tensions among the powerful at the heart of the extended national family in Freyre's *Casa-grande e senzala.* Leôncio's sexual pursuit of a young woman raised in the same house as he was, as a "sister," also points to the incest that often characterized these liaisons.

Even taking into consideration the frustrations felt by the planters' wives in the face of competition by the supposedly seductive slave women,[70] of which Guimaraes takes note in his portrayal of Leôncio's mother, the power differential between the slave-owning *senhoras* and their female charges is never far away. Upon the death of her favorite slave, Juliana, the mother takes over the young Isaura and cherishes and raises her as if she were the daughter she herself never conceived. Her benevolence, however, it must be mentioned, is contoured by the hard edge of ownership. Although she endows the "daughter of my soul," as she refers to Isaura, with music, dance, literature, art, and foreign languages, Isaura remains a human pet and drawing room showpiece (17). As the *senhora* indicates on one occasion, she is a bird that she has no intention of letting out of her cage while she remains alive, for fear that she might not return. Her demands that Isaura exclude sad slave songs from her repertoire seem just as invasive and mentally controlling as her son's projections on the young woman's body.

---

70. Juliana, like Sab's mother, is presented as the active agent in the relationship with the Portuguese administrator at the sugar mill to which she is banished for punishment (17).

Guimaraes's attenuated engagement with slavery once more receives direct expression when he introduces Isaura's savior, the millionaire bachelor Alvaro. Alvaro is a liberal with republican leanings and is described as almost socialist. He is also a "passionate abolitionist" who has freed his slaves and created a colony of paid workers on one of his plantations (57). Alvaro's example of remunerated black labor that does not result in a loss to the planters, and which provides the ex-slaves with white tutelage in the arts of freedom, is presumably the model for republican, postslavery Brazil. The vision of black sharecroppers allows Guimaraes to address present slavery without delving into the unsavory details of how slave-grown sugar and coffee made Alvaro's family wealthy in the first place, and also enriched the Brazilian empire. If overlooking the agency of black labor in creating the nation means that blacks are somehow absorbed into the national body, it makes Guimaraes a precursor to the more explicit statements of black extinction in Brazil, due to Darwinist evolutionism and Positivism that would be articulated early in the new century. For several Brazilian social scientists, natural selection, sexual selection, and white immigration would make Brazil white in a period of from one hundred to three hundred years.[71] To the degree, then, that Isaura, the daughter of a mulatto woman and a Portuguese father, is white enough to be confused with an Andalusian or a Neapolitan, she can be considered a "perfect Brazilian" (21). Unlike Avellaneda's Sab, the reference does not deny her mixed heritage, it merely underscores the evolutionist premise. For her male admirers, the mole on her face is a beauty mark. For her female rivals it is a telltale sign of her African forbears. For Guimaraes, the mole is a metonymic indication of the (remaining) black spot on the face of the nation.

Guimaraes's raciology is probably the lesser aspect in a larger scheme of human hierarchy, however. Isaura's superiority is clearly a function of whiteness, as we see in the pointed contrast with the sexualized *mulata* Rosa, and in the fact that, even when seen working among the other slaves, one would assume, naturally, that she is the mistress on account of her dignified bearing. But there is an overriding physiognomist theoretical framework influencing the creation and behavior of Guimaraes's characters that is worth noting. His reference to Johan Kasper Lavater in the description of the greedy and morally corrupt Martinho, the presumptive slave catcher, gives a clear indication of the Swiss pseudoscientist's presence in Guimaraes's thought. Lavater's 1781 *Essai sur la physiognomie* had articulated a centuries-old asso-

71. David Brookshaw, *Race and Color in Brazilian Literature*, 54.

ciation between an individual's external physical features and his or her character or internal disposition. Visual intuition and taste, based on the Greek model of physical beauty and perfection, is what allowed one to read the body's surface and discern moral rank among members of the human species.[72] Just as Isaura's bewitching beauty inspires references to her as a fairy, an angel, or a goddess, her antithesis would be Belchior the gardener, another putative lover, who was hunchbacked, bowlegged, hairy, and ill spoken. Accordingly, for Leôncio, the worst punishment imaginable for Isaura, in the face of her persistent rejections, would be to force a marriage between the two. Predictably, the Romantic heroine threatens suicide at the prospect. If Isaura, in the final analysis, is the perfect Brazilian for her beauty, polish, and desirability, we must also remember that she was the perfect slave. The narrator takes pains to detail her competence in the domestic tasks—cooking, weaving, washing, ironing, and other work she shares with the other female slaves—even as he insinuates that her sense of duty in fulfilling these tasks is also a mark of her inner nobility. Taking into consideration her reiterated submissiveness and lack of rebelliousness as a slave, one is given to suppose that as a free woman with the shackles gone, she would indeed embody the perfect model of republican womanhood; competent in the domestic sphere, yet acquiescent in relation to the patriarchal order. Mulattoness, in this case, as in that of the cosmetically whitened Sab and in Manzano's racial self-promotion, assumes a purportive agency in the quest for privilege under the rubric of race in Latin American nineteenth-century writing.

72. Mosse, *Final Solution,* 24–25.

4

Negrism, Modernism, Nationalism, and a Palesian Paradox

To free the slave is discovered to be tolerable only in so far as it freed his master.

W. E. B. Du Bois, "The Souls of White Folk"

Ballagas and the Map of Black Poetry

In this chapter I want to examine two intriguing paradoxes surrounding *negrismo,* Latin America's "black" poetic movement of the period 1925–1940, and the way it wrote blackness. The first paradox concerns the question of the predominantly white authorial presence in a movement variously labeled as *poesía negroide* (Negroid poetry), *poesía mulata* (mulatto poetry), or *poesía afro-antillana* (Afro-Antillean poetry). The implications of the transracial trajectory of the genre are of central interest, especially regarding its dominant hermeneutical narrative, and the question of the definition or redefinition of national cultural identity in Cuba and Puerto Rico. The second paradox derives in some important respects from the first. Indeed, given its ongoing ramifications, it might just as well be seen as an example of the first, for the matter of the transracial "gesture" is at the heart of the current canonizing thrust in relation to Puerto Rican Luis Palés Matos. Palés is a white poet whose *negrista* poetry, while it is his most highly visible claim to fame, is at the same time perceived by some critics as an obstacle to the fullest appreciation of his oeuvre, since it deflects critical attention from his other, "non-raced" work. This produces the second paradox.

Regarding the movement as a whole, it is important to point out that in much of *negrismo,* both as primary text and as hermeneutic, there is a discernibly Orientalist mechanism at work. That is to say, taking Said's disquisition into account regarding the power-based, authoritative, and reductive reproduction of tropes of the East by the West, in *negrismo* there appears a similar perceptual and representational dynamic on the part of the Hispano-Caribbean literati relative to its black subjects. Following Said, then, we may well speak of the poetics of *negrismo* as a Negrist poetics, to take into account what the movement implies in terms of writing, power, and difference. Of course, a primary consideration here in relation to the East-West divide is that *negrismo*'s writing self and racialized Other for the most part do not inhabit geographical spaces that are literally oceans apart. And it is precisely its national contour, its geography, its implied polity, and the internal history generated by the two that would distinguish the Negrist text from the Orientalist text in transracial discourse. At the heart of *negrismo*'s interracial gesture lies the question of intent. For whom is the *negrista* text written? And what becomes of its potential for racial rapprochement in the final analysis?

The transracial writing I examined in Chapter 1 reflected the process of national self-definition in Golden Age Spain since the literature of the period largely set out the conditions of the "domestication" of the incoming blacks. The reappearance in the twentieth century of this kind of literary crossover in Spain's former colonies Cuba and Puerto Rico would also turn out to be fundamental to national self-definition, albeit with important differences. *Negrismo*'s discourse would be conditioned by the severe race and class divisions inherited from the intervening centuries of slavery, and the hindrances to nation building, in both Cuba and Puerto Rico, that were consonant with the new imperial regimen initiated by the Spanish-American War of 1898. The turn-of-the-century primitivist vogue radiating outward from the European metropolitan center to the (post)colonial periphery in the Caribbean and the rest of Latin America would constitute the most important consideration in the new interracial initiative. It would help make *negrismo* an important launching pad for a new discourse around race and the nation in these two Caribbean countries, especially considering their late abolition of slavery,[1] the general embrace of racial hierarchy in nineteenth-century Latin America in which they participated, as well as the earlier dynamics of racial domination in the Iberian Peninsula.

Primitivism itself involved an ambivalent discursive and artistic involvement with colonially subjected non-European Others. Its earliest showcases were the turn-of-the-century world's fairs, which placed on exhibition not only cultural realia, masks, sculpture, religious artifacts, and so on, but also, occasionally, recreations of native life in its tribal setting. Exotic human beings accompanied exotic animals from Africa, Asia, and Oceania at these and similar shows, the former often being exhibited with the latter in zoos. While this display of trophies of victory overseas was a statement of imperial triumphalism, continuing an age-old tradition of conquest, it also presented pacified images of an erstwhile enemy whose immobilization had been called for in the shrill tones of colonialist propaganda scant years before. "Stop African savagery! Abolish human sacrifice," had been the invocation that, for example, preceded the incursions on the Ashanti, the Dahomey, and the Benin.[2] For blacks, the process signaled an important imagistic permutation. They would move from being the noble savages of Romanticism and Abolitionism of previous decades to the viciously ignoble targets of high imperialism at the end of the century. The subsequent trafficking of the same natives as harmless exotica, of ethnographic and even zoological interest, would eventually produce their further revalidation as cultural alternatives as the carnage of the First World War created a crisis of confidence for European civilization.

With the primitivist vogue, African cultural artifacts began to appear in museums, studios, and homes of European collectors and aesthetes by the beginning of the century, quickly creating, in the postwar period, a critical mass in which all areas of artistic endeavor in Europe were noticeably answering its call. Modernist pioneer Pablo Picasso's incorporation of African masks in his 1907 *Les Demoiselles d'Avignon* and his general Cubist aesthetic

1. Cuba's *teatro bufo* of the nineteenth century combined elements of Spanish Golden Age burlesque and current Jim Crow minstrelsy of the U.S. South. It was not, however, accompanied by the kind of nationalistic self-reflection that came with *negrismo*. Slavery was abolished in Puerto Rico in 1873 and in Cuba in 1886.

2. The Colonial Exhibition in Amsterdam in 1883 featured a group of twenty-eight Surinamese, while for the world's fair at Antwerp in 1884 a Congolese village was reconstructed. At the Paris Exposition of 1900, several African villages were represented, complete with a replica of a "tower of sacrifice," in the Dahomeyan village. See Jan Nederveen Pieterse, *White on Black: Images of Africa and Blacks in Western Popular Culture*, 95–96, 80.

are remarkable examples of this. So, too, are the Negro music and dancing and the African masks and drumming that became standard features of Dadaist iconoclasm at the famous Cabaret Voltaire in Zurich a decade later. Black music, proclaimed an enthusiastic George Anthiel in 1931, had created an empire as it spiraled out from its African center, recreated itself in the Americas, and finally descended upon a spiritually exhausted postwar Europe. To be sure, with the eruption of ragtime at the 1893 Chicago World's Fair and the spread of jazz, the blues, and myriad black vernacular dance forms, the entertainment culture in the United States was transformed. Soon to follow were the sober strains of many contempory European composers in Paris. There was also a noteworthy quest after African folklore as manifested in ethnographer Leo Frobenius's collection *Der Schwarze Dekameron* (1910) and that of Blaise Cendrars's *Anthologie nègre* (1920). In the United States, black orality turned out to be no less attractive to the modernist linguistic rebelliousness of elite writers T. S. Eliot and Ezra Pound later that decade.[3]

Estranged British aesthete Nancy Cunard summed up the curious mix of desire and denigration underlying primitivism's multigenred and multinational cross-racial impulse in her 1931 review of Harlem, the cultural capital of the black American world: "[I]t is the zest that the Negroes put in[to life], and the enjoyment that they get out of things that causes... envy in the ofay. Notice how many of the whites are unreal in America; they are *dim*. But the Negro is very real; he is *there*. And the ofays know it. That's why they come to Harlem—out of curiousity and jealousy and don't-know-why. This desire to get close to the other race has often nothing honest about it."[4] The response to black otherness, seen as a manifestation of ontological fullness by white Occidental selfhood, would thus range from the ponderous tomes of philosopher Oswald Spengler's *The Decline of the West* (1922), who welcomed the cycle of cultural renewal that primitivism portended, to the mundanity of the stages and dance floors of Harlem, whose

---

3. Michael North reports in *The Dialect of Modernism: Race, Language, and Twentieth-Century Literature,* that "after his interest in African art became well known, Picasso enjoyed spreading the rumor that he actually was of African descent" (65). The painter subsequently denied African influence on his work. See also Tristan Tzara, "Zurich Chronicle (1915–1919)"; and George Anthiel, "The Negro on the Spiral." North discusses Eliot and Pound in chapter 4.

4. Nancy Cunard, "Harlem Reviewed," 49–50. Hugh Ford comments on Cunard's association with black musician Henry Crowder and his introduction of her to the African American vernacular (introduction to *Negro: An Anthology,* xv).

essence would be so energetically pursued in Carl Van Vechten's 1926 novel, *Nigger Heaven.*

Cuban Afrologist Fernando Ortiz is a critical component of *negrista* discourse in both its Puerto Rican and its Cuban expressions. Prime examples of traditional Latin American intellectuality, Ortiz's writings on Afro-Hispanic, primarily Afro-Cuban culture reflect both faces of *negrista* ambivalence. They are revealed first in his early racist ethnography (which I discuss in Chapter 5) and subsequently in his role as the catalyst behind the Cuban cultural elite's embrace of blackness as a potentially legitimate national cultural heritage in the 1930s. Ortiz's summer trip to the United States and Europe in 1928 was an important, if unacknowledged, point of departure for the new black arts in Cuba. Upon his return, he wrote up a travel report that was published twice in as many months in Havana. "El arte africanoide de Cuba" first appeared in *Social* in February 1929 and then again in March in the *Diario de la marina.*

"El arte" registered Ortiz's dismay at the enthusiasm with which the metropolitan avant-garde had gone primitive. As he observed, the excitement was not limited to blackness as mere artistic motif for whites; blacks were even creating a stir as performers and as a general human presence. In a suggestive metaphor, he compared the electrically lit modern Europe, spellbound by African drumming, to a primordial moonlit African night entranced by tribal tom-toms, unwittingly thereby primitivizing civilization's self-proclaimed center.[5] The trope, of course, could just as well apply to the *negrismo* of the Caribbean Lettered City in turn, regarding their rediscovery of their black compatriots. Having researched and published on various aspects of Afro-Cuban culture over the preceding three decades, and considering his current post as director of the journal *Archivos del folklore cubano,* Ortiz was perhaps even more qualified than composer George Anthiel to appreciate the transatlantic connection between Argentine tango, the Cuban *son,* and such North American dances as the Charleston.

The trip, however, helped make at least three things clear. The first was that black culture in Cuba might not be such a blight on the face of the nation as he himself and the rest of Cuban officialdom had been maintaining for decades. Second, and following historical precedent in which the *habanera* had seduced Bourbon Spain, Cuban *mulato* musical culture could foreseeably

---

5. Two years later, Nicolás Guillén's "La canción del bongó" would use the same metaphor in the lines: "This is the song of the bongo / he who is highest will respond if I call" *(Esta es la canción del bongo / el que más alto sea responde, si llamo yo)* (in Nicolás Guillén, *Nicolás Guillén: Obra poética 1920–1972,* 1:116).

occupy a place of prestige in metropolitan artistic circles, in the same way that the musics of other diasporic sources were doing. In fact, the enthusiasm invested in the materialization of this particular insight resulted, in less than a decade, in the lifting of the ban on Afro-Cuban carnival processions, which had the hoped-for salutary effect on tourist revenues in the island. It also further catalyzed the acceptance, commercialization, and internationalization of Afro-Cuban musical genres like the *son,* the conga, and the rumba, while ensuring fame and fortune for many of their white practitioners like Eliseo Grenet, Moisés Simons, and Xavier Cugat.[6] Finally, the Cuban poems on black themes, which had been a trickle until then, grew, over the next decade, into a movement proper, enough to warrant critical attention and preservation in anthologies. Apart from Nicolás Guillén and Emilio Ballagas, the latter of whom I discuss below, the Cuban poets with individual collections were Ramón Guirao (*Bongó,* 1934) and Vicente Gómez Kemp (*Acento negro,* 1934).

The collections of *negrista* poetry as an exemplary instance of the politics of race and authority in Latin America are most fully appreciated in the context of the anthologies emerging from the broader poetics of blackness that characterized the intercontinental avant-garde movement of the 1920s and 1930s. This is especially so given the importance of voicing and racial representation to the field, and the exercise of canonical power implied in the editorial selection and presentation of the texts. My interest, therefore, in what remains of this section, is in highlighting the question of the naming and framing of *negrista* anthologies, principally by Emilio Ballagas, the movement's earliest and arguably most influential anthologist, and in exploring the implications that his presumptions have had on the genre. As Michel-Rolph Trouillot has remarked in his analysis of a similar hermeneutical narrative: "Terminologies demarcate a field politically and epistemologically. Names set up a field of power."[7]

In James Weldon Johnson's introduction to *American Negro Poetry,* there is a noteworthy sense of racial vindication and celebration. Johnson's collection, an important precursor to the anthology *The New Negro* (1925) by Alain Locke, another Harlem Renaissance publication whose writers would in turn also help inspire the *Négritude* movement of the early 1930s, looked

6. Regarding Afro-Cuban musical genres, see Robin D. Moore, *Nationalizing Blackness: Afrocubanism and Artistic Revolution in Havana, 1920–1940.* James Weldon Johnson, in his preface to *The Book of American Negro Poetry,* would also stress the influence of contemporary black American music on successful British dancer and choreographer Vernon Castle (11).

7. Michel-Rolph Trouillot, *Silencing the Past: Power and the Production of History,* 115.

to establish black literature in America as having both a contemporary pres-ence as well as historical depth. Johnson's anthology would not only show-case current talents such as Sterling Brown, Countee Cullen, and Langston Hughes, it would highlight, as well, hitherto overlooked poets, like the ex-slave George Horton, who was born in 1797, the same year as Juan Fran-cisco Manzano, and who, like him, committed his poetry to memory before he learned to write. Underscoring the canonical importance of Phyllis Wheat-ley, female slave poet and only the second woman to publish a volume of poetry in America (1773), was also of importance to Johnson. Johnson felt that literature, as an artifact of high culture, could be the means of demon-strating what he called the "intellectual purity" of blacks. Consequently, black poets might be better off reaching beyond the limitations of dialect as a medium of expression. In this regard, the conventional and even recondite language of his collection would also serve to combat the bozalic image of the "singing, shuffling, banjo-playing" Negro of the minstrel tradition. His introduction, at the same time, claimed a central place within the broader American culture, for what he termed "Aframerican" folkways. Here he pointed to the ongoing process of appropriation by white performers of such forms as ragtime, the cake walk, the turkey trot, and so on, and the fact that they were currently the most highly paid exponents of these genres.[8] As already stated, a similar process was also taking place in the Hispanic Caribbean.

Alain Locke, in his turn, was no less assertive. While the anthology *The New Negro* shared with Johnson's collection the middle-class, college-educated authorial preference, Locke's political position-taking in his introduction was firm in terms of both its self-conscious racial solidarity and its declara-tion of an essential Americanness. Jim Crow segregation in housing had allowed for a steady buildup of a black population in the Harlem section of Manhattan. Black migrants from the American South, Africa, and the West Indies had produced a great "race-welding," which African American partici-pation in the recent war helped translate into a heightened sense of political possibility. Locke's declaration that "the American mind must reckon with a fundamentally changed Negro" not only expressed this new attitude, but also addressed the white collaborators and supporters of the Harlem Renaissance, insinuating coalitions that might go beyond what was merely literary, to contemplate more concrete realms of social activism. Avoiding the pitfalls of a politics of racial separatism à la Marcus Garvey, whose Back to Africa movement was by then in decline, Locke opted to confront American democ-

8. Johnson, *Book of American Negro Poetry,* 9, 41.

racy in terms of its own postulates of equal rights. Notwithstanding such ideals, however, he still saw a positive role for the American Negro in African development, calling it one of the "most constructive and universally helpful missions that any modern people can lay claim to."[9]

Nancy Cunard's foreword to her collection *Negro: An Anthology* (1934) is equally pertinent to the discussion of the politics of race and authority in contemporary avant-garde race literature, especially because it took the longer view of antiracist struggle and identified the book with the Abolitionism of the previous century. Cunard, scion of a wealthy British family, moved beyond infatuation with the motifs of primitivism after her visit to Paris in 1920, and adopted an openly radical position on behalf of racial and social justice. Conspicuously framed by Langston Hughes's famous poem on nationalist assertion "I too (am America)" and a blistering critique of British imperialism in South Africa by noted Pan-African activist George Padmore, her anthology embodies widely diasporic concerns. Its intercontinental scope, which, apart from entries from the United States, included material from Africa, the Caribbean, Europe, and South America, was only matched by the variety of its disciplinary approaches. History, ethnology, protest journalism, literature, and folklore combined to justify the claim by Hugh Ford, who wrote decades later that this was an editorial first. Predictably, a publication dedicated to addressing the "indignities and injustices done to the race," of biracial authorship but declaredly "for the black race," and overtly communistic in orientation, had difficulty in finding a publisher.[10]

But all of the above was hardly new, for a black countercultural episteme had begun to be articulated "almost as soon as blacks could write," as Henry Louis Gates Jr. points out. Gates pushes back the New Negro initiative to the antebellum slave narratives, documenting not only the significant literary production of the Reconstruction, but also the ongoing racial introspection and self-examination in the writing of black magazines from the turn of the century up to 1925. The extended "New Negro" initiative, then, is of great historiographic significance. This is especially so, given the corresponding

---

9. Alain Locke, ed., *The New Negro*, 7. By 1925, the leader of the United Negro Improvement Association was about to be imprisoned, and the once-flourishing Back to Africa campaign had suffered a severe setback due to the failure of the association's Black Star Line and the Black Cross Navigation and Trading Company. Garvey was deported subsequently from the United States. A belated attempt to reorganize in London was unsuccessful. See E. David Cronon, *Black Moses: The Story of Marcus Garvey and the Universal Negro Improvement Association;* and Locke, *New Negro*, 14.

10. Ford, introduction to *Negro*, xvi, xi.

paucity of literary production from black Latin America. The assimilationist pressures experienced by black writers like Juan Francisco Manzano (writing from bondage), or the "cult of whiteness" practiced in the Parnassianism of Brazil's João da Cruz e Sousa or in Panama's Modernist poet Gaspar Octavio Hernández in the latter nineteenth century, are indicative not only of the demands of cultural conformity, they also remind us of how exclusionary literary practice was. In this regard, the rebellious lyric of Brazil's premier abolitionist, Luis Gama, the "Nappy-Headed Orpheus" *(Orfeu de carapinha)*, and the oppositional, multigenred work of Colombia's Candelario Obeso stand as vitally important Latin American antecedents to twentieth-century negritude and broader Afro-latino discourse.[11]

This background to *negrismo* is important because it illuminates the moment of (re)discovery in Hispanic literature of the black muse, and it helps us understand the tensions attending the editorial packaging of the poetic materials at hand, both in terms of the symbolic ownership of the genre and in terms of the implications for an interracial dialogue on black/white race relations in Latin America. In the United States, the culture of Jim Crow, which added to the escalation of racist hostilities after the war, made the continuing claim of a space of racial articulation by the spokespersons of the Harlem Renaissance a sine qua non, as pointed out in relation to Johnson. The new sense of independence with which the New Negro movement was imbued also allowed it to at least articulate, if not dictate, terms for interracial dialogue as we saw with Locke. It would be the absence of analogous literary forums for Afro-latinos, or of an equally conspicuous history of legal racial segregation in post-Emancipation South America or the Hispanic Caribbean, that would produce the rhetoric of interracial representability in *negrista* criticism as the avatars of the Lettered City once again followed Europe's literary lead and adopted primitivism.

Effectively, much of *negrista* subjectivity is arrived at by way of the prism of folklore, with a stereotypical and repetitive apprehension of racial character and situation, and scant attention to the problematics of black life. As editor of the *Orbita de la poesía afrocubana 1928–37 (Antología),* Ramón Guirao's opinion is informative. Although he saw in *negrismo*'s transracial writing an opportunity for genuine social and racial rapprochement, he looked with suspicion at the faddish orientation of the movement and criti-

---

11. Henry Louis Gates Jr., "The Trope of the New Negro and the Reconstruction of the Image of the Black," 131. See also Luis Gama, *Primeiras trovas burlescas e outros poemas;* and Candelario Obeso, *Cantos populares de mi tierra.*

cized its superficiality and its penchant for caricature: "We have acquired the dark merchandise from other aesthetic marketplaces and we have passed it through customs without taking stock of our own reality of blackness." He added, "Our Afrocreole poetry is an echo of the European vogue. It is more a consequence than a result of our own initiative. This poetic modality, imported by white Creoles, responds intrinsically to their condition as racial transplants who have forgotten, in their lack of originality, everything that surrounds them in order to transmigrate more readily to things European."[12]

The paradox of blacks as a degraded social reality, suddenly turned object of aesthetic contemplation, especially considering the attention then being generated in local print media by the North American New Negro phenomenon, demanded a rational response from the elite white *negrista* practitioners. Where Guirao hinted at the movement's promise for "sincere [interracial] dialogue," fellow poet and anthologist Emilio Ballagas elaborated a curious rationale for the white authorial presence. It emerged as a white "right to represent." Ballagas had been the compiler of the earliest multiethnic anthology, the *Antología de la poesía negra hispanoamericana* (1935), which appeared after a collection of his own *negrista* poems, the *Cuaderno de poesía negra,* the year before. The *Antología de la poesía negra hispanoamericana* preceded by a decade his wider-reaching *Mapa de la poesía negra americana* (1946). Along with the omnipresent Fernando Ortiz, he was the first to elaborate a rationale around *negrismo*'s multiethnic authorship. His introduction to the 1935 collection marked the first anthological confrontation with the question of the naming of the genre, its definition, and what turned out to be, in the final analysis, its "ownership." His introduction, first of all, took care to stress the inexactitude of the title. Calling it "BLACK POETRY . . . is not quite accurate," he opined, as he registered the fact that white poets also were writing on the black theme.[13]

A similar opinion had been expressed a year prior by Ortiz: "I don't believe that this recent poetic current flowing from the depths of our people is *black*. It is quite simply *mulatto*, the product of an indissoluble bond between Africa and Castile in its emotion, its rhythm, its vocabulary, its syntax, its ideas, its tendencies." Since there was no black literature that was native to the Americas, this poetry was, like the *bongó*, syncretic, and thus *mulata* by definition. *Black* poetry, Ballagas would suggest later, was African, inspired

---

12. Ramón Guirao, introduction to *Orbita de la poesía afrocubana 1928–37 (Antología)*, xviii, xxii.
13. Ibid., xix; Emilio Ballagas, ed., *Antología de la poesía negra hispano-americana*, 20.

by African sources, and expressed by Africans. Ortiz, however, was hard put to go beyond his ethnographic metaphor of the syncretic and consistently explain why some of the poems he discussed, whether by white, black, or mulatto poets, were authentic examples of "mulatto poetry" *(poesía mulata),* and some were not. Ballagas the poet took a more elaborate approach to the question. On the issue of *negrismo's* racially heterogeneous authorship, his prologue to the 1935 anthology declared that once the white poet saw his black subject, as it were, "from the inside" *(desde dentro),* he could be a genuine practitioner of the genre. In fact, he proposed, the ability to "faithfully trans-late the Afro-Cuban spirit," had been made available through the scientific studies undertaken by Fernando Ortiz, who was the "highest authority" on the matter of black psychology, music, language, and customs. Fernando Ortiz had apparently provided a blueprint of the Afro-Cuban "psyche" or "spirit."[14] This, ostensibly, was a single, ontologically quantifiable entity. In other words, racial ventriloquism was feasible—one just had to do the research. Negrist discourse, both as poetry and as hermeneutic, had been put in motion.

In a subsequent article, suggestive for its desire to free black poetry of the racial marker, he shifted focus momentarily to the integrity of the poetic word, suggesting that attaching a racial label to it would be an affront to poetry itself. "There is no such thing, properly speaking, and in terms of the philosophy of art, as a black poetry, as there's no white poetry." If there was an incursion into "difference" by contemporary mainstream poets—García Lorca vis-à-vis the gypsies in Spain, Mexican poets and the indigenous peoples, Cuban *negristas* and blacks in Cuba—it could all be explained as a function of class and in traditions that placed popular culture within the purview of poets. Apparently overlooking the fact that his analogy evoked a racialized power differential in all three cases, he continued by saying that the indul-gence in vernacular culture as voice and motif in this poetry was not done with the intention of offending its subjects. On the contrary, the intention was to "glorify" them. The racial label was really of a secondary order in this genre. The day would come, he anticipated, when critics, poets, and the public would be able to dispense with the racial marker and speak of a black poetic "song" with no need to refer to color.[15]

---

14. Fernando Ortiz, "La poesía mulata. Presentación de Eusebia Cosmé, la recitadora," 210; Fernando Ortiz, "Más acerca de la poesía mulata: Escorzos para su estudio," 33, and Emilio Bal-lagas, "Situación de la poesía afroamericana," 5, 32. See also Ballagas, *Antología,* 14, 18.

15. Ballagas, "Poesía negra liberada," 5–6.

The 1946 essay "Situación," and the introduction to the *Mapa de la poesía negra americana* of the same year, revisited the question of white authors. In the former, he asserted that "[t]his sensibility of the man of color can be capably expressed by blacks and mulattos from their own intuitive lyrical core, and just as well by whites, though by way of a reflex phenomenon, so subtle sometimes, that it presupposes not only a fortunate identification, but (establishes) to what extent setting aside the historicist and sociological burden can restore the idea of the oneness of humanity and the Christian idea of our common origin."[16] Again, racial ventriloquism was feasible. Just do the research and feel the feeling. On this occasion, in addition to "explaining" the white presence in a nominally black poetry, he again attached a hierarchy of values to the aesthetics of the movement, suggesting that history, sociology, and politics should be subjected to higher, more ethereal considerations of artistic purity.

It is significant that—notwithstanding his earlier critique of the denigrated caricature of the black subject in the tradition of Cuban *bufo* theater, and by contemporary white writers limited by their external apprehension of blacks—Ballagas, in "Situación," went on to claim what seem to be (white) Hispanic generative rights over black poetry. "The black thing *began* in the [Iberian] Peninsula, first as humanity, then as literary fact. The black poetry being cultivated in the Hispanic Antilles, in Cuba, Santo Domingo, and Puerto Rico *is nothing but Spanish poetry.* It is not only so in its language— often altered for humorous effect—dressed up in Africanist emotions, *but its original creative spurt also came from Spain.*" At this point we should consider the international visibility and audibility of the black poets of the Harlem Renaissance, to whom he often alluded; Ballagas's effort to remove "blackness" from the racial label of the poetry and to otherwise deracialize it; and his detailed legitimation of the white authorial presence. The question thus arises as to whether, in stressing the movement's Spanish origins, he was not creating an alternate, specifically Hispanic geography for *poesía negra.* Such a poetic map might preserve the privilege of the white signifying elite of which he was a part. His bemoaning the "historicist mania" in the movement's criticism, and his curious inclusion in his *Mapa de la poesía negra americana* of such contemporary Spanish poets as Alfonso Camín and Frederico García Lorca, and of Golden Age poets Góngora and Lope de

---

16. Ballagas, "Situación," 6. He repeats the statement in *Mapa de la poesía americana*, 9, but without the religious reference.

Vega, suggests that he was attempting to preserve this privilege. This observation is not to suggest that "white" poets cannot write "black" poetry. As far as I am aware, there are no racial barriers to the human imagination. It does point, however, to the general absence of black writers in a nominally black genre, and to the fact that Afro-Cubans, as a constituency, were in a sense being spoken for. "Any statement will invoke the structures of power allied with the social location of the speaker," Linda Martín Alcoff reminds us, "aside from the speaker's intentions or attempts to avoid such invocations." *Negrismo,* like any other discursive event, involved "not only the text or utterance, but also [its] position within a social space that includes the persons involved in, acting upon, and/or affected by the words."[17]

In the face of the de facto appropriation of the hypothetical space of black lyrical voicing, the declaration by both *negrista* anthologists that the movement was over by the end of the decade was to have a conspicuous role in the future canonical displacement of Afro-latino literature. In over a hundred general anthologies of Spanish American poetry published between 1940 and 1980, only two black poets appear. They are Nicolás Guillén, who emerged in the *negrista* period, and Plácido de la Concepción Valdés, a nineteenth-century poet; both are Cuban. Between 1935 and 1937, Ortiz, in addition to his other historical and ethnographic work, would publish a series of articles on what had by then become permanently inscribed as "mulatta poetry," or *poesía mulata.* This included reviews of the recital of the popular female *negrista* performer mulatto Eusebia Cosme and of collections by white poets Vicente Gomez Kemp and Luis Palés Matos, of Cuba and Puerto Rico respectively.[18] His role as public intellectual and culture broker is probably most evident in his setting up of the Sociedad de Estudios Afrocubanos in 1937 and in the reauthorization, in the same year, of the tradition of carnival processions, or *comparsas,* in Havana.

The reauthorization of the black *comparsas* and their elevation to the status of official folklore was significant because it represented a complete turn-

---

17. Ballagas, "Situación," 30, 9; Linda Martín Alcoff, "The Problem of Speaking for Others," 105, 102.

18. Ortiz, "La poesía mulata"; Ortiz, "Más acerca de la poesía mulata"; and Fernando Ortiz, "Luis Palés Matos." See also Guirao, introduction to *Orbita de la poesía afrocubana,* xix; Ballagas, "Situación," 45; Aurora de Albornoz and Julio Rodríguez-Luis in *Sensemayá: La poesía negra en el mundo hispanohablante (antología),* 9. See also Mullen, *Afro-Cuban Literature,* 167. The work of Nancy Morejón, awarded the Cuban National Award for Literature in 2002, has also been included in recent anthologies.

about from previous official positions. When Antonio Beruff Mendieta, the mayor of Havana, with Ortiz's enthusiastic endorsement, authorized the reintroduction of *comparsas,* it came in the wake of the long-standing ban of 1884 and after vigorous campaigns at the turn of the century against Afro-Cuban *santería* and related religious practices. These culminated in the prohibition of such street processions at both the municipal and national levels. Manifestations of this nature were held to be barbarous and damaging to the image of a civilized Cuba. The reinstallation of the tradition, however, was accompanied by Ortician rhetoric regarding the need to conserve "old folkloric traditions," as was customary in civilized nations like Spain and England, even in spite of their intrinsic elements of barbarity, as in the case of Cuba. The mayor recognized their potential for tourism as Cuba's "second industry" and offered monetary awards to the best groups.[19] Ortiz's response to Beruff, upon consultation, had been in the affirmative on both counts.

Bearing in mind *negrismo*'s dominant bacchanalian stereotype of sun-soaked song and dance and *mulato/a* hypersexuality, elite endorsement of the *comparsa* may well be seen as a material corollary to white control of its discursive antecedent. Reaction from the black middle class was significant. Newspaper columnist Alberto Arredondo was quick to point out that, besides the prizes to individuals or groups of performers, the masses of black Cubans stood to gain very little from the Afro-Cuban vogue. On the contrary, he suggested in his article "El arte negro a contrapelo," the new culture craze perpetuated unflattering images of blacks and detracted from the resolution of more substantive social issues. He would much rather see blacks celebrating with whites on the road to economic equality, than see them in a carnival parade. The ideal of a culturally and racially integrated nation was not served by the vogue, either, since there were no white people to be seen in the still-stigmatized street dances, although, as pointed out above, white

---

19. See, for example, Aline Helg, *Our Rightful Share: The Afro-Cuban Struggle for Equality, 1886–1912,* 111–16. Robin Moore cites municipal ordinances, issued by mayors Nicasio Estrada Moro (1900) and Fernando Freyre de Andrade (1913), prohibiting *comparsa* processions, drums of African origin, and the "immoral" and "lascivious" dances associated with them. A presidential decree was subsequently applied against them by President Gerardo Machado in 1925 (Moore, *Nationalizing Blackness,* 66–72). See also Fernando Ortiz, "Informe del doctor Fernando Ortiz, Presidente de la Sociedad de Estudios Afrocubanos, aprobado por la Junta Directiva de dicha Sociedad, pronunciándose en favor del resurgimiento de las comparsas populares habaneras," 12; and "Comunicación del Alcalde de la Habana al Presidente de la Sociedad de Estudios Afro-cubanos, solicitando la opinión y el consejo de dicha sociedad sobre el resurgimiento de las comparsas populares habaneras," 7.

artists were conspicuously benefiting from select aspects of the trend. While Ortiz could be seen as promoting the interests of blackness in the Sociedad de Estudios Afrocubanos, Arredondo reminded his readers, he could also be seen as doing the same for whiteness through the Instituto Hispano Cubano de Cultura. Ortiz had founded both institutions. Racial and cultural separation, therefore, seemed entrenched even among the agents and agencies that were promoting black culture. For Arredondo, this top-down "Afrocubanism," to the degree that it was a hindrance to black emancipation, was also a hindrance to national progress.

If the black and mulatto bourgeoisie was alarmed at *negrismo's* exploitation under cover of ethnography or folklore, its representatives also felt that the movement's highlighting of the "primitivity" of blackness was inimical to their interest in assimilating into cultured "white" society. Throughout the life of the new republic, dominant Hispanic culture in Cuba had demanded that Afro-Cubans put behind them the barbarism of their slave ancestors and become a part of modern "civilization." *Negrismo,* by reifying blackness as a series of retrograde images associated with the cultural practices of the slave, could have a negative effect on the country as a whole. Suspicious of the new folklore and of its articulation as art, and alarmed at the idea floated by the Communist party of creating a territorial "black belt" in Oriente province, the members of the black middle class stressed their essential Cubanness. We are not African, proclaimed the writer Juan Luis Martín. The "Afro" in *Afro-Cubanism* is an epistemological falsehood. "[B]efore cultivating race, it is better to cultivate (the idea of) the nation...an entirely black atmosphere does not exist (in Cuba), therefore the so-called 'Afro-Cuban' poetics does not respond to a racial reality.... [Y]ou cannot apply anything differently to blacks than you would to whites, neither in social nor in political terms," he argued.[20]

In the face of black (bourgeois) protestations, in the media, that were both against race and against racism, the precise positions taken by blacks on these matters within the white-dominated republic of letters assume much importance. Of related interest is ascertaining to what extent the metaphor of interracial solidarity, Ballagas's *desde adentro* postulate, as a key to trans-

---

20. Juan Luis Martín, "Falsa interpretación afrocubana," 7. The idea of the "black belt" was put forward in a resolution coming out of the Confederación Nacional Obrera de Cuba and was published in June 1934. It would relocate blacks and mulattos ostensibly for self-determination as a national minority, creating thereby two separate and racially identified countries. See Moore, *Nationalizing Blackness,* 7; and Alejandro de la Fuente, *A Nation for All: Race, Inequality, and Politics in Twentieth-Century Cuba,* 192.

racial writing, was borne out in the anthologies themselves. The first issue may be answered primarily through reference of the work of mulatto poet Nicolás Guillén. Guillén, the *negrista* poet of most enduring fame, was less nuanced and more direct on the matter of racism than the above writers, as he confronted white cultural hegemony in Cuba. The racially affirmative tenor of his work from 1929 to 1935 is the closest thing in *negrismo* to the assertiveness earlier referred to in the Harlem Renaissance. But bearing in mind the canonical association of the three anthologies under discussion, it is certainly significant that they only included "Sabás," one of the more controversial poems from his 1934 collection, *West Indies Ltd.* This was in Ballagas's 1935 anthology. The overt militancy of others, such as "Canción de los hombres perdidos," "Nocturno en los muelles," "Caminando," and "Balada de Simón Caraballo," seem to have been avoided by the *negrista* editors.

Notwithstanding Ballagas's theory of interracial sensibility and solidarity, there was certainly no esprit de corps among *negrista* practitioners that might have made them cultivate an agenda against social and racial oppression. This is not to say that there was no opportunity for such an agenda to develop, either in 1930s Cuba or in the Cuba of the preceding three decades, for that matter. The infamous Red Summer of 1919, which saw twenty-six anti-black riots across America's cities north and south, underlay such powerful poetic statements as "If We Must Die," "America," and "The White House" by Claude McKay. No one would know, however, by reading *negrista* poetry, of the thousands of Afro-Cubans massacred in 1912 for aspiring to equal rights and justice under the banner of the Partido Independiente de Color, or of the "campaign of racist violence" that overtook the island in 1933 and 1934.[21] Rather, many of *negrismo*'s writer-subject presumptions are borne out precisely in one of the poems that sought to memorialize the movement. Asturian poet Alfonso Camín, then residing in Cuba, claimed by a later *negrista* editor as "the true initiator of the black poetry in Cuba" has left what is perhaps the most unsubtle expression of much of what is taken for granted in the transracial aspect of the genre. It appears in his claim for proprietorial rights and cultural capital in *negrismo,* and his simultaneous objectification, appropriation, and subordination of black subjectivity. "Negro," reads Camín's poem of the same name, "don't you forget tomorrow / that I was the first singer of the black song / in the Antilles" (Negro: no olvides mañana / que yo fui el primer pregón / negro en la tierra antillana). Camín's poetic persona goes on to claim that it was he who spread the fame

---

21. See Helg, *Our Rightful Share,* and De la Fuente, *Nation for All,* 204.

of the genre abroad, "to run the wide seas" (a correr la mar lejana), hence the admonition that the *negro* not forget the supposed debt of gratitude.[22]

If Fernando Ortiz had provided the blueprint for the spirit and psyche of blacks, as Ballagas suggested, he had also provided their language in his 556-page *Glosario de afronegrismos* (1924). *Negrista* racial ventriloquism would use black folklore and the vernacular as a sort of base or metatextual foundation that would prove its authenticity. Indeed, anonymous ritual chants and fragments of carnival songs and folk dialogues from the eighteenth and nineteenth centuries make up the entire first section of the Guirao anthology. Bits of Afro-Cuban ritual interspersed into the poems, *cabildo* chants, and black colloquial speech constitute a multileveled neobozalic oral register for Cuban *negrista* verse. This Afro-Antillean idiom would establish a linguistic bridge to the poetic subject. In the three anthologies under discussion, however, it is the glossaries—the key to the ostensibly hermetic code of the black referent—that seal the poetic subject's otherness in the final analysis, even as they establish the discursive link between the writers and their implied white audience. In the dramatic narrative recreation of a *ñañigo* initiation, for example, Alejo Carpentier captures the mystique of the esoteric ceremony while he manages to maintain its exotic flavor. The poem "Liturgia" is replete with ritual personae and performance dialogue:

> La Potencia rompió,
> Yambá o!
> Retumban las tumbas
> en casa de Ecué...
>
> Endoco endiminoco,
> Efimere bongó
> Enkiko baragofia
> Yamba ó!
>
> Hierve botija!
> calienta pimienta!
> siete cruces
> arden ya
> con pólvora negra
> —incienso arará—.
>
> [The Power broke through,
> Yamba Oh!

22. Hortensia Ruiz del Vizo, ed., *Black Poetry of the Americas (A Bilingual Anthology)*, 22.

The drums resound
in the house of Ecue . . .

Endoco endiminico,
Efimere bongo
Enkido baragofia
Yamba Oh!

The jug boils!
The pepper heats up!
seven crosses
already burn
with black powder
—Arara incense—.][23]

In similar fashion, Guillén rewrote a traditional chant for killing snakes, of the sort recorded by Guirao,[24] and communicates the supposedly atavistic awe inspired by the reptile as well as the collective urge to kill it. Apart from the choral voicing of the call-and-response of traditional African orality, his "Sensemayá: Canto para matar una culebra" would also put on display an essential element of *negrista* language, the rhythmic percussion that recreated the effect of African drums. This was often achieved in the movement through the creative use of onomatopoeia, or by way of made-up words known as *jitanjáfora*:

Mayombe-bombe-mayombé!
Sensemayá, la culebra . . .
Mayombe-bombe-mayombé!
Sensemayá, no se mueve . . .
Mayombe-bombe-mayombé!
Sensemayá, la culebra . . .
Mayombe-bombe-mayombé!
Sensemayá, se murió.

[Mayombe-bombe-mayombé!
Sensemayá, the snake . . .
Mayombe-bombe-mayombé!
Sensemayá, it does not move . . .

23. In Guirao, *Orbita de la poesía afrocubana,* 77–78.
24. See "Canto para matar culebras," in Guirao, *Orbita de la poesía afrocubana,* 7. Guirao's rearranged "Canto" had actually been part of a nineteenth-century symbolic Día de Reyes (January 6) carnival performance. See Alejo Carpentier, *La música en Cuba,* 267.

Mayombe-bombe-mayombé!
Sensemayá, the snake . . .
Mayombe-bombe-mayombé!
Sensemayá, it died.][25]

Again, cradlesongs, delivered in dialect, repeat the folk motif and are cultivated by the poets of the genre.[26] Afro-Cuban Ignacio Villa's "Drumi, Mobila" is a particularly noteworthy example of the pursuit of black vernacular in this vein of *negrismo:*

No yora, Mobila,
Que tu mamá ta la campo,
Y horita ta bení pa cá.

Si nene drumi
Cuando mamá sale,
E trae regalito pa tí,
E trae to lo nunie pa tí,

Y si nene no drumi,
Chimbilicó
Cheche Calunga
Lo ranca lo pitico
Y lo come.

[Doan cry, Mobila
You mudda deh in the fiel'
And she comin' here just now.

If baby sleep
When Mommy go out
She gon' bring nice present fo' you
She gon' bring all the doggie fo' you

An' if baby doan sleep,
Chimbilico!
Cheche Calunga
Gon' take way all you little whistle
An' eat you up.][27]

25. In Guirao, *Orbita de la poesía afrocubana,* 104.
26. See, for example, "Para dormir a un negrito," by Emilio Ballagas, and "Canción de cuna para dormir a un negrito," by Ildefonso Pereda Valdés, a Uruguayan poet; both in Ballagas, *Antología,* 49, 53.
27. Two and a half decades later, 1958, Guillén would reprise the theme of the lullaby. But while his cradlesong maintained the parent-child intimacy and the socializing intention of the

The ubiquitous Ortician fingerprint is once more evinced in this regard. In 1929, his decision to publish a collection of *pregones* or cries of black street vendors as they hawked their wares, in spite of the obvious (quasi)ethnographic interest, took on a curious sense of "harvesting," given primitivism's voguish character and his recent trip to Europe. The *pregones* were reprinted from the *Diario de la marina* in his *Archivos del folklore cubano.*[28] As with the poets, Ortiz's enthusiasm over their purported aesthetic value, their musicality, and their humorous content, all betray the distance between the elite intellectualism of the movement and the subalternized materiality of its subjects. Not surprisingly, the *pregón,* as an objet trouvé of black orality, would subsequently become the theme of two poems.

Of the two, Ballagas's "Pregón" ("Street Vendor's Cry") is the better example.[29] The poem opens and closes with the call of the peddler to the housewife: "¡Casera!" (Housewife!). The peddler brings a variety of tropical fruit: "¡Piña, guanábana, mango! / ¡Mamey, platanito, manzano!" (Pineapple, custard apple, mango! / Mammee, banana, apple!), and Ballagas effects a brilliant synesthesial conceit as he blends the aroma of the fruit with their appetizing look and the sound of the *pregón.* Sound and smell thus radiate across the sunlit tropical day and, together with the brightly colored fruit, titillate the appetite of the consumers: "Cuando pregona el melon / y lo vuelve a pregonar, / en el rojo del melón / nos enciende el paladar" (When he calls out "Melon"/ and calls it out again / in the redness of the melon / our taste buds are turned on). There is no direct contact or dialogue in the poem, however, with the *pregonero,* the vendor himself, who remains anonymous. The speaker's primary interest is in the *pregón,* in its artistic value, and in the variety of sensations it awakens as it passes.

The *pregón,* in effect, is personified as it goes by, "en ruedas de brisa y sol" (on wheels of breeze and sunlight). In reality, of course, there is no such thing as "wheels of breeze and sunlight." Since the wheels of the fruit cart are quite possibly wooden, the job of the vendor, as he pushes it in the stultifying

---

genre, the child here is not put to sleep. The exhortation this time is for him to wake up *(despertar),* or more suggestively to "rise up," instead of going to sleep, as the poet visualizes a completely different role both for lullaby and for parent. Just as suggestive is the fact that the poem is written in standard Spanish, but with an epigraph from Ballagas's neobozalic antecedent ("Drumi mi nengre / mi nengre bonito"). The intertextual link that the epigraph establishes with the former poem, and its deliberate departure from the vernacular, would make it seem that Guillén is casting an ironic backward look at *negrista* nativism.

28. Fernando Ortiz, "Pregones populares," 375.

29. The other "Pregón" was by Nicolás Guillén. It also appeared in Ballagas's 1935 anthology.

Caribbean heat, shouting as he peddles his wares, is quite likely a very unpoetic one. When he is incorporated into the narrative, it is almost incidental. He appears as an appendage of the personified *pregón,* which, we are told, "drags a lip" *(hala una bemba)* behind it. The lip, in turn, "drags a Negro" *(arrastra un negro)* in its wake. The man himself, then, occupies a minor role in a more complex poetic conceit. He is merely apprehended in the poem as a blur of "sweat and shine" and is rendered invisible in spite of the colorful materiality of his presence. Additionally, notwithstanding the collective allure of his merchandise—"el rojo del melón nos enciende el paladar" (the red of the melon turns our taste buds on)—neither his labor nor the service he provides is acknowledged by the speaker.

The dismissal of the *pregonero* in this poem might well be seen as a violation of the spirit of the movement, given the nationalist and humanistic rhetoric about *negrismo* that came from both Ballagas and Ortiz, that is, even if we associate this disregard for the fruit seller with the indifference of consumer culture. The racialized morphology of the *negro* further undermines the case for humanism and "racial rapprochement," in the genre. Ballagas's synecdochial use of the derogatory term *bemba* to refer to the vendor's mouth ("the cry drags a lip / and the lip drags a Negro behind it"), does two things. First, it isolates the lips/mouth of the black subject, already an aberration in the racist colonial imaginary, in the visual economy of the poem. The image of disproportionately large lips is further exaggerated by the stretching and swelling implied if, as the poem states, the lips drag the rest of the body of the black man behind it. Second, this image bears a close affinity to the caricaturesque iconography of blackface, which would continue to figure in the depiction of blacks in print media in Latin America for years to come.

Negrista ambivalence is again evinced in Ballagas's poetic eulogy to the renowned black female dancer María Belén Chacón, though there is sympathy expressed this time for the hardworking subject, a washerwoman who succumbed to pneumonia. However, in spite of the compassion, it is clear that her loss to the speaker is felt primarily in terms of the pelvic. Evidently an admirer with some degree of familiarity with her, he laments: "Ya no veré mis instintos / en los espejos alegres y redondos de tus dos nalgas" (I'll no longer see my instincts / in the round happy mirrors of your two buttocks). Ballagas's "Elegía a María Belén Chacón" joins several *negrista* poems, including ones written by black writers, whose main characteristic in treating the black or mulatto woman is an unblushing prurience and an uninhibited familiarity.

Depicted in a primarily one-dimensional role as dancer, in a carnival procession, or at a dance, her value is that of a richly erotic and mobile icon, expressed by way of an exaggerated emphasis on hips, breasts, eyes (to reflect her inner fire), and buttocks. In Ballagas's "Kite Dance" ("El baile del papalote"), the mulatto woman is a vigorous, if sometimes graceful dancer, who ascends in proportion to her intake of alcohol. Toy that she is, however, she is subjected to the control of the flyer of the kite, who manipulates her flight from his end of the string. When the rum begins to compromise her gracefulness, and the "wind" threatens to carry her away, he reins her in to his arms. In José Antonio Portuondo's "Mari Sabel," the direct control gives way to erotic speculation, as the dancer's rum-inspired and epileptic movements eventually break the restraints of her clothing. Before her body is finally exposed, however, the leering eyes of the male onlookers, described as "navajazos de miradas" (slashing, knifelike looks), had already "desgarraron tu bata" (ripped [her] smock to shreds). Hernández Catá's "Rumba" repeats the libidinous gaze of the male group, the presumption of easy availability, and the thinly veiled threat of sexual violence behind the desire for the *negra:* "Cien ojos buscan los caminos / que conducen a sus entrañas" (A hundred eyes seek the pathways / that lead into her). In *negrismo*'s representation of black women, the paradigmatic association of the female muse with chastity, ranging from the unrequited love(rs) of the medieval courtly lyric to the heavy symbological investment in white beauty in nineteenth-century Modernism, has been disrupted. Its overt lasciviousness and the symbolic violence it demonstrates could only come from the generations of real racial and social domination that preceded the movement.

Emilio Ballagas, to conclude on the matter of the anthologies, as poet, anthologist, and commentator on *poesía negra,* provided, with the perhaps unwitting assistance of Fernando Ortiz, the ethnographer, the most important ideological legacy to subsequent liberal scholarship on the topic. The resurgence of interest in Africana studies produced by the civil rights era in this country influenced the production of several new *negrista* anthologies, mostly in the intercontinental style of his *Mapa.* The most notable of them were by Rosa E. Valdés-Cruz, *La poesía negroide en América* (1970), Hortensia Ruiz del Vizo, *Black Poetry* (1972), and José Luis González and Mónica Mansour, *Poesía negra de América* (1976). By the time the *Sensemayá* anthology of Aurora de Albornoz and Julio Rodríguez-Luis was published in 1980, Ballagas's main ideas, repeated and elaborated upon by the mentioned anthologists, had been elevated to the status of "doctrine" for the critical appreciation of *negrista* texts, which these critics repeat almost verbatim.[30]

30. Albornoz and Rodríguez-Luis, *Sensemayá,* 9.

The reason for this repetition may lie in the attractiveness to the liberal critical posture, of Ballagas's authoritative claim to exaltation of the ethnic Other, and the comfort levels inspired by his theory of interethnic representability. Both precepts come clothed in the sanitized notion of harmonious racial integration and cultural synthesis in Cuba and the Hispanic Caribbean. The Negrist point of departure of these positions, however, is all too evident. In this regard, the simplistic generalizations and the institutionalizing impulse are again evinced in Valdés-Cruz's assertion regarding the subjects of the poetry: "There are differences in the matter of cultural and racial integration between Cuban blacks and North American blacks, which have come about under different socioeconomic, social, and political conditions in the two countries. *That is why Cuban blacks are always predisposed toward happiness and celebration, and not moaning and complaining.*" Valdés-Cruz's blanket assumptions about the experiences of blacks in Cuba, and indeed the United States, are as dismissive of the complexities attendant to the constitution of these subjectivities as they are condescending. Cuban critic José Juan Arróm, for his part, was no more candid about the colonial past when he tried to rationalize the Cuban interracial posture on the basis of a shared and purportedly equitable sense of community and national history. Speaking ostensibly as a critic of the exotic content of Europe's primitivism, and in vindication of his own compatriots' sincerity regarding the topic, he claimed in 1942, "[T]he black had long-standing roots of four hundred years. The white Cuban did not see blacks as an African with a necklace of crocodile teeth, *but as a Cuban who was just as much Cuban as he was, a citizen of the same republic that they had together forged by dint of the machete.*"[31] Again an entire history of black long-suffering and struggle is dismissed in one fell hermeneutic swoop.

Ballagas's transracial representability was also the basis for diminishing the importance of the European vanguard in this literary "discovery" of the black compatriot, and it has prompted the assertion that there is a historiographic debt of gratitude owed by subsequent Afro-latino writers to the largely white *negrista* movement. To the degree that such a configuration leaves the premises of racial and authorial privilege unchallenged, however, and supports the appearance of democratic or vindicatory intentions in this poetry, it contributes to the creation of appropriately mollified forms of social consciousness in relation to *negrismo* and its extratextual referents in

---

31. Rosa E. Valdés-Cruz, *La poesía negroide en América,* 67; José Juan Arróm, "La poesía afrocubana," 393 (emphasis mine in both quotes).

Latin American culture.[32] At the same time, it skirts important questions related to black alterity and to accountability in discourse.

A significant example of Ballagas's influence on criticism across the decades may be found in the curious assertion in *Sugar's Secrets,* to the effect that, "[L]ittle is gained by debating whether Afro-Antilleanism was a truly indigenous movement or an imported intellectual fad." Its writer goes on to say, "[D]ismissing white negrista poets while praising writers of African descent for their presumably more authentic portrayals of blacks may help consolidate present ideological positions, but only at the expense of dehistoricizing and depoliticizing both the issues and the literature."[33] For this study, however, Afro-Antilleanism was both an indigenous movement and an imported intellectual fad, and the ways in which it was each of these things is central to its analysis. Since *negrismo*'s importedness speaks directly to previous black disenfranchisement and marginalization in Caribbean and Latin American life and letters, there is much to be gained in establishing the impact of the fad, and the nature and level of foreign influence. Undoubtedly local authors and subjects mark the movement as "indigenous," but at the same time it is important to emphasize how much the awareness of the black compatriot was stimulated by the Africanist vogue of the metropolitan vanguard. It was this European revaluation that accorded acceptability and validity to select aspects of the African New World presence, which in turn would play a role in subsequent postcolonial myths of inclusion. The contradictions attendant to the movement's indigenousness and its importedness suggest that a (re)historicizing and (re)politicizing of the issues is indeed central to the matter at hand, especially since both history and politics are integrally tied to positionality, power, and ethnicity in *negrista* writing.

Puerto Rico: *Burundanga?*

In the foundational essays and theses of Puerto Rico's generation of the 1930s, whose premise of white racial superiority and whose Hispanophilia had their clearest expression in Antonio Pedreira's book *Insularismo,* Luis Palés Matos is the only writer around whom a discourse of cultural recognition of the black presence might be built. Palesian exceptionalism has maintained

32. See, for example, Vera Kutzinski, *Sugar's Secrets: Race and the Erotics of Cuban Nationalism,* 153. On the management of social consciousness, see Glenn Jordan and Chris Weedon, *Cultural Politics: Class, Gender, Race, and the Postmodern World,* 117–18.

33. Kutzinski, *Sugar's Secrets,* 153.

the attention of intellectuals today involved in creating a consensus about the relationship between race and the Puerto Rican nation. Many critics see his thought as being conscientiously and diametrically opposed not only to a retrograde and racist Pedreira, but also to the Eurocentric antecedents of the nineteenth century and, in effect, deserving of the recognition and centrality that befits its anti-imperialism and its broadly democratic tenor. The ostensible value of Palesian ideology to the nation thus lies in the fact that it is neither of the old colonial regime, nor of the new "postcolonial" one, but assumes, rather, the racial and cultural vernacular "Afro-Antilleanism" *(afro-antillanismo),* or just "Antilleanism" *(antillanismo),* as its center. It is an ideology that is linked to and partially inspired by the antibourgeois international appeal of the Cuban revolution and its apparent achievement of racial democracy, and it is located, more specifically, in the iconic aura of Cuba's biracial national poet, Nicolás Guillén, a contemporary of Palés and an exemplar of *negrista* verse.

If the advocating of a mulatto national identity by the country's intellectual elite seems to have the earmark of an invention of ethnicity, it is to be borne in mind that this elite imagination of the nation is taking place in the context of a profoundly ambivalent history regarding the island's racial makeup and character. The poetic celebration of a white, male, national selfhood, which had pivotal articulations in 1844 and 1958,[34] and which existed alongside a less deeply rooted tradition of nostalgic Indianism, was rudely interrupted by essayists Isabelo Zenón Cruz and José Luis González in recent decades. Whereas Zenón Cruz's *Narciso descubre su trasero* (1975) made a frontal attack on the conceit of whiteness in Puerto Rico, González's *El país de cuatro pisos* (1982) decentered the Spanish premise in the national genealogy and highlighted the foundational role of black labor and black culture in the early centuries of the colony. Much more than the diffuse Palesian defense of a Negroid poetics in the 1930s, its own virtue notwithstanding, Zenón Cruz and González have anchored the idea of a black presence and contribution to the national ontology in an irreversibly commonsensical and concrete manner.

34. See Manuel Alonso's Eurocentric sonnet "Un puertorriqueño" (1844), and María Teresa Babín's assertion, in *Panorama de la cultura puertorriqueña,* that the *jíbaro,* or white Puerto Rican peasant, represents "that which is most pure, resistant, and intrinsic about Puerto Rican nationality" (quoted in Zenón Cruz, *Narciso,* 1:65). Zenón Cruz highlights the Indianism of the 1930s through the 1950s in Puerto Rican literature as a process that ignores and displaces the black presence.

This is by no means meant to suggest that blackness as a racial identifier has acquired, as a result, any greater acceptability, at any level of the broader Puerto Rican polity, than, say, a hundred years ago. In fact, the enduring colonial anxiety of whitening was unequivocally expressed as recently as the 2000 census, during which an estimated 80.5 percent of Puerto Ricans identified themselves as racially white, a percentage higher, it might be observed, than in the United States. One recalls that a hundred years before, José Julio Henna, head of a delegation to the U.S. Congress, had also asserted that "almost eighty percent" of Puerto Ricans were "Caucasians," though a somewhat less enthusiastic member of that august body, in 1916, expressed the opinion that 75 to 80 percent of the island's population was "African or had an African strain in their blood." An equally memorable statement in this national self-portrait would be Augusto Malaret's 1937 description of Puerto Rico as the "whitest of all the Antilles," in a comparison with Cuba and the Dominican Republic.[35]

In a state, then, that bespeaks a sort of national neurosis on the matter of race, a purportedly liberationist, Palés-inspired, left-of-center consensus around mulatto national racial identity might be seen as apposite and relevant and might even assume some urgency. Indeed, inborn credibility of the Palesian proposal is enhanced to the degree that it can be inscribed around supportive signs like Afro–Puerto Rican musical genres such as the *plena, bomba,* or *salsa,* Afro–Puerto Rican cuisine, as well as *boricua,* the Afro-flavored national vernacular that the poet notably incorporated into his work.[36] Following the Guillén precedent, Luis Palés Matos thus emerges as an appropriate vehicle or cultural icon upon which to build an Afro-Antillean doctrine of racial and cultural homogeneity. It is puzzling, therefore, that Palés's primary contemporary critical supporter, Mercedes López-Baralt (one notes the articles, the monographic study, as well as her authoritative 1995 critical edition of his poetry), should lament his ongoing marginal status vis-à-vis the Puerto

35. See José Javier Pérez, "La raza: Reflejo de lo que se quiere ser y no se es." More than the U.S. binary and its appropriateness for Puerto Rico or Latin America in general, I am more concerned to note here the perennial flight from blackness discussed in Chapter 2. See also Godreau, "La semántica fugitiva," for a discussion that is critical of the exclusion of intermediate categories such as *mestizo, trigueño, mulato,* and so on. Miriam Jiménez Román quotes the Caucasian identity claim in "*Un hombre (negro) del pueblo:* José Celso Barbosa and the Puerto Rican 'Race' toward Whiteness," 20. See also Kelvin Santiago-Valles, "Policing the Crisis in the Whitest of All the Antilles," 44.

36. See Juan A. Guisti Cordero, "AfroPuerto Rican Cultural Studies: Beyond *cultura negroide* and *antillanismo*"; and Julio Marzan, *The Numinous Site: The Poetry of Luis Palés Matos,* 32.

Rican literary canon. Notwithstanding his literary genius and his trans-generational influence and appeal, which the critic takes pains to detail, the issue as to why Palés has not yet been consecrated as national poet (à la Guillén) prompts at least two questions in light of the racial ambivalence outlined above. The first one has to do with whether or not the racial muse might have tainted Palés's historiographic persona as poet. The second one is, if it has, to what degree?

In the rest of this chapter, I want to suggest that when both liberal and neoliberal critics of Palés fail to convincingly resolve the tensions arising from the poet's transracial initiative, the failure stems from their reluctance to confront the demons spawned by colonial production as they are invoked by Palesian Negrism.[37] I feel that it is what is responsible for the euphemism, doublespeak, and often dismissal and diminishment of the racial factor in a discourse *(negrismo)* that fundamentally defines itself by way of considerations around race. Palesian exceptionalism as part of a generalized reluctance to acknowledge the true extension of race in the poet's work is inevitably related to the real state of race relations in Puerto Rico, as experienced on a daily basis by those subjects constructed as "other" in a normative nonblack ontology. Whereas in Tomás Blanco's classic 1937 treatise, racial prejudice in Puerto Rico is described as an "innocent game of children," "healthily euphemistic" in tenor, and where the term *negro* is not offensive but an expression of "tender affection," Kelvin Santiago-Valles points to the "long past of discrimination and a present of brutal (though furtively racialized) police persecution." In addition, militarized police actions that involve the deployment of the U.S. National Guard in neighborhoods that are poor and black, and racial terrorism in the form of street graffiti calling for the murder of the generally darker Dominican immigrants hardly support a rhetoric of happy racial integration and tolerance in Puerto Rico.[38]

In the face of this kind of reality, an Afro-Antilleanist or "mulatto" discourse built around the work of the poet may well be read as a demagogic

---

37. By "liberal" critique here, I refer to the first generation of Palés critics, that of his contemporaries, like Tomás Blanco and Margot Arce, on the racial question in his poetry. In acknowledging his recognition of blackness in Puerto Rican culture, they are "liberal" in relation to the often-acrid rejections that characterized the period. Graciany Miranda Arcilla, "La broma de una poesía prieta en Puerto Rico," is the most extreme expression of this rejection. By "neoliberal," I refer to the present generation of Palesian critics (such as Mercedes López-Baralt, Julio Marzán, Carmen Vásquez Arce), whose revisionist thrust takes the work of the former a step further and makes him into a culture hero.

38. Blanco, *El prejuicio racial en Puerto Rico,* 4, 12, 14; Santiago-Valles, "Policing the Crisis," 43, 51.

shift in emphasis of the traditional Hispanophilia of the dominant sectors in Puerto Rico, especially to the extent that this shift might serve ruling-class projections of racial democracy while obscuring real racialized power and oppression. The selective discursive deployment of elements of the Afro-Antillean cultural repertoire, those that are textual as well as those that are extratextual, may similarly be seen as helping to effect the persuasive function in the Gramscian hegemonic operation built around the binary of consent and coercion. While intellectuals, educational institutions, the media, and even orchestrated and institutionalized activities of popular culture promote a rhetoric of cultural fusion, unemployment, discrimination, and continued criminalization and marginalization of blackness, much like the census flight from a black identity, manage to perpetuate black liminality. Insofar as the illusion of happy fusion becomes operational then, discrimination becomes an acknowledged but "isolated" reality, and racially motivated protest is made to seem aberrant, unpatriotic, or the function of black hypersensitivity. In stressing the importance to the maintenance of hegemony of the "armour of coercion" in any given social formation, Stuart Hall, after Gramsci, reminds us that "[T]he dominant system must . . . continually make and remake itself so as to 'contain' those meanings, practices and values which are oppositional to it. . . . [However] whatever the concessions the ruling 'bloc' is required to make to win consent and legitimacy, its fundamental basis will not be over-turned." The apparent enigma of Palés's being a "marginalized canon" is therefore resolved once we recognize the abiding power of Hispanophilia and the dominance of whiteness in Puerto Rico, notwithstanding the incessant invocations of mulattoness and/or Antilleanness on the part of the neoliberal critical front. For all his brilliance, in other words, the poet from Guayama, the racially tinged "Witchdoctors' Town" *(la Ciudad Bruja),*[39] may well have been deemed unfit to sit at the head of the Puerto Rican Parnassus.

In accordance with its Negrist trajectory, the rhetorical dressing up of Palés for national canonhood has been a studied and ongoing operation. To the degree that the black element in his work, though proportionally smaller (22 percent), represents a transracial discursivity born of the colonial contract, its spatial, temporal, and contextual referents unavoidably assume critical import. It is not surprising, therefore, that this element has become central to his vindication, a process that involves discrete and interrelated elements

---

39. Miranda Arcilla's analysis of population censuses from 1910–1930 made him predict that in about forty years (thus about 1975) blacks would have disappeared from the Puerto Rican landscape through miscegenation ("La broma de una poesía prieta," 3). See also Stuart Hall, "Culture, the Media, and the 'Ideological Effect.'"

of nationalist consecration, aesthetification, and sanitization. Accordingly, he is strenuously belauded not only for being the first *negrista* poet, but also for being the one who, in Julio Marzán's opinion, "performed the literary moves that set the stage for Guillén to surface." It is a promotion in which one notes the adamancy of the claim to anteriority as well as its nationalist purport. Rosa Valdés-Cruz repeats the assertion of his primacy, stressing that Palés was the first in introducing the "crucial period" of the genre. Mercedes López-Baralt, for her part, dispenses with the reference to the time the movement gathered momentum, ostensibly from 1926, and refers her readers to an earlier poem of 1917, "Danzarina africana," to illustrate her claim that he was the genre's "unquestionable initiator." This revisionist gesture, apparently, has no room for Cuban Felipe Pichardo Moya's poem, "La comparsa," published in the Havana journal *Gráfico,* in 1916. The López-Baralt thesis goes even further. It takes us beyond Emilio Ballagas's assertion of white authorial importance in the specifically *Hispanic* map of black poetry, as discussed above, to claim primacy for Palés in a wider Afro-diasporic geography, naming, in this case, Jamaican Claude McKay and African American Langston Hughes.[40]

Allied to the declaration that Luis Palés Matos is a regional and international literary originator of black poetry is the claim he was also the first promoter of an antiracist cultural fusion *(mestizaje)* in Puerto Rico and was someone who celebrated black culture at some personal risk. Marzán thus eulogizes him for being a "a white man who, in the [hostile environment of the] 1920s, dared to reflect publicly on his culture's African roots." Likewise, he is credited with giving voice to the forgotten and disenfranchised and for being a champion of anti-imperialism. Here again, the López-Baralt postulate is significant in its suggestion that, by virtue of his defense of the relevance of a black poetic muse in the Hispanic Antillean aesthetic, Palés can be referred to as a poet of negritude. It is a stunning claim. Even though *negritud* is a Hispanization of the French term *Négritude* and can cover a similar semantic area in its broad reference to blackness, the critic's deployment of the term can hardly claim to have been a linguistic lapse, especially bearing in mind the reference to poet Aimé Césaire that accompanies it.[41]

40. See Marzán, "The Poetry and Antipoetry of Luis Palés Matos," 511; and Marzán, *Numinous Site,* 15; Valdés-Cruz, *La poesía negroide,* 113; Mercedes López-Baralt, *El barco en la botella: La poesía de Luis Palés Matos,* 22. See also López-Baralt, *El barco,* 23, for the reference to McKay and Hughes.

41. Marzán, *Numinous Site,* 31; Carmen Vásquez Arce, "*Tuntún de pasa y grifería:* A Cultural Project"; López-Baralt, *El barco,* 25, 18.

What is important about the reference, however, is that in making Palés appear to share the passion and commitment of negritude as counterideology, it pulls a mask over the real source of his interest in the black muse. Also, it tends to detract from and diminish the anguish over genocide and ancestral loss for diasporic Africans and Afro-descendants that Césaire and other poets have expressed, not to mention the Martinican poet's courageous indictment of colonialism and slavery, and the symbolic capital that he earned over the decades as poet and politician.

Effectively, the not insignificant strain of antiblack derision and hostility in Palés's poetry, which has brought the charge of racism by some of his critics, has met with not a little resistance from his apologists. It appears frequently in essays that promote the nationalist agenda and is underscored in the two monographs by Marzán and López-Baralt dedicated to his work. Resistance to the bias and reductionism of such highly charged poems as "Bombo," "Lagarto Verde," and "Ñam-Ñam" ranges from a straightforward diminishment of the racial factor to the more sophistic approach that would even set it aside, since racial difference, as Rubén Rios reminds us, is so elusive. López-Baralt, in turn, challenges the competency of the readers who see Negrophobia in Palesian verse, and she proposes that their readings fail to appreciate the poet's use of irony, which is, in her opinion, really directed at subverting Western values, rather than making fun of black people. The racial reading, which she dubs "pedestrian," is presumably of a lesser order: "In spite of the efforts of the best Palesian criticism, it is still necessary to combat literal readings of the *Tuntún,* which are frequent."[42]

Julio Marzán also joins the complaint against the racial focus on Palesian verse, arguing that it detracts from the finer qualities of his work and diminishes him in status. His protest is even more direct in that it takes on Palés's principal detractor, Isabelo Zenón Cruz, a Puerto Rican intellectual who happened to be black, and dismisses Zenón Cruz's charge of racism as "specious," as the result of an incomplete and out-of-context reading. Interestingly enough, although Marzán would acknowledge the presence of *some* prejudice in Palés, it does not appear to him to be significant enough to disturb a fair-minded and unbiased reader. His appeal to reason (with this implied unbiased interlocutor) is apparent in his discussion of Palés's mock-heroic depiction of black majesty in "Bombo" and "Elegía del duque de la mermelada." "Is

42. Rubén Ríos Avila, *La raza cósmica del sujeto en Puerto Rico,* 147; Mercedes López-Baralt, "Preludio en Boricua, o la ironía como programa poético en el *Tuntún* palesiano"; López-Baralt, *El barco,* 53, 167.

this a racist poem?" he asks; "Is Palés's romantic interpretation of the tribal African as a noble savage a bad thing—or simply an outdated one? Is being compared to an ape any different from being compared to a frog, an ox, or a rooster? Is the Duke being ridiculed for underneath being like an ape, or was it for his aping Westerners, or was it for forsaking his numen?"[43]

The question, it seems, is not as convoluted as the critic would suppose. The insinuation that all readers of Luis Palés Matos subscribe to a white "racial contract," that those who cry foul at his imagery miss the subtlety of its irony, or that a black critic like Zenón Cruz did not know what he was talking about when he said that some of Palés's poems are "offensive to blacks," is an affront to the intellect of all these categories of readers. The last charge is clearly linked to the presumption that black people are incapable either of recognizing the signs of their oppression or of defining their reality. Related to it is the frequency with which the accusation of bias is forestalled by critics who insist on using the term *exaltar* (to exalt, to glorify), which we first saw in Ballagas, when speaking of Palés's intentions vis-à-vis black culture in his poetry. The trivialization and relativization of the animal tropes in Palés also springs from the same source, especially considering the potent historical role of the simian metaphor in the racist imagination. Even the pretended problematization by Marzán of the protests against Palés's portrayal of Haitian postcolonial mimicry falls flat, for its premise is not that colonial mimicry in itself is alienating, but that blacks betray their own (savage) nature in attempting to behave and look like sophisticated Westerners. This latter argument dates back at least to Rosa E. Valdés-Cruz, whose analysis included references to an Afro-Hispanic world that was at once "simple and natural" and characterized by rhythm, explosive happiness, and sexuality: "But the thing that Palés cannot accept is that Negroes would wish to imitate the white man and stop being black; it is then that they lose their majesty and grandeur. They then lose all the respect that they have gotten from the poet who now speaks with sarcasm and humor. . . . Palés sings here with painful irony for their disguises by which they seek to change their natural selves."[44] Race as an unchanging biological same, then, is what determines the black numen for Marzán and like critics, and atavism is its unavoidable order.

If nationalist value and racial sterilization are deemed important to the rehabilitation of the poet, it is the artistic dimension of his work that his

---

43. Marzán, *Numinous Site,* 41, 82.
44. See Zenón Cruz, *Narciso,* 2:100, Valdés-Cruz, *La poesía negroide,* 27, 23, 143–44.

apologists in the final analysis would rather underscore, hence their invocation of critical theory to establish its virtues and their stress on its technical attributes. Accordingly, Palés's use of myth, rhythm, irony, imagery, and intertextuality confirm Barthian prescriptions regarding real literary quality and the "Barthian pleasures of the text," and a Bakhtinian lens is imported to explain the subversive quality of his humor. In the same vein, a seat is sought for him among the more important bards of Latin America for his baroque ingenuity and for being an unsung innovator of what Chilean poet Nicanor Parra once termed "antipoetry."[45]

A more candid look at the problematics of Palesian appreciation might, in my opinion, give greater consideration to the colonial determinant insofar as it impacted, not only on Palés as a white *criollo* writing in 1930s Puerto Rico, but also on the way in which the primitivism of the modernists found echo in the Caribbean periphery. Appreciating the Negrist intention, both in the writing and reading of blackness, is again central to this process. Luis Palés Matos, much like the other intellectuals of his generation, was acutely sensitive to the impact of U.S. imperialism on the cultural and political destiny of Puerto Rico, and he shared in the pessimism that characterized their outlook. For Pedreira, the national tragedy revolved around three interrelated issues: ethnology, biology, and history, all of which were apparent in the generalized miscegenation initiated by Spanish colonists, whose legacy was a population of mixed-bloods. Miscegenation, since it put the superior whites, with their intelligence, nobility, and other higher attributes, into contact with the natural abjection of the slaves, had been a "difficult marriage." For Pedreira, mulattos, precisely because they were neither black nor white, were indecisive, uncreative, and incapable of leadership. Also, no contribution to an autonomous, modern Puerto Rico could be expected from the descendants of the black slaves, since they, with a history of being led and fed and provided for, were unaccustomed to and incapable of thinking for themselves. Like the mulattos, they were too cowardly for virile history-making action, an asset, again, of whiteness. "At the core of our population," he lamented, "one will find without great effort a great biological struggle of contrary and countercohesive forces, which have militated against our definitive formation as a people." Race mixture, he punned finally, was "con-fusion."[46]

45. López-Baralt, *El barco,* 28; Marzán, *Numinous Site,* 9.

46. Antonio S. Pedreira, *Insularismo: Ensayos de interpretación puertorriqueña,* 46, 50, 45. The following page citations are to this volume.

Biology and ethnography apart, Pedreira's pessimism was also provoked by the uninspiring economic prospects for Puerto Rico, based on the island's lack of natural resources and its distance from the rest of the international marketplace. Puerto Rico, in his opinion, was overpopulated, its agricultural land was exhausted, it was too small for a profitable tourist industry, and it had no real ports for trade. Additionally, it was a tragedy that although the U.S. presence had brought some modernization and material progress, this had been too costly in terms of traditional high culture. Old Hispanic values had been eroded to the point where music, painting, museums, and literature had lost their prestige in private and public life, and worse, the cultivation of culture was no longer being appropriately funded in civic society. In a lamentation reminiscent of José Enrique Rodó at the turn of the century, he said: "Today we are more civilized, but yesterday we were more cultured." Pedreira linked the loss of high culture in Puerto Rico to U.S. democratizating tendencies and to the negative impact this was having on the cultural elite, not only in symbolic terms, but also materially. The threat that was becoming increasingly manifest was one of progressive equality. That "superior men" were losing their traditional guarantees in society and were being placed at a disadvantage by what he considered mediocrity was unconscionable.[47]

The most burdensome existential challenge for the male creole, in terms of a putative national project, however, was Puerto Rico's inhospitable tropical climate. The heat decomposes us and makes us old prematurely, Pedreira claimed, and it is counterinducive to intellectual exploits and had reduced the white man to a state of mental vegetation. Four hundred years after the colonial project was initiated, white creoles, in a curious example of environmental determinism, were still trapped in a state of *aplatanamiento*, that is, of acclimatization to the "new" environment. At a time when, interestingly enough, race-thinkers like José Vasconcelos in Mexico and Brazil's Gilberto Freyre were articulating their own versions of civilization in the tropics, Pedreira was bemoaning its impossibility. Bearing in mind the island's lack of racial pedigree (its "con-fusion"), its physical insularity, and its multilateral isolation, what Puerto Rico added up to, for the white creole, could be expressed in one word that was highly evocative and multivalent: *burundanga*, which he quoted from his contemporary, Luis Palés Matos. The term, taken from the Puerto Rican vernacular, defines a hodgepodge of things that are

47. Ibid., 99, 101–2.

not only worthless, but also repugnant.[48] It appears in the poem "Canción festiva para ser llorada." As part of a refrain that sums up the (white) speaker's existential response to Afro-Antillean racial and cultural hybridity, and the generalized unhappiness of the postcolonial condition, it is as terse and brutal as it is poignant.

> Cuba-ñañigo y bachata—
> Haití-vodú y calabaza—
> Puerto Rico–burundanga—
>
> [Cuba-ñañigo and bachanal
> Haiti-voodoo and calabash—
> Puerto Rico–burundanga]

That Pedreira in his sense of isolation and disaffection could identify so intimately not only with the letter, but also with the spirit of Luis Palés Matos on the national question, is a key element in the discussion regarding the foundational discourse of the 1930s. Some commentators have apparently lost sight of this fundamental affinity between the two writers in the proposal of a supposedly binary relationship in their thinking relative to the black presence in Puerto Rico. If Palés's purported defense of the black muse has been misleading, however, it only confirms his own ambivalence regarding the African presence in the Caribbean and in Puerto Rico. The Palesian "celebration" of blackness has traditionally been seen in his defense of the autochthonous as an object of poetic expression and in the unprecedented inclusion of black subjects that his work represented for Puerto Rican literature. Neither event constitutes, in my opinion, an unqualified glorification of the black muse or of black subjectivity. Palés's Afro-Antillean aesthetic was expressed in a November 13, 1932, interview with Angela Negrón and again in a brief article that the writer published two weeks later, "Hacia una poesía antillana." On both occasions, Palés pointed to the black presence in the Hispanic Caribbean, adding, on the latter occasion, that it constituted the specifically Antillean difference vis-à-vis other Hispanic cultures. It was important for him for this "spiritual homogeneity" to be acknowledged and to be articulated in the region's poetry.[49]

---

48. Ibid., 57, 102. Manuel Alvarez Nazario defines *burundanga* as "an admixture of things that are useless or of little worth; something repugnant, rubbish" (*El elemento negroide en el español de Puerto Rico*, 324).

49. Luis Palés Matos, "Hacia una poesía antillana," 100.

It bears pointing out, however, that these insights were hardly original. His reference to what Fernando Ortiz, in 1940, would formally denominate Afro-Hispanic "transculturation" was an ongoing discursive and research project that had appeared since 1906 with Ortiz's *Hampa afro-cubana: Los negros brujos (apuntes para un estudio de entnología criminal),* a text with which Palés was familiar, and which he even cited. Besides, his vindication of the Afro element in the broader Hispano-Caribbean mix, in defiance of traditional Eurocentric referentiality, has an unmistakable resemblance to the proethnic call made a year earlier by Nicolás Guillén in his introduction to his second collection, *Sóngoro Cosongo.* There is more than just coincidence in Guillén's assertion that it did not matter to him that the racially reactionary might object to his black aesthetic, and Palés's anticipation, a year later, of the scandal that his own new Afro-oriented creed might provoke. Taking into consideration that his first Africanist poem, "Danzarina africana," was written in 1917, it seems strange that Palés should have waited until 1932 to declare that white Antilleans are really culturally black at heart, in spite of what they might otherwise say, that is, a year after the Guillén prologue had declared that "we are all like the sapodilla"—a little brown.[50]

The primitivist vogue is the other key element in the question of what we might call Palés's authorial self-construction at the *negrista* conjuncture. José de Diego Padró, his closest artistic collaborator, has pointed to Palés's voracious appetite for information from the literary world abroad, as well as his cosmopolitan pretensions, isolated, as he was, in his limiting island environment. As his glossary to *Tuntún* indicates, there is an almost academic methodicalness to his pursuit of sources of information on African and diasporic black culture, which encompasses ethnography, psychology, linguistics, and travel writing. He even cites the *Encyclopaedia Britannica* and the Spanish *Espasa* encyclopedia as references. The transracial writings of José Mas, Vachel Lindsay, Eugene O'Neill, Blaise Cendrars, Leo Frobenius, William Seabrook, Carl Van Vechten, John Vandercook, among others, were all reflected in his work, as his earliest critics assert. So, too, was his particular enthusiasm for the sonorous qualities of Lindsay's dramatic "The Congo," when he heard the poem performed by fellow poet Muñoz Marin. The subsequent recording and dramatization of his own "Tembandumba" and "Danza negra," with additional Africanized lyrics, a cast of characters,

50. Palés cites *Los negros brujos* in his glossary as one of his references. It is logical to suppose that he had access to other writings by Ortiz. See the "Vocabulario" section of the 1937 edition of *Tuntún de pasa y grifería: Poemas afroantillanos,* 125. See also Angela Negrón Muñoz, "Hablando con don Luis Palés Matos," 89; and Guillén, *Obra poética 1920–1972,* 1:114.

and a "black" soundtrack with drums and voices, is a direct reflection of his enthusiasm for this "found poetry." It is hard not to conclude that the performance of these poems, as part of the outreach program of Puerto Rico's Department of Education in 1935, marks an important Negrist instantiation through its linkage of pedagogy, persuasion, and state power. The endorsement of the content of *Tuntún*, of Palés's new "negroid" authorial persona, and of the performance of generations of black professional reciters, or *declamadores*, further advance the Negrist project. Following the initial legitimizing gesture of famous Spanish actor González Marín, who recited Palés to rave reviews, they naturalize the Palesian epistemology of blackness.[51]

The early lyrical experiments that were the product of Palés's all-night bohemian exchanges with de Diego Padró and other members of their coterie evince their interest in both the overseas avant-garde and the ersatz primitivism that accompanied it. *Diepalismo,* the short-lived movement that combined their names in 1921, accented sound over sense in a dadaesque display of plasticity and onomatopoeia. Their poetic manifesto, the "Orquestación diepálica," went as follows:

> ¡Guau! ¡Guau! Au-au, au-au, au-au, huuummm...
> La noche. La luna. El campo...huuummm...
> Zi, zi, zi-zi, co-quí, co-quí, co-co-quí...
> Hierve la abstrusa zoología en la sombra.
> ¡Silencio! Huuuuuummmmm...
>
> [Bow, Wow! Au-au, au-au, au-au, huuummm...
> The night. The moon. The countryside...huuummm...
> Zi, zi, zi-zi, co-quí, co-quí, co-co-quí...

51. Of the early critics, see, for example, Tomás Blanco, "Poesía y recitatación negras"; and Margot Arce, "Más sobre los poemas negros de Luis Palés Matos." For Diego Padró's comments regarding Vachel Lindsay's effect on Palés, see José de Diego Padró, *Luis Palés Matos y su trasmundo poético,* 23. See also contemporary reviews on González Marín, by Rafael Montañez, on Cuban reciter Eusebia Cosme, by Carmelina Vizcarrondo and Nilita Vientos Gastón, on Dominga de la Cruz Carillo by Jorge Font Saldaña (1938), as well as a later one on Puerto Rican Juan Boria by Jaime Torres Torres (1993). Montañez's review is particularly revealing in that it cites the approbatory comment of Spanish literary icon Miguel de Unamuno regarding Marín's convincing portrayal of savagery in his rendition of "Ñam-Ñam." Unamuno reportedly went to his room and shouted, "You're an animal, Pepe González," 15. Unamuno's prologue to José Mas's travelogue *En el país de los bubis* was similarly congratulatory of the writer, ostensibly for the truth in representation of Spain's African colony of Equatorial Guinea. He remarked that, through Mas, "you can feel the animal, almost vegetal tragedy of the black race" (3). The essentialist primitivist link in Palés is inescapable if we consider the iconography that accompanied the individual publication of the poems, for example, "Candombe" (1936) and "Canción festiva para ser Llorada" (1937), in the *Puerto Rico Ilustrado.*

The abstruse zoology boils in the shadows.
Silence! Huuuuuummmmm . . .]

The "pre-Cubist Intention" of their second and last joint production pre-
saged Diego Padró's overtly primitivist ode to Hottentot culture which followed and the acoustic imagery that would later be associated with Palés
and *negrismo* as a whole. Diego Padró's evocation of blackness and a primordial Africa as a motif mutual to both artists, is seen in his "Tun-tún-
tún . . . cuntúncuntún . . . Danzas en el corazón de las selvas oscuras" (Tun-
tún-tún . . . cuntúncuntún . . . Dances in the heart of the dark jungles).[52]
Palés expanded his own *Tuntún de pasa y grifería* trope into a book of poems.

There is every reason to appreciate Diego Padró, Palés's companion and
cocreator, as a privileged observer of the poet, insofar as his reminiscences
demystify the pretended revolutionary Afrocentricity of the latter. This is
especially true in relation to his emphasis on the fact that the black muse
was a welcomed creative opportunity for Palés. Like contemporary Spanish
poets Lorca and Alberti, he could exploit the popular-ethnic vein in his
home, Puerto Rico, notwithstanding his aristocratic intellectuality and his
deeply felt affiliation to Western values. Again, this observation is not meant
to suggest that as an Antillean one cannot simultaneously embrace these two
aspects of the region's broad historico-cultural heritage. It is just to propose
that black cultural and racial vindication is not necessarily the place to look
for the Palesian interest in the black muse. On the contrary, his search for
artistic originality through the *negrista* fashion and his response to the national
crisis of the 1930s emerge as two axes of a prolonged contemplation on the
black compatriot and the regional community. If Puerto Rico's tropical heat
stifled creativity and induced paralysis for Pedreira and others, Palés the poet
would counteract the general malaise by becoming a voyager in the spirit.
He would activate a travel motif, as one of his editors observed, going first to
the Nordic regions, and then to Africa. Art, according to Jaime Benítez,
would be his "escape hatch."[53]

Palés's ambivalent feelings regarding the Caribbean are summarized in his
long poem "Canción festiva para ser llorada." It is a "festive song," to be
sung, paradoxically, through tears; it is one in which the poet's bitterness, a

---

52. Diego Padró, *Luis Palés Matos,* 27. The full title of the "pre-Cubist" poem is "Intra-
objetivismo de intención precubista" (28).

53. Ibid., 50–51; Jaime Benítez, "Luis Palés Matos y el pesimismo en Puerto Rico: Doce
años después," 27.

constant throughout his entire oeuvre, is dominant. The "Canción" discursively recreates the transnational Caribbean as a house, under the proprietorship, significantly, of the poetic speaker, a white male *criollo*. Although the reference to the Sinclair Lewis character Babbitt sets the narrative temporally in the early twentieth century during the U.S. "postcolonial" presence, the poem's ideological core is squarely colonial, as is indicated in the division of labor projected by the speaker onto the rest of the community of islands. Accordingly, in this "neocolonial" house, the role of the black and mulatto women remains the same as in the days of slavery. The islands of Martinique and Guadaloupe are racialized and feminized and inscribed as black domestic workers, each one in an area of the dwelling determined by the speaker.

> . . . Martinica y Guadalupe
> me van poniendo la casa.
> Martinica en la cocina
> y Guadalupe en la sala.
> Martinica hace la sopa
> y Guadalupe la cama.
> buen calalú, Martinica,
> que Guadalupe me aguarda.

> [. . . Martinique and Guadaloupe
> arrange the house for me
> Martinique in the kitchen
> and Guadaloupe in the living room.
> Martinique makes the soup
> and Guadaloupe makes up the bed.
> Nice callaloo, Martinique,
> let Guadaloupe wait for me.]

The complement to forced domestic labor, however, according to the colonial contract, is the sexual availability of the black woman, hence the candid reference to sex (in this case, cunnilingus) with Guadalupe the *mulata*. Not surprisingly, her erotic usefulness is registered in an offhand manner. As the pun on *pan* and *tort(ill)a* indicates, she belongs to a secondary plane of desirability.[54]

54. In its normal articulation, the idiom goes: "A falta de pan, tortilla" (Tortilla, if there's no bread). In this case, *torta* would also be a reference to female genitals, per the Puerto Rican vernacular.

En qué lorito aprendiste
ese patuá de melaza,
Guadalupe de mis trópicos,
mi succulenta tinaja?
a la francesa, resbalo,
sobre tu carne mulata
que a falta de pan, tu torta
es prieta gloria antillana.

[From what parrot did you learn
that patois like molasses,
Guadalupe of my tropics,
my succulent earthen jar?
I slide over your mulatto meat
in the French style
your cake is dark Antillean glory,
tortilla, if there's no bread.]

The (con)text might invoke a supposition of colonial nostalgia in the Palesian speaker, and of a past in which white male sexual predation was the unquestioned norm, given the contours of the sexual economy of slavery. In this scenario, the sexual exploitation of the black woman, defined as a "domestic animal" in "Pueblo negro," another of his poems, did not qualify for the vindication that might characterize her abuse as rape, hence the casual tone of the speaker in these lines. Effectively, *mulata* love is reiterated in "Mulata-Antilla," as "love unhurried and untrammelled." In the case of "Canción festiva," the supposition of white male sexual chauvinism in the speaker would be true to the degree that, traditionally, whiteness presupposed land tenure and its associated privileges. In the more objective context of Palés's biography, however, one would have to take into account his own family's descent into poverty, precisely as a result of the inherent instability of (capitalist) colonial production.[55]

The crude irony of a *criollo* clan fallen upon such hard times that their lone "domestic animal," Lupe, would steal eggs so that the family, one of literary pretensions, might be afforded much needed protein, exposes the

---

55. In the postslavery scenario, some domestic workers were paid and some went unpaid, especially if they needed room and board. Sexual exploitation remained the norm. See testimonials in Elizabeth Crespo's "Domestic Work and Racial Divisions in Women's Employment in Puerto Rico, 1899–1930." Palés's father came from a landowning, planter family. Guayama had had its moment of prosperity as a sugar producer between 1830 and 1846. See Guillermo A. Baralt, *Esclavos rebeldes: Conspiraciones y sublevaciones de esclavos en Puerto Rico (1795–1873),* 116.

underside of the colonial mastertext of white conquistador dominance. In a household where both parents were poets and three sons future bards, their poverty counterposes the aura of literati cultural capital to the more mundane materiality of their collective physical need. The casual reductionism of making (fellow colonies) Martinique and Guadaloupe into *negras* thus responds as much to fantasy as it does to reality. As in other aspects of the cross-racial impulse, in it desire commingles clearly with derogation. The analogy with Cervantes's *Don Quixote* characters Maritornes and Dulcinea that the speaker employs here is particularly important:

> Sólo a veces Don Quijote
> por chiflado y musaraña
> de tu maritornería
> construye una dulcineada.

> [Only sometimes Don Quixote
> In his oddball absentmindedness
> might make something sweet
> out of your distasteful nature.]

In seeing himself as Quixotic for forcibly (re)making these supremely repugnant black women into the ideal female model of Cervantes's Dulcinea, he underscores the sense of alienation and displacement that his generation projected for the white male *criollo* writer in the colonial world.[56]

As it does with the women, the "Canción" offers an unflattering inscription of black men. It also racializes other Caribbean countries that, effectively, have a majority black population. Santo Domingo, St. Kitts, the Lesser Antilles, St. Thomas, and Curaçao are thus depicted through menial imagery that alludes to the slave past as well as the tourist economies that continue to define these islands as vulnerable, insignificant entities, especially bearing

56. Lupe, described in Palés's unfinished autobiographical novel, "Litoral: reseña de una vida inútil," as a "fat, black woman," had been acquired by the grandfather when she was twelve years old and had served the clan since then. She had been a mammy figure and was now a cook. Her current services were unpaid, hence his description of her as being "impelled by the simple spirit of service inherent to her race and by the maternal affection she has for us." My application of the poet's metaphor of the domestic animal to her is motivated by this unpaid itinerant service she provided and by his recollection that if, during her frequent visits to the house, she returned at night, she would huddle in the damp cold outside until daybreak. See Palés, "Litoral," 67, 69.

In *Don Quixote*, Maritornes was short, cockeyed, half-blind, and hunchbacked, and had such bad breath that unless one were a mule driver, it would make one vomit. Daniel Grünberg, in reviewing the Cervantes analogy, maintains, following López-Baralt and Marzán, that Palesian use of the grotesque in describing black people, is meant to glorify *(exaltar)* them ("Dulcinear la maritornería, la exaltación de lo grotesco en *Tuntún de pasa y grifería*," 138, 143).

in mind their collective susceptibility to hurricanes. Santo Domingo, for example, becomes the guitar-playing gardener in the Caribbean house, while the Lesser Antilles are dancing little marmosets *(titís),* and St. Kitts is the neighborhood "clown" *(el bobo de la comarca).* Jamaica and Curaçao are symbolized through rum, the by-product of sugarcane, the historical reason for their black populations. As with the other territories, the song and dance and condiments of the spice-producing islands make them appear as diminutive racialized regional fixtures in the international division of labor. In the sardonic signifying voice of the white Puerto Rican, whose former associations with hegemony are now dislocated by the new imperial regimen, the widening consciousness that the imperial transition has wrought has also made the Antillean house a place of discomfiture. Puerto Rico's new subjection helps explain how the surface happiness of the tourist islands brings a grimace of pain to the speaker. His adoption of the Quixotic mask reveals both his marginality and the self-conscious strategy required to endure an uncomfortable reality. It is interesting that Haiti is not named in the "Canción" as integral to the circuit of tourism and small-scale agricultural production in which twentieth-century neocolonial capital placed the countries of the Caribbean basin. Despite its recent subjection to the imperial project with the 1915–1934 occupation, it is Haiti's symbolic status as site of the only successful slave revolution (1791–1804) that the poem evokes. Again, the prism of race dominates, and Haitian icons of liberation like Toussaint-Louverture and Dessalines represent a menacing, animalistic force, and Macandal's epic religious and ideological role in the Haitian revolution is portrayed in terms of cannibalism and voodoo mania.

Tuntún's rootedness in the imagery of the past is reflected in the evocation in "Canción" of aspects of the consciousness of the former planter class in its domineering mode, or, alternatively, in its moments of anxiety when under the specter of slave revolt. Its duality attests to the epistemological splittage that the colonial legacy has imposed. Colonial nostalgia would further be evinced in the poet's predilection for a narrative of cultural disparagement that serves to shore up a displaced racial selfhood in a world that often gives the appearance of having been turned upside down. In the expansion of *Tuntun's* racial imagery to encompass a diasporic geography of blackness, Nigricia, it is important to stress the degree to which the book's dominant tropes of black rape, irreligion, cannibalism, and drunkenness fit into a preexisting Afro–Puerto Rican template. That is to say that the nineteenth-century ethnography, the colonial travel writing, or the primitivist texts of Modernism, alluded to above, that Palés consulted, are by no means projected to, or from, an epistemological *tabula rasa*. Palés, in *Tuntún de pasa y grifería*, would thus function in the mode of the raconteur who has ingested and is selectively retelling their stories.

The first indication of *Tuntún* as palimpsest remits us once more to Lupe, the sometime servant in the Palesian family home and the speaker of the original text of the poet's wide-ranging black narrative source. Lupe, as mammy and storyteller, provoked a fascination in the young Palés with the black world of magic, fantastic creatures, and exotic "African" refrains. Of particular resonance was a bedtime story about a disobedient boy who was lost in the forest; he was about to be devoured by witchdoctors when he was saved in the nick of time by his faithful dogs. In his unfinished autobiographical novel, "Litoral," in the scene of the *baquiné*, or wake, for the dead black child, Palés's adolescent narrator is startled to discover that the same phrase that accompanied the climactic moment of cannibalism in the bedtime story, is also a part of the *baquiné* ritual. There is an eerie flashback as he and his brother involuntarily join in the chant, "Adombe, gangá mondé, / ¡Adombe," to the astonishment of the other white onlookers, while Lupe, now in a totally different guise as high functionary in an alien rite, turns and smilingly recognizes them. The moment is important because it highlights the suppression of blackness in what is a fundamentally heterogeneous cultural identity in the poet, originated in the input of the repressed black mammy or mother figure, which has broader nationwide implications. The narrator's earlier assertion, upon arrival at the scene of the wake, that they felt they were "as if in another world: the world of blacks," marks the *baquiné* as a site of conflict, as indeed it marks other sites of cultural hybridity. Bearing in mind the negative symbolic value of the *Gran Ciempiés*, or high priest, at the event, the drinking, the Africanized chants, and the (not so) surreptitious sex of the couples in the nearby cane fields, it does not seem excessive to posit a recoil from the hybrid identity in the self-portrait of the artist as a grown man, notwithstanding his purported vindication of the black cultural presence. It is the sort of contradiction that defines colonial ambivalence.[57]

---

57. Palés, "Litoral," 92, 89. The degree of Lupe's repression is perhaps measured in the fact that in neither of the references made to her by Tomás Blanco, *Sobre Palés Matos,* 15, or Diego Padró, *Luis Palés Matos,* 21, is she named. Palés's negative reaction to blackness may indeed have its source in the poet's own mixed genealogy, notwithstanding the insistence of some critics as to his white racial identity. His reference to "my two races" in "Mulata-Antilla" might therefore be more than metaphorical, especially considering Puerto Rican vernacular lore regarding African traces in his family tree. The anxiety of being white, but not quite, then, is what might be behind the sometimes vicious humor concerning black subjectivity.

It is therefore significant that the refrain *Adombe gangá mondé* should reemerge in Palés's poem "Falsa canción de baquiné," where the title's confession of "falseness" repositions the speaker on the outside of the black cultural community. We recall that *Tuntún*'s "Preludio en Boricua," spatially located in Puerto Rico, had also admitted to the reader that much of the narrative to follow was made up, and its narrator disingenuous. When *Adombe gangá mondé,* a phrase that means "now we are going to eat," reappears, it does so with two important contextual variations. In Lupe's bedtime bogeyman story, it was spoken by the witchdoctors to announce their cannibalistic intentions, which were eventually frustrated by the arrival of the dogs. In the "Falsa canción," the implicit transracial projection of the tale, internalized by its interlocutor, the young Palés, has now been made explicit by the older Palés. If the identity of the putative victims in Lupe's original story was ambiguous, in the "Falsa canción" they are clearly white. There are no dogs to interrupt the sequence of events here, either. Further, the cannibal utterance is in the imperative mood, portending execution of the command to eat the white victims. It has a Francophone/Haitian inflection as well.

> Ahora comamos carne blanca
> Con la licencia de su mercé
> Ahora comamos carne blanca...
>
> [Now let's eat white meat
> With the permission of your worship
> Now let's eat white meat...]

That the cannibal scene can be so overtly resemanticized as *Haitian* builds on the supposition articulated in the *baquiné* chapter of the novel that the ceremony has its origin in Haitian vodoo death rituals.[58] The deflection is significant insofar as it pushes voodoo and cannibalism out of Puerto Rico, the "whitest of the Antilles," and disavows the very regional homogeneity extolled by Afro-Antilleanism theory. Besides, it erases Lupe as a specifically Afro-Puerto Rican culture bearer.

Tuntún de pasa y grifería's exploration of blackness traces a negatively charged semantic arc that leaves Puerto Rico and the Antilles, reaches down

---

58. Palés's poetic prelude reads, "Tuntún of nappy-headedness, / this book that goes to your hands... / I composed one day... / little that is of lived reality, / and much tell-tale and fable" (*Tuntún,* 47). Palés speculates in his glossary that the phrase may mean either "now we are going to eat," or "now we are going to dance" (ibid., 125). See author's footnote regarding the origin of the cannibal scene (Palés, "Litoral," 88).

to South America, and crosses the Atlantic to Africa in a diasporic mapping that the poet refers to as "Nigricia." The term *Nigritia* had been used by slave traders to designate their zone of activity in West Africa. They used it also to refer to the entire continent.[59] As a "toponym," *Nigritia* followed other outsider-imposed designations, like *Ethiopia, Lybia,* and *Guinea,* which named Africa on the basis of one of its regions, before Europeans came to a clearer cartographic sense of the continent's full extension. Here Palés extends the part-for-the-whole procedure to project an essential black spirit, Nigricia's numen, that has presumably spread abroad along with its human constituents. Nigricia's numen—primitive, telluric, and atavistic, especially when appreciated through the prism of religion—turns out to be the diametrical opposite of the spirit of good that is the Judeo-Christian deity. Palés's poem "Numen," in fact, makes Nigricia's ritualistic tribal dancing into a sort of Black Mass, as its participants are possessed by the devil, the "great original beast." Another poem, "Danza negra," continues this association of dance and the "black soul" *(alma negra)* with the otherworldly. Although its refrain *Calabó y bambú / Bambú y calabó* (Calabó and bamboo / Bamboo and Calabó) locates this poem initially on the island of Fernando Póo, and reveals part of its inspiration in José Mas's 1931 travelogue *En el país de los bubis,* it is clear that the poem's allusions to Tombouctou, Haiti, Martinique, the Congo, and Cameroon are all meant to trace the imagined, extended nation of blackness inscribed by *Tuntún*. References to Cuba, Brazil, and Uganda, throughout the collection, complete this task. Despite the spatially disperse location(s) of Nigricia's black subjects, however, or the time elapsed since some of them have left the African source, what unites them all is the sign of the primitive.

Communal black dance, whether satanic or saturnalian, is often an occasion for cannibalism in Palesian discourse, and in the poem "Ñam-Ñam," voracious man-eating as cultural quintessence again seems to dominate his characterization of the African continent as a whole. Cannibalism, as a primary trope that separates the civilized from the savage, us from them, is what marked the distinction between Romans and Christians, Christians and Jews, and more recently Europe and its colonial others, Peter Hulme reminds us. The sign of the cannibal, inflated by the hearsay factor, came over time to outstrip its referent, and to overshadow the "body of the man-eater, and the practice of man-eating itself." This process is very much in evidence in German ethnographer Georg Schweinfurth's 1878 account of

---

59. Blake, *Europeans in West Africa,* 28, for example, uses the term *Nigritia* in this sense.

the Niam-Niam, an influential source for early twentieth-century encyclopedia definitions, assimilated and subsequently rearticulated by Palés. Schweinfurth himself had been preceded by French explorers' "intelligence" at midcentury. French travel writers had identified the Niam-Niam as people with tails, a finding that seemed to corroborate the observation of an earlier Dutch explorer in 1677, confirming existing associations of Africa with the monstrous, which had existed in Western discourse since Pliny, Herodotus, and Homer. Predictably, for Schweinfurth, neither the energetic denial by the Niam-Niam chiefs of the practice of anthropophagy among their people, nor his own lack of personal proof, were of any avail against tradition and the fearsome physical aspect of these dreadlocked natives.[60] The mythmaking tenor of his account is unmistakable, and it justifies the following extended citation:

> Long before Mehemet Ali, by dispatching his expeditions up the White Nile had made any important advance into the interior of the unknown continent; before even a sailing-vessel had ever penetrated the grass-barriers of the Gazelle; at a time when European travellers had never ventured to pass the frontiers of that portion of Central Africa which is subject to Islamism—whilst the heathen negro countries of the Soudan were only beginning to dawn like remote nebulae on the undefined horizon of our geographical knowledge; that tradition had already been circulated about the existence of a people with whose name the Mohammedans of the Soudan were accustomed to associate all the savagery which could be conjured up by a fertile imagination. The comparison might be suggested just as at the present day, in civilised Europe, questions concerning the descent of men from apes form a subject of ordinary conversation, so at that time in the Soudan did the Niam-niam serve as common ground for all ideas that pertained to the origin of man.

Since *nyam* designates foods as well as the act of eating in African and Afro-Caribbean language, an actual tribal grouping whose name duplicates the

60. Pieterse, in *White on Black,* describes cannibal humor (the image of the white explorer or missionary and the natives dancing around the cooking pot) as "the most worn cliché about non-western peoples" (114). See also Peter Hulme, "Introduction: The Cannibal Scene," 24; and Ted Motohashi, "The Discourse of Cannibalism in Early Modern Travel Writing," 85. The 1911 edition of the *Encyclopaedia Britannica,* which speaks of the "cannibalistic propensities" of the Niam Niam or Azande people, cites Schweinfurth's travelogue as one of the sources for its entry (635). The corresponding entry for the 1994 edition proffers: "They had a reputation for cannibalism in the past" (754). The question that arises regarding the Niam-Niam, perhaps, is how does one lose a reputation for cannibalism?

inherent semantic ambivalency of the term must have seemed uniquely opportune for the poet, especially bearing in mind its baser connotations.[61]
For Palés, then, Africa presented synecdochially through the Niam-Niam,
becomes a man-eating machine, as it grunts and devours its dinner of white
intruders. In a perversion of self-vindication, the poem's Negrist premise
reinforces the colonial division of talents among humankind.

> Asia sueña su nirvana,
> América baila el jazz,
> Europa juega y teoriza,
> Africa gruñe: ñam-ñam.

> [Asia dreams its nirvana
> America dances jazz
> Europe plays and theorizes
> Africa growls: nyam nyam.]

The prelude to the book had indicated a nonchalant distraction in the
Palesian narrative excursion on black subjectivity, but here it comes to assume a somewhat less casual tone, as *Tuntún* proceeds to signify on black
diasporic culture. The contemporary antiblack discourse, exemplified above
in Schweinfurth's assumption of European cultural supremacy, reveals a distinct textual and subtextual presence in the book, to which has been added
the poet's peculiar penchant for irony. The more or less playful and conde-
scendingly emitted racial slurs embedded in the title, *Tun-tún de pasa y
grifería ("y otros parejeros tuntunes"),*[62] give way to consistent references to
the congenitally malodorous armpits of the black female and to the simian
origin of black people as a whole. If name-calling *(grifo, pasa, cocolo, Babilongo, cuadrumana),* is an elementary part of the process of degradation in
humor, the Palesian stress on the lower bodily functions as part of his characterization of these subjects adds to the discursive assault on the invented
Africa of colonial discourse, to which his *Tuntún* has contributed. Accordingly, the deceased boy child of the "Falsa canción de baquiné," who would

---

61. Georg Schweinfurth, *The Heart of Africa: Three Years' Travels and Adventures in the
Unexplored Regions of Central Africa from 1868 to 1871,* 1:271. Richard Alsopp, ed., *Dictionary
of Caribbean English Usage,* describes *nyam* as "to eat [something] as crudely as an animal would,"
410–11.

62. The syntax in these two lines sardonically joins the noun *grifo* (mulatto) through wordplay to *parejero.* In Puerto Rico, referring to someone as a *grifo parejero* is an indication that the
speaker believes the "uppity" *(parejero)* mulatto is doing or saying something to look or be white
and thus threaten the racial order.

be reanimated in an afterlife in Guinea, will grow up to be an invincible warrior and dancer if he drinks the urine of an alligator. Upon the application of goat's feces to his body, he will also become irresistible to women. In "Bombo," the mythical chieftain shares a similar depictional fate. Ostensibly all-powerful, his bodily excretions guarantee happiness to those who would ingest them: "Happy will he be who drinks from the swamp / where He submerges his rear end." The mock-heroic procedure applied herein to this figure of black "majesty," evinced in the poem's conspicuous use of the formal *venid* (*venid hermanos al balele:* "come brethren to the dance"), and the anti-Cartesian glaze over Bombo's jaundiced, sleepy eye, point unerringly to the hostility hidden behind many of the expressions of humor in *Tuntún*. For Freudian psychoanalysis, laughter is often a facade for lethal intentions, and unmasking a fraud by way of the joke consists precisely in "showing that what he pretends to be is quite different from what he really is."[63]

Palés's most malicious puns are reserved for the postcolonial Haitian elite, presented in "Lagarto Verde" and "Elegía del duque de la mermelada." Inflated titles such as "Madame Cafolé" and "Monsieur Haití" contrast conspicuously with the repeated monkey images—*monada* (monkeyface), *tití* (marmoset), *orangután* (orangutan), and *mono* (monkey)—to establish just how grotesque it is that these descendants of African slaves might pretend to be aristocrats. Effectively, the earlier designation of them in the prelude as an "aristocracy of primates," or an "aristocracia macaca," is repeated, as are references to cannibalism and atavism. In portraying the Duque de la Mermelada as a savage whose outer trappings of civilization do nothing to suppress his innate barbarity, Palés is at one with modernist writer Eugene O'Neill's *Emperor Jones,* who strips his protagonist of his royal finery until he is reduced to a loincloth to symbolize his jungle status. The analogy might just as well be made with John Vandercook's *Black Majesty: The Life of Christophe, King of Haiti,* which satirizes foundational Haitian president, Jean Jacques Dessalines. Vandercook reported Dessalines's conspicuous inappropriateness for high culture as he attempted to execute the minuet under the guidance

---

63. For his characterization of black women, see the poems "Elegía del duque de la mermelada," "Pueblo negro," "Ten con ten," and "Mulata-Antilla." "Babilongo" and "cuadrumana" ("quadrumanous") are to be found in "Majestad negra" and "Elegía del duque de la mermelada," respectively. *Cocolo,* in the Puerto Rican vernacular, is a derogatory term used to identify blacks; in this case from the Lesser Antilles. *Babilongo,* which appears in the glossary, represents a voodooesque personage, or spirit of evil, while blacks are described as quadrumanous as early as the 1917 poem "Esta noche he pasado." See also Neve, "Freud's Theory of Humor"; and Feinberg, *Secret of Humor,* 59.

of imported instructors as follows: "Hour after hour every day they tried to lead the sweating master of the blacks through the intricacies of the latest Paris dances. Jean Jacques was squat and as strong as a gorilla, but he was not graceful. He could ride a horse at full gallop down a rock-strewn hillside under a raking cannon fire; he could swing a sword and rout an army with a bellow rent hoarsely from the cavern of his chest—but guide his foot in a minuet, not at all."[64]

William Seabrook proceeded in similar vein in his portrayal of the "faultlessly attired" former president Sudre Dartiguenave, who "liked to be told that he resembled Napoleon III." It was enough, however, for the head of state to be confronted by evidence of a curse on his stairway ("two charred sticks crossed and fastened together with a bit of string"), for him to be reduced to a quivering mass of superstitious fear. President Guillaume Sam, in turn, when facing insurgents, would also leap "like an ape" over a stone wall to seek safety.[65] The resemblance of this image to the Duque de la Mermelada in his aristocratic boots and gloves, powerfully impelled to go clambering over the cornice of the palace, or of the Condesito's superstitious vulnerability to the term "green lizard" *(lagarto verde)* in the poem of the same title, may be coincidental. It undoubtedly springs, however, from the same source of prejudice. That Haitian postcolonial mimicry is critiqued so soundly as "monkey business" by the Caribbean intellectual and his apologists is best seen against the unstintingly celebratory discourse of this very constituency regarding the European cultural legacy.

Tembandumba, the queen for a day of the carnival parade, in her hyperbolized voluptuousness, and her almost manic and mechanized harlotry, completes *Tuntún*'s derisive contemplation of "black majesty." The stunning image of her in the poem "Majestad negra," as a "dark sugarmill of sensual harvest" *(prieto trapiche de sensual zafra),* at once links the subject to the sugarcane crusher, the primordial object of Caribbean colonial production, and to the automatic physical and symbolic dimension of an industrialized sexuality. The phallic connotation herein imposed on sugarcanes as they enter her/the mill for grinding revert unerringly to universal male anxieties regarding the *vagina dentata.* Tembandumba's poem, like the others in the series, mockingly holds up the black subject, not in terms of a vindicatory entrance into the world of Puerto Rican letters, but through the distortion of the grotesque, as antipoetic topics. Together they constitute what Philip Thomson's analysis

64. John Vandercook, *Black Majesty: The Life of Christophe, King of Haiti,* 92.
65. William Seabrook, *The Magic Island,* 113, 279.

of the role of the grotesque in humor calls "a kind of negative example, the other side of the coin of the beautiful and the sublime."[66]

In conclusion, if art was a way out for Luis Palés Matos, given the crisis accosting the Puerto Rican intellectual elite of the 1930s, it would seem that his black subjects performed the role of lyrical scapegoat in providing the libidinal release that laughter avails us. There is no overstating the poet's deeper existential response to his time and place, nor its fundamental affinity with that of his peers. The anxiety of belonging and the desire for escape from the sterility and monotony of his native Guayama gave his lyric a nihilistic and even suicidal tenor at times, to which poems like "Topografía" and "Humus" are eloquent testimony. In Palesian critical discourse, the question of speaking for the Other, unlike in the Cuban case, is sidestepped by the broader national and regional metaphor of Afro-Antilleanism, and it is eventually evaded by the authentication and verisimilitude afforded especially by its black reciters, or *declamadores*. It is still pertinent to note, however, that the blackness that it represents has been invented by the discourse of power, which in the final analysis goes unchallenged by Palés. That is to say that Palesian author location, due in part, perhaps, to the poet's self-absorption, precludes the sense of solidarity that even Ballagas was able to invoke. It is this absence of solidarity and the assault on alterity that, in the final analysis, separates Palesian *negrismo* from the ideological projection of *Négritude*. In this regard, perhaps the most glaring lacuna in the laudatory critical appreciation of Luis Palés Matos is its failure to account for the absence of enslaved Africans and Afrocreoles in Puerto Rico as agents of history in his poetry. Their struggles and frustrations under the colonial regimen of racial terror and forced labor, or even the martyrdom of slave conspirators Cubelo and Juan Bautista in Guayama, his birthplace, in 1822, are as absent from the dominant discourse as they are from his purported defense of the black cultural premise. Black voicing in *Tuntún* is restricted to the cannibalism of *Adombe ganga mondé,* the purportedly parroted patois of the Francophone Antilleans, and the incomprehensible wall of sound that black diasporic languages represent.[67] In Palés, racial ventriloquism has stumbled against the speech of the Other.

66. Thomson, *Grotesque,* 15. See also H. R. Hayes, *The Dangerous Sex: The Myth of Femenine Evil.*

67. See *Esclavos rebeldes: Conspiraciones y sublevaciones de esclavos en Puerto Rico (1795–1873).* I am indebted to Joseph Dorsey for pointing out this reference. See "Pueblo negro" for example, and the real and symbolic distance that black language in the poem suggests between poetic subject and object.

In the consideration of his poetry under the multivalent metaphor of *burundanga*, it is useful to return to his series of courtship poems to Maria, his second wife, and appreciate the degree to which the female muse, in the starkness of lyrical emotion, erases the divide between art and autobiography. In the poems dedicated to her, Maria is consistently characterized, not only by way of more or less standard tropes alluding to her transcendent beauty, her chastity, and her overall praiseworthiness. She is even deified as the restorer of the lost faith of the poetic speaker, and the harbinger of his eventual happiness. It is perhaps significant, also, that in the series of twenty-eight poems, at least twelve of them reiterate the tropology of her whiteness. In a broad poetic narrative that even questions the possibility that poetry might flourish in the inhospitable human and topographic landscape of Puerto Rico, the symbolic importance of such a figure is to be noted. If in the presence of the *mulata* the poetic speaker is forced into the Quixotic mode as a way of compromise and survival, the arrival of Maria, the living and long-awaited muse, can only mean one thing. In the racially tainted Antillean jungle, to return to Edgar Rice Burroughs's foundational trope of colonial writing, Tarzan has found Jane.[68]

68. See the discussion of Tarzan's white pedigree in Hulme, "Introduction: The Cannibal Scene." It is what is responsible for the inhibitions that would preclude him from the cannibalism and rape that characterize the animalized blacks and other jungle denizens around him.

5

Menegildo, Macandal, and Marvelous Realism

OF ICONICITY AND OTHERNESS

There is no drama like the drama of history.
C. L. R. James

There's not a breathing of the common wind that will forget thee.
William Wordsworth, "To Toussaint L'Ouverture"

Anthropology, Time, and Racial Tolerance

Whereas the colonial regimen of forced labor required a particular kind of subpersonhood, that of objectification, and the (top-down) literary abolitionism of the nineteenth century needed to be tempered by the timidity, abjection, and lactification *(mulatez)* of the protagonists, new Latin American republics were, on the whole, faced with an altered racial episteme in which the *negro* was no longer a thing but a citizen. In the case of Cuba, assertive turn-of-the-century propositions for racial equality would both constitute a challenge to the constitution and the guarantees it enshrined, and cause acute discomfort for a ruling elite concerned over the possibility of the loss of white racial privilege that had been naturalized under the aegis of coloniality. With a politicized new black subjectivity fueled by an overwhelming participation in the rebellion against Spain, and by no means desirous of disavowing modernity (as in some sort of postcolonial cultural maroonage),

212

but pursuing, instead, full and equitable participation in civil society, the question for this elite of how to retain cultural and political dominance would become paramount. An important aspect of the mandate they put into effect would center around the question of suffrage and the need to control the significant black vote in a bipartite system of a Liberal party and a Conservative party, who, in turn, were always mindful of the U.S. hegemon and its equation of political stability in the island with a particular racial status quo. The reorganization of racialized power in the early Cuban republic would thus signify a distinct reversal of the process of racial democratization set in motion by black soldiery during the interrupted struggle for independence and most famously articulated by national hero José Martí. It would eventually equate to a betrayal of the emerging nation's highest principles of a nation with all and for all.

Fernando Ortiz was a singularly important intellectual and ideological (re)source in early republican Cuba's racial episteme. His overwhelmingly anthropologized discursivity was doubly foundational. On the one hand, it coincided with the birth of the nation, and on the other, its self-referential presumption and authority, originated in the lettered city of which he was an outstanding exemplar, claimed and was accorded the permanence and truth-value of the scientific. Ortiz's descriptive and taxonomical account of Afro-Cuban culture in *Hampa afro-cubana: Los negros brujos (apuntes para un estudio de etnología criminal)* (1906) and in his other early works provided both the pre-text and the metatext for *negrismo*. Significantly, also, his participation—particularly by way of *Los negros brujos,* in the broader national dialogue of the first three decades of the century—helped establish the negative ideological and semantic parameters of the textual *negro* for the discourse of racial domination. In this chapter, I read Ortiz's *Los negros brujos* alongside Alejo Carpentier's novel *Ecue-Yamba-O,* written some twenty-five years after, taking account of the evolving discourse of national and cultural identity that both texts inscribe, and the permutations of blackness that they reflect, vis-à-vis a racialized and dominant white national selfhood.[1] *Los negros brujos* and *Ecue-Yamba-O* allow us to follow the real-world challenges to racial coexistence, most graphically materialized in the so-called race war of 1912, the presence of which hangs like a specter over the two works; in the one case, because it had not yet occurred, and in the other, because it

1. By 1925, Ortiz 'had also written *Hampa afro-cubana: Los negros esclavos,* "La fiesta afro-cubana del 'Día de Reyes,'" and *Los cabildos afrocubanos,* among others. Alejo Carpentier began *Ecue-Yamba-O* in 1927 during a period of incarceration under the Machado administration; he later finished it in France and published it in Spain in 1933.

appeared, a scant decade and a half later, to have been erased from memory. Carpentier's *El reino de este mundo* (1948), although more commonly associated with the cultural-nationalist or regionalist aesthetic of "marvelous realism" or *lo real maravilloso,* also bears the partisanist political trace of anthropologized *negrista* discourse, as I shall argue.

Haitian poet and critic René Depestre has made, to his credit, one of the most cogent observations regarding *negrismo* and its cross-racial writership during the resurgence of interest in the movement in the 1960s. After indicating the degree of transculturative attraction to the Afro-Cuban heritage that the white *negristas* evinced, he added, pointedly, that the movement displayed "neither anger nor rebelliousness."[2] The ability to successfully separate the political from the aesthetic is undoubtedly a striking feature of the genre, and could only have been achieved by way of the silencing and/or co-optation of the referent, as indicated earlier. The more or less obvious absence or paucity of black literary voices in early republican Cuba, as a result of slavery and the colonial premise, would therefore offer only a partial explanation of this silence, which, as we will see, has both a material, political dimension, and a symbolic, discursive one. Whereas the events of 1912 effectively squashed attempts at independent political mobilization for black racial betterment, the criminalization of blackness that preceded these events, and the suggestively anthropophagous *reincorporation* of a depoliticized Afro-Cubanness by way of *negrista* arts a decade and a half after, constitutes a more complete explanation both for the movement's lack of black writers and its lack of political assertiveness.

In spite of Fernando Ortiz's probably pivotal role in the articulation of a generalized antiblack sense of Cubanness, or *cubanía,* through his early work on criminology, his participation in the inscription of a blackness that was inimical to the nation and that might be profitably dispensed with in the country's political and cultural interest is rarely recognized. On the contrary, it is his antiracist heroism and Ortiz's inspired deployment of the tools of science in his work as a "defender of freedoms" that Alberto Pamies stresses in his prologue to *Los negros brujos.* Juan Marinello is of a similar opinion regarding this "highest service" rendered to the nation by Ortiz. Critics have pointed out the degree to which the writer's prolificacy and the variety of his research endeavors have tended to create an aura of unimpeachability around him and preclude critical analysis of his race-thinking. He is known variously as Cuba's third discoverer (after Columbus and Alexander Von

---

2. Dépestre, "Problemas de la identidad del hombre negro en las literaturas antillanas," 38.

Humboldt), as "Mister Cuba," or as the person who over six decades defined the essence of Cubanness. His lengthy essays on music, sociology, anthropology, criminology, and Afro-Cuban history and culture have also consecrated his intellectual persona to the degree that most readers know more by reading "about him," as Mullen observes, than by actually reading him.[3] The ideological biases of his early work, however, have tended to be overlooked in the process of his sacralization, as has the evolution in his thought as he became more familiar over time with his objects of study, Cuba's citizens of African descent.

If racial ventriloquism in *negrismo* was achieved on the basis of the removal of the referent from the realm of agency, it remains to be established just how this removal was effected, and what was the role of Ortician anthropology in the process. As an anthropologist, Ortiz at the turn of the century was intriguingly situated between the unabashed ethnocentrism of nineteenth-century travelogues and ethnographic accounts, from which he quoted extensively, and the professional self-effacement, cultural relativism, and field research that came to be regarded as required norms for anthropological practice by midcentury.[4] Notwithstanding his manifest biases, however, the writer of *Los negros brujos* insisted on his "dispassionate objective observation." The purportedly scientific intention of the treatise, however, is no doubt compromised by the writer's confessed concern that his insights serve the interests of the state. In much the same way in which he gave the nod to the Positivism of Italian criminologist Cesare Lombroso in his introduction to the work, Ortiz's invocation of the "newborn country" would make explicit his endorsement of Tomás Estrada Palma, the republic's first president, who started a campaign, in 1902, against *ñáñigos, brujos,* and Africa-derived expressions of culture.[5] Riding in the wake of a journalistic crusade in 1904 against these practitioners of Afro-Cuban folk culture, and effectively giving this campaign his seal of approval as a metropolitan-trained local intellectual, *Los negros brujos* would help legitimize their subsequent persecution. The book would also place him on the discursive continuum, located largely

3. Alberto N. Pamies, prologue to *Hampa afro-cubana: Los negros brujos (apuntes para un estudio de etnología criminal),* xv; Juan Marinello, "Don Fernando Ortiz: Notas sobre nuestro tercer descubridor"; Gustavo Pérez-Firmat, *The Cuban Condition: Transition and Identity in Modern Cuban Literature,* 1–31; Edward Mullen, "*Los negros brujos:* A Reexamination of the Text," 113.

4. Instructive in this regard are James Clifford, "On Ethnographic Authority"; Talal Asad, introduction to *Anthropology and the Colonial Encounter;* and Mary Louise Pratt, "Fieldwork in Common Places."

5. Fernando Ortiz, *Hampa afro-cubana: Los negros brujos (apuntes para un estudio de etnología criminal),* 154, 253. Hereinafter page citations will be provided parenthetically in the text.

in the news media, through which these practices had been criminalized since the 1890s.

The disciplinary label under which the disquisition inserts itself, however, is a primary indication of how questionable its discursive grounding is. If the science of criminology itself implies supposedly objective criteria in selecting its objects of study, the always already aberrant nature of the racialized Other is highlighted in the disturbing redundancy contained in the articulation of the field of "criminal anthropology," as it attempts to specify those whom it would analyze. Ortiz's anchor in nineteenth-century Positivism is apparent both in his legitimizing invocation of Lombroso in the introduction of the book, as well as in the racialized application of Lombroso's theory of the born criminal. The first of the two-part prologue to the book reproduces Lombroso's letter to the author in which he expresses his approval of his disciple's analysis—"I believe your ideas on atavism in black sorcery to be exactly right" (1). Ortiz responds to this with effusive expressions of gratitude and appreciation.

Los negros brujos, the first of a projected three-part series to focus on the Cuban underworld or *hampa,* was premised on the author's intention of providing "original and valuable data" for the new science of criminal anthropology and sociology (21). The value and originality of this contribution was presumed to lie in the preponderance of extant studies on the white (European) underworld and on the black subjects' presumably being evolutionary throwbacks to an earlier stage of human development. Ernst Haeckel's now-discredited theory of recapitulation shows why the notion of the "born criminal" was so attractive to Lombrosian criminology. Recapitulation theory sought to explain queries arising from observations of metamorphosis and ontogeny. During the transformation of a tadpole to a frog, or of an embryo to a mature human being, the entire evolutionary process of the species appeared to be condensed within the life cycle of a single individual, in a sense repeating (recapitulating) the main phases of the history of the group.[6]

This formulation, when applied to the human species, allowed for the "scientific" ranking of, say, a white child, a contemporary primitive, and the savage that supposedly preceded them both, in a hierarchic scale of moral, cultural, and intellectual development. Consequently, criminality, for the Lombrosan school of thought, was an index of the immoral and the uncivilized, and a vestige of an earlier era. It was further interpreted as "the normal

---

6. Piet de Rooy, "Of Monkeys, Blacks, and Proles: Ernst Haeckel's Theory of Recapitulation," 29–30.

behavior of inferior persons." In like manner, persons considered insane, and other such social categories like beggars, were regarded as unfit, aberrations on the evolutionary road to either extinction or perfection, depending on one's viewpoint. Piet De Rooy's study of Haeckel concludes: "Recapitulation proved capable of serving as a general theory of biological determinism, and once this route was taken, it was possible to compare all 'lower' groups, non-white races, women (of all races), Mediterranean Europeans and the proletariat, with white Europeans or prehistoric forbears."[7]

Ortiz's close adhesion the general Lombrosian Positivist paradigm lets him set up the basic oppositions among the Cuban people. He could thus separate the numerically fewer—and more refined—elements of Spanish nobility, from the general vice and aggression that characterized the lower-class adventurers and conquistadors who colonized the island and the enslaved Africans who were subsequently added to the population. Both races, he asserts,

> became fused in these groups that were psychologically the same or at least similar, and today Cuban society develops psychically along a subtle gradient that has whites, whose attributes place them at the level of civilized man, to the black African who, were he to be returned to his country, would go back to celebrating libations with the cranium of his enemy. . . . Due to a reciprocal influence between both races, the blacks began to acquire more and more elements of progress, which made them wake up from their secular sleepiness and partially emerge from the social subsoil where their lack of culture kept them, and the white race Africanized its lowest class. (17–18)

Paradoxically, Ortiz's reference to syncretism and a cultural continuum, and the seeming ability of his black subjects to benefit from a more "enlightened" environment, appeared alongside a raciological principle that also saw savagery as a fixed feature of their makeup. Religious fetishism and the crimes it produces is "in the mass of their blood," he asserted at another point (230). According to him, this explains why all blacks coming to Cuba ended up forming part of the criminal underworld. It also explains why they are congenitally unfit for an evolved religion like Catholicism, despite their incorporation of superficial elements of Christianity into their so-called religious rituals. Even if the criminality of Cuba's blacks is less densely concentrated than that of, say, blacks from Africa, Jamaica, Haiti, or the southern United States, on account of the exposure of Cuba's blacks to white demographic

7. Ibid., 31, 30.

and cultural influences, their acculturation remains only skin deep. Atavism guarantees that their savagery is just beneath the surface. This is the reason why, in early Ortician usage, the neologism *afrocubano* speaks not to a morphology of alterity and inclusion but of opposition and distinction. As the author stresses on several occasions in the course of the text, the *afro-* prefix represents a barbarous human addendum tacked on to a preexistent civilized Cubanness or *cubanía,* one of "savages brought to a civilized country" (231).

Insofar as black criminality is ultimately the main focus of *Los negros brujos,* the nature of the offenses described, as well as the reliability of the author's sources and his recommendations for correcting the social ills they represent, are all significant. So too, in the final analysis, is his long-lasting legacy as a contributor to the creation of icons of black criminality in Cuba.[8] His position in a broader discursive Negrist continuum, then, even before writing the *negro* takes shape as a literary fad in the 1920s, is evident. Ortiz describes the individual *brujo* as being irrevocably on the outside of law and order and civilization: "[He is] almost always a criminal, perennial swindler, often a thief, a rapist and murderer in some cases, a violator of graves when he can. Lecherous to the highest degree of savage corruption, polygamous and concubinary, lascivious both within and outside of religious practice, and a fomenter of prostitution. Considering his general exploitation of uncultured minds and those of his various concubines, [he is] a true social parasite" (229).

Ortiz's listing of *brujería* infractions and the recommendations against them further indicate the anthropologist's unwillingness to move beyond an uncompromising rejection of what he sees as an alien cultural ensemble. The lists are an important indication not only of the author's role as criminologist, but also of his manifest sense of unity with civil authorities vis-à-vis the cultural practices that attracted his attention as anthropologist in the first place.

In a chapter dedicated to newspaper reports on black criminal activity from dozens of towns across Cuba, he presents a variety of activities and contexts of Afro-Cuban folklife that uniformly elicit arrest, detention, fines, or prison terms for the individuals concerned. Deemed to be indicative of the practice of obeah, these activities include ritual singing and dancing as well as the possession of an assortment of articles used in worship and in concocting charms and curses. The use of hearsay as reliable evidence by the

8. Josaphat B. Kubayanda, in *The Poet's Africa: Africanness in the Poetry of Nicolás Guillén and Aimé Césaire,* points to a tendency in contemporary criminology and anthropology in Cuba to associate "lawlessness and criminal behavior" with Afro-Cuban religions like the Palero, Abakuá, and the association of Ñáñigos (112); see also McGarrity, "Race, Culture, and Social Change," 199.

authorities, however, and the arbitrary arrest and punishment of the accused, which often included children, reveals more about the ingrained racial biases of the legal system of turn-of-the century Cuba than about the purported criminality of the community it targeted. Likewise, Ortiz's elevation of anecdotal accounts, which often came from unnamed sources, to the status of objective data, and his use of newspaper reports that were clear cases of media sensationalism reveals his own lack of impartiality.[9]

For Ortiz, police action on the question of the obeahmen, and legislation on the phenomenon of *brujería* in general in Cuba, needed to be rationalized and modernized. Instead of merely going after the criminal byproducts of *brujería,* such as fraud, prostitution, end even murder, in his opinion, it was the source of the problem that needed to be tackled. Legislation should therefore be introduced to specifically target obeah *as* obeah, bearing in mind that the ancillary crimes mentioned were not always committed in the course of its practice. Among the seashells, powders, coconuts, crucifixes, candles, dried leaves, roots, and so on that were seized from the homes and altars of individuals, and which were the cause of alarm among the authorities and among the wider population, were human and animal bones, also. The association of *brujería* with necrophilia and with the ritualistic murder of white children by black obeahmen, purportedly for the preparation of curative *embós,* is the most conspicuous of the crimes discussed in *Los negros brujos* and is probably the text's most important underlying motif. Ortiz points to the fact that at least eight murders of white boys and girls were reported in the press between 1904 and 1923.

If obeahmen in their role as diviners might be regarded as swindlers, or if they were held to be quacks and an unacceptable source of popular influence for illegally practicing medicine, being associated with grave robbing and child murder identified them with the violation of a most forbidding cultural taboo. Here again, however, racism in its institutional guise, both juridical and journalistic, came into evidence. The significance of the murders was exaggerated by the white mainstream press as part of a campaign of hysteria

---

9. The standard rendering of *brujería* in academic discussions is "witchcraft" or "sorcery," and *brujo* is usually defined as "(male) witch" or "sorcerer." Since these terms carry specific European connotations, however, I have opted to include also the use of the Anglo-Caribbean terms *obeah, obeahman,* and *obeahwoman.* Ortiz acknowledges the Yoruba origin of the term *obi,* which refers to an elder or father figure, and which was resemanticized under the Manichean culture of coloniality to represent someone involved in evildoing (123). One report from Taco-Taco, Cuba, dated 1902, reported on a case of *brujería* or obeah, in which a black cat, frogs, and pins were extracted from a girl during an exorcism (182).

and race-baiting whose objectives extended beyond mere news coverage, forming part of a continuing offensive against attempts at black emancipation. The crusade tapped into deep-seated fears of black assertiveness that went back as far as the Haitian revolution; these fears had been revived by the loyalist press during the 1890s to demonize not only the black foot soldiers in the insurgency, but also the movement's most important military figure, the mulatto general Antonio Maceo. Maceo, along with his brother José, was often accused of wanting to turn Cuba into a black dictatorship. The child murders would provide further fuel for the crusade in the press as the Partido Independiente de Color started mobilizing in 1909. Since some of the alleged child victims were female, anxiety over black political independence, already associated with a descent into barbarism, was further overlain with panic over *brujería*'s linkage to rape by blacks. Hence the security of white women—and ultimately the entire white family structure—seemed under threat. That some of the child murders were subsequently found to have been committed by the relatives of the white victims and the corpses mutilated to make them seem to be the work of black obeahmen, however, reveals the depth and widespread nature of racist sentiment.[10] It also points to the consciously propagandistic role of the media as agents of knowledge production and dissemination.

Judging from his repeated reference to the murder of the child Zoila, which was sensationalized in the press for months after its occurrence in November 1904, it is clear that this event was an important stimulus to Ortiz's draconian recommendations for the solution of the problem of *brujería*. Zoila supposedly had been killed by obeahmen so that her heart and blood could be used in the preparation of curative *embós*. Again, for someone with legal training, Ortiz's unquestioning acceptance of sensationalist reports in the yellow press situates him squarely with the panic and racial prejudice that produced the verdict of capital punishment for two of the accused, Domingo Bocourt and Víctor Molina. As Aline Helg has pointed out, mob justice, scanty circumstantial evidence, and rumor-mongering were major elements in this affair.[11]

After Zoila, Ortiz proposed a campaign in which the obeahmen, and the entire culture of *brujería,* including its clients, should be eliminated. Citing the practice as evidence of "evolutionary deficiency" (230), he asked: "Could

10. See Helg, *Our Rightful Share;* and Silvio Castro Fernández, *La masacre de los independientes de color,* 134.
11. Helg, *Our Rightful Share,* 109–11.

there be any reason that might justify the toleration in Cuban society of a barbarity that stains and holds back its civilization?" (241). According to the nineteenth-century paradigm of biological determinism and pathogenesis he followed, black witchcraft was evidence of the illness affecting Cuba's social body. Imprisonment, he suggested, should therefore be deployed as a means of quarantining obeahmen, who should remain isolated even in jail, in order to not contaminate other inmates. Incarceration would also prevent the leaders from contaminating their followers. In this way the necessary de-Africanization of black Cubans, and indeed of Cuban society as a whole, might begin. Ortiz's analysis of the problem of black religious criminality, in the name of scientific "modernity," purportedly shunned extreme traditional responses to witchcraft such as burning at the stake, mass exile, or the garrote. His solution, instead, favored forced labor along with mass incarceration. In the interest of science, again, his enlightened despotism would further recommend not the destruction of the idols and other artifacts of *brujos,* as was often the case when they were seized, but their preservation in museums (246).

There is little gainsaying the symbolic violence or the gendered, classist, and racialized nature of the task of social engineering, which fell to society's "leading classes" (249), in Ortiz's dissertation, or in his call for the destruction of the "infectious foci," of *brujería.* Nor is it possible to ignore his clamor for the social elimination of the obeahmen and of the social parasitism they represented (235). Additionally, while it was aimed ostensibly at *brujería* and its adherents, it is clear that his message applied to all those not willing to sign on to the social contract of modernity and the European model of what it meant to be civilized. To the degree that Ortician anthropological discourse saw de-Africanization as a solution to Cuba's purported problem of underdevelopment or backwardness, however, it merely represented a "scientific" reprise of historian Antonio Saco's calls for a white Cuba made some seventy years earlier. Effectively, in a speech on the "decadence" of Cuba in 1924, he would invoke the hundred-year struggle undertaken by the Sociedad Económica de Amigos del País to make Cuba white. At the time he wrote *Los negros brujos,* he was firmly in agreement with the Europe-oriented immigration policies currently in effect. In a 1906 article, he suggested that as far as immigrants were concerned, "*race* is probably the most fundamental area that we must take into consideration."[12] Blacks and Asiatics

12. Fernando Ortiz, "La inmigración desde el punto de vista criminológico," 55 (emphasis in the original).

are more delinquent than whites, he claimed, their primitive psyches are not as developed as the latter. Their immigration should be blocked, therefore, and Northern Europeans should be imported so that they might bring life and progress to Cuba.

The evolutionist binary at work in Ortiz's projection of a "civilized" white Cuba beset by a "barbarous" black Cuba brings to mind Johannes Fabian's analysis of the rhetorical strategies of anthropological discourse. Seeing both temporal and spatial relegation of the anthropological object to the past in this discourse, Fabian suggests that for the anthropologist and his interlocutor, the primitive lives in another "Time." The profoundly political content of what Fabian calls the "denial of coevalness" to the anthropologized Other is most starkly registered by Ortiz. In *Los negros brujos,* he not only relegates Afro-Cuban religion and its adherents to a static preteritive state, but also further completes their social erasure by encasing their cultural paraphernalia in a museum, the socioculturally designated house of the past. The mirage of diachronic separateness created by anthropological discourse is, however, exploded through Fabian's observation that "What are opposed, in conflict, in fact, locked in antagonic struggle, are not the same societies at different stages of development, but different societies facing each other at the same time."[13] For *Los negros brujos,* in the context of a newly independent nation in which the anthropological Other is not located in far-off lands but instead shares the same national space and time, racial coexistence is revealed to be at the heart of the crisis. Real, rather than rhetorical racial equality, turns out to be its ultimate challenge.

In *Los negros brujos,* Fabian's further assertion that the anthropologist's object of discourse is mostly to be seen and not heard is borne out in the photographs of the alleged *brujos,* all unnamed except for Bocourt, that Ortiz reproduces. It is also there in the multiple illustrations of black artifacts that Ortiz provides his reader (137). Significantly, again save for Bocourt, none of the informants from whom Ortiz has gleaned information regarding Afro-Cuban deities and their functions, is acknowledged. It is the different societies facing each other, however, and the way Ortician discourse participates in the dominant discourse at the moment of the reassertion of racialized power in the first decade of republican life, and also in the discourse of *negrista* vindication, that I am primarily concerned with. Their cultural "difference" and their lives on the margins of society might have been primarily responsible for the criminalization of Afro-Cuban *brujos* in the new republic, as had been

---

13. Johannes Fabian, *Time and the Other: How Anthropology Makes Its Object,* 3, 155.

the case with the *ñáñigos* a decade before. There is no denying the centrality of the black veterans of the Liberation Army to the material and symbolic birth of the nation, however. Neither can one deny their desires for politico-cultural integration into a basically Occidentalist Cubanness, regardless of their declarations of black racial pride. National hero José Martí's vision of a multiracial "ownership" of the nation had been clear in its stipulation that those who were capable of laying down their lives for the nation were deserving of the vote.[14] Given the example that the unsung black martyrs had set for Martí himself through their insurgency, and the legitimate expectations of those who survived to see the postwar period, the implications for democracy, racial politics, and suffrage at the juncture of statehood turn out to be of paramount importance.

The P.I.C. and the Limits of Racial Tolerance

The Partido Independiente de Color, originally constituted in August 1908 as the Agrupación Independiente de Color to formalize their members' struggle against the discrimination that kept blacks on the fringes of the new republic, followed in the footsteps of a similar preindependence organization. This was the Directorio General de Sociedades de la Raza de Color, which had also fought against the multilateral manifestations of prejudice since 1887. Included among the leadership and membership of both groups were veterans of the insurgency. Generals Pedro Ivonnet and Evaristo Estenoz, formerly of the Liberation Army, for example, led the P.I.C. The party was persecuted ostensibly for being in violation of the 1910 Morúa amendment that forbade race-based political organizations and was ruthlessly annihilated in 1912 when it staged an armed protest to repeal the Morúa law. Although the veiled and overt accusations that it was a racist party that had instigated a race war formed the basis of government reports, of current media coverage, and of dominant historiography around the

---

14. Ortiz had spent five of his first twenty years in Cuba. Most of the artifacts he had contact with had been in Madrid's *Museo de Ultramar.* Recent *ñáñigo* persecution is to be seen in the fact that they had been targeted for deportation during the Independence war. Hundreds were imprisoned without trial. Helg, *Our Rightful Share,* 107. Despite their sometimes ambivalent response to the dominant discourse of black barbarism, the P.I.C. cultivated an iconography that included Olorún-Olofí, the Yoruba creation god. For Martí's nationalism, see Tomás Fernández Robaina, *El negro en Cuba, 1902–1958: Apuntes para la historia de la lucha contra la discriminación racial,* 27.

events of 1912, both aspects of the premise are false. Membership was never racially exclusive, since it included persons who identified themselves as "white." Besides, the party consistently declared through its publications that its objective was not "to rule" but to be "governed well." Significantly, it was the Morúa precept that represented an infraction, by the Cuban Congress, of the constitutional right to the freedom of thought and association that was put into action by the *Independientes*.[15] It is also significant that a countering amendment, proposed in 1910 by Conservative congressman Lino D'ou, which (following the logic of Morúa) would have outlawed a wide range of de facto white racist organizations in Cuba at the time, was rejected by both parties. The real problem for the P.I.C. was that, with blacks representing close to a third of the electorate, and thus a vital swing vote for the two major parties, an *independent* black political organization would in all likelihood have upset the racial balance of power in Congress. It would have seriously jeopardized the kind of control over the black electorate that Liberals and Conservatives enjoyed through their client relationship with token black politicians.

The protest was fueled to a significant degree by President José Miguel Gómez's broken promises of employment and inclusion, after black veterans had overwhelmingly supported his armed protest against the fraudulent re-election bid of Estrada Palma in 1906. Considering the ostentatious awards accorded white veterans of lesser rank since the end of the mobilization against Spain, this new betrayal by Gómez, and the fact that a public sector job was all many of them could hope for as a means of sustenance, the new status quo must have been particularly rankling. This would have been especially so, taking into account that the existing state of affairs was backed by the United States. The government's aggressive pursuit of Spanish immigrants after the massive investment of the black soldiery in the war for independence against Spain must also have been a source of resentment. Effectively, the resurgence of Spaniards in public life was quite noticeable, especially in the mercantile arena, and in the tobacco and sugar industries. By 1899, Afro-Cuban numbers had fallen to just under a third of the national population, after being almost fifty percent in 1877, and 200,000 Spanish immigrants would come to Cuba between 1902 and 1910. Congressional appropriation

---

15. Quoted in Castro Fernández, *La masacre*, 14. See also Fernández Robaina, *El negro en Cuba;* and Helg, *Our Rightful Share.* Even the conservative newspapers of the time denounced the Morúa bill as unconstitutional (Helg, *Our Rightful Share,* 166).

of a million dollars in 1906 to subsidize white immigration, especially after the all-white government of Estrada Palma had rejected a request by the United Fruit Company to import Jamaican laborers for plantations in Oriente, was as clear an indication as any of the prevailing racial policy.[16] Additionally, segregation and discrimination persisted in several areas of public life, primarily in employment, but also in ballrooms and public baths, social clubs, the baptismal registry, and primary and secondary education.

The P.I.C.'s agenda, endorsed by their conspicuously growing membership, reflected the crisis as many blacks saw it. The result was that their demonstration of May 20, 1912, in Oriente, primarily a show of force aimed at pressuring the government to recognize their legality, provoked a nationwide wave of repression in which some three to five thousand P.I.C. members, often unarmed, were slaughtered over a two-month period. This included a particularly gruesome episode in which hundreds of innocent blacks were hunted down and taken for target practice by government forces and a white voluntary ad hoc militia under General José de Jesús Monteagudo. In a generalized climate of racial terrorism, even to speak ill of white people in public was to risk life and limb. Considering that their platform included the nationalization of employment, free and compulsory education for all, legislation controlling child labor, land reform, trial by jury, an end to selective immigration, and inclusion of blacks in the diplomatic corps, it becomes clear that in protesting against structural inequalities they were not, as Afro-Cubans, "breaking the fragile boundaries of Cuban racial democracy," as one historian put it.[17] What they were breaking, rather, were the limits of white tolerance in openly challenging racial hegemony.

That race trumped class and other considerations in the massive white anti-P.I.C. mobilization of 1912 establishes beyond a doubt that the rather dubious notion of racial democracy is a limiting tool in the analysis of early republican Cuba's internal politics. The active coalition of the white Liberals and Conservatives, of journalists, and of a mostly white militia, in which even some black members were on one occasion murdered and the perpetrators pardoned, constitute an ample demonstration of the white racial contract as the operative political principle dominating the event. The unequivocal intentions of the U.S. gunboats and marines dispatched to the

16. Thomas, *Cuba*, 515, 497.

17. Official estimates of P.I.C. dead are in excess of two thousand. Guillermo Lara of the P.I.C. puts the figure at five thousand. See Castro Fernández, *La masacre*, 3; and De la Fuente, *Nation for All*, 76.

island, their material interests notwithstanding, only confirms this perception, especially considering the rhetoric of racial derogation that accompanied the U.S. occupation in 1902 and again in 1906.

Aline Helg has identified the iconography of caricature and stereotyping as primary journalistic mechanisms aimed at transforming all blacks into a common and personal threat in the imagination of whites, thus facilitating the racist mobilization that ensued. The reductivist procedure, which sublimates racial hostility and fear in other instances to produce laughter, as we have seen in other historical circumstances under study in this book, is here channeled towards aggression. Under the ontological tyranny of the stereotype, at the moment of actualization of prejudice, all other descriptors of the racialized subject cease to have importance. Much like the Martí-articulated doctrine of a nation with all and for all, the P.I.C.'s rather idealistic goals for the entire nation were dismissed once the reductivist propaganda machinery had activated the prejudice required to direct deadly force at them. Racial terrorism continued in 1919, when a Jamaican was lynched for giving candy to a white girl and alleged *brujos* were discovered dead while in police custody, indicating that the mobilization against the P.I.C. was less about sanctioning the purported illegality of the party—it was more about achieving a race-based goal of intimidation. Historians of the period and cultural critics are in general agreement that it was the last time in Cuba's history that independent black voices were raised in collective protest.

Afro-Cubanism: Antidotal Bongo?

More than a decade later, Fernando Ortiz, in a 1924 speech to the Sociedad Económica, protested against what he termed Cuba's slide into barbarism. In this case, it was not the racialized underworld or *hampa* to blame. Culture, he lamented, was being defeated at every level, both sociopolitically and economically. Over the preceding decade, theft had gone up, suicide rates had gone up, and there was such a low percentage of convictions stemming from homicide cases that a feeling of impunity seemed to have developed among the criminal element of society. Citing a correlation between presidential pardons for convicted murderers and the electoral cycle, he jibed that the Supreme Court had become the Supreme Patron of crime. Further, the ongoing loss of Cuban land to foreign enterprises for sugar cultivation was a scandal, as was the fact that foreigners also had the controlling stake in mining, railways, telephones, banking, and shipping. With 50 percent illiteracy, the state of public education in Cuba was disastrous, he complained, especially considering the fact that the "negritos" of the neighboring Caribbean islands and the blacks and "redskins" of the United States showed higher levels of literacy.[18]

U.S. capital investment in the sugar industry since the turn of the century had been prodigious. The expansion of sugar cultivation, especially in the eastern province of Oriente, is reflected in the 536 percent increase in capital investment in 1913–1928, most of it being North American. The displacement of Cuban landowners by the new latifundists was, therefore, equally notable. By 1928, 75 percent of Cuban sugar exported would be from mills owned by North Americans. Ortiz's anxiety over Cuba's increasing economic subjection to U.S. interests was well founded. So too, was his concern over bribery and corruption in high places. As Thomas points out, electoral fraud was commonplace. The number of votes cast could exceed the number of registered voters, as happened in several municipalities in the 1921 general elections. The term "military advisers," he adds, was merely a euphemism for amnestied thugs deployed to guarantee the polling outcome. Even the national lottery was regarded as a source of personal enrichment for those in charge of its administration. Senators, as a matter of course, handled the lottery's lucrative collectorships for personal gain, and its director general could expect to make as much as $2.5 million a year. International loans extended for financing government projects were no different. In the case of President Mario Marcía Menocal (1913–1921), these were converted into opportunities that allowed his personal fortune to grow from $1 million to close to $40 million during his tenure.[19] In fact, it was the involvement of his successor, Alfredo Zayas, in the sale of the ruined Santa Clara convent site in 1922 (a deal from which the president profited personally by approximately $1 million), that catalyzed the protest of writer Alejo Carpentier and other like-minded young intellectuals and linked Ortiz to a younger generation of artist-activists.

18. Ortiz, "La decadencia cubana; conferencia de propaganda renovadora pronunciada en la Sociedad Económica de Amigos del País la noche del 23 de febrero de 1924." Paradoxically, but perhaps predictably, it was the same black West Indians that he regarded as the "worst and most uncivil elements" (41) that the sugar lobby was bringing into the country.

19. For a discussion of U.S. capital investment in the early-twentieth-century Cuban economy, see Gérard Pierre-Charles, *Génesis de la revolución cubana,* 31; see also Thomas, *Cuba,* 547, 525.

The *minoristas,* of which Carpentier was a member, was one of several civic-minded organizations, such as the Movement of Veterans and Patriots, the Falange for National Action, and Ortiz's Committee of National and Civil Renovation, all formed in 1923, that would react to the national crisis. The *minorista* group included José Antonio Fernández de Castro, Jorge Mañach, Juan Marinello, Emilio Roig de Leuchsenring, Francisco Ichaso, Féliz Lizaso, Felipe Pichardo Moya, and José Zacarias Tallet, who, like Carpentier, had also been involved in the famous Protest of the Thirteen against Zayas's Santa Clara scandal. Their manifesto combined heterogeneous but comple-mentary goals not uncommon among other organizations of progressive young intellectuals in contemporary Latin America. Following the movement for university reform five years earlier in Argentina, they called for auton-omy in institutions of higher learning and an end to university sinecures. They also targeted the administration's corrupt electoral practices and the country's domination by U.S. capital, coming out at the same time in sup-port of the dispossessed small landowners and agricultural workers. In the area of art, the *minoristas* strenuously vindicated national themes while call-ing for an infusion into national cultural life of the new artistic and scientific trends from abroad.[20] In 1927, Carpentier, along with Mañach, Marinello, Ichaso, and Martí Casanovas, would edit Cuba's official vanguard journal, the *Revista de Avance,* which lasted through 1930.

Several studies have attested to *Avance*'s cosmopolitanism. The journal promoted international Hispanic writers of the stature of Federico García Lorca, César Vallejo, and Mariano Azuela, and it introduced its readership, through translation, to other international icons such as Bertrand Russell and Carl Jung, as well as the writing of John Dos Passos, Ezra Pound, Blaise Cendrars, and Paul Morand. What is perhaps most important to point out here is its cultural nationalism and the fact that it served as a forum for *negrista* verse by such poets as Ramón Guirao, Emilio Ballagas, Carpentier himself, and Regino Pedroso. Carpentier, adopting the antibourgeois atti-tude typical of the vanguard, directly invoked Ortiz once when talking about Afro-Cubanism's rediscovery of the black motif in Cuban literature. "Fernando Ortiz, in spite of differences in age, used to mingle with the boys. His books were read. Folklore was acclaimed. Precisely because it dis-pleased intellectuals of the old school, one went with reverence to *ñañigo* initiations and praised the *diablito* dance." By 1929, even Ortiz himself had

20. See "Declaración del grupo minorista," in Nelson T. Osorio, *Manifestos, proclamas y polémicas de la vanguardia literaria hispanoamericana,* 248–50.

seemed to shift his perception of negative difference from one premised on fixed and unchanging racial characteristics to one of culture.[21] As pointed out earlier, his trip to Europe the previous summer had nudged him toward a less reactionary position regarding the value of the African legacy.

The "celebration" of blackness by the Afro-Cuban movement was by no means unproblematic. If in the pages of *Avance* and other contemporary publications *negrismo* did not express the sense of paranoia generated by Afro-Cuban culture in the first two decades of the century, the Afro-oriented cultural-nationalist impulse of the *vanguardistas* was certainly not enough to overcome their phobia against black immigrants from neighboring islands. Repeated essays from *Avance's* editorial section, "Directrices," bemoaned the arrival of Haitian and Jamaican laborers. From these it is clear that the presence of the Jamaicans and Haitians was objectionable, first, because it was an expression of U.S. sugar expansion in Cuba, and because they competed with locals for jobs in the employment marketplace. More importantly, the "Directrices" declared that the newcomers themselves were a blight and were therefore unwelcome. A 1927 article, published in a Madrid newspaper by reporter Luis Araquistain, regarding the apparent difficulty of successfully placing Spanish immigrants in Cuba, inspired a commentator to express concern over the increasing "Africanization" of the island. Essayist Ramiro Guerra, in a local lecture, deplored the twin menace of the new latifundism and its imported labor force. Guerra's observations seemed to magnify the menace that the new laborers represented. After hearing Guerra and reading Ariquistain, the editors of *Avance* expressed their indignation at the black invaders and their embarrassment at Cuba's not being a sufficiently accommodating host for (Hispanic) whiteness: "Now we ask: if all of us listened emotionally to the words of Dr. Guerra, convinced that he was giving us a warning from the heart of a Cuban in pain, and we understand the need for precautionary measures; if we all know that [our] land is being taken away from us and that another inferior race is threatening us, what could surprise us in those words of Ariquistain?" Again, the editors in "Directrices: Cuba, caso antillano" struck a note peculiarly reminiscent of the Ortiz of two decades before as they came back to the question of the intruders: "If the Haitian and the Jamaican were intellectually and spiritually advanced, their

---

21. Quoted in Roberto González-Echeverría, *Alejo Carpentier: The Pilgrim at Home,* 48. In a purportedly antiracist statement in 1929 to the Sociedad económica de amigos del país, "Ni racismos ni xenofobias," in which his recurrent motif is "Culture, not race," Ortiz acknowledges the racial diversity among the Hispanic collective. He still, however, thinks that the idea of someone conceiving of himself or herself racially as "black Spanish" to be laughable.

importation would not sadden us and even less would their treatment as equals. It is not precisely the blackness of their skins that bothers us. In short: however one looks at our process of blackening, the truth of it is undeniable, and so it is obvious that Cuba has consequently been left in a very depressing situation. The great sore is there for the world to see. How long must we wait for the dignifying surgery?[22] The editorial bears an all-too-obvious hint at the horrendous events of 1912.

The impulse among *Avance's vanguardistas* to applaud the country's black folklore while balking unabashedly at the presence of black foreigners, might indeed seem contradictory. But the conflict is not explained on the grounds of the foreignness of the latter and the "patriotic" preferences of the former. Applause notwithstanding, Afro-Cubans in Carpentier's *Ecue-Yamba-O* fared no better. Carpentier's deployment of the bongo as symbolic cultural "antidote" to Wall Street, a metaphor much endorsed by critics, leaves key questions unanswered.[23] If the proposal is that the bongo is to be the shield or protector of the nation against the all-pervasive Yankee presence, one is prompted to ask: By what process, first of all, does a marginalized and persecuted cultural artifact suddenly occupy a commanding central space in the national episteme? Second, given the new importance of the formerly denigrated bongo, does the status of the bongo player, or *bongosero*, change accordingly? Could it be that the "nationalized" bongo as antidote, in supporting a supposition of racial togetherness, homogeneity and democracy, points, rather, towards a sort of anthropophagous in-corporation of the Other? A look at the strikingly anthropologized narrative in *Ecue-Yamba-O* suggests that in spite of the contemporary framing of the novel, and its not insignificant critique of the nation's political crisis, its black characters remain overwhelmingly outside of the "time" of the omniscient narrator. His reluctance to let them effectively share the nation space in coeval terms militates powerfully against their ability to confront the threat of the imperial Other as part of a homogenous national front, assuming, that is, that anyone or anything within a mere ninety miles of the empire could remain impervious to its influence.

The structure of Carpentier's first novel reveals, more than anything else, the influence of Fernando Ortiz the anthropologist as the source of the folkloric raw material for *negrismo,* or as the "intellectual father" of the *minoristas,*

22. "Directrices: Tierra y población en las Antillas," 87–88; "Directrices: Cuba, caso antillano," 289.

23. See Kutzinski, *Sugar's Secrets;* and Paul B. Miller, "*Blancas y negras:* Carpentier and the Temporalities of Mutual Exclusion."

as one critic described him.[24] *Ecue-Yamba-O* is a sort of bildungsroman, which, as it tells the coming-of-age story of the protagonist, Menegildo Cué, also traces the progression of his unceremonious demise and "rebirth" through his son. Menegildo was born on a rural farm that supplied the San Lázaro sugar mill, was forcibly relocated to Havana to serve time as the result of a crime of passion, and met a premature end as he became embroiled in the city's *ñáñigo* underworld upon his release. Aside from the fairly straightforward plot, every possible opportunity in the story is taken by the narrator to delve into the peculiarities of the Afro-Cuban cultural ethos, in both rural and urban settings. Plot development even seems contrived, at times, to facilitate these descriptions. Plot and structure apart, the portrayal of the main characters turns out to be irrevocably primitivist.

The novel is set two years after the government proclamation permitting Haitian laborers to enter the country. The mention in chapter 1 of the First World War further frames it chronologically, especially since the dispossession suffered by the Cué family and other small landholders was directly related to the rise in demand for Cuban sugar occasioned by the decline in European beet sugar production that the war caused.[25] Carpentier's avant-garde critique of the culture of corruption in the novel is also noteworthy. It is vividly exemplified through Menegildo's cousin Antonio, a picaresque distortion of the model of bourgeois morality, who is apparently meant to typify the norm for black survival and success required by the times. *El negro Antonio* (black Antonio), as he is dubbed, is a petty thief–become–shoeshine entrepreneur. He is also a *ñáñigo*, a reelection broker for whichever party would hire him, a minor agent in the lottery, and a pimp. When we first meet him in the text, he is described with some irony as being "at the peak of his career" (116). The role of blacks as a constituency within the political pecking order is further exemplified with the references to the parties in the black neighborhoods that are sponsored by the electoral candidates, their link to the broader demagogic machinery, and the benefits that these lower-level voters derive from their political affiliations.

The liberal and progressive pose of the narrator presenting this critique of the contemporary Cuban condition in the novel, however, turns out to be less liberal and progressive regarding slavery and the past. The harsh reality

---

24. Pérez-Firmat, *Cuban Condition*. The following page citations from Carpentier, *Ecue-Yamba-O* will be taken from the 1968 edition.

25. There was an estimated 60 percent loss in Cuba's rural properties during 1899 and 1905. Almost all the black peasantry in Oriente province was dispossessed as a result of the penetration of U.S. capital.

of slavery days, as remembered by Menegildo's grandfather Luí, are curiously counterposed by his recollections of a benevolent and enlightened master who believed in equality and who gave his faithful servant Juan Mandinga, Luí's father, his last name and his own plot of land after abolition. Thus insinuated into the narrative is the narrator's endorsement of the mainstream myth of the white founding fathers as good and beneficent slaveholders whose intrinsic belief in liberty propelled the anticolonial struggle and provided an apparently seamless transition into the era of independence. This narrative is therefore not complicated by details of Mambi participation or the struggles for black liberation that ran parallel to the anticolonial fight for freedom.

If the corrupt and semicomical *negro* Antonio and the good house slave Juan Mandinga are the products of a patronizing narrator, and are located in the chronological time of the narrative, the novel's anthropologized discursivity clearly places the other black characters in preteritive anthropological time. Much like Ortiz's *Los negros brujos,* the pages of *Ecue-Yamba-O* are interspersed by illustrations and photographs of *santería's* hybrid artifacts. These are presumably a lyrical stand-in for research and are meant to lend a degree of objectivity and credibility to the narrative. They range from the pictures of the altar of Beruá, the *brujo,* to esoteric *ñañigo* drawings or *firmas,* to the script and icon that accompany the *santería* prayer for the Anima Sola. The narrative also accompanies Menegildo himself through the rites of passage that mark his development, and these moments are used as opportunities to articulate the Afro-Cuban vision of the cosmos. An early indication of the novel's anthropological organizing principle is seen in the lizard that falls on his stomach as a newborn, which functions as an ill omen. When at age three he is bitten by a crab, Beruá is summoned, and we witness the application of folk medicine in the form of the snake fat that is applied to the wound and the recitation of the prayer to the Justo Juez.[26] The earlier omen overrides the latter prayer, however, since as it turns out, the prayer's request for protection "from witchcraft, from sudden death, from knife wounds" goes unheeded (31). Menegildo's initiation at age eight into the world of work and into the music and dance of his people, the beginning of his sex life with Longina, Beruá's medical attentions when he is waylaid for cuckolding the Haitian, and his final ceremony of acceptance

26. Use of the Justo Juez prayer was widespread in the Iberian Peninsula and in Latin America. It is evidence of religious syncretism in Cuba and the Hispanic Caribbean. See Anna Susana Speratti-Piñero, *Pasos hallados en El reino de este mundo,* 118.

into the *ñañigo* brotherhood are all significant moments of his anthropolo-gized life cycle. They afford the narrator the opportunity to show off his "insider's" knowledge of Afro-Cuban culture.

The overarching anthropological perspective is memorably expressed at one point through the diachronic link that the communal music makes with primeval Africa. The purportedly essentialist power of the cultural source is such that it is unaffected even by the brutal conditions of transat-lantic transplantation. Black music is a force of nature. In the words of the narrator, it can make the sun "pause" in the sky: "Half a league away from the sugar chimneys, that music emerged from remote times, pregnant with intuition and mystery. The almost animal instruments and the black litanies merged beneath the sign of an invisible jungle. Delayed by some kind of invocation, the sun paused on the horizon" (32). Menegildo himself gives particularity to this perspective; shortly after, we are told that his father chased away the rural guardsman who had come to find out why, at eight, he was not going to school. The narrator makes it clear that he was already a "doctor" in the rhythms and cadences of his people (31). From the narra-tor's standpoint, the fact that he was illiterate and could not even draw an X to sign his name was unimportant. Western education as an integral aspect of modernity and the twentieth-century state was apparently irrelevant to the Afro-Cuban subject. In a passage that presages Carpentier's speculations on marvelous realism and the Haitian revolution, animism and prelogic can conjure up unstoppable forces, and black magics offer an effective counter-weight to the white magics of modernity: "Just as how white men have filled the atmosphere with encoded messages, the tempos of symphonies and courses in English, black men . . . know that the air is a seamless fabric that transmits invoked forces" (55).

Later, Menegildo is candidly described as totally lacking in social aware-ness, with a sense of being that is limited to the bodily fullness of (black) male adolescence: "[H]e felt himself full, hard and bursting at the seams, with that essential reality that belongs to heat or to cold . . . his bronchia, his sex, all gave him a sense of life that excluded all metaphysical worry" (188). Following the metaphorical time of anthropology, he is stuck in the binary of mind and body. Even when he functions within the chronological time of the narrative, his representation displays a disturbing ambivalence. In spite of his earlier description as being incapable of and disinterested in intellectual matters, he expresses dominant white prejudices against the Haitian and Ja-maican newcomers, who he describes as cocky, animalistic, and savage. He also muses over the gross injustice that their presence represents, especially taking into consideration the economic grief caused to black families whose breadwinners are dislodged by these foreigners willing to take lower wages than Cubans for the available jobs. While a feeling of resentment by locals against foreigners who compete for limited resources is entirely plausible whatever the stripe of the parties concerned, in this case the position adopted by Menegildo seems a distortion of historical perspective. It scapegoats the incoming laborers for the failings of the early republican elites and their collusion with imperial forces, in that neither the cost to the national economy in the policy of courting white immigrants, nor the twin effect of the white racial contract as blacks feel the brunt of a renewed Hispanic racist exclusion as well as that of Yankee Jim Crowism, get his attention. Further, Menegildo's black-on-black xenophobia not only misrecognizes the plight of the international proletariat, with whose vulnerability he has much in common, but also is premised on the erasure of the earlier struggles of the Independent Party of Color for equal rights and justice in the republican regimen. Considering the damage done to the project of a deracialized nation for all in 1912, the belated invocation of the bongo that he and his family inspire some twelve years after the racist massacre of the P.I.C. is at best suspect.

If the instinctual and unlettered Menegildo seems to be an unlikely bearer (or beater) of the bongo of national liberation at the hour of imperialist cultural penetration, Salomé, his mother, seems just as firmly set as he is in the contours of the primitive. As she and her family endure wrenching poverty and as she proves susceptible to the designs of both man and nature, the multiple motifs of her personality are never developed, and a full psychological treatment never emerges. Salomé is limited to brief, if dramatic, expressions in the vernacular, which, while they satisfy her characterological function in the economy of the narrative, seem also geared to demonstrate the competence of the narrator in the Afro-Cuban dialectal register. Overcome by the ferocity of the storm, which has made a mess of her hut and its contents, all she manages is a series of animalistic howls: "Oh, me gawd! Oh, me gawd!" (45). Again, superstitious and apprehensive at the thought of another woman capturing the attentions of her teenage son, she warns him brusquely: "Woman bad" (76).[27]

27. The original text reads, "¡Ay dio mio!" and "La mujere son mala." It is not my intention to give the impression that only blacks drop their *s*'s or speak "in a particular way" in Cuba. Vernacular culture is too mobile for racial restrictions. My position, however, is that speech is an aspect of racialized character development in this novel.

Salomé is more memorable though, as an exemplum of naturalistic black sexuality. Here, the striking nonchalance of her portrayal as procreator is only partly due to the extreme material poverty of the rural environment. Her delivery of the baby Menegildo is singularly uncomplicated. Bringing the child into the world signified no more than a pause in the rhythm of her everyday chores, as not even the midwife that she sends for at the last possible moment turns out to be necessary. Apparently a minor inconvenience that requires neither clean linen, boiled water, nor postpartum repose, for her, childbirth was an amply rehearsed ritual: "This was very familiar ground for Salomé" (18). Several chapters later, her sisters, who come to visit the wounded Menegildo with their numerous progeny, are described as worthy members of her clan, since "[t]hey bred like fishes" (108). Similarly, Menegildo's animalization is only partly the result of environmental factors and the naturalistic bent of the narrative. If we see him abandoned in the yard as a baby, where the dog licks his body, a pig nudges him out of the way, and a hen scratches his stomach, that is only one aspect of his characterization as a rural black. His copulation with sheep as an adolescent is the detail that completes the animalistic continuum set up by his mother's portrayal. It also confirms black bestiality through sex.

One of *Ecue-Yamba-O*'s earliest critics, Carpentier's fellow *minorista* Juan Marinello, opined in 1937 that the novel was torn between the writer's ambition—his desire to show that he was au courant with the avant-garde spirit and style—and his interest in exploring the Afro-Cuban dilemma. These objectives produced a certain tension within the novel, and as a result, while it satisfied the requirements of the European taste for the exotic, it did not do justice either to the black constituency upon which it was based or to the nation. Marinello lamented its reductivism, saying that the novelistic Menegildo could at best represent only one of many possible aspects of blackness, and that *Ecue-Yamba-O,* for skirting the national and racial drama that the topic offered, did not fulfill its promise as an Afro-Cuban novel. As is well known, Carpentier himself was ambivalent about the work, at one point defending his familiarity with the Cués in real life and at another point acknowledging the superficiality of his portrayal of them. To be sure, he nearly disavowed the novel, saying that it was the work of an amateur, akin to a musician practicing his scales, and adding that the reason that he authorized a new edition was to correct the errors of a highly flawed pirated version of 1968. It is important to recognize that Carpentier was concerned that a corrected edition of his first novel indicate its time of writing, 1927, so that it could not be confused with his more mature, later work. It is also significant that his reflections on a hypothetical postrevolutionary Menegildo took care to credit the revolution with giving black Cubans their inalienable dignity and humanity.[28]

Notwithstanding the gains of the revolution, his observation continues to overlook Afro-Cuban agency in the historical process, or to recognize that dignity and humanity were intrinsic aspects of the historical trajectory of the struggles of blacks. A comparison between his self-satisfied preliterate persona who dies a pointless death due to gang violence, and the valiant efforts of the black press to articulate an antiracist and inclusive national ideology before and during the period of P.I.C. insurgency provides a measure of the lacunae in Carpentier's representation of the contemporary Afro-Cuban ethos. His denial of coevalness to his black literary constituency, seen primarily in the dead-end deterministic model of *ñañigo* life in Havana, owes as much to the Ortician anthropological pre-texts as it does to the effect of the dominant antiblack discourse of the early republic. It is a perspective that depends on the elision and erasure of black political agents and agency.

Haiti: Knowing the Unthinkable

Carpentier, as Marinello suggested, may have misrecognized the opportunity for an American epic in the ingredients provided by the international literary ethos and the political contours of early republican Cuba and fallen prey to a somewhat distorted paradigm of black subjectivity in *Ecue-Yamba-O*. Although he makes more concrete claims to knowing in the prologue of *El reino de este mundo,* his second novel, a close reading of the text prompts a similar conclusion. Carpentier's assertion of intimacy with Menegildo and family offers an appropriate point of departure for discussion of a novel whose historicist premise has for the greater part preempted further inquiry into the nature of his interpretation of the events described therein. It is worth revisiting, even if briefly. Prior to his disavowal of *Ecue-Yamba-O* as amateurish, Carpentier had defended, with a significant sense of assertiveness, his familiarity with the black family that peopled his narrative. In his frequent visits to the countryside, and in open rupture of contemporary interracial protocol, the black Menegildo had been his childhood playmate. The writer even felt comfortable enough, having been a welcome presence

---

28. Carpentier, prologue to *Ecue-Yamba-O* (1989 edition), 12.

in the Cué household, to use the names of Usebio, Salomé, and Luis in the novel, without changing them, as he states. Notwithstanding the presumed closeness, however, he also acknowledged, in retrospect, a superficiality regarding the quality of this knowledge. Their inner pains and struggles, their repressed resentments, and what their ancestral beliefs and practices really meant for *them,* had all escaped him. He thought he knew the Cués, but his knowledge was that of an outsider, he later admitted. Considering his change of opinion on the issue of the familiarity with the Cués and black Cuban culture in general, the question of the meaning and the intention behind the writer's subsequent claim to "extremely rigorous documentation" in *El reino de este mundo* and of a respect for "historical truth" acquires significance.[29] To what degree is this declaration of knowing regarding Haitian history and culture to be taken literally, one might ask, and what room did the very assertiveness of the statement leave for possible retraction in the future?

The question of the degree to which the assumption of discursive authority in regard to Haiti might or might not commit the writer is already answered in part by Carpentier's earlier reference to his *Ecue-Yamba-O* phase as being poorly informed and long past. Presumably here the maturity of the intervening years and the time invested in researching the background to the second novel would have shored up Carpentier's competence regarding Haitian black culture and the worldview of the protagonists in the revolution. One might note, in addition, that in the interim, in Paris in 1936, he wrote the script and helped produce a documentary on voodoo. But what is actually done with his research, in the production of a textuality that itself represents new knowledge, constitutes the body out of which the rest of the above question must be answered. The claim to knowledge, and the related issue of the interpretation and representation of the Haitian and ultimately the Latin American reality in Carpentier, is an important one. Although it has probably not received the critical attention it deserves, it is crucial to the final significance of his work as a product of the Latin American lettered city, and as one who helped chart the aesthetic direction of the twentieth-century Latin American novel.[30]

Carpentier's reflections in 1966 on his visits to China, the Middle East, and Eastern Europe are illustrative in this regard. In his travels, his sense of

29. Ibid.; Alejo Carpentier, *Novelas y relatos, Alejo Carpentier,* 54.
30. Critic Emir Rodríguez Monegal describes the prologue to *El reino de este mundo* as the "prologue to the new Latin American novel" ("Lo real y lo maravilloso en *El reino de este mundo,* 619).

disappointment and frustration at not arriving at a complete comprehension of the cultural world around him is noteworthy. In the essay, the Cartesian logocentricity of the writer becomes evident as he laments over the language barrier that kept him as an outsider while he traveled in the Orient. More than any other cultural signs, it was the written text and his own lack of literary antecedents in the respective languages that posed the difficulty. It would require a lifetime, or the next twenty years at least, he mused, for someone in his position to acquire the expertise he desired. The meaning of this competence was just as important as its acquisition. Mastery over the respective languages of Iran or the People's Republic of China would do more than provide access to the hermetic tomes of Arabic literature or the meaning behind Chinese masks and animal motifs; for a writer, it would enable the translation of these worlds, enable, in a sense, their possession.[31]

It is significant that in the same essay, Carpentier referred to the baroque architecture, the literature, the theater, and the music of Leningrad and Prague as being "my [cultural] property," again, notwithstanding the different languages that prevented their fullest comprehension. That his sense of estrangement in the Soviet Union was greatly diminished on account of his own cultural background and the prominence of such icons as Pushkin, Dostoyevsky, and Tolstoy in dominant Western culture, is understandable. But it was in Latin America where the fullness of identity was ultimately available for the Cuban. In contrast to these "foreign," European sites, it was the Latin American cultural and historical landscape that had long promised to fill the void of information and identity. Importantly, the decision during his earlier years in Paris to read "nothing but American texts" responded to an ardent desire to discover and to "express the American world." It had come in reaction to the sense of displacement that he had experienced when confronted by cultural and racial chauvinism in Europe in the 1930s. "I was saturated with Europe," he declared in a 1945 interview, "I felt I was beginning to lose my footing." His sense of New World belonging and allegiance stayed with him and was reiterated as late as 1975, in a lecture called "The Baroque and Marvelous Realism." Here he restated the uniqueness and evocative nature of Latin American points of reference such as the famous Mayan towers of Tikal, the Zapotec acropolis at Monte Albán, the Mixtec ruins at Mitla, and Henri Christophe's imposing fortress, the Citadel, at Milot, Haiti. The sheer size of Christophe's structure, the circumstances surrounding its construction, and other associated facts of the Haitian revolution, such as

31. Alejo Carpentier, "De lo real maravilloso americano," 87–89.

the legendary Macandal, whose followers were convinced of his immortality and his powers of metamorphosis, all proved to be the final catalyst for Carpentier's second novel.[32]

Marvelous realism and the Latin American baroque, along with Carpentier's invocation of a continental imaginary as novelistic raw material, which his 1966 discussion on Europe served to introduce, suggest a reality that turns out, arguably, to be not as self-evident as the writer might be implying. It would clearly take more than just the community created by the colonial language(s) to constitute the homogenous whole that he had in mind when he addressed the novelists of Latin America and encouraged them to exploit the continent's resources.[33] Whereas in his trip to the Orient he had spoken of himself as gawking like a common tourist, it bears pointing out that it was also as a tourist that he had marveled at the Citadel and witnessed the Petro and Rada drums of Haiti. His celebration of Meso-America's pre-Colombian ruins might have been significant as part of a break from surrealism and its predictable metaphors, with the legendary feats of Mexican president Benito Juárez or of Bolivian guerrilla Juana Azurduy gaining importance thereby as potential creative sources for his brand of New World-ism, or *novomundismo*. Carpentier's projection of Latin America as a seamless site of sameness, however, where historically constituted race, class, or gender privileges are immaterial, leaves much to be explained. In other words, the supposed newness and authenticity of these points of reference, vis-à-vis the old colonial world, or their purportedly postcolonial symbolic value to the literati on this side of the Atlantic, is not to be confused with a necessarily emancipatory intention on the writer's part, notwithstanding the vindicatory implications of the gesture. I believe that the much-commented *El reino de este mundo* is an example of this authorial ambivalence.

In *El reino de este mundo,* in spite of Carpentier's insistence on its "minutely detailed collation of dates and chronologies" and the novel's structuring around historical facts and figures, the creative liberties he took have long

32. Ibid., 89. See also González Echeverría, *Alejo Carpentier,* which cites the 1945 interview, 38. The Citadel is described in the novel as a "mountain on top of a mountain," 93. It covers an area of ten thousand square meters and has walls up to forty meters high. The structure has been under restoration by the United Nations as one of the World Heritage sites. The ranges of cannon and the mounds of cannonballs are silent testimony to the political will of the revolution. Carpentier visited Haiti in 1943 upon the invitation of a French colleague, Louis Jouvet. He recounts: "I was in Pauline Bonaparte's house, in Sans Souci, in the Citadelle la Ferriere.... What more does a novelist need to write a book? I began to write *El reino de este mundo.*" César Leante, "Confesiones sencillas de un escritor barroco," 26.
33. Alejo Carpentier, "The Baroque and the Marvelous Real," 107.

been detailed. The historical existence of characters, place names, events, and elements of Haitian folklore and voodoo culture that frame the work, however, guide the exegesis of many contemporary readers who still take the prologue literally. That this is so highlights the cognitive impact of Carpentier's manipulation of the historical archive in his novel. Inversely, however, it also forces us to consider the emphases and erasures that the novel reveals, as well as the ideological intent inherent to these emphases and erasures. Far from being inert and inconsequential, silences or exclusions in *El reino de este mundo,* as in any act of historical recuperation, are the other face of a dialectical practice that make them just as meaningful as its inclusions and emphases, as Michel-Rolph Trouillot might argue.[34] They evince the writer's agency, as, among a plethora of people and events, he decides which elements will constitute his narrative.

Perhaps the most notable example of this process is the novel's focus on Henri Christophe, the cook-become-king, rather than on other protagonists of the revolution, say, Dessalines, who was at the head of the final push that led to independence in 1804, or, more importantly, Toussaint-Louverture, the liberator who had withstood and overcome Europe's best armies during the previous decade of fighting. It is to the drama and tragedy surrounding Henri Christophe's reign that the creative writer turned instead, making a moral tale out of its failures and making its limitations a symbol of the revolution. A controversial and extraordinary figure even in a time of uncommon events and characters, Christophe's portrayal in history and in legend has varied from despised megalomaniac, on the one hand, to fondly remembered national hero, on the other. Coming on the heels of the only slave revolution is history, his assumption of kingship must have been final proof for the colonial episteme, of the world upside down. It is therefore significant, as Speratti-Piñero observes, that Carpentier "almost always" chose the interpretations of Christophe that came from his detractors, "avoiding practically everything that might have nuanced his image or been of benefit to it."[35]

---

34. Carpentier, prologue to *Novelas y relatos,* 54. See also Speratti-Piñero, *Pasos hallados,* for a discussion of the historical framework that structures the novel. González-Echeverría states, regarding the prologue's truth value, "[A]nyone who has read Carpentier with some care will not hesitate to take these words quite seriously. . . . [T]he story he tells is verifiable, documented" (*Alejo Carpentier,* 135). See also Naomi Sokoloff, "The Discourse of Contradiction: Metaphor, Metonymy, and *El reino de este mundo*"; and Trouillot, *Silencing the Past,* 48.

35. Speratti-Piñero, *Pasos hallados,* 35, 47. For Toussaint-Louverture as hero, see C. L. R. James, *The Black Jacobins: Toussaint L'Ouverture and the San Domingo Revolution.*

A biased portrayal of Christophe may be organically linked to what Carpentier found to be marvelous (though paradoxically real) about the Haitian revolution. The character's leap from rags to royalty in the slave colony, his Napoleonic regalia, and his massive fortress impress the imagination no less than do the organizational genius and the maroon-based poison war of the legendary Macandal or the uniqueness of the rebellion itself, with its voodoo subtext. However, it is quite conceivable that the prism of the marvelous, through which the novel is articulated, responds to a reluctance to fully acknowledge the material and symbolic significance of the event in real-world political terms. This is especially so, taking into account the degree to which the revolution shook the pillars of colonialism and threatened the most basic assumptions of slavery and racism.

Michel-Rolph Trouillot has argued that the Haitian revolution was considered unthinkable, not only among the planter class in Saint Domingue on the eve of the insurrection, but also among the most liberal of contemporary French philosophers, even as it happened. The blackout in Western historiography on the subject is notorious. The "most radical political revolution of the Age," Trouillot adds, is most strikingly absent from Eric Hobsbawm's *Age of Revolutions* (1789–1843), from Larousse's *Great Events of World History,* and from the national historiography of France and England. These were the colonial powers that sustained the greatest losses in trying to recapture what was up until 1789 the most valuable piece of real estate on the planet. When indeed the occurrence is mentioned in such sources, the accounts tend toward trivialization or a draining of the event of its political content. "When reality does not coincide with deeply held beliefs," Trouillot concludes, "human beings tend to phrase interpretations that force reality within the scope of these beliefs. They devise formulas to repress the unthinkable and to bring it back within the realm of accepted discourse."[36]

The most remarkable discursive feature about *El reino de este mundo,* and undoubtedly the source of its literary and historiographic claim to fame, is the magical prism through which the story is articulated. What is marvelous dominates what is real in its epistemological scheme. The text expresses admiration for the historical kingdoms of Africa—of Popo, Arada, the Nagós, and the Fulah—and of the exceptional Mandingo ruler, the Kankan

36. Trouillot, *Silencing the Past,* 73. In 1789 Britain's export trade amounted to 27 million pounds and that of France 17 million, 11 million of which was generated through its colony of Saint Domingue. Britain's entire colonial trade was worth 5 million pounds at the time. See James, *Black Jacobins,* 50.

Muza, for example. Although these references may be important in and of themselves, their significance in the text has more to do with establishing a lineage and context for the charismatic and miraculous Macandal and for presenting the idea of Africa as mythical source of extrarational powers. In the old continent, mythically termed the Gran Allá, kings are also fierce warriors—they produce hundreds of heroic progeny, their weaponry contains the secrets of metals, and they speak the language of trees and clouds.[37] But this power and potency are dependent upon the favor of the gods, whose displeasure would presage failure and defeat in their endeavors. It is important that in the novel the god compact and the (super-)human protagonism make the transatlantic voyage. African mysticism is transferred to Haiti through voodoo. What is important here is that the discourse of myth is the prism through which the black revolution might become acceptable.

The gods, subsequently, are appropriately prominent in the voodoo-centric Haitian revolution. Effectively, the triumph of the Loas had been announced in Macandal's apocalyptic predictions. Similarly, in Boukman's invocation at the ceremony at Bois Caiman, where the final decisions to initiate hostilities were made, Boukman had declared that a covenant was established between the initiates on this side and the gods on the Other Shore. The ever-present Ti Noel finally acknowledged the fruits of these premises upon his return to Haiti from Cuba. Dessalines's victory was due to a "vast coalition entered into by Loco, Petro, Ogoun Feraille, Brise—Pimba, Caplou—Pimba, Marinette Bois—Chèche, and all the deities of powder and fire." With these and other similar assertions of the determinacy of the magical, the force of the insurgents' spiritual resources notwithstanding, the material plane of operations, featuring the military planning and strategizing recedes from primary consideration.[38] The political dimension of the struggle becomes secondary. Rather, the war is waged on the plane of the

37. Macandal represents a perfect example of this two-sided treatment as his mobilization and his revolutionary work through the means of poison are set against the revelation that (ostensibly) during the period of his metamorphoses the hypervirile Mandingo has fathered a child with the face of a boar.

38. I quote from Harriet de Onís's translation, Alejo Carpentier, *The Kingdom of This World*, 109. Subsequent page citations will appear parenthetically in the text. Regarding the determinacy of the magical, it is significant that Macandal's ability to remain a maroon for some twelve years, and his ingenuity in organizing a network to distribute and administer poison to the planter families nearly throughout the colony wide takes a back seat to his religious charisma and the magic of his lycanthropy. Carolyn E. Fick speaks to his vision and feats of mobilization in the struggle against the colonials in *The Making of Haiti: The Saint Domingue Revolution from Below*, 60–63.

gods, as Ogún Badagri, the Dahomey-derived warrior-deity and master of Lightning and the Storm, overcomes the Goddess of Reason.

Insinuated into the narrative at the same time, however, is the discourse of cannibalism. While the rebels get drunk and soak their arms in the blood of their oppressors, the jubilant Loas in the parallel spirit world are also inebriated by the victory. Macandal had predicted that they would bury their faces in the blood of the whites, and drink "until their lungs were full" (42). That black gods would follow in the footsteps of their human creators simply exemplifies the logic of the primitivist perspective. Indulging in the antiblack tropological archive turns out to be a consistent rhetorical tendency in *El reino de este mundo*. It undercuts the superficial rhetoric of cultural vindication that has led some critics to see the novel as a celebration of negritude. Ti Noel, the link to all the important characters and events in the text, and therefore a key support to the premise of verisimilitude mentioned above, is the bearer of the fundamental message of the story.[39] Upon his return to Haiti, he discovered that one slave regimen, the colonial one, has been replaced by another, the postcolonial one. The revolution itself has been a wasted effort, especially since, as a slave on Lenormand de Mezy's plantation, he was better off than how he found himself under Christophe's monarchy, subjected to forced labor on the ubiquitous fortress. Ti Noel's reflections, overtly racialized in the text, which emphasizes his chagrin at having *blacks* as slave masters, have set the forced-labor construction of the Citadel against the slavery that produced the edifice of colonial capitalist accumulation. In the comparison, the latter has been less harmful to its victims. At least in the earlier regime, the life of the enslaved carried some value, since it represented some capital outlay on the part of the slaveholder. It is significant that at this point the omniscient narrator does little to share with us the reasons behind the urgency of the fort's construction, as he emphasizes the new monarch's capriciousness and his megalomania. His downfall is sure, however, for he has abandoned his voodoo gods, has embraced the West, and has "betrayed his race."[40]

39. In the prologue, Carpentier advises us that *El reino de este mundo* covers almost the space of a lifetime. Ti Noel is there from several years before Macandal's capture in 1757, through the Bois Caiman ceremony in August 1791. He leaves with Lenormand de Mezy shortly after the uprising and returns in the latter years of Christophe's reign, which had begun in 1811. The last dateable event concerns the queen and princesses in Italy in about 1834. He dies shortly thereafter.

40. This is a fairly common assessment of the novel. See, for example, Salvador Bueno, "Carpentier en la maestría de sus novelas y relatos breves"; Ana María Hernández de López, "En torno a los principios y el sacrificio por la justicia en Alejo Carpentier"; and Graciela Limón, "Haitian Gods, African Roots: Identity and Freedom in Alejo Carpentier's *The Kingdom of This World.*"

As indicated earlier, the narrative spans an epistemological space between its own interior reality and the wider history of which it purports to be a synecdoche. While its integrity as a work of fiction is in a sense inviolable, its pretensions to nonfictionality are not. Its reductions of the larger history are therefore to be noted, as is its scant attention to the complexities of the process. It is perhaps a convenience of emplotment that Ti Noel's absence in Cuba, when he accompanies the fleeing Lenormand de Mezy, coincides with the crucial period of anticolonial military confrontation and the establishment of the new republic. Perhaps more than the challenges of maintaining freedom, as under Christophe, the insurgents at that time faced the task of acquiring it and then establishing the bases for its maintenance. Although the details of Toussaint-Louverture's military campaigns and the governorship and of the early republic are beyond the scope of this discussion, a few of its aspects are relevant as elements of the challenge of the postcolonial transition that the book sidesteps. They include, among other things, Haiti's obstacles to international diplomatic recognition, the ongoing menace of reconquest and reenslavement, the question of the nature and policy of a postslavery economy, and the problem of national identity, bearing in mind the inherited caste and class divisions.

An idea of the unrelenting hostility of the colonizers vis-à-vis the now-independent nation is provided in a communication from the French first consul to the minister of Marine in 1807. It shows that after Napoleon had lost nineteen generals and well over fifty thousand troops, and four years after governor Rochambeau's final ouster, the revolution was still considered "impossible" in the world of officialdom. "Everything must be prepared for the restoration of slavery," said First Consul Decrès: "This is not only the opinion of the metropolis, but it is also the view of England and other European powers." French emissaries were sent to other slave-owning nations (Spain, Holland, and the United States) and appealed to the racial contract so that diplomatic relations might be forestalled and any commercial relations with the new nation discontinued. "The existence of an armed negro people, occupying places that they have despoiled by the most criminal acts, is a horrible spectacle for all white nations," declared Charles-Maurice de Talleyrand, French ambassador to the United States, to General Louis Turreau in Washington.[41] Official recognition of Haiti by the United States

41. Quoted in Mats Lundhal, "Toussaint L'Ouverture and the War Economy of Saint Domingue, 1796–1802," 2. See also Hilary Beckles, "Divided to the Vein: The Problem of Race, Colour, and Class Conflict in Haitian Nation-Building, 1804–1820," 496.

would not come until after the Civil War, and the Vatican would delay recognition of the new state for half a century. It would take a reparations commitment of 150 million francs, signed by President Boyer in 1825, to satisfy France's claims for losses suffered by its colonists. The debt was not fully paid until 1922. Of course, in 1804 it was hardly necessary for these postcolonial events to alert Dessalines of the urgent need to preserve the integrity of the newly won independence. The protracted war of liberation had been a sufficiently gruesome experience for him to decide to erect forts on Haiti's tallest mountains, to be prepared for the always-possible return of the colonizers. The origin of the Citadel lay in this initiative.

The paramountcy of military preparedness for self-preservation determined Haiti's foreign policy as well as its internal politics. For its leaders, the overthrow of the colonial regimen in Saint Domingue inexorably meant the constitution of a modern state over and against previous modes of social organization allowed by the limited scope of maroon society. In this regard, Toussaint-Louverture's interest in political independence within the framework of a revolutionary France, in comparison to the geographic and political isolation of the seventeenth-century Palmares maroon "republic" in Brazil, for example, represented a pragmatic political compromise. It would organically include French metropolitan elements for what they meant in terms of capital and technological input. The war had left a shattered economy and cumulative losses of over a billion francs. Main towns like Le Cap, Port-de-Paix, Gonaives, and Saint-Marc had been reduced to ashes, and a significant part of the labor force had been eliminated, as had sources of capital and the material infrastructure of the agricultural industry, including sugar mills, irrigation works, and draft animals.[42]

It was due to the militarization of government and of production that coffee, sugar, and cotton exports, down to 2.8, 1.2, and 0.7 percent of 1789 levels, respectively, could rebound to 45, 38, and 58 percent of what they were just before the uprising. At the time of Toussaint-Louverture's death in

---

42. Beckles, "Divided to the Vein," 495. Zumbi's Palmares maroon settlement in seventeenth-century Brazil is perhaps the most noteworthy alternative construction effected by freedom-seeking Africans in the colonial Americas, apart from Haiti. As Price demonstrates in *Maroon Societies,* military defense was the primary concern of all such settlements. That Africans might lay independent claim to territory outside of the structure of slavery and colonialism was inconceivable for their erstwhile captors. See James, *Black Jacobins,* regarding Toussaint-Louverture's reluctance to break completely with France, especially chapter 13. Economic strategies, including the questions of land distribution and of small-scale production versus large scale production and its political implications, are discussed by Robert K. LaCerte, "The Evolution of Land and Labour in the Haitian Revolution, 1791–1820."

1803, in Napoleon's prison at Fort Joux, France, Philadelphia banking institutions held over 6 million francs in his name for future purchases of war matériel.[43] Even given Toussaint-Louverture's Herculean military successes, his constant sloganeering, and his appeals to the populace for self-sacrifice for the recovery of agricultural production, the combined problems of self-defense, the economy, land distribution, profit-sharing, and national unity may well have proven too complex for his leadership to resolve, even if he had survived. Like Ti Noel trying to enter the world of the geese, the problem of Haiti was how to enter modernity without a past. For Carpentier, writing across race and dealing with events that seemed too magical to be real, the problem was how to make his characters leave anthropological time and enter current, actual time.

In the narrative, Christophe inevitably belongs to both worlds. As tyrant and presumptive traitor of his voodoo gods, it is only logical that he be appropriately punished, according to the framework of African myth that the book had earlier established. This explains the pins in the voodoo doll and the forceful personification of the drums of the Great Pact on the night of his suicide, as they express the will of his oppressed subjects. The drums, we recall, had represented the High Powers of the Other Shore, which had been invoked against the colonial oppressors when Boukman led the historic ceremony on the night of Bois Caiman. Here they are turned against the unrighteous monarch and precipitate his demise. Christophe, however, as black king, is also a noisome and ubiquitous irruption into modernity. Symbolizing both the defeat of European colonialism and the turnover from slavery to sovereignty, and, given the impossibility of creating diachronic separateness, for Carpentier's Negrist narrative his *presence* is to be somehow denied. Denial of coevalness for the Haitian monarch would therefore be expressed through an emphasis on his colonial mimicry through a racialized caricatural rhetoric, aimed at stressing the incongruity of both black king and court.

Accordingly, the scenario that greets Ti Noel's astonished eyes as he approaches the rose-colored palace of Sans Souci is one of awe and wonderment. There are black horsemen in military uniforms that are more Napoleonic than Napoleon. They go by in a cloud of gold dust. The architectonic details of the edifice, the dance orchestra, the church with its officious ministers, and the other pompous personages strutting hither and thither all set the tone for denial through hyperbolic affirmation of the

---

43. Lundhal, "Toussaint L'Ouverture," 9, 3.

blackness of the entire ensemble. The climax of one of the book's more memorable passages comes with the assertion that even the Immaculate Conception is black. In this striking paradox, the world has again turned upside down with the incongruity of African bodies occupying the symbols of European high culture. Christophe himself is shown sweaty and uncomfortable in church, in the sweltering tropical heat, with his tightly buttoned swallowtail coat overladen with decorations. Marie-Louise, his wife, is more explicitly unbecoming as royalty. As things fall apart, she is shown to resort unceremoniously to her peasant roots. In a panicked response to his stroke, she abandons queenly etiquette and squats in the antechamber over a wood fire to make him a root brew. Similarly in Europe, when her servant Soliman becomes ill, she concocts him some bush tea with herbs specially sent over by the new President Boyer. In neither case do her remedies achieve the desired result. That she is out of place in the role of royalty *à la européen* is clearly depicted by her almost comical ignorance of the Latin liturgy proffered by Juan de Dios González, Christophe's new Catholic archbishop, and the readiness with which she dispenses with her high heels as she scrambles to safety with her daughters after the king's fatal gunshot. Even with the perspective of a study such as the present one, one would be hard put to defend the colonial mimicry of the Haitian postindependence aristocracy; however, it is certainly relevant to recognize the paradox entailed in the fact that the ironic take on Christophe's cultural mimetism ensued from a Latin American lettered tradition that was itself defined by mimicry both in form and fashion.

In a cast whose characterization is given short shrift, Ti Noel gets the most attention. This is due evidently to his role as witness throughout the entire narrative, as the one who brings the novel's final philosophical message. For many critics, *El reino de este mundo* is a sort of morality tale or a thesis novel. Through his experience of several cycles of oppression, and faced by the inability to escape into the world of the animals, the revelation that Ti Noel shares is that humanity's greatest task and triumph is in confronting injustice in the here and now, instead of dreaming of happiness in a future world. In heaven there is no greatness to be achieved. It is a universal message that has risen above the racialized nature of the oppression, first by whites, then by blacks, and finally by the mulatto Agrimensors who approach him in the settlement where he has squatted to make his private kingdom. If the moral economy of the story makes the conclusion a reasonable one, Ti Noel himself is not as convincing as a philosopher. Aside from his tutelage under Macandal, there is not much in his development over the several decades of the book to suggest that he is capable of the kind of intellectual sophistication that the message implies.

When we meet him, he is declaredly illiterate and mentally challenged, and with the eruption of violence at de Mezy's plantation, there is little to separate him from the savage behavior of the other revolting slaves. Although he does not join in the general melee of food and frolic, he slakes his long thirst for wine and promptly goes upstairs to rape the slave master's wife. There had not been much of an investment in sexual protocol with his own future "wife," either, when he took her (three times) in the stables following Macandal's execution. In spite of a twenty-year relationship with this woman (a cook at the Mezy residence), which has produced twelve children, neither she nor his offspring are named in the narrative, and there is a remarkable lack of intimacy or even dialogue among them, outside of the mention of his passing on some of Macandal's stories. Additionally, although he participates in the historic ceremony at Bois Caiman, the moment seems to have little resonance in his consciousness, and he does not engage in dialogue with any of the other rebels. Similarly, his eventual senility as an older individual, his talking to the animals, and his donning the remnants of kingly garments, looted from Sans Souci, do little for his profile as a visionary.

One of the later images of Ti Noel, the one who survived it all, has him sitting atop the three volumes of the *Grande Encyclopédie,* which he had converted into his regular seat for chewing sugarcane. The scene is poignantly suggestive of the bankruptcy of the new Haitian condition, more than of a passing low in the cycle of future revolutionary rebirth. The juxtaposition of unprocessed sugarcane and the compendium of Western knowledge, with the worn-out and unlettered black man, are an eloquent expression of their mutual lack of complementarity. In the final analysis, the degree to which the Carpenterian version of the Haitian revolution stumbles on its premises of vindication and verisimilitude reveals, like in *Ecue-Yamba-O,* another novelistic split down the middle, in that it raises multiple questions concerning the half that never was told. Carpentier, originally a *negrista* poet, shows that neither the movement itself nor the exoticism of its transracial impulse had gone away after the poetry lost momentum. With him, even when undergirded by "research" and framed by verisimilitude, the questions of authority and representation of the Other remain(ed) ideologically charged and prone to exotification and prejudice. In the potentially epic narrative of antislavery agency, the written *negros* have still not managed to enter unfettered into the realm of the heroic.

Conclusion

The texts that, in their varying narrative guises, constitute the writing of the *negro* open an important window on race-making in the Luso-Hispanic world and the modern world in general. On account of the implied permanence of the printed word, they may also be seen as potentially permanent instantiations of a dominant, white, racist discourse, which, at particular historical moments, was unselfconsciously overt and at others was articulated under the aesthetic cover of the literary. The racist trace in these literary texts, again potentially evident to all categories of readers, is often circumscribed, institutionally even, by peculiarities of cognition that tend to attenuate and/or obfuscate its more deleterious dimensions. For example, one result of the transracial script is the production of a Negrist discourse, at the level of both art and hermeneutics, in which denigration passes for glorification, or in which antislavery writing is less about the emancipation of the oppressed than it is about the celebration of its lettered creators.

To the extent that there exists a cognitive dysfunction in literary critique that ignores, misrecognizes, and misapprehends the traumas of being black in a world of racialized oppression, this dysfunction may be seen as part of the inverted epistemology that sustains racial domination. In this scheme, moral and ethical norms supporting whiteness are seen to be inoperative when dealing with its presumably inferior Others. For Mills, writing on this double standard, racist domination functions through an agreement "to misinterpret" the world. "One has to learn to see the world wrongly," he suggests, "but with the assurance that this set of mistaken perceptions will be validated by white epistemic authority, whether religious or secular."[1]

1. Mills, *Racial Contract,* 18.

This skewed process of cognition is a fundamental aspect of the white racial contract, which interpellates whites across the globe and invites them to subscribe to its premise of superiority and its desire for domination. Mills's invocation of a white constituency that is *not* a signatory to the contract of whiteness and its political appeal is just as important, in that it speaks to the potential for widening the counterinstitutional consensus regarding the purpose and meaning of the texts in question. It also helps clear the path for ways of narrating race that do not subscribe to the precept of racial hierarchy.

Regarding Latin American letters, one of the important sources for the misreading of race is the racial democracy principle, which in its denial of racialized oppression starts off on the wrong hermeneutical foot, thereby underscoring the validity of the theory of willful racial misunderstanding. Decolonizing the canon and the broader discursive archive thus acquires its relevance as an ongoing exercise, that is, beyond trend-driven academic or publishing cycles. This is so especially if we consider the place of the culture of letters in modernity's technology of word and image, and its connection to the racialized aspect of social and politico-economic domination.

Within the regions studied in this book, Argentina, although I have not given it detailed attention, is as dramatic an example of the intersection of race, writing, and national formation as any other, especially if we take into account the broader ideological atmosphere of the nineteenth century and its particular applications to that country. Argentine founding father Juan Alberdi's famous 1852 maxim, "to govern is to populate," reveals his view of incoming migrants to Argentina in white and racially exclusive terms. A century and a half later, the successful career of this idea was evinced in a declaration, by one of Alberdi's successors, regarding the "essentially European roots" of Argentine "man." In Argentina, said ex-president Carlos Menem at the University of Maastrich in 1993, "we have no blacks." One might say that Menem's statement represents either a willed ignorance regarding the national constituency, or a return to the genocidal projections of such noted nationalist ideologues as José Ingenieros and Domingo Faustino Sarmiento, who preceded him in the eighteen hundreds. It can, of course, be both things at the same time. The crude reality of these projections was reinforced in August 2002, in the detention of an Afro-Argentine woman at the Ezeiza national airport on the suspicion that the passport she was carrying was false. María Magdalena Lamadrid was not allowed to use the travel document, which she legitimately possessed, on the precept that since she was black, she "could not be Argentinean." The immigration official proceeded to add insult to injury by further inquiring if she spoke Spanish and whether or not she was Peruvian. Recalling the *bozal* of colonial times, who was so deemed because he spoke no language "but his own," one wonders to what category would his or her American descendant correspond, when even ownership of the language of their national home centuries later cannot be taken for granted. The officer's presumption that Lamadrid might be Peruvian further underscores the historical dilemma of diaspora and exile. Ironically, María Magdalena "Pocha" Lamadrid is president of a black activist group, Africa Vive (Africa Lives), one of whose objectives is to organize a census that would finally put a reliable number to the thousands of surviving Argentineans of African descent. When she was detained, she was on her way to Panama to participate in a conference on the life and work of Martin Luther King Jr.[2]

Menem's denial of a black presence in Argentina, to which he is reputed to have added, "that is a problem that belongs to Brazil,"[3] offers an interesting counterpoint in the discussion of the African diaspora and the Latin American nation-state in other locations. In Brazil, Colombia, Ecuador, Honduras, and Nicaragua, for example, the *mestizaje* and the top-down "racial democracy" mantras are finally losing ground in favor of a more frontal recognition of white privilege, of the need for racial equality, and of the pluricultural realities of the nation. The tradition of exclusion seems to want to reassert itself in Argentina, but in Brazil and in other areas of the continent recently experiencing redemocratization, the tradition of delusion, of "racial democracy," seems finally headed toward demise. It is significant that it was in 1988, on the centenary of the abolition of slavery in Brazil, that national recognition of the cultural patrimony of the *quilombos* was begun and the process for titling of lands still held by the descendants of maroons was initiated. Since then, with the creation of the Palmares Cultural Foundation and the National Institute for Agrarian Reform, at least 65 out of 1,265 sites inventoried by the foundation have received titles.

2. Reported by Rolando Rivière in the Argentine daily *La Nación*, November 26, 1993, and by Yanina Kinigsberg for *Clarín*, August 24, 2002, respectively. Estimates on the numbers of Afro-Argentines today vary from five hundred thousand to more than one million. Until the middle of the nineteenth century, they constituted up to 30 percent of the population of the capital, Buenos Aires. Their numbers later plunged, mainly due to massive participation of black males in the war of the Triple Alliance in 1865–1870, and because of the yellow fever epidemic in 1871. A poignant 2002 documentary, *Afroargentinos,* reports on the history and presence of blacks in Argentina.

3. Quoted in *Afroargentinos.*

While this is by no means an overwhelming number, it nonetheless gives concrete and symbolic value to an initiative that was too long overdue. The state-sanctioned efforts to introduce a Brazilian brand of affirmative action are just as important.[4]

The twin processes, land titling and affirmative action, represent a historic shift in the dynamic of (black) racial subjectivity and national formation in Brazil, especially in relation to the colonial and postcolonial antecedent in the cases this study has addressed. They are important also to the degree that they are the product of decades of effort by black activist groups, public intellectuals, leftist social science researchers, and NGOs, as well as the stimulus of the 2001 World Conference on Racism in Durban. In this regard, the participation of the Brazilian state has been incalculable, especially under the presidency of Fernando Henrique Cardoso (1995–2003), a former sociologist and antiracist sympathizer. That thousands of Brazilians of African descent might now emerge from remote areas where there is no electricity or running water, and where they live on subsistence farming or fishing, speaks volumes on the question of the historical determinants to their condition. The areas where they live have been earmarked for improvement through the provision of access to education, health care, and other basic services; of technical assistance in the form of machinery, equipment, and irrigation systems; and of technical and arts and craft training. That many of these areas in Brazil (and Colombia, Ecuador, and Central America as well) are potentially rich in natural resources such as timber or exploitable minerals, or show promise for cattle ranching or ecotourism, points to a joint public and private sector interest with transnational implications; this, too, constitutes an interesting facet of the phenomenon of land titling.

Regardless of the pros and cons of the complex situation of Brazilian *quilombo* dwellers or their counterparts in other places, it is clear that the twenty-first century will complete their passage from maroonage to modernity, and that the impetus that guaranteed their survival over the centuries and helped underwrite their agency as social actors up to the present will have a determinative role in the future. As the descendants of maroons enter the "time" of the nation—not as ethnographic curiosities, but as people with a history of struggle and a counterinstitutional consciousness—they will

---

4. Titling of former maroon lands in the Colombian *chocó* region of the Pacific, which was written into law in 1993, is far more advanced than in the Brazilian case; see Eva Thorne, "The Politics of Afro-Latin American Land Rights."

continue to shape the political horizon in their countries of residence, along with other subaltern groups with similar objectives. Similarly, the poets, authors, and critics who are aligned in greater or lesser measure with this transformational impulse will continue to explore the meaning of race in their lives and work. They will also challenge the racist archive and the imagination that feeds it, as alternative writings of the pluricultural landscape inevitably emerge.

Works Cited

Afroargentinos. Dir. Jorge Fortes and Diego Ceballos. Buenos Aires: Filma-gen Producciones, Lagartija Muda Producciones, 2002.

Alba Bufill, Elio. "La Avellaneda y la literatura antiesclavista." *Círculo: Revista de Cultura* 19 (1990): 123–30.

Albornoz, Aurora de, and Julio Rodríguez-Luis. *Sensemayá: La poesía negra en el mundo hispanohablante (antología).* Madrid: Editorial Orígenes, S.A., 1980.

Alencar, José de. *O guarani, Iracema, Ubijara.* Rio de Janeiro: Instituto Nacional do Livro, 1977.

Alsopp, Richard, ed. *Dictionary of Caribbean English Usage.* Oxford: Oxford University Press, 1996.

Althousser, Louis. "Ideology and Ideological State Apparatuses." In *Critical Theory since 1965,* ed. Hazard Adams and Leroy Searle, 239–51. Tal-lahassee: University Press of Florida, 1986.

Alvar, Manuel. *Léxico del mestizaje en hispanoamérica.* Madrid: Ediciones Cultura Hispánica, 1987.

Alvarez Nazario, Manuel. *El elemento negroide en el español de Puerto Rico: Contribución al estudio del negro en América.* San Juan: Instituto de Cultura Puertorriqueño, 1961.

Amistad. Dir. Stephen Spielberg. Glendale, Calif.: DreamWorks SKG, 1997.

Amorim, António. "Escravos africanos em Portugal: Que descendentes (lhes) deixaram (ter)?" In *Os negros em Portugal—sécs. XV a XIX,* ed. Ana Maria Rodrigues and Joaquim Soeiro de Brito, 19–24. Lisbon: National Commission for the Commemoration of the Portuguese Dis-coveries, 2000.

Anthiel, George. "The Negro on the Spiral." In *Negro: An Anthology,* ed. Nancy Cunard, 214–19. New York: Frederick Ungar Publishing, 1970.

Araujo, Nara. "Raza y género en *Sab.*" *Casa de las Américas* 33, no. 90 (1993): 42–49.

Arce, Margot. "Más sobre los poemas negros de Luis Palés Matos." *Revista Bimestre Cubana* 37–38 (1936): 30–39.

Arredondo, Alberto. "El arte negro a contrapelo." *Adelante: Revista Mensual* 3, no. 26 (1937): 5–6, 20.

Arróm, José Juan. "La poesía afrocubana." *Revista Iberoamericana* 4 (1942): 379–408.

Asad, Talal. Introduction to *Anthropology and the Colonial Encounter,* ed. Talal Asad, 9–19. New York: Humanities Press, 1973.

Avellaneda, Gertrudis Gómez de. *Sab.* Prologue and notes by Mary Cruz. Havana: Editorial Arte y Literatura, 1976.

———. *Sab and Autobiography.* Trans. and ed. Nina M. Scott. Austin: University of Texas Press, 2000.

Azim, Firdous. *The Colonial Rise of the Novel.* London: Routledge, 1993.

Balibar, Etienne, and Immanuel Wallerstein. *Race, Nation, Class: Ambiguous Identities.* London: Verso, 1991.

Ballagas, Emilio. *Cuaderno de poesía negra.* Santa Clara, Cuba: Imprenta La Nueva, 1934.

———. *Mapa de la poesía negra americana.* Buenos Aires: Editorial Pleamar, 1946.

———."Poesía negra liberada." *Revista de la UNAM* 18 (1937): 5–6.

———. "Situación de la poesía afroamericana." *Revista Cubana* 21 (1946): 5–60.

Ballagas, Emilio, ed. *Antología de poesía negra hispano-americana.* Madrid: M. Aguilar, 1935.

Baralt, Guillermo A. *Esclavos rebeldes: Conspiraciones y sublevaciones de esclavos en Puerto Rico (1795–1873).* Río Piedras, Puerto Rico: Ediciones Huracán, 1982.

Barradas de Carvalho, Margarida. "L'idéologie religieuse dans la 'Crónica dos feitos de Guiné' de Gomes Eanes de Zurara." In *Bulletin des études portugaises.* Amadora: Livraria Bertrand, 1956.

Barreda Tomás, Pedro. "Abolicionismo y feminismo en la Avellaneda: Lo negro como artificio narrativo en *Sab.*" *Cuadernos Hispanoamericanos* 342 (1978): 613–23.

Barreto, Luis Felipe. "Gomes Eanes de Zurara e o problema da 'Crónica da Guiné." *Studia* 47 (1989): 311–69.

Barthelemy, Anthony. *Black Face, Maligned Race: The Representation of Blacks in English Drama from Shakespeare to Southerne.* Baton Rouge: Louisiana State University Press, 1987.

Beckles, Hilary. "Caribbean Anti-Slavery: The Self-Liberation Ethos of Enslaved Blacks." *Journal of Caribbean History* 22, nos. 1, 2 (1998): 1–19.

———. "Divided to the Vein: The Problem of Race, Colour, and Class Conflict in Haitian Nation-Building, 1804–1820." In *Caribbean Freedom: Economy and Society from Emancipation to the Present,* ed. Hilary Beckles and Verene Shepherd, 494–503. Princeton: Markus Weiner Publishers, 1996.

———. "Emancipation by War or Law? Wilberforce and the 1816 Barbados Slave Rebellion." In *Abolition and Its Aftermath: The Historical Context, 1790–1916,* ed. David Richardson, 80–104. London: Cass, 1985.

Behn, Aphra. *"Oroonoko" and Other Writings.* Oxford: Oxford University Press, 1994.

Beltrán, Gonzalo Aguirre. *Cuijla: Esbozo etnográfico de un pueblo negro.* Mexico: Fondo de Cultura Económica, 1958.

———. *La población negra de México.* Mexico: Fondo de Cultura Económica, 1972.

Benítez, Jaime. "Luis Palés Matos y el pesimismo en Puerto Rico: Doce años después." In *Tuntún de pasa y grifería: Poemas afroantillanos,* 9–41. San Juan: Biblioteca de Autores Puertorriqueños. 1974.

Benítez-Rojo, Antonio. "¿Cómo narrar la nación? El círculo de Domingo Delmonte y el resurgimiento de la novela cubana." *Cuadernos Americanos* 45, no. 3 (1994): 103–28.

———. "Power/Sugar/Literature: Toward a Reinterpretion of Cubanness." *Cuban Studies* 16 (1980): 1–31.

Benjamin, Walter. *Illuminations.* Ed. Hannah Arendt. New York: Harcourt, Brace and World, 1968.

Bennett, Louise. *Jamaica Labrish.* Kingston: Montrose Printery, 1966.

Bergmann, Jörg. *Discreet Indiscretions: The Social Organization of Gossip.* New York: Aldine de Gruyter, 1993.

Bernardino de Sahagún, Fray. *Historia general de las cosas de Nueva España.* Introduction and notes by Alfredo López Austin and Josefina García Quintana. 2 vols. Madrid: Alianza, 1988.

Bernd, Zilá. *Literatura e identidade nacional.* Porto Alegre, Brazil: Editora da Universidade, 1992.

Beverley, John. "After Communism." *Boundary 2: An International Journal of Literature and Culture* 26, no. 3 (1999): 39–46.

————. *Against Literature.* Minneapolis: University of Minnesota Press, 1993.

Bhabha, Homi. "The Other Question." *Screen* 24, no. 4 (1983): 19–36.

Blake, John William, trans. and ed. *Europeans in West Africa, 1450–1560.* 2 vols. London: Hakluyt Society, 1942.

Blanco, Tomás. *El prejuicio racial en Puerto Rico.* San Juan: Editorial Biblioteca de Autores Puertorriqueños, 1940.

————. "Poesía y recitación negras." *Revista Bimestre Cubana* 37–38 (1936): 24–30.

————. *Sobre Palés Matos.* San Juan: Biblioteca de Autores Puertorriqueños, 1950.

Boose, Lynda. "'The Getting of a Lawful Race': Racial Discourse in Early Modern England and the Unrepresentable Black Woman." In *Women, "Race," and Writing in the Early Modern Period,* ed. Margo Hendricks and Patricia Parker, 35–54. London: Routledge, 1994.

Bourdieu, Pierre. *Language and Symbolic Power.* Trans. Gino Raymond and Matthew Adamson. Cambridge: Harvard University Press, 1991.

Bourdieu, Pierre, and Jean-Claude Passeron. *Reproduction: In Education, Society, and Culture.* Trans. Richard Nice. London: Sage, 1990.

Bowser, Frederick. "Colonial Spanish America." In *Neither Slave nor Free: The Freedmen of African Descent in the Slave Societies of the New World,* ed. David Cohen and Jack Greene, 19–58. Baltimore: Johns Hopkins Press, 1972.

Boxer, C. R. *The Portuguese Seaborne Empire, 1415–1825.* New York: Alfred A. Knopf, 1969.

Boyarin, Daniel. "What Does a Jew Want; or, The Political Meaning of the Phallus." In *The Psychoanalysis of Race,* ed. Christopher Lane, 211–40. New York: Columbia University Press, 1998.

Branche, Jerome. "Soul for Sale? Contrapunteo cubano en Madrid." *Revista Estudios* 19 (2002): 163–86.

————. "Sub-*poena:* Slavery, Subjection, and Sufferation in Juan Francisco Manzano." In *Nineteenth-Century Literature,* ed. Russel Whitaker. Detroit: Gale Publishing. Forthcoming.

Branche, Jerome, ed. *Lo que teníamos que tener: Raza y revolución en Nicolás Guillén.* Pittsburgh: Instituto Internacional de Literatura Iberoamericana, 2003.

Bremer, Federika. "The Homes of the New World: Impressions of America." In *Slaves, Sugar, and Colonial Society: Travel Accounts of Cuba, 1801–1899,* ed. Louis A. Pérez Jr., 116–19. Wilmington: Scholarly Resources, 1992.

Brenan, Gerald. *The Literature of the Spanish People: From Roman Times to the Present.* Cambridge: Cambridge University Press, 1962.

Brookshaw, David. *Race and Color in Brazilian Literature.* Lanham, Md.: Scarecrow Press, 1986.

Buck-Morss, Susan. "Hegel and Haiti." *Critical Inquiry* 26 (2000): 820–66.

Bueno, Salvador. "Carpentier en la maestría de sus novelas y relatos breves." In *Novelas y relatos: Alejo Carpentier,* 7–44. Havana: Editorial Pueblo y Educación, 1974.

———. *Domingo del Monte, ¿Quién fue?* Havana: Ediciones Unión, 1986.

———. "La lucha contra la esclavitud y su expresión literaria." *Unión* 1 (1986): 48–56, 1986.

———. *Las ideas literarias de Domingo Delmonte.* Havana: Editoral Hercules, 1954.

———. Prologue to *Acerca de Plácido.* Havana: Editorial Letras Cubanas, 1985.

Burkholder, Mark, and Lyman Johnson. *Colonial Latin America.* New York: Oxford University Press, 1998.

Burton, Richard D. E., and Fred Reno, eds. *French, and West Indian: Martinique, Guadeloupe, and French Guiana Today.* Charlottesville: University Press of Virginia, 1994.

Bush, Barbara. *Slave Women in Caribbean Society, 1650–1838.* Bloomington: Indiana University Press, 1980.

Cahill, David. "Colour by Numbers: Racial and Ethnic Categories in the Viceroyalty of Peru, 1532–1824." *Journal of Latin American Studies* 26, no. 2 (1994): 323–46.

Camín, Alfonso. *Maracas, y otros poemas.* Mexico: La Impresora Azteca, 1952.

Camões, Luís de. *Os lusíadas.* São Paulo: Victor Civita, 1979.

Carpentier, Alejo. "The Baroque and the Marvelous Real." In *Magical Realism: Theory, History, Community,* ed. Lois Parkinson Zamora and Wendy B. Faris, 89–108. Durham: Duke University Press, 1995.

———. "De lo real maravilloso americano." In *Tientos y diferencias,* 85–99. Havana: Ediciones Unión, 1966.

———. *Ecue-Yamba-O: Novela afro-cubana.* Buenos Aires: Editorial Xanadu, 1968.

———. *Ecue-Yamba-O.* Madrid: Alianza Editorial, 1989.

———. *El reino de este mundo.* Barcelona: Seix Barral, 1984.

———. *The Kingdom of This World.* Trans. Harriet de Onís. New York: Noonday Press, 1999.

———. *La música en Cuba.* Havana: Editorial Pueblo y Educación, 1989.

————. *Novelas y relatos, Alejo Carpentier.* Havana: Editorial Pueblo y Educación, 1974.

Carrera, Magalí. *Imagining Identity in New Spain: Race, Lineage, and the Colonial Body in Portraiture and Casta Paintings.* Austin: University of Texas Press, 2003.

Cartey, Wilfred. *Black Images.* New York: Teachers College Press, 1970.

Cassuto, Leonard. *The Inhuman Race: The Racial Grotesque in American Literature and Culture.* New York: Columbia University Press, 1996.

Castañeda, Digna. "The Female Slave in Cuba during the First Half of the Nineteenth Century." In *Engendering History: Caribbean Women in Historical Perspective,* ed. Verene Shepherd, Bridget Brereton, and Barbara Bailey, 141–54. New York: St. Martin's Press, 1995.

Castellano, Juan R. "El negro esclavo en el entremés del Siglo de Oro." *Hispania* 44 (1961): 55–65.

Castor, Susy. *Migración y relaciones internacionales (el caso haitiano-dominicano).* Mexico: Facultad de Ciencias Políticas y Sociales, U.N.A.M, 1983.

Castro Alves, Antonio de. *The Major Abolitionist Poems.* Ed. and trans. Amy A. Peterson. New York: Garland Publications, 1990.

Castro Fernández, Silvio. *La masacre de los independientes de color.* Havana: Editorial de Ciencias Sociales, 2002.

Cepero Bonilla, Raúl. *Azúcar y abolición.* Barcelona: Edición crítica, 1976.

Césaire, Aimé. *Return to My Native Land/Cahier d'un retour au pays natal.* Paris: Présence Africaine, 1971.

Chandler, Richard, and Schwartz Kessel. *A New History of Spanish Literature.* Baton Rouge: Louisiana State University Press, 1961.

Chasca, Edmund de. "The Phonology of the Speech of the Negroes in Early Spanish Drama." *Hispanic Review* 14 (1946): 323–29.

Chaves y Rey, Manuel. *Cosas nuevas y viejas (apuntes sevillanos).* Prologue by José Nogales. Sevilla: Tipografía Sanceda, 1904.

Clifford, James. "On Ethnographic Authority." In *The Predicament of Culture: Twentieth-Century Ethnography, Literature, and Art,* 21–54. Cambridge: Harvard University Press, 1988.

Cohen, William. *The French Encounter with Africans: White Response to Blacks, 1530–1880.* Bloomington: Indiana University Press, 1990.

"Comunicación del Alcalde de la Habana al Presidente de la Sociedad de Estudios Afro-cubanos, solicitando la opinión y el consejo de dicha-sociedad sobre el resurgimiento de las comparsas populares habaneras."

In *Las comparsas populares del carnaval habanero, cuestión resuelta,* ed. Antonio Beruff Mendieta, 7–8. Havana: Molina y Cia., 1937.

Conrad, Robert Edgar. *Children of God's Fire: A Documentary History of Black Slavery in Brazil.* Philadelphia: Pennsylvania University Press, 1994.

Cortés López, José Luis. *La esclavitud negra en la España península del siglo XVI.* Salamanca, Spain: Ediciones Universidad de Salamanca, 1989.

Cotarelo y Mori, Emilio, ed. *Colección de entremeses, loas, bailes, jácaras y mojigangas desde fines del siglo XVI a mediados del XVIII.* Madrid: Casa Editorial Bailly/Bailliére, 1911.

Covarrubias, Sebastián de. *Tesoro de la lengua castellana o española.* 1611. Reprint, ed. Martín de Riquer. Barcelona: Horta, 1943.

Crespo, Elizabeth. "Domestic Work and Racial Divisions in Women's Employment in Puerto Rico, 1899–1930." *Journal of El Centro de Estudios Puertorriqueños* 8, nos. 1, 2 (1996): 30–41.

Crone, C. R., ed. and trans. *"The Voyages of Cadamosto," and Other Documents on Western Africa in the Second Half of the Fifteenth Century.* London: Hakluyt Society, 1937.

Cronon, E. David. *Black Moses: The Story of Marcus Garvey and the Universal Negro Improvement Association.* Madison: University of Wisconsin Press, 1974.

Cruz, Mary. "*Sab,* su texto y su contexto." Prologue to *Sab,* by Gertrudis Gómez de Avellaneda, 11–120. Havana: Editorial Arte y Literatura, 1976.

Cunard, Nancy. "Harlem Reviewed." In *Negro: An Anthology,* ed. Nancy Cunard, 47–55. 1934. Reprint, New York: Continuum Publishing, 1996.

DeCosta, Miriam. "The Portrayal of Blacks in a Spanish Medieval Manuscript." *Negro History Bulletin* 37, no. 1 (1974): 193–96.

DeCosta, Miriam, ed. *Blacks in Hispanic Literature: Critical Essays.* Port Washington, N.Y.: Kennikat Press, 1977.

DeCosta-Willis, Miriam, ed. *Singular Like a Bird: The Art of Nancy Morejón.* Washington, D.C.: Howard University Press, 1999.

De la Fuente, Alejandro. *A Nation for All: Race, Inequality, and Politics in Twentieth-Century Cuba.* Chapel Hill: University of North Carolina Press, 2001.

———. "Slave Law and Claims-Making in Cuba: The Tannenbaum Debate Revisited." *Law and History Review* 22, no. 2 (summer 2004): 339–69.

———. "Two Dangers, One Solution: Immigration, Race, and Labor in Cuba, 1900–1930." *International Labor and Working-Class History* 51 (1997): 30–49.

Del Monte, Domingo. "Estado de la población blanca y de color de la isla de Cuba en 1839." In *Escritos,* ed. J. A. Castro, 1:144–59. Havana: Cultural, 1929.

Dentith, Simon. *Bakhtinian Thought: An Introductory Reader.* London: Routledge, 1995.

Depestre, René. "Problemas de la identidad del hombre negro en las literaturas antillanas." *Revista Casa de las Américas* 53 (1969): 19–28.

De Rooy, Piet. "Of Monkeys, Blacks, and Proles: Ernst Haeckel's Theory of Recapitulation." In *Imperial Monkey Business: Racial Supremacy in Social Darwinist Theory and Colonial Practice,* ed. Jan Brenan et al., 7–34. Amsterdam: VU University Press, 1990.

Díaz, María Elena. "Beyond Tannenbaum." *Law and History Review* 22, no. 2 (summer 2004): 371–76.

Diego Padró, José de. *Luis Palés Matos y su trasmundo poético.* Río Piedras, Puerto Rico: Editorial Puerto, 1973.

"Directrices: Tierra y población en las Antillas." *Revista de Avance* 1, pt. 2, no. 16 (1927): 87–88.

"Directrices: Cuba, caso antillano." *Revista de Avance* 3, no. 29 (1929): 287–89.

Domarus, Max, ed. *Hitler: Speeches and Proclamations, 1932–1945.* Vol. 1. London: I. B. Tauris, 1990.

Domínguez Ortiz, Antonio. *The Golden Age of Spain, 1516–1659.* Trans. James Casey. New York: Basic Books, 1971.

———. "La esclavitud en Castilla durante la edad moderna." In *Estudios de historia social de España,* ed. Carmelo Viñas y Mey, 369–427. Madrid: CSIC, 1952.

Donnan, Elizabeth. *Documents Illustrative of the History of the Slave Trade to America.* 4 vols. Washington D.C.: Carnegie Institute of Washington, 1932.

Drake, St. Clair. *Black Folk Here and There: An Essay in History and Anthropology.* Vol. 2. Berkeley and Los Angeles: University of California Press, 1990.

Drescher, Seymour. "Public Opinion and the Destruction of British Colonial Slavery." In *Slavery and British Society, 1776–1846,* ed. James Walvin, 22–48. Baton Rouge: Louisiana State University Press, 1982.

Duno, Luis. *Solventando las diferencias: La ideología del mestizaje en Cuba.* Madrid: Iberoamericana, 2003.

Durham Seminario, Lee Ann. *The History of the Blacks, the Jews, and the Moors in Spain.* Madrid: Playor, 1975.

Eanes de Zurara, Gomes. *The Chronicle of the Discovery and Conquest of Guinea*. 2 vols. Trans. Charles Raymond Beazley and Edgar Prestage. New York: Burt Franklin, 1896–1897.

————. *Crónica de Guiné*. Lisbon: Agência Geral das Colónias, 1949.

Elbl, Ivana. "Cross-Cultural Trade and Diplomacy: Portuguese Relations with West Africa, 1441–1521." *Journal of World History* 3, no. 2 (1992): 165–204.

————. "A Man of His Time (and Peers): A New Look at Henry the Navigator." *Luso-Brazilian Review* 28, no. 2 (1991): 73–89.

Ellis, Robert. "Reading through the Veil of Juan Francisco Manzano: From Homoerotic Violence to the Dream of a Homoracial Bond." *PMLA* 113 (1998): 422–35.

Encyclopaedia Britannica: A Dictionary of Arts, Sciences, and General Information. 9th ed. Vol. 17. Edinburgh: Adam and Charles Black, 1884.

————. 11th ed. Vol. 19. New York: University Press, 1911.

————. Chicago: Encyclopaedia Britannica, 1994.

Escalante, Aquiles. *El palenque de San Basilio: Una comunidad de descendientes de negros cimarrones*. Baranquilla, Colombia: Editorial Mejoras, 1979.

Eze, Emmanuel Chukwudi. "The Color of Reason: The Idea of Race in Kant's Anthropology." In *Anthropology and the German Enlightenment*, 196–237. Lewisburgh, Pa.: Bucknell University Press, 1995.

Eze, Emmanuel Chukwudi, ed. *Race and the Enlightenment*. Cambridge: Blackwell Publishers, 1997.

Fabian, Johannes. *Time and the Other: How Anthropology Makes Its Object*. New York: Columbia University Press, 1983.

Fanon, Franz. *Black Skin, White Masks*. Trans. Charles Lam Markmann. New York: Grove Press, 1968.

Feinberg, Leonard. *The Secret of Humor*. Amsterdam: Rodopi, 1978.

Fenichel, Otto. *The Collected Papers of Otto Fenichel*. Vol. 1. New York: Norton, 1953.

Fernández Robaina, Tomás. *El negro en Cuba, 1902–1958: Apuntes para la historia de la lucha contra la discriminación racial*. Havana: Editorial de Ciencias Sociales, 1990.

Fick, Carolyn E. *The Making of Haiti: The Saint Domingue Revolution from Below*. Knoxville: University of Tennessee Press, 1990.

Fiola, Jan. "Race Relations in Brazil: A Reassessment of the 'Racial Democracy' Thesis." University of Massachusetts at Amherst, Program in Latin American Studies, Occasional Papers Series, 1999.

Fischer, Sibylle. *Modernity Disavowed: Haiti and the Cultures of Slavery in the Age of Revolution.* Durham: Duke University Press, 2004.

Fivel-Démoret, Sharon Romeo. "The Production and Consumption of Propaganda Literature: The Cuban Anti-Slavery Novel." *Bulletin of Hispanic Studies* 66 (1989): 1–10.

Font Saldaña, Jorge. "Dominga de la Cruz Clarillo, nueva intérprete del verso negroide." *Puerto Rico Ilustrado,* 1938.

Foot, Michael, and Isaac Kramnic, eds. *The Thomas Paine Reader.* New York: Penguin Books, 1987.

Ford, Hugh. Introduction to *Negro: An Anthology,* ed. Nancy Cunard. New York: Continuum Publishing, 1996.

Fra Molinero, Baltasar. *La imagen de los negros en el teatro del Siglo de Oro.* Madrid: Siglo XXI Editores, 1995.

Franco, José Luciano. "La conspiración de Aponte, 1812." In *Ensayos históricos,* 125–90. Havana: Editorial de Ciencias Sociales, 1974.

Frank, Andre Gunder. *World Accumulation, 1492–1789.* New York: Monthly Review Press, 1992.

Freud, Sigmund. "Jokes and the Comic." In *Comedy: Meaning and Form,* ed. Robert W. Corrigan, 167–73. New York: Harper and Row, 1981.

———. *Jokes and Their Relation to the Unconscious.* New York: Norton, 1963.

Freyre, Gilberto. *The Masters and the Slaves: A Study in the Development of Brazilian Civilization.* New York: Alfred A. Knopf, 1956.

———. *O escravo nos anúncios de jornais brasileiros do século XIX.* São Paulo, Brazil: Companhia Editora Nacional, 1979.

Friol, Roberto. *Suite para Juan Francisco Manzano.* Havana: Editorial Letras Cubanas, 1977.

Galeano, Eduardo. *Las venas abiertas de América Latina.* Havana: Casa de las Américas, 1971.

Gama, Luis. *Primeiras trovas burlescas e outros poemas.* Sao Paulo, Brazil: Martins Fontes, 2000.

García, Enildo. "Cartas de Domingo del Monte a Alexander H. Everett." *Revista de Literatura Cubana* 7, no. 13 (1989): 105–48.

———. "Romanticismo antillano: Domingo del Monte y 'The Harvard Connection.'" *Círculo: Revista de Cultura* 22 (1993): 68–78.

Gates, Henry Louis, Jr. "Introduction: Writing 'Race' and the Difference It Makes." In *"Race," Writing, and Difference,* ed. Henry Louis Gates Jr., 1–20. Chicago: University of Chicago Press, 1985.

———. "The Trope of the New Negro and the Reconstruction of the Image of the Black." *Representations* 24 (1988): 129–55.

Giacomini, Sonia Maria. "Ser escrava no Brasil." *Estudos Afro-Asiáticos* 15 (1988): 145–79.

Gilman, Sander. *Difference and Pathology: Stereotypes of Sexuality, Race, and Madness.* Ithaca: Cornell University Press, 1985.

Gilroy, Paul. *The Black Atlantic: Modernity and Double Consciousness.* Cambridge: Harvard University Press, 1993.

———. *"There Ain't No Black in the Union Jack": The Cultural Politics of Race and Nation.* Chicago: University of Chicago Press, 1991.

Giroux, Henry, and Susan Searles. "Race Talk and the Bell Curve Debate: The Crisis of Democratic Vision." *Cultural Critique* 34 (1996): 5–26.

Godreau, Isar. "La semántica fugitiva: 'Raza,' color y vida cotidiana en Puerto Rico." *Revista de Ciencias Sociales* 9 (2000): 52–71.

———. "Peinando diferencias, bregas de pertenencia: El alisado y el llamado 'pelo malo.'" *Caribbean Studies* 30, no. 1 (2002): 82–134.

Gómez de Avellaneda, Gertrudis. *Sab.* Prologue and notes by Mary Cruz. Havana: Editorial Arte y Literatura, 1976.

———. *Sab and Autobiography.* Trans. and ed. Nina Scott. Austin: University of Texas Press, 1993.

González, José Luis. *El País de cuatro pisos.* Río Piedras, Puerto Rico: Ediciones Huracán, 1980.

González, José Luis, and Mónica Mansour. *Poesía negra de América.* Mexico: Ediciones Era, 1976.

González del Valle, José Zacarías. *La vida literaria en Cuba (1836–1840).* Havana: Publicaciones de la Secretaría de Educación, 1938.

González-Echeverría, Roberto. *Alejo Carpentier: The Pilgrim at Home.* Ithaca: Cornell University Press, 1977.

Goody, Jack. "Writing, Religion, and Revolt in Bahia." *Visible Language* 20, no. 3 (1986): 319–45.

Granada, Germán de. "Sobre el origen del 'habla de negro' en la literatura peninsular del siglo de oro." *Prohemio* 2, no. 1 (1971): 97–109.

Grant, Helen F. "The World Upside-Down." In *Studies in Spanish Literature,* ed. R. O. Jones, 103–36. London: Tamesis Books, 1973.

Greenfield, Sidney M. "Madeira and the Beginnings of New World Sugar Cane Cultivation and Contribution to Discourse on Race and Slavery." In *Caribbean Slavery in the Atlantic World: A Student Reader,* ed. Verene A. Shepherd and Hilary McD Beckles, 42–54. Kingston: Ian Randle Publishers, 2000.

Grégoire, Henri. *On the Cultural Achievements of Negroes.* Trans. T. Cassirer and Jean-François Brière. Amherst: University of Massachusetts Press, 1996.

Grünberg, Daniel. "Dulcinear la maritornería, la exaltación de lo grotesco en *Tuntún de pasa y grifería.*" *Estudios, Revista de Investigaciones Literarias y Culturales* 10, no. 19 (2002): 135–44.

Gubar, Susan. *Racechanges: White Skin, Black Face in American Culture.* New York: Oxford University Press, 1997.

Guillén, Nicolás. *Nicolás Guillén: Obra poética 1920–1972.* Vol. 1. Havana: Editorial de Arte y Literatura, 1974.

Guimaraes, Bernardo. *A escrava Isaura.* Rio de Janeiro: Ediouro, S.A., [n.d.].

Guirao, Ramón, ed. *Orbita de la poesía afrocubana 1928–37 (Antología).* Havana: Ucar, García y Cía. 1938.

Guisti Cordero, Juan A. "AfroPuerto Rican Cultural Studies: Beyond *cultura negroide* and *antillanismo.*" *Centro: Journal of El Centro de Estudios Puertorriqueños* 8, nos. 1, 2 (1996): 56–77.

Haberly, David. "Abolitionism in Brazil: Anti-Slavery and Anti-Slave." *Luso-Brazilian Review* 9 (1972): 30–47.

———. *Three Sad Races: Racial Identity and National Consciousness in Brazilian Literature.* Cambridge: Cambridge University Press, 1983.

Hair, P. E. "Columbus from Guinea to America." *History in Africa* 17 (1990): 113–29.

Hall, Kim. *Things of Darkness: Economies of Race and Gender in Early Modern England.* Ithaca: Cornell University Press, 1995.

Hall, Stuart. "Culture, the Media, and the 'Ideological Effect.'" In *Mass Communication and Society,* ed. James Curran, Michael Gurevitch, and Janet Woollacott, 315–48. London: Edward Arnold, 1977.

———. *Race, the Floating Signifier.* Dir. Sut Jhally. Northampton, Mass.: Media Education Foundation, 1996.

———. *Representation and the Media.* Dir. Sut Jhally. Northampton, Mass.: Media Education Foundation, 1997.

———. "The Spectacle of the 'Other.'" In *Representation: Cultural Representations and Signifying Practices,* ed. Stuart Hall, 223–80. London: Sage Publications, 1997.

Handelsman, Michael. *Lo afro y la plurinacionalidad: El caso de Ecuador visto desde su literatura.* Quito, Ecuador: Abya Yala, 2001.

Hannaford, Ivan. *Race: The History of an Idea in the West.* Washington, D.C.: Woodrow Wilson Center Press, 1996.

Haring, Clarence. *The Spanish Empire in America.* New York: Harcourt, Brace, and World, 1963.

Harris, Cheryl. "Whiteness as Property." *Harvard Law Review* 106, no. 8 (1993): 1709–1721.

Hayes, H. R. *The Dangerous Sex: The Myth of Feminine Evil.* New York: G. P. Putnam's Sons, 1964.

Helg, Aline. *Our Rightful Share: The Afro-Cuban Struggle for Equality, 1886–1912.* Chapel Hill: University of North Carolina Press, 1995.

———. "Race in Argentina and Cuba, 1880–1930: Theory, Policies, and Popular Reaction." In *The Idea of Race in Latin America, 1870–1940,* ed. Richard Graham, 37–69. Austin: University of Texas Press, 1990.

Hernández Cuevas, Marco Polo. *African Mexicans and the Discourse on Modern Nation.* Dallas: University Press of America, 2004.

———. "The Afro-Mexican and the Revolution: Making Afro-Mexicans Invisible through the Ideology of Mestizaje in *La Raza Cósmica.*" *PALARA* 4 (2000): 59–83.

Hernández de López, Ana María, ed. "En torno a los principios y el sacrificio por la justicia en Alejo Carpentier." In *Narrativa hispanoamericana contemporánea: Entre la vanguardia y el posboom,* 31–46. Madrid: Editorial Pliegos, 1996.

Herrnstein, Richard, and Charles Murray. *The Bell Curve: Intelligence and Class Structure in American Life.* New York: Free Press, 1994.

Hughes, Langston. *The Big Sea.* New York: Hill and Wang, 1979.

Hulme, Peter. "Introduction: The Cannibal Scene." In *Cannibalism and the Colonial World,* ed. Francis Barker, Peter Hulme, and Margaret Iversen, 1–38. Cambridge: Cambridge University Press, 1998.

Impey, Olga Tudorica. "Del duello de los godos de Espanna: La retórica del llanto y su motivación." *Romance Quarterly* 33, no. 3 (1986): 295–307.

Insúa, Alberto. *El negro que tenía el alma blanca.* Madrid: Espasa-Calpe, 1958.

Jackson, Richard L. *The Black Image in Latin American Literature.* Albuquerque: University of New Mexico Press, 1976.

———. *Black Writers in Latin America.* Albuquerque: University of New Mexico Press, 1979.

James, C. L. R. *The Black Jacobins: Toussaint L'Ouverture and the San Domingo Revolution.* New York: Vintage Books, 1963.

Jaramillo Uribe, Jaime. "Mestizaje y diferenciación social en el nuevo reino de Granada en la segunda mitad del Siglo XVIII." *Anuario Colombiano de Historia Social y de la Cultura* 2 (1965): 21–48, 195–213.

Jensen, Larry R. *Children of Colonial Despotism: Press, Politics, and Culture in Cuba, 1790–1840.* Tampa: University of South Florida Press, 1988.

Jiménez Román, Miriam. "*Un hombre (negro) del pueblo:* José Celso Barbosa and the Puerto Rican 'Race' toward Whiteness." *Journal of El Centro de Estudios Puertorriqueños* 8, nos. 1, 2 (1996): 8–29.

Johnson, Charles. "A Phenomenology of the Black Body." In *The Male Body: Features, Destinies, Exposure,* ed. Laurence Goldstein, 121–36. Ann Arbor: University of Michigan Press, 1994.

Johnson, James Weldon, ed. *The Book of American Negro Poetry.* New York: Harcourt, Brace, Jovanovich, 1931.

Johnson, Lemuel. *The Devil, the Gargoyle, and the Buffoon: The Negro as Metaphor in Western Literature.* New York: Kennikat Press, 1971.

Jordan, Glenn, and Chris Weedon. *Cultural Politics: Class, Gender, Race, and the Postmodern World.* Oxford: Blackwell, 1995.

Karasch, Mary C. *Slave Life in Rio de Janeiro, 1808–1850.* Princeton: Princeton University Press, 1987.

Katzew, Ilona, et al., eds. *New World Orders: Casta Painting and Colonial Latin America.* New York: Americas Society Art Gallery, 1996.

Kelly, Edith L. "The Banning of *Sab* in Cuba: Documents from the Archivo Nacional de Cuba." *The Americas: A Quarterly Review of Inter-American Cultural History* 1, no. 3 (1945): 350–53.

———. "La Avellaneda's *Sab* and the Political Situation in Cuba." *The Americas: A Quarterly Review of Inter-American Cultural History* 1, no. 3 (1945): 303–16.

Kennedy, James. "Luiz Gama: Pioneer of Abolition in Brazil." *Journal of Negro History* 59, no. 3 (1974): 225–67.

Kinigsberg, Yanina. "Una mujer denunció que la discriminaron por ser negra." *Clarín* (Buenos Aires), August 24, 2002.

Kirkpatrick, Susan. "Gómez de Avellaneda's *Sab:* Gendering the Liberal Romantic Subject." In *In the Feminine Mode: Essays on Hispanic Women Writers,* ed. Noel Valis and Caril Maier, 115–30. Lewisburg, Pa.: Bucknell University Press, 1990.

Konetzke, Richard, ed. *Colección de documentos para la historia de la formación social de hispanoamérica.* 5 vols. Madrid: Consejo Superior de Investigaciones Superiores, 1953–1962.

Kristeva, Julia. *Nations without Nationalism.* New York: Columbia University Press, 1993.

Kubayanda, Josaphat B. *The Poet's Africa: Africanness in the Poetry of Nicolás Guillén and Aimé Césaire.* New York: Greenwood Press, 1990.

Kutzinski, Vera. *Sugar's Secrets: Race and the Erotics of Cuban Nationalism.* Charlottesville: University Press of Virginia, 1993.

Labrador-Rodríguez, Sonia. "La intelectualidad negra en Cuba en el siglo XIX: El caso de Manzano." *Revista Iberoamericana* 62, no. 74 (1996): 13–25.

LaCerte, Robert K. "The Evolution of Land and Labour in the Haitian Revolution, 1791–1820." In *Caribbean Freedom: Economy and Society from Emancipation to the Present,* ed. Hilary Beckles and Verene Shepherd, 42–47. Princeton: Markus Weiner Publishers, 1996.

Lahon, Maria Cristina Neto Didier. "Os escravos negros em Portugal." In *Os negros em Portugal—sécs. XV a XIX,* ed. Ana Maria Rodrigues, 71–78. Lisbon: National Commission for the Commemoration of the Portuguese Discoveries, 2000.

Leante, César. "Confesiones sencillas de un escritor barroco." In *Homenaje a Alejo Carpentier: Variaciones interpretativas en torno a su obra,* ed. Fernando Alegría et al., 11–32. New York: Las Américas Publishing, 1970. 11–32.

———. "Dos obras antiesclavistas cubanas." *Cuadernos Americanos* 4 (1976): 175–88.

Letter from a West-India Merchant to a Gentleman at Tunbridg, concerning that Part of the French Proposals, which Relates to North-America, and particularly Newfoundland. London, 1712.

Lewis, Gordon. *Main Currents in Caribbean Thought.* Baltimore: Johns Hopkins University Press, 1983.

Lewis, Marvin A. *Afro-Argentine Discourse: Another Dimension of the Black Diaspora.* Columbia: University of Missouri Press, 1996.

———. *Afro-Hispanic Poetry, 1940–1980: From Slavery to "Negritud" in South American Verse.* Columbia: University of Missouri Press, 1983.

———. *Afro-Uruguayan Literature: Post-Colonial Perspectives.* Lewisburg, Pa.: Bucknell University Press, 2003.

———. *Ethnicity and Identity in Contemporary Afro-Venezuelan Literature: A Culturalist Approach.* Columbia: University of Missouri Press, 1983.

———. *Treading the Ebony Path: Ideology and Violence in Contemporary Afro-Colombian Prose Fiction.* Columbia: University of Missouri Press, 1987.

Lewis Galanes, Adriana. "El album de Domingo del Monte (Cuba, 1838/39)." *Cuadernos Americanos* 451, no. 452 (1988): 255–65.

Limón, Graciela. "Haitian Gods, African Roots: Identity and Freedom in Alejo Carpentier's *The Kingdom of This World." Journal of Caribbean Studies* 9, no. 3 (1993): 195–201.

Linebaugh, Peter. "All the Atlantic Mountains Shook." *Labour/Le Travailleur* 10 (1982): 87–121.

Lipski, John. "The Golden Age 'Black Spanish': Existence and Coexistence." *Afro-Hispanic Review* 5, nos. 1, 2, 3 (1986): 7–12.

Locke, Alain, ed. *The New Negro.* New York: Atheneum, 1968.

Locke, John. "Of Property." In *Two Treatises of Government,* ed. Peter Laslett, 285–302. New York: Cambridge University Press, 1988.

Lope de Vega y Carpio, Félix. *El negro del mejor amo.* In *Lope de Vega, Comedias, XI,* ed. Donald McGrady. Madrid: Turner, 1993.

López-Baralt, Mercedes. *El barco en la botella: La poesía de Luis Palés Matos.* San Juan: Editorial Plaza Mayor, 1997.

———. "El extraño caso de un canon marginal: La poesía de Luis Palés Matos." Introduction to *La poesía de Luis Palés Matos: Edición crítica,* 1–18. Puerto Rico: Editorial de la Universidad de Puerto Rico, 1995.

———. "Preludio en Boricua, o la ironía como programa poético en el *Tuntún* palesiano." *Revista de Estudios Hispánicos* 17, no. 18 (1990): 329–38.

Luis, William. "The Antislavery Novel and the Concept of Modernity." *Cuban Studies/Estudios Cubanos* 1, no. 1 (1981): 33–47.

———. *Literary Bondage: Slavery in Cuban Narrative.* Austin: University of Texas Press, 1990.

———. "La novela antiesclavista: Texto, contexto y escritura." *Cuadernos Americanos* 236 (1981): 103–16.

Luis, William, ed. *Voices from Under: Black Narrative in Latin America and the Caribbean.* Westport, Conn.: Greenwood Press, 1984.

Luis Martín, Juan. "Falsa interpretación afrocubana." *Adelante* 3, no. 2 (1937): 7.

Lundhal, Mats. "Toussaint L'Ouverture and the War Economy of Saint Domingue, 1796–1802." In *Caribbean Freedom: Economy and Society from Emancipation to the Present,* ed. Hilary Beckles and Verene Shepherd, 2–11. Princeton: Markus Weiner Publishers, 1996.

Mansour, Mónica. *La poesía negrista.* Mexico: Ediciones Era, 1973.

Manuel de Macedo, Joaquim. *As vítimas-algozes: Quadros de escravidão.* São Paulo: Editora Scipione, 1991.

Manzano, Juan Francisco. *The Autobiography of a Slave/Autobiografía de un esclavo.* Ed. Ivan A. Schulman; trans. Evelyn Picon Garfield. Detroit: Wayne State University Press, 1996.

———. *Obras: Juan Francisco Manzano.* Ed. José Luciano Franco. Havana: Instituto cubano del libro, 1972.

Marinello, Juan. "Don Fernando Ortiz: Notas sobre nuestro tercer descubridor." *Bohemia,* April 18, 1969, 52–60.

———. "Una novela cubana." In *Literatura hispanoamericana: Hombres— meditaciones,* 167–78. Mexico: Ediciones de la Universidad Nacional de México, 1937.

Marotti, Georgio. *Black Characters in the Brazilian Novel.* Los Angeles: UCLA Center for Afro-American Studies, 1987.

Martín Alcoff, Linda. "The Problem of Speaking for Others." In *Who Can Speak? Authority and Critical Identity,* ed. Judith Roof and Robyn Wiegman, 97–119. Urbana: University of Illinois Press, 1995.

Marzán, Julio. *The Numinous Site: The Poetry of Luis Palés Matos.* Cranbury, N.J.: Associated University Presses, 1995.

———. "The Poetry and Antipoetry of Luis Palés Matos." *Callaloo* 18, no. 2 (1995): 506–23.

Mas, José. *En el país de lo bubis.* Prologue by Miguel de Unamuno. Madrid: Editorial Pueyo, 1931.

McGarrity, Gayle. "Race, Culture, and Social Change in Contemporary Cuba." In *Cuba in Transition: Crisis and Transformation,* ed. Sandor Halebsky, et al., 193–205. Boulder, Colo.: Westview Press, 1992.

McKee Evans, William. "From the Land of Canaan to the Land of Guinea: The Strange Odyssey of the 'Sons of Ham.'" *American Historical Review* 85, no. 1 (1980): 15–43.

Mellor, Anne K. "'Am I Not a Woman and a Sister?' Slavery, Romanticism, and Gender." In *Romanticism, Race, and Imperial Culture, 1780–1834,* ed. Alan Richardson and Sonia Hofkosh, 311–29. Bloomington: Indiana University Press, 1996.

Miller, Beth. "Avellaneda, Nineteenth Century Feminist." *Revista/Review Interamericana* 4 (1974): 177–83.

Miller, Paul B. "*Blancas y negras:* Carpentier and the Temporalities of Mutual Exclusion." *Latin American Literary Review* 29, no. 58 (2001): 23–45.

Mills, Charles. *The Racial Contract.* Ithaca: Cornell University Press, 1999.

Miranda Arcilla, Graciany. "La broma de una poesía prieta en Puerto Rico." *Alma Latina,* February 1933, 5, 43.

Molloy, Sylvia. *At Face Value: Autobiographical Writing in Spanish America.* Cambridge: Cambridge University Press, 1991.

Monguió, Luis. "El negro en algunos poetas españoles y americanos anteriores a 1800." *Revista Iberoamericana* 44 (1951): 240–50.

Montañez, Rafael. "González Marín." *Puerto Rico Ilustrado,* n.d.

Moore, Robin D. *Nationalizing Blackness: Afrocubanismo and Artistic Revolution in Havana, 1920–1940.* Pittsburgh: University of Pittsburgh Press, 1997.

Morner, Magnus. *Race Mixture in the History of Latin America.* Boston: Little, Brown and Company, 1967.

Mosby, Dorothy E. *Place, Language, and Identity in Afro–Costa Rican Literature.* Columbia: University of Missouri Press, 2003.

Mosse, George. *Toward the Final Solution: A History of European Racism.* New York: Howard Fertig, 1985.

Motohashi, Ted. "The Discourse of Cannibalism in Early Modern Travel Writing." In *Travel Writing and Empire: Postcolonial Theory in Transit,* ed. Steve Clark, 83–99. London: Zed Books, 1999.

Mudimbe, Valentin. "*Romanus Pontifex (1454)* and the Expansion of Europe." In *Race, Discourse, and the Origin of the Americas: A New World View,* ed. Vera Hyatt and Rex Nettleford, 58–67. Washington D.C.: Smithsonian Institution Press, 1995.

Edward Mullen, *Afro-Cuban Literature: Critical Junctures.* Westport, Conn.: Greenwood Press, 1998.

Mullen, Edward, ed. *The Life and Poems of a Cuban Slave: Juan Francisco Manzano, 1797–1854.* New Haven, Conn.: Archon Books, 1981.

———. "*Los negros brujos:* A Reexamination of the Text." *Cuban Studies* 17 (1987): 111–32.

Murray, David R. *Odious Commerce: Britain, Spain, and the Abolition of the Cuban Slave Trade.* Cambridge: Cambridge University Press, 1980.

———. "The Slave Trade, Slavery, and Cuban Independence." *Slavery and Abolition* 20, no. 3 (1999): 106–26.

Nebrija, Antonio de. *Gramática de la lengua castellana.* Madrid: Editora Nacional, 1980.

Negrón Muñoz, Angela. "Hablando con don Luis Palés Matos." In *Luis Palés Matos y su trasmundo poético,* ed. José de Diego Padró, 85–92. Río Piedras, Puerto Rico: Ediciones Puerto, 1973.

Neve, Michael. "Freud's Theory of Humor, Wit, and Jokes." In *Laughing Matters: A Serious Look at Humor,* ed. John Durand, 35–43. England: Longman, 1988.

Nicholas V, Pope. "The Bull Romanus Pontifex." In *European Treaties bearing on the History of the United States and Its Dependencies to 1648,* ed. Frances Gardiner Davenport, 20–26. Washington, D.C.: Carnegie Institution of Washington, 1917.

North, Michael. *The Dialect of Modernism: Race, Language, and Twentieth-Century Literature.* New York: Oxford University Press, 1994.

Obeso, Candelario. *Cantos populares de mi tierra.* Bogota: Ministerio de Educación Nacional, 1950.

Olsen, Margaret M. "*Negros horros* and *cimarrones* on the Legal Frontiers of the Caribbean: Accessing the African Voice in Colonial Spanish American Texts." *Research in African Literatures* 29, no. 4 (1998): 52–72.

———. *Slavery and Salvation in Colonial Cartagena de Indias.* Gainesville: University Press of Florida, 2004.

O'Neill, Eugene. *Four Plays by Eugene O'Neill.* New York: Penguin Putnam, 1998.

Ortiz, Fernando. "Defensa cubana contra el racismo antisemita." *Revista Bimestre Cubana* 70, no. 1 (1955): 97–107.

———. "El arte africanoide de Cuba." *Diario de la Marina* 3 (1929): 6.

———. "El fenómeno social de la transculturación y su importancia en Cuba." *Revista Bimestre Cubana* 46, no. 2 (1940): 273–79.

———. *Glosario de afronegrismos.* Havana: Imprenta El Siglo XX, 1924.

———. *Hampa Afro-Cubana: Los negros brujos (apuntes para un estudio de etnología criminal).* 1906. Prologue by Alberto N. Pamies. Havana: Editorial de Ciencias Sociales, 1975.

———. *Hampa afro-cubana: Los negros esclavos; estudio sociológico y de derecho público.* Havana: Revista bimestre cubana, 1916.

———. "Informe del doctor Fernando Ortiz, Presidente de la Sociedad de Estudios Afrocubanos, aprobado por la Junta Directiva de dicha Sociedad, pronunciándose en favor del resurgimiento de las comparsas populares habaneras." In *Las comparsas populares del carnaval habanero, cuestión resuelta,* ed. Antonio Beruff Mendieta, 9–20. Havana: Molina y Cia., 1937.

———. "La decadencia cubana; conferencia de propaganda renovadora pronunciada el la Sociedad Económica de Amigos del País la noche del 23 de febrero de 1924." *Revista Bimestre Cubana* 19, no. 1 (1924): 17–44.

———. "La fiesta afrocubana del 'Día de Reyes.'" *Archivos del Folklore Cubano* 1, no. 2 (April 1924): 146–65.

———. "La inmigración desde el punto de vista criminológico." *Derecho y Sociología* 1 (1906): 54–64.

———. "La poesía mulata. Presentación de Eusebia Cosme, la recitadora." *Revista Bimestre Cubana* 34, noa. 2–3 (1934): 205–13.

———. "La sinrazón de los racismos." *Revista Bimestre Cubana* 70, no. 1 (1955): 161–83.

———. *Los cabildos afrocubanos.* Havana: Imprenta la Universal, 1921.

———. "Los factores humanos de la cubanidad." *Revista Bimestre Cubana* 35, no. 2 (1940): 61–186.

————. *Los negros curros.* Havana: Editorial Ciencias Sociales, 1995.

————. "Los últimos versos mulatos." *Revista Bimestre Cubana,* 35, no. 3 (1935): 321–36.

————. "Luis Palés Matos: *Poemas afroantillanos:* Publicaciones recibidas." *Estudios Afrocubanos* 1 (1937): 156–59.

————. "Martí y las razas de librería." *Cuadernos Americanos* 55, no. 3 (1945): 185–98.

————. "Más acerca de la poesía mulata. Escorzos para su estudio." *Revista Bimestre Cubana* 37, no. 2 (1936) 23–39, 218–27.

————. "Ni racismos ni xenofobias. Discurso en la sesión solemne del 9 de enero de 1929, en la Sociedad Económica de Amigos del País de La Habana, conmemoración del 136 aniversario de la fundación de dicho instituto patriótico." *Revista Bimestre Cubana* 24, no. 1 (1929): 6–19.

————. "Pregones populares." *Archivos del Folklore Cubano* 4, no. 4 (1929): 375.

Osorio, Nelson T. *Manifiestos, proclamas y polémicas de la vanguardia literaria hispanoamericana.* Caracas: Biblioteca Ayacucho, 1988.

Otero, Lisandro. "Delmonte y la cultura de la sacarocracia." *Revista Iberoamericana* 152, no. 53 (1990): 723–31.

Pagden, Anthony. *Lords of All the World: Ideologies of Empire in Spain, Britain, and France, c. 1500–c.1800.* New Haven, Conn.: Yale University Press, 1995.

Painter, Nell Irvin. "Representing Truth: Sojourner Truth's Knowing and Becoming Known." *Journal of American History* 81, no. 2 (September 1994): 461–92.

Palés Matos, Luis. "Hacia una poesía antillana." In *Luis Palés Matos y su trasmundo poético,* ed. José de Diego Padró, 99–107. Río Piedras, Puerto Rico: Ediciones Puerto, 1973.

————. "Litoral: Reseña de una vida inutil." In *Luis Palés Matos: Obras, 1914–1959,* vol. 2, *Prosa,* 15–157. Río Piedras, Puerto Rico: Editorial de la Unversidad de Puerto Rico, 1984.

————. *Tuntún de pasa y grifería: Poemas afroantillanos.* San Juan: Imprenta Venezuela, 1937.

————. *Tuntún de pasa y grifería: Poemas afroantillanos.* San Juan: Biblioteca de Autores Puertorriqueños, 1974.

Pamies, Alberto N. Prologue to *Hampa afro-cubana: Los negros brujos (apuntes para un estudio de etnología criminal),* by Fernando Ortiz, vii–xxiii. Havana: Editorial de Ciencias Sociales, 1975.

Parcas Ponseti, Helena. "Sobre la Avellaneda y su novela *Sab.*" *Revista Iberoamericana* 28 (1962): 347–56.

Patterson, Orlando. *Slavery and Social Death: A Comparative Study.* Cambridge: Harvard University Press, 1995.

Pedreira, Antonio S. *Insularismo: Ensayos de interpretación puertorriqueña,* ed. Mercedes López-Baralt. San Juan: Editorial Plaza Mayor, 2001.

Pequeño larousse en color. Paris: Ediciones Larousse, 1976.

Pérez, José Javier. "La raza: Reflejo de lo que se quiere ser y no se es." *El Nuevo Día,* August 21, 2001, 12.

Pérez Firmat, Gustavo. *The Cuban Condition: Translation and Identity in Modern Cuban Literature.* Cambridge: Cambridge University Press, 1989.

Pessoa Monteiro, Marília. "A mulher negra escrava no imaginário das elites do século XIX." *Clio: Revista de Pesquisa Historica* 12 (1989): 93–102.

Pierre-Charles, Gérard. *Génesis de la revolución cubana.* Mexico: Siglo Veintiuno Editores, 1978.

Pieterse, Jan Nederveen. *White on Black: Images of Africa and Blacks in Western Popular Culture.* New Haven, Conn.: Yale University Press, 1992.

Pike, Ruth. "Sevillian Society in the Sixteenth Century: Slaves and Freedmen." *Hispanic American Historical Review* 47, no. 3 (1967): 344–59.

Poliakov, Leon. *Aryan Myth: A History of Racist and Nationalist Ideas in Europe.* Trans. Edmund Howard. London: Chatto and Windus Heineman for Sussex University Press, 1974.

———. "Racism from the Enlightenment to the Age of Imperialism." In *Racism and Colonialism: Essays on Ideology and Social Structure,* ed. Robert Ross, 55–64. The Hague: Mentinus University Press, 1982.

Pratt, Mary Louise. "Fieldwork in Common Places." In *Writing Culture: The Poetics and Politics of Ethnography,* ed. James Clifford and George E. Marcus, 27–50. Berkeley and Los Angeles: University of California Press, 1986.

———. *Imperial Eyes: Travel Writing and Transculturation.* London: Routledge, 1992.

Prescott, Laurence. *Candelario Obeso y la iniciación de la poesía negra en Colombia, 1985.* Bogota: Instituto caro y cuervo, 1985.

———. *Without Hatreds or Fears: Jorge Artel and the Struggle for Black Literary Expression in Colombia.* Detroit: Wayne State University Press, 2000.

Price, Richard. *Maroon Societies: Rebel Slave Communities in the Americas.* Baltimore: Johns Hopkins University Press, 1996.

Quevedo y Villegas, Francisco de. *Obras completas.* Vol. 2. Ed. Felicidad Buendía. Madrid: Aguilar, 1967.

Quiñones Benavente, Luis. "Entremés famoso: El negrito hablador, y sin color anda la Niña." In *Colección de entremeses, loas, bailes, jácaras y mojigangas desde fines del siglo XVI a mediados del XVIII,* ed. Emilio Cotarelo y Mori, 605–7. Madrid: Casa Editorial Bailly/Bailliére, 1911.

Rama, Angel. *La ciudad letrada.* Hanover: Ediciones del norte, 1984.

Ramos, Julio. *Paradojas de la letra.* Caracas: Ediciones eXcultura, 1996.

Read, Jan. *The Moors in Spain and Portugal.* London: Faber and Faber, 1974.

Reis, José João. *Slave Rebellion in Brazil: The Muslim Uprising of 1835 in Bahia,* trans. A. Brakel. Baltimore: Johns Hopkins Press, 1993.

Reis, Roberto. *A permanência do círculo: Hierarquia no romance brasileiro.* Niterói, Brazil: Editoria Universitaria, 1987.

Reynosa, Rodrigo de. *Coplas.* Madrid: Taurus, 1970.

Ríos Avila, Rubén. *La raza cómica del sujeto en Puerto Rico.* San Juan: Ediciones Callejón, 2002.

Rivière, Rolando. "Menem, estudiantes y milagros." *La Nación,* November 26, 1993.

Rodney, Walter. *How Europe Underdeveloped Africa.* Washington, D.C.: Howard University Press, 1982.

Rodríguez, Ileana. "Romanticismo literario y liberalismo reformista: El grupo de Domingo Delmonte." *Caribbean Studies* 20 (1980): 35–56.

Rodríguez Monegal, Emir. "Lo real y lo maravilloso en *El reino de este mundo." Revista Iberoamericana* 37 (1971): 619–49.

Rout, Leslie B., Jr. *The African Experience in Spanish America: 1502 to the Present Day.* Cambridge: Cambridge University Press, 1976.

Rueda, Lope de. *Teatro completo.* Introduction by Arturo Souto Alabarce. Mexico: Editorial Porrúa, 1974.

Ruiz del Vizo, Hortensia, ed. *Black Poetry of the Americas (A Bilingual Anthology).* Miami: Ediciones Universal, 1972.

Russell, P. E. "Toward an Interpretation of Rodrigo de Reinosa's 'poesía negra.'" In *Studies in Spanish Literature of the Golden Age,* ed. O. R. Jones, 225–46. London: Tamesis Books, 1973.

Russell-Wood, A. J. R. "Before Columbus: Portugal's African Prelude to the Middle Passage and Contribution to Discourse on Race and Slavery." In *Race, Discourse, and the Origin of the Americas: A New World View, 1492,* ed. Vera Hyatt and Rex Nettleford, 134–68. Washington, D.C.: Smithsonian Institution Press, 1995.

————. "Iberian Expansion and the Issue of Black Slavery: Changing Portuguese Attitudes, 1440–1770." *American Historical Review* 83, no. 1 (1978): 16–42.

Saco, José Antonio. "Análisis por don José Antonio Saco de una obra sobre el Brasil, intitulada, *Notices of Brazil in 1828 by Rev. Walsh* author of a Journey from Constantinople, etc. (Noticias del Brasil en 1828 y 1829 por el presbítero R. Walsh, autor de un viaje a Constantinopla, etc.)." In *José Antonio Saco: Acerca de la esclavitud y su historia,* ed. Eduardo Torres-Cuevas, Arturo Sorhegui, 173–208. Havana: Editorial de Ciencias Sociales, 1982.

————. "Justa defensa de la Academia Cubana de Literatura, contra los ataques que se le han dado en el Diario de La Habana, desde el 12 hasta el 23 de abril del presente año, escrita por Don José Antonio Saco e impresa en Nueva Orleans por Mr. St.-Romes, oficina de El Courier año de 1834." In *Colección de papeles científicos, históricos, políticos y de otros ramos sobre la isla de Cuba ya publicados, ya ineditados,* vol. 3, 25–65. Havana: Editorial Nacional de Cuba, 1963.

————. "La supresión del tráfico de esclavos africanos en la isla de Cuba, examinada con relación a su agricultura y a su seguridad, por don José Antonio Saco." In *José Antonio Saco: Acerca de la esclavitud y su historia,* ed. Eduardo Torres-Cuevas, Arturo Sorhegui, 208–56. Havana: Editorial de Ciencias Sociales, 1982.

Said, Edward. *Orientalism.* New York: Vintage Books, 1979.

Sánchez-Eppler, Karen. "Bodily Bonds: The Intersecting Rhetorics of Feminism and Abolition." *Representations* 24 (fall, 1988): 28–59.

Santa Cruz, Nicomedes. *Décimas y poemas: Antologia.* Lima: Campodónico Ediciones, S.A., 1971.

————. "El negro en Iberoamérica." *Cuadernos Americanos* 451, no. 52 (1988): 7–46.

Santiago-Valles, Kelvin. "Policing the Crisis in the Whitest of All the Antilles." *Journal of El Centro de Estudios Puertorriqueños* 8, nos. 1, 2 (1996): 42–57.

Santos Domínguez, Luis Antonio. "La minoría morisca: Apuntes de sociolingüística histórica." *La Corónica: A Journal of Medieval Spanish Language and Literature* 14, no. 2 (spring 1986): 285–90.

Saunders, A. C. de C. M. *A Social History of Black Slaves and Freedmen in Portugal, 1441–1555.* Cambridge: Cambridge University Press, 1982.

Scarry, Elaine. *The Body in Pain: The Making and Unmaking of the World.* New York: Oxford University Press, 1985.

Schlau, Stacy. "Stranger in a Strange Land: The Discourse of Alienation in Avellaneda's *Sab*." *Hispania* 69 (1986): 495–503.

Schmidt-Nowara, Christopher. *Empire and Antislavery: Spain, Cuba, and Puerto Rico, 1833–1874.* Pittsburgh: University of Pittsburgh Press, 1999.

Schwartz, Stuart. "Colonial Identities and the Sociedad de Castas." *Colonial Latin American Review* 4, no. 11 (1995): 185–201.

Schweinfurth, Georg. *The Heart of Africa: Three Years' Travels and Adventures in the Unexplored Regions of Central Africa from 1868 to 1871.* 2 vols. London: Sampson Low, Marston, Searle, and Rivington, 1878.

Seabrook, William. *The Magic Island.* New York: Paragon House, 1989.

Sentaurens, Jean. *Seville et le théâtre: De la fin du moyen age à la fin de XVIIe siècle.* Talence, France: Lille, Atelier national de reproduction des thèses, Université de Lille, 1984.

Seshadri-Crooks, Kalpani. "The Comedy of Domination: Psychoanalysis and the Conceit of Whiteness." In *The Psychoanalysis of Race,* ed. Christopher Lane, 353–79. New York: Columbia University Press, 1998.

Silverman, Maxim. "Mechanisms of Oppression: Interview with Albert Memmi." In *Race, Discourse, and Power in France,* ed. Maxim Silverman, 29–39. Aldershot, Hants, England: Avebury, 1991.

Skidmore, Thomas E. "Racial Ideas and Social Policy in Brazil, 1870–1940." In *The Idea of Race in Latin America, 1870–1940,* ed. Richard Graham, 7–36. Austin: University of Texas Press, 1990.

Smart, Ian. *Central American Writers of West Indian Origin: A New Hispanic Literature.* Washington, D.C.: Three Continents Press, 1984.

Snowden, Frank. *Before Color Prejudice: The Ancient View of Blacks.* Cambridge: Harvard University Press, 1983.

Snowdon, Peter. "The Moor That Meets the Eye." In *Al-Ahram Weekly On-Line* 17, no. 469 (February 2, 2000).

Sokoloff, Naomi. "The Discourse of Contradiction: Metaphor, Metonymy, and *El reino de este mundo*." *Modern Language Studies* 16 (1986): 39–53.

Solomianski, Alejandro. *Identidades secretas: La negritud argentina.* Rosario: Beatriz Viterbo Editora, 2003.

Sommer, Doris. "Sab c'est moi." *Genders* 2 (1988): 111–26.

Spengler, Oswald. *The Decline of the West.* New York: Alfred A. Knopf, 1939.

Speratti-Piñero, Emma Susana. *Pasos hallados en El reino de este mundo.* Mexico: El Colegio de México, 1981.

Spillers, Hortense J. "Mama's Baby, Papa's Maybe: An American Grammar Book." *Diacritics* 17, no. 2 (1987): 65–81.

Stabb, Martin. *In Quest of Identity: Patterns in the Spanish American Essay of Ideas, 1890–1960*. Chapel Hill: University of North Carolina Press, 1967.

Stannard, David E. *American Holocaust: Columbus and the Conquest of the New World*. New York: Oxford University Press, 1992.

Stephens, Thomas. *Dictionary of Latin American Racial and Ethnic Terminology*. Gainsville: University Presses of Florida, 1989.

Stinchcomb, Dawn. *The Development of Literary Blackness in the Dominican Republic*. Gainesville: University Press of Florida, 2004.

Stowe, Harriet Beecher. "Sojourner Truth: The Libyan Sibyl." *Atlantic Monthly,* April 1863, 473–81.

Suárez y Romero, Anselmo. *Francisco: El ingenio, o las delicias del campo*. Havana: Editorial de Arte y Literatura, 1974.

Sweet, James H. "The Iberian Roots of American Racist Thought." *William and Mary Quarterly* 54, no. 1 (1997): 143–66.

Tanco y Bosmeniel, Félix. "Petrona y Rosalía." In *Cuentos cubanos del siglo XIX,* ed. Salvador Bueno, 103–31. Havana: Editorial Arte y Literatura, 1975.

Tannenbaum, Frank. *Slave and Citizen: The Negro in the Americas*. New York: Vintage Books, 1946.

Teyssier, Paul. *La langue de Gil Vicente*. Paris: Librairie C. Klincksieck, 1959.

Thomas, Hugh. *Cuba; or, The Pursuit of Freedom*. New York: Da Capo Press, 1998.

———. *The Story of the Atlantic Slave Trade, 1440–1870*. New York: Simon and Schuster, 1997.

Thompson, Alvin. "The Berbice Revolt, 1763–64." In *Themes in African-Guyanese History,* ed. Winston McGowan, James Rose, and David Granger, 77–106. Georgetown, Guyana: Free Press, 1998.

Thomson, Philip. *The Grotesque*. London: Methuen, 1972.

Thorne, Eva. "The Politics of Afro-Latin American Land Rights." Manuscript read at the Latin American Studies Association 25th International Congress, Las Vegas, 2004.

Thornton, John. "Perspectives on African Christianity." In *Race, Discourse, and the Origin of the Americas: A New World View, 1492,* ed. Vera Hyatt and Rex Nettleford, 169–98. Washington, D.C.: Smithsonian Institution Press, 1995.

Tiffin, Chris, and Alan Lawson. "The Textuality of Empire." Introduction to *De-Scribing Empire: Postcolonialism and Textuality*, 1–14. London: Routledge, 1994.

Torres Torres, Jaime. "Poema de negrura, sudor y caña." In *El Nuevo Día* (San Juan), July 18, 1993.

Trouillot, Michel-Rolph. *Silencing the Past: Power and the Production of History.* Boston: Beacon Press, 1995.

Twinam, Ann. *Public Lives, Private Secrets: Gender, Honor, Sexuality, and Illegitimacy in Colonial Spanish America.* Stanford: Stanford University Press, 1999.

Tzara, Tristan. "Zurich Chronicle (1915–1919)." In *Dada Painters and Poets: An Anthology*, 2d ed., ed. Robert Motherwell, 235–54. Boston: G. K. Hall, 1981.

United Nations. *Report of the World Conference against Racism, Racial Discrimination, Xenophobia, and Related Intolerance.* Durban, South Africa, August 31–September 8, 2001. New York: United Nations, 2002.

Valdés-Cruz, Rosa E. *La poesía negroide en América.* New York: Las Américas Publishing, 1970.

Vandercook, John. *Black Majesty: The Life of Christophe, King of Haiti.* New York: Harper and Brothers, 1928.

Van Vechten, Carl. *Nigger Heaven.* New York: Octagon Books, 1973.

Vasconcelos, José. *La raza cósmica.* Mexico: Espasa Calpe, 1999.

Vásquez Arce, Carmen. "*Tuntún de pasa y grifería:* A Cultural Project." In *The Cultures of the Hispanic Caribbean,* ed. Conrad James and John Perivolaris, 86–103. London: Macmillan Education, 2000.

Verlinden, Charles. *The Beginnings of Modern Colonization.* Trans. Yvonne Freccero. Ithaca: New York, 1970.

Vientós Gastón, Nilita. "El arte de Eusebia Cosme." *El Mundo,* 1938.

Villaverde, Cirilo. *Cecilia Valdés.* Havana: Editorial Letras Cubanas, 1984.

Viveros Vigoya, Mara. "Y así nació este libro." In *Mots pour Nègres mots des noir(e)s: Enjeux socio-symboliques de la nomination en Amérique Latine,* ed. Victorien Lavou Zoungbo and Mara Viveros Vigoya, 7–11. Perpignan, France: Presses Universaires de Perpignan, 2004.

Vizcarrondo, Carmelinda. "El arte de Eusebia Cosme." *El Mundo,* 1938.

Wallerstein, Immanuel. "The Construction of Peoplehood: Racism, Nationalism, Ethnicity." In *Race, Nation, Class: Ambiguous Identities,* ed. Etienne Balibar and Immanuel Wallerstein, 71–85. London: Verso, 1991

Walsh, Robert. *Notices of Brazil in 1828 and 1829*. Boston: Richardson, 1831.

Walvin, Jack. "The Propaganda of Anti-Slavery." In *Slavery and British Society, 1776–1846*, ed. Jack Walvin, 49–68. Baton Rouge: Louisiana State University Press, 1982.

Weber de Kurlat, Frida. "El tipo cómico del negro en el teatro prelopesco, fonética." *Filología* 8 (1962): 139–68.

————. "El tipo de negro en el teatro de Lope de Vega: Tradición y creación." *Nueva Revista de Filología Hispánica* 19 (1970): 337–59.

West, Cornel. *Prophesy Deliverance: An Afro-American Revolutionary Christianity*. Philadelphia: Westminster Press, 1982.

White, Hayden. *The Content of the Form: Narrative Discourse and Historical Representation*. Baltimore: Johns Hopkins University Press, 1987.

————. "The Historical Text as Literary Artifact." In *Critical Theory since 1965*, ed. Hazard Adams and Leroy Searle, 295–409. Tallahassee: University Presses of Florida, 1986.

Williams, Eric. *Capitalism and Slavery*. Chapel Hill: University of North Carolina Press, 1994.

Williams, Lorna Valerie. *The Representation of Slavery in Cuban Fiction*. Columbia: University of Missouri Press, 1994.

Williams, Robert A., Jr. "Documents of Barbarism: The Contemporary Legacy of European Racism and Colonialism in the Narrative Traditions of Federal Indian Law." In *Critical Race Theory: The Cutting Edge*, ed. Richard Delgado and Jean Stefancic, 98–109. Philadelphia: Temple University Press, 2000.

Woodson, Carter G. "Attitudes of the Iberian Peninsula (in Literature)." *Journal of Negro History* 20, no. 2 (1935): 190–243.

Ximénez de Enciso, Diego. *El Encubierto y Juan Latino: Comedias de Don Ximénez de Enciso*. Ed. Eduardo Julio Martínez. Madrid: Aldus, S.A., 1951.

Yarbro-Bejarano, Yvonne. *Feminism and the Honor Plays of Lope de Vega*. West Lafayette, Ind.: Purdue University Press, 1994.

Yellin, Jean Fagan. *Women and Sisters: The Antislavery Feminists in American Culture*. New Haven, Conn.: Yale University Press, 1989.

Zambrana, Antonio. *El negro Francisco*. Havana: Editorial Letras Cubanas, 1979.

Zavala, Iris M. "Representing the Colonial Subject." *Re/Discovering Colonial Writing*, ed. René Jara and Nicholas Spadaccini, 323–48. Minneapolis: Prisma Institute, 1989.

Zenón Cruz, Isabelo. *Narciso descubre su trasero: El negro en la cultura puerto-rriqueña.* 2 vols. Humacao, Puerto Rico: Editorial Furidi, 1975.

Zeuske, Michael. "Hidden Markers, Open Secrets: On Naming, Race-Marking, and Race-Making in Cuba." *New West Indian Guide/Nieuwe West—Indische Gids* 76, nos. 3, 4 (2002): 211–42.

Index